Lecture Notes in Artificial Intellig

T0238239

Subseries of Lecture Notes in Computer Science
Edited by J. G. Carbonell and J. Siekmann

Lecture Notes in Computer Science
Edited by G. Goos, J. Hartmanis and J. van Leeuwen

Nada Lavrač   Stefan Wrobel (Eds.)

Machine Learning: ECML-95

8th European Conference on Machine Learning
Heraclion, Crete, Greece, April 25-27, 1995
Proceedings

 Springer

Series Editors

Jaime G. Carbonell
School of Computer Science
Carnegie Mellon University
Pittsburgh, PA 15213-3891, USA

Jörg Siekmann
University of Saarland
German Research Center for Artificial Intelligence (DFKI)
Stuhlsatzenhausweg 3, D-66123 Saarbrücken, Germany

Volume Editors

Nada Lavrač
Artificial Intelligence Laboratory, J. Stefan Institute
Jamova 39, 61000 Slowenia
E-mail: nada.lavrac@ijs.si

Stefan Wrobel
Institut für Angewandte Informationstechnik, GMD
Schloß Birlinghoven, D-53754 Sankt Augustin, Germany
E-mail: stefan.wrobel@gmd.de

CR Subject Classification (1991): I.2.6, I.2.3-4, I.2.8, F.2.2

ISBN 3-540-59286-5 Springer-Verlag Berlin Heidelberg New York

CIP data applied for

Typesetting: Camera ready by author
SPIN: 10485707   45/3140-543210 - Printed on acid-free paper

Foreword

The Eighth European Conference on Machine Learning, ECML-95, held in Heraclion, Crete, 25–27 April 1995, continues the tradition of earlier EWSL (European Working Session on Learning) and ECML conferences, being the major European scientific forum for presenting the latest advances in Machine Learning research.

The scientific program of ECML-95 consists of four invited lectures (by Rudolf Kruse, Donald Michie, Tom Mitchell and Stellan Ohlsson), 14 papers presented at plenary sessions and 26 posters with short plenary presentations. In the proceedings, the invited lectures and 14 selected papers are published as full papers, and posters are published as extended abstracts. In total, 38% of the 104 papers submitted to ECML-95 were accepted for presentation and publication, reflecting the continued high standard of ECML conferences. Each submitted paper was reviewed by three referees, and final decisions were made at the Program Committee meeting in January 1995, attended by 12 PC members.

We wish to thank all the researchers for submitting their papers, the PC members and additional referees for the help in the reviewing process, and the European Network of Excellence in Machine Learning for the financial support which made the PC meeting possible. We are also very grateful to our colleagues who provided invaluable organizational support. Darko Zupanič and Dunja Mladenić from J. Stefan Institute prepared summary review materials for the PC meeting. Josef Börding and Ulrike Teuber provided administrative support in paper management at GMD. Luzia Sassen designed the poster, and Marcus Lübbe helped with the World-Wide Web.

ECML-95 was organized by the Institute of Computer Science, Foundation for Research and Technology – Hellas (FORTH), Science and Technology Park of Crete, Vassilika Vouton, Heraklion, Greece. Our gratitude goes to the Local Chair Vassilis Moustakis (FORTH), the members of the Organizing Committee Lena Gaga, Michalis Blazadonakis, Stelios Orphanoudakis, George Potamias and Maria Prevelianaki, and all other individuals who helped in the organization of the conference.

Finally, we would like to acknowledge all the sponsors of ECML-95 for supporting this scientific event.

February 1995

Ljubljana   Nada Lavrač
Sankt Augustin   Stefan Wrobel

Program Chairs

Nada Lavrač, J. Stefan Institute, Ljubljana, Slovenia
Stefan Wrobel, GMD, Sankt Augustin, Germany

Local Chair

Vassilis Moustakis, ICS FORTH, Heraclion, Crete, Greece

Program Committee

F. Bergadano (Italy)	I. Bratko (Slovenia)	P. Brazdil (Portugal)
W. Buntine (USA)	L. De Raedt (Belgium)	W. Emde (Germany)
J.G. Ganascia (France)	K. de Jong (USA)	Y. Kodratoff (France)
I. Kononenko (Slovenia)	W. Maass (Austria)	R. L. de Mantaras (Spain)
S. Matwin (Canada)	K. Morik (Germany)	S. Muggleton (UK)
E. Plaza (Spain)	L. Saitta (Italy)	D. Sleeman (UK)
W. Van de Velde (Belgium)	G. Widmer (Austria)	R. Wirth (Germany)

Organizational Support

Michalis Blazadonakis, FORTH
Josef Börding, GMD
Lena Gaga, FORTH
Marcus Lübbe, GMD
Dunja Mladenić, JSI
Stelios Orphanoudakis, FORTH
George Potamias, FORTH
Maria Prevelianaki, FORTH
Luzia Sassen, GMD
Ulrike Teuber, GMD
Darko Zupanič, JSI

Sponsors

Commission of the European Union (Support of Conferences)
MLnet, ESPRIT European Network of Excellence in Machine Learning
Foundation for Research and Technology - Hellas (FORTH), Heraclion
GMD, Sankt Augustin
J. Stefan Institute, Ljubljana

Additional Reviewers

E. Alberdi	D. Alexis	K.D. Althoff
J.L. Arcos	M. Bain	S. Bell
C. Bento	G. Bisson	R. Boswell
M. Botta	P. Brockhausen	L. Carbonara
C. Carry	P. Compton	D. Conklin
L. Console	A. Cornuejols	V. Corruble
V. Cutello	P. Edwards	M. El Attar
S.L. Epstein	C. Feng	B. Filipič
J. Franklin	J. Fürnkranz	J. Gama
A. Giordana	S. Grolimund	D. Gunetti
J. Han	A. Hoffmann	R. Holte
K.P. Jantke	G.H. John	A. Jorge
M. Keane	J.U. Kietz	V. Klingspor
R. Kohavi	K. Koperski	M. Kovačič
M. Kukar	G. Le Blanc	C. Ling
B. Lopez	H. Mühlenbein	A. Mahidadia
E. McCreath	H. Mignot	F. Mitchell
J. Morin	I. Moulinier	G. Nakhaeizadeh
C. Nedellec	R. Oehlmann	G. Paass
C.D. Page	M. Pendrith	B. Pfahringer
U. Pompe	M. Potter	J.R. Quinlan
G. Ramalho	B.L. Richards	A. Rieger
M. Robnik	P.Y. Rolland	C. Rouveirol
D. Roverso	M. Sahami	C. Sammut
J. Sarma	E. Sommer	A. Srinivasan
I. Stahl	J. Stehr	E. Steurer
B. Tausend	J. Thomas	L. Torgo
C. Torras	T. Urbančič	H. Vafaie
G. Venturini	A. Voss	S. Weber
D. Wettschereck	F. Wysotzki	J.D. Zucker

Table of Contents

III Extended Abstracts

Part I:

Invited Papers

Reasoning and Learning in Probabilistic and Possibilistic Networks: An Overview *

Jörg Gebhardt and Rudolf Kruse

Department of Mathematics and Computer Science
University of Braunschweig
D-38106 Braunschweig, Germany
Email: gebhardt@ibr.cs.tu-bs.de

Abstract. Graphical modelling is a powerful framework for reasoning under uncertainty. We give an overview on the semantical background and relevant properties of probabilistic and possibilistic networks, respectively, and consider knowledge representation and independence as well as evidence propagation and learning such networks from data.
Whereas Bayesian networks and Markov networks are well-known for a couple of years, we also outline the perspectives of possibilistic networks as a tool for the efficient information-compressed treatment of uncertain *and* imprecise knowledge.

1 Introduction

Due to its simplification of multivariate data analysis, graphical modelling is being increasingly recognized as an appropriate framework for both knowledge representation and inference under uncertainty [65]. Applications can be found in all areas of analysing dependent observations, for example, in regression analysis, spatial analysis, and expert systems. As a consequence of its primary origin in multivariate statistics, the most advanced numerical approaches to the structured handling of uncertain information have been obtained in the field of probabilistic graphical models [4].

Referred to uncertain reasoning in knowledge-based systems, *Bayesian networks* are established as a powerful tool [40]. They provide a well-founded normative framework in the presence of *uncertain*, but *precise* data. On the other hand, extending pure probabilistic settings to the treatment of *imprecise (multivalued)* information usually restricts the computational tractability of inference mechanisms. Since the explicit modelling of imprecise data is more and more claimed as being necessary for industrial practice, it is reasonable to investigate graphical models related to alternative uncertainty calculi. Under the aspect of efficiency, such uncertainty calculi should provide a justified form of *information compression* and *simplification* in order to support reasoning under uncertainty

---
* This work has partially been funded by CEC-ESPRIT III Basic Research Project 6156 (DRUMS II)

and imprecision without essentially affecting the expressive power and correctness of decision making procedures.

Possibility theory [14] seems to be very promising for this purpose. It is a good choice for systems that accept *approximate* instead of crisp reasoning, characterized by a non-significant sensitivity concerning slight changes of information. From this it follows that possibility theory may grow up to play the same role in the field of uncertain reasoning in knowledge-based systems as nowadays *fuzzy control* as a tool for (information-compressed) interpolation between crisp points in vague environments in the field of control engineering [33].

Related to the mentioned perspectives, this paper gives a brief comparison of probabilistic and possibilistic networks: Section 2 addresses the semantic background and relevant properties of probabilistic networks, and summarizes how to perform inference in such networks. Furthermore, the problem of inducing probabilistic networks from a database of sample cases is considered. Section 3 deals with the same topics referred to *possibilistic networks*. Some additional remarks in Section 4 conclude the discussion.

2   Probabilistic Networks

Graphical models provide a unified qualitative framework for representing and reasoning with uncertainty and independencies. The qualitative part of a graphical model is a graphical representation of dependencies between variables, expressed, for example, by a directed acyclic graph (DAG), an undirected graph (UG), or a chain graph. Each structure reflects a certain kind of independence in the way that conditioning on evidence (obtained through instantiation of a subset of variables) can be realized by efficient local propagation algorithms, related, for example, to the vertices involved in a hyperedge of a dependency hypergraph, rather than by inefficient global conditioning procedures. For this reason, graphical models are always referred to a notion of *(conditional) independence* that has to be specified for the particular uncertainty calculus under consideration [7, 40].

Let V denote a finite set of variables taking their values ω_v on attached domains Ω_v, $v \in V$. Furthermore, let Ω denote their joint domain, and Ω_A the marginal domain of all variables in $A \subseteq V$. Finally, let $\omega_A = (\omega_v)_{v \in A}$ denote a possible state in Ω_A, and $\omega = (\omega_v)_{v \in V}$ a possible state in Ω.

In this paper, we refer to finite domains only, which means that we confine to the important case of *discrete graphical models* with V being the underlying set of vertices.

In pure probabilistic approaches, uncertain knowledge about the quantitative dependencies between the variables in V are formalized with the aid of a probability distribution P on Ω. Conditional independence, encoded by the qualitative part of a probabilistic graphical model, is defined as follows:

Let A, B, and C be three disjoint subsets of variables in V.
A is called *conditionally indpendent of B given C w.r.t. P*, abbr. $I_P(A, B|C)$, iff

$$P(\omega_{A \cup B}|\omega_C) = P(\omega_A|\omega_C) \cdot P(\omega_B|\omega_C) \tag{1}$$

whenever $P(\omega_C) > 0$, $\omega \in \Omega$.

Equation (1) reads as follows: The marginal conditional probability on $\Omega_{A \cup B}$, given any instantiation of the variables in C, equals the product of the marginal conditional probabilities on Ω_A and Ω_B, respectively, referred to the same instantiation of the variables in C.

Given an *independence model* M, that is, a set of conditional independence statements about the variables in V, the task is to find a graphical representation G such that the topology of G reflects the properties of M [40, 56].

A probabilistic graphical model can be equated with the set of probability distributions on Ω that satisfy the constraints implied by G. Two probabilistic graphical models are equivalent, if their underlying sets of satisfying probability distributions are equivalent, i.e. they constitute the same joint probability distribution P on Ω.

Among the various approaches to probabilistic graphical models, for example, influence diagrams used to represent decision processes [54, 44, 26], we restrict ourselves to the special case of *Bayesian networks* and *Markov networks*, respectively, which are an advanced and widely discussed framework for knowledge representation and propagation in probabilistic expert systems.

Bayesian Networks The most popular kind of a probabilistic graphical model in artificial intelligence is the *Bayesian network*, also called *belief network* [40]. A Bayesian network consists of a directed acyclic graph $G = (V, E)$, and a set of conditional probability distributions $P_v(\omega_v | \omega_{par(v)})$, $v \in V$, where $par(v) = \{v' \in V | (v', v) \in E\}$ denotes the set of all parents of v in G.

Since G is directed, Bayesian networks are appropriate to represent direct causal dependencies between variables, which in many cases is quite natural for the purpose of knowledge representation in probabilistic expert systems that support, for example, diagnostic reasoning (abductive inference) in medical applications.

Bayesian networks specify a conditional decomposition of the joint probability distribution P on Ω:

A strictly positive probability distribution P on Ω *factorizes* w.r.t. a directed acyclic graph $G = (V, E)$, if

$$P(\omega) = \prod_{v \in V} P(\omega_v | \omega_{par(v)}). \tag{2}$$

In this case, P satisfies the *global Markov property*, saying that, for any disjoint subsets A, B, and C of V, such that C separates A from B in the moral graph induced by A, B, and C, we have $I_P(A, B|C)$ [34].

In this sense, a Bayesian network is also a graphical representation of a Markov chain. Alternatively, the Markov property can be expressed in terms of the concept of *d-separation* [62].

It can be shown that $P(\omega) = \prod_{v \in V} P_v(\omega_v | \omega_{par(v)})$ constitutes the factorizing probability distribution of a Bayesian network, where $P(\omega_v | \omega_{par(v)})$ equals $P_v(\omega_v | \omega_{par(v)})$, whenever $P_v(\omega_{par(v)}) > 0$. For this reason, equation (2) can be seen as the *interpretation* of a Bayesian network.

Markov Networks An alternative form of probabilistic graphical models refers to undirected graphs $G = (V, E)$ and is called *Markov network* [40]. It represents Markov random fields, used, for instance, in imaging and spatial reasoning [2] and stochastic models in neural networks [27].

Similar to Bayesian networks, the aim is to get a decomposition of the joint probability, but now in terms of a *potential representation* of P:

A strictly positive probability distribution P on Ω *factorizes* according to an undirected graph $G = (V, E)$, if

$$P(\omega) = \prod_{C \in cliques(G)} \phi_C(\omega), \qquad (3)$$

with *cliques*(G) denoting the set of *maximal cliques* on G. A maximal clique on G is a subgraph of G that is fully connected, but not strictly contained in other fully connected subgraphs of G. The function ϕ_C depends on ω through ω_C only.

It can be shown that P factorizes, if and only if any variable $v \in V$ is independent of $V - \{v\} - neighbours(v)$, where $neighbours(v) = \{v' | \{v, v'\} \in E\}$ [24]. The latter condition is called the *local G-Markovian property* [18].

Similar to DAGs, factorization also implies the *global Markovian property*, saying that, for any disjoint subsets A, B, and C of V, such that C separates A from B in G, we have $I_P(A, B | C)$. Equation (3) can therefore be viewed as the *interpretation* of a Markov network.

2.1 Reasoning in Probabilistic Networks

DAGs and UGs represent conditional independence relations in fundamentally different ways. In particular, there are UGs that represent a conditinal independence relation that cannot be represented by a single DAG, and vice versa. On the other hand, every dependence model that is isomorphic to a chordal graph G, which means that every cycle in G of at least length four has an edge joining two nonconsecutive vertices, is also isomorphic to a DAG.

Chordal graphs constitute the class of *decomposable models* [40], which have the useful property that the cliques of their Markov networks form a tree.

These special structures supported the development of efficient inference engines for probabilistic graphical models. Their main purpose is to provide a computational simple conditioning of P. Simplicity of computation means that due to the factorization property of the joint probability distribution P considered in the probabilistic graphical model, conditioning can be performed stepwise on marginal probability distributions referred to only few variables.

Oriented at the way the human mind reasons, J. Pearl [39] developed a local propagation algorithm that works in singly connected Bayesian networks. S. Lauritzen and D. Spiegelhalter [35] approached the same problem from a pure mathematical point of view. Their proposed method works directly and efficiently in an arbitrary sparse Bayesian network. It involves the transformation of the given DAG into a triangulated UG, and the creation of a tree whose vertices are the cliques of this triangulated graph. To realize the propagation process, probabilities in the original Bayesian network are updated by message passing among the vertices of this tree of cliques.

Flexible softwaretools for applying the method are, for example, HUGIN [1, 31] and BAIES [6].

An alternative technique for local computation in hypertrees in the more general framework of *valuation-based systems (VBS)* [47] has been proposed in [51, 46] and implemented in PULCINELLA [43].

2.2 Learning Probabilistic Networks from Data

For many application fields, the need to specify probabilistic networks is considerable, so that an automatic induction of the qualitative part (the structure) and the quantitative part (the conditional probability distributions) using underlying background knowledge could alleviate such specification difficulties.

Some modelling problems arise from the fact that various kinds of a priori information about the network can be available, expert knowledge as well as an additional database of sample cases, both to be considered in a unified framework for realizing the network induction process.

If we restrict ourselves to a pure data-oriented approach, then the typical assumption is that of a given database $\mathcal{D} = (D_1, \ldots, D_m)$ of m partial observations $D_j \subseteq \Omega_{A_j}$ of independent random variables with common distribution P.

The data are *complete*, if $A_j = V$ for all $j = 1, \ldots, m$, *partially incomplete* (with missing values), if $V = A_1 \cup \ldots \cup A_m$, and *incomplete* (with hidden variables), if $V \neq A_1 \cup \ldots \cup A_m$.

The network induction process consists of constructing a network within a selected class of networks that best fits the database with respect to a chosen (information-theoretical) optimality criterion.

Quantitative network induction refers to estimating the joint probability distribution P from a parametrized family of probability distributions, given a specific network structure.

A lot of research has been done in this field, referred to basic methods such as maximum likelihood, maximum penalized likelihood, or fully Bayesian approaches, involving different computational techniques of probabilistic inference such as the expectation maximization (EM) algorithm, Gibbs sampling, Laplace approximation, and Monte Carlo methods. For an overview, see [3, 55].

Qualitative network induction is learning a network structure from a database of sample cases. In very general terms, the corresponding methods can be classified in three groups, either based on linearity and normality assumptions [42], the extensive testing of conditional independence relations (CI tests) [63], or taking a Bayesian approach [5, 36]. The first group is quite restrictive, CI tests tend to be unreliable unless the volume of data is enormous, and they become rapidly computationally infeasible with increasing number of vertices. Bayesian learning requires debatable a priori assumptions (for example, default uniform priors on distributions, uniform priors on DAGs) and also tends to be inefficient unless Greedy search methods are used.

A quite promising forward search Bayesian learning algorithm is $K2$ [5], which approximates the most probable structure of a Bayesian network in $O(mn^2u^2r)$ time, where r is the maximum cardinality of the considered domains, and u a presupposed upper bound on the number of parents each vertex may have. $K2$ has successfully been applied, but needs a pre-ordering of the vertices. For this reason, hybrid algorithms, combining CI tests (for finding a vertex ordering) and $K2$ (for constructing the Bayesian network with respect to this vertex ordering) have been developed [52]. $K2$ works with complete and crisp data, i.e. $|D_j| = 1$, $j = 1, \ldots, m$, whereas the treatment of missing values and hidden variables is only clear from a theoretical point of view [5].

An alternative algorithm, using a backward search strategy, is described in [30].

An important topic, namely determining the sample size needed to accept the result delivered by structure induction algorithms on a chosen statistical significance level has so far not been considered in a sufficient way. Besides the problem of measuring distances between structures, an additional problem is that of evaluating Markov equivalent DAGs, which are indistinguishable from data alone.

3 Possibilistic Networks

3.1 Possibility Distributions

A *possibility distribution* π on a universe of discourse Ω is a mapping from Ω into the unit interval, i.e. $\pi : \Omega \to [0, 1]$ [67].

From an intuitive point of view, given a possibility distribution π as an imperfect specification of a state $\omega_0 \in \Omega$, for any $\omega \in \Omega$, $\pi(\omega)$ quantifies the possibility degree of truth of $\omega = \omega_0$. The case $\pi(\omega) = 0$ means that $\omega = \omega_0$ is impossible, $\pi(\omega) = 1$ means that $\omega = \omega_0$ is possible without any restrictions, and $\pi(\omega) \in (0, 1)$ means that $\omega = \omega_0$ is partly possible, since there is evidence that supports $\omega = \omega_0$ as well as evidence that contradicts $\omega = \omega_0$.

A possibility distribution π induces a partial ordering on the possible states, which is less informative than a probability distribution on Ω, so that the *measure of possibility* $\Pi(A)$ of a finite event $A \subseteq \Omega$ is simply defined as the maximum of $\pi(\omega)$ for all $\omega \in A$.

Recent years of research provided different proposals for the semantics of a *theory of possibility* as a framework for reasoning with uncertain and imprecise data. Among the numerical approaches, we like to mention possibility distributions as epistemic interpretation of fuzzy sets [67], the axiomatic view of possibility theory based on the concept of a possibility measure [14], Spohn's theory of epistemic states [58], possibility distributions as one-point coverages of random sets [38, 28], contour functions of consonant belief functions [45], falling shadows in set-valued statistics [64], and possibility theory based on likelihoods [13].

The view of a possibility distribution as an *information-compressed* representation of an uncertain and imprecise specification of a state ω_0 of interest can be clarified in a random set framework that generalizes traditional approaches given in [59, 12, 9].

Let $(C, 2^C, P), C = \{c_1, c_2, \ldots, c_m\}$, denote a finite probability space, and $\gamma : C \to 2^{\Omega}$ a set–valued mapping. C is interpreted as a set of contexts that are distinguished for set-valued specifications of ω_0. The contexts are supposed to describe different physical and observation-related frame conditions, which are, for example, formalized by logical propositions.

The relation $\gamma(c_j)$ is assumed to be the *most specific correct set-valued specification* of ω_0, implied by the frame conditions that describe c_j. This says that $\omega_0 \in \gamma(c)$ is guaranteed to be true for $\gamma(c)$, but for no proper subset of $\gamma(c)$. The quantity $P(\{c_j\})$ is the (subjective) probability of applying c_j for the specification of ω_0. The resulting *random set* $\Gamma = (\gamma, P)$ is an imperfect (set-valued and uncertain) specification of ω_0. Let π_Γ denote the *one-point coverage of* Γ (the *possibility distribution induced by* Γ), defined as

$$\pi_\Gamma : \Omega \to [0,1], \pi_\Gamma(\omega) = P(\{c \in C \mid \omega \in \gamma(c)\}).$$

In a complete modelling, the contexts in C must be specified in detail, so that the relationships among all contexts c_j and their context–dependent specifications $\gamma(c_j)$ of ω_0 are clarified. On the other hand, if the contexts are unknown or ignored, then $\pi_\Gamma(\omega)$ is the total mass of all contexts c that provide a correct specification $\gamma(c)$ of ω_0, and this quantifies the *possibility of truth* of "$\omega = \omega_0$" [20, 19].

The (information-compressed) imperfect knowledge about ω_0, represented by π_Γ, can be specialized in the way that uncertainty is excluded by stating α-*correctness of* Γ *w.r.t.* ω_0, which means that there exists a subset $C' \subseteq C$ of contexts such that $P(C') \geq \alpha$ and $\forall c' \in C' : \omega_0 \in \gamma(c')$. In this case, the α-*cut* $[\pi_\Gamma]_\alpha = \{\omega \mid \pi_\Gamma(\omega) \geq \alpha\}$ of the possibility distribution π_Γ turns out to be the most specific correct set-valued specification of ω_0, given the representation Γ of our background knowledge about ω_0, and the α-correctness assumption w.r.t. ω_0 [21].

Operating on possibility distributions can be performed within the pure random set background [9, 28], but has the disadvantage that it is not conform with the *extension principle* [66], which from a semantical point of view has been claimed as the adequate way of generalizing operations from crisp or imprecise (set-valued) data to the possibilistic setting [15, 33]. For this reason, it seems to be more convenient to base the interpretation of possibility degrees on the above mentioned concepts of α-correctness and maximum specificity, strongly oriented at the meaning of the underlying contexts in C. For an extensive presentation of this view of possibility theory, we refer to [21, 23]. It verifies the extension principle not just as a principle, but as a theorem in the underlying formal and semantical framework. Special aspects of possibility measures for decision making have been considered in [22].

3.2 Possibilistic Graphical Models

Possibilistic graphical models can be introduced in a similar way as probabilistic graphical models. The main difference consists in the change from probability distributions to possibility distributions, so that there is the need for an appropriate concept of *possibilistic independence*.

Although well-known for a couple of years [29], a unique concept of possibilistic independence has not been fixed yet. For some recent discussions, see [16, 17]. In our opinion, the main problem is to recognize that possibility theory is a calculus for uncertain *and* imprecise reasoning.

For comparison, note that using a single *probability distribution* covers only modelling of *uncertain*, but *precise* data. In a corresponding way, relational database theory applies *relations* in order to represent *imprecise*, but *certain* information about dependencies among variables. Due to their restrictions to distinguishable kinds of imperfect data, the two frameworks supply different concepts of independence, which are probabilistic independence and lossless-join decomposability. Probabilistic independence may be viewed as an *uncertainty-driven* type of independence, whereas lossless-join decomposability [37, 60] reflects an *imprecision-driven* type of independence.

Since possibility theory addresses both kinds of imperfect knowledge, concepts of possibilistic independence can be uncertainty–driven or imprecision–driven, so that there are at least two ways of introducing and justifying them.

Concerning the treatment of imperfect information, one should consider two levels of reasoning, namely the *credal level*, where all operations on our pieces of knowledge take place, and the *pignistic level*, where the final step of decision making follows [53]. Imprecision-driven possibilistic independence is strongly oriented at the credal level, applying the extension principle as the basic concept of operating on possibility distributions, and avoiding normalization, which would change their meaning from quantifying absolute to relative degrees of possibility. In opposite to this, an uncertainty-driven approach to possibilistic independence should be referred to the pignistic level, taking decision making aspects into account and thus quantifying the relative degrees of possibility of events. On this level, the need of normalization is obvious.

With respect to this consideration, in [8] two definitions of possibilistic independence have been justified, namely uncertainty-driven possibilistic independence based on *Dempster's rule of conditioning* [45], specialized to possibility measures, and imprecision-driven possibilistic independence that coincides with the well-known concept of *possibilistic non-interactivity* [14], which is a generalization of the lossless-join-decomposition property to the possibilistic setting.

Due to its consistency with the extension principle, we confine to possibilistic non-interactivity. As a concept of possibilistic independence it can be formalized as follows:

Let A, B, and C be three disjoint subsets of variables in V.

A is called *conditionally independent* of B given C w.r.t. π, abbr. $I_\pi(A, B|C)$, iff

$$\pi(\omega_{A\cup B}|\omega_C) = min\{\pi(\omega_A|\omega_C), \pi(\omega_B|\omega_C)\} \qquad (4)$$

whenever $\pi(\omega_C) > 0$, $\omega \in \Omega$, with $\pi(\cdot|\cdot)$ denoting the non-normalized conditional possibility distribution, i.e.

$$\pi(\omega_A|\omega_C) = max\{\pi(\omega')|\omega' \in \Omega, \omega'_A = \omega_A, \omega'_C = \omega_C\}.$$

It has to be emphasized that both mentioned types of possibilistic independence satisfy the so-called *semi-graphoid axioms* [41] of symmetry, decomposition, weak union, and contraction, which were proposed as basic properties that
any concept of conditional independence should have [7, 57, 54].
Possibilistic independence based on Dempster's rule additionally satisfies the intersection axiom and is therefore a *graphoid* [17]. But note that the intersection
axiom is related to uncertainty-driven independence as used in probability theory. Hence, relational independence does not satisfy this axiom, and therefore it
cannot be satisfied by possibilistic non-interactivity as its more general type of
imprecision-driven independence.

Factorization of possibility distributions is similar to factorization of probability distributions by changing the product to the min-operator.

3.3 Reasoning in Possibilistic Networks

The axiomatic framework of *valuation-based systems (VBS)* [47, 50] is able to
represent various uncertainty calculi such as probability theory, Dempster-Shafer
theory, and possibility theory. Conditional independence in VBSs has been defined in [48] and shown to satisfy the graphoid axioms in [49]. Possibilistic independence in VBSs corresponds to uncertainty-driven possibilistic independence
based on Dempster's rule. Hence, using this type of possibilistic independence,
a local propagation algorithm for hypertrees, developed in the setting of VBSs
[51, 46], can directly be applied to possibilistic networks that have or can be
transformed into this structure (note the correspondence between hypertrees,
Markov trees, and join trees). The general algorithm has been implemented in
the PULCINELLA system [43].

Choosing possibilistic non-interactivity as the appropriate type of possibilistic independence in order to hold consistency with the extension principle, the
VBS approach has to be slightly modified, since no normalization takes place.
The related local propagation algorithms for hypertree structures are considered
in [33] and implemented in the tool POSSINFER [33].

3.4 Learning Possibilistic Networks from Data

Inducing the qualitative part (the structure) and the quantitative part (the conditional possibility distributions) of a possibilistic network from a database of
sample cases has not been studied in much detail yet. A first result concerning
this topic is presented in [23]. It refers to the semantic background of possibility
distributions considered in Section 3.1, and defines a possibilistic interpretation
of a database $\mathcal{D}$ of complete, potentially imprecise sample cases, so that, in op-
posite to the methods mentioned in Section 2.4, $|D_j| > 1$ is accepted. Based
on this interpretation, the task is to find a possibilistic network that best fits
$\mathcal{D}$ relative to a class of possibilistic networks and a chosen optimality valuation. An obstacle for the corresponding structure induction methods is the fact
that there are already serious complexity problems in the more special case of
structure identification in relational data: If we are given a hypergraph H and

a relation R, then only in cases where H is tractable (for instance, if H is a hypertree), one can (tractably) decide whether H induces a lossless join decomposition of R. On the other hand, the lossless join decomposition of a relation into a structure taken from a *class* of dependency hypergraphs turns out to be a harder problem, which is presumably intractable even in cases where each individual member of the class is tractable [11]. As a consequence, at least from the viewpoint of efficiency, *heuristics* for inducing possibilistic networks from data have to be tolerated.

In our approach, the valuation of a DAG or an UG with respect to a given database is referred to the amount of information that has to be added to the network in order to identify any possible state $\omega \in \Omega$ as the unknown state ω_0 of interest, assuming a uniform distribution on Ω. Due to the involved handling of imprecise data, the underlying information measure is *Hartley information* [25], generalized to the uncertainty calculus of possibility theory. In [23], we present the theoretical background and a Greedy search algorithm for inducing DAG structures of possibilistic networks in $O(n^2 m r)$ time without any a priori ordering of the vertices. This algorithm has successfully been applied for reconstructing a non-singly connected DAG with 22 vertices and 24 arcs, based on a generated database of 700 samples [23]. The reconstruction is perfect, except from those dependencies, where a unique directing of arcs is not possible, since not expressable in a database.

4 Concluding Remarks

In this overview, we discussed various aspects of reasoning and learning related to probabilistic and possibilistic graphical models. Whereas probabilistic networks deal with uncertain, but precise information, possibilistic networks – for reasons of efficiency – accept a well-founded type of information compression, reducing exact reasoning to only approximate reasoning, which has turned out to be sufficient for many purposes in practice.

Current research interest concerns the automatic construction of graphical models from expert knowledge and available databases of sample cases. In more general terms, this is a well-known problem in the field of *Machine Learning*, where several techniques of concept learning from examples have been discussed. On the other hand, the special properties of the considered network structures and uncertainty calculi restrict the applicability of general machine learning methods. Within the addressed numerical settings, *probably approximately correct (PAC) learning* [61] seems to be convincing at least with respect to its underlying probabilistic framework. In PAC learning, there are some nice complexity results [32, 10] that could be of some interest for limiting the number of sample cases needed in a database in order to guarantee a certain approximation quality of the obtained network. Nevertheless, pure statistical methods of learning probability distributions and verifying probabilistic independence seem to be appropriate. In a similar way, the induction of possibilistic networks from data can be oriented at the specific properties of possibility theory.

References

1. S.K. Andersen, K.G. Olesen, F.V. Jensen, and F. Jensen. HUGIN — A shell for building Bayesian belief universes for expert systems. In *Proc. 11th international joint conference on arificial intelligence*, pages 1080–1085, 1989.

2. J. Besag, J. York, and A. Mollie. Bayesian image restauration with two applications in spatial statistics. *Ann. Inst. Statist. Math.*, 43(1):1–59, 1991.

3. W. Buntine. Operations for learning with graphical models. *Journal of Artificial Intelligence Research*, 2:159–225, 1994.

4. P. Cheeseman and R.W. Oldford, editors. *Selecting Models from Data*, volume 89 of *Lecture Notes in Statistics*. Springer-Verlag, 1994.

5. G. Cooper and E. Herskovits. A Bayesian method for the induction of probabilistic networks from data. *Machine Learning*, 9:309–347, 1992.

6. R. Cowell. BAIES - a probabilistic expert system shell with qualitative and quantitative learning. In J. Bernardo, J. Berger, A. Dawid, and A. Smith, editors, *Bayesian Statistics 4*, pages 595–600. Oxford University Press, 1992.

7. A. Dawid. Conditional independence in statistical theory. *SIAM Journal on Computing*, 41:1–31, 1979.

8. L.M. de Campos, J. Gebhardt, and R. Kruse. Syntactic and semantic approaches to possibilistic independence. Technical report, University of Granada and University of Braunschweig, 1995.

9. J. Kampé de Fériet. Interpretation of membership functions of fuzzy sets in terms of plausibility and belief. In M.M. Gupta and E. Sanchez, editors, *Fuzzy Information and Decision Processes*, pages 13–98. North–Holland, 1982.

10. S. Decatur. Learning in hybrid noise environments: Using statistical queries. In *Proc. 5th Int. Workshop on Artificial Intelligence and Statistics*, pages 175–185, Fort Lauderdale, 1995.

11. R. Dechter and J. Pearl. Structure identification in relational data. *Artificial Intelligence*, 58:237–270, 1992.

12. A.P. Dempster. Upper and lower probabilities induced by a multivalued mapping. *Ann. Math. Stat.*, 38:325–339, 1967.

13. D. Dubois, S. Moral, and H. Prade. A semantics for possibility theory based on likelihoods. Annual report, CEC–ESPRIT III BRA 6156 DRUMS II, 1993.

14. D. Dubois and H. Prade. *Possibility Theory*. Plenum Press, New York, 1988.

15. D. Dubois and H. Prade. Fuzzy sets in approximate reasoning, Part 1: Inference with possibility distributions. *Fuzzy Sets and Systems*, 40:143–202, 1991.

16. L. Farinas del Cerro and A. Herzig. Possibility theory and independence. In *Proc. of the Fifth IPMU Conference*, pages 820–825, 1994.

17. P. Fonck. Conditional independence in possibility theory. In R.López de Mántaras and D. Poole, editors, *Uncertainty in Artificial Intelligence, Proc. of the Tenth Conference*, pages 221–226. Morgan and Kaufmann, 1994.

18. M. Frydenberg. The chain graph markov property. *Scandinavian Journal of Statistics*, 17:333–353, 1990.

19. J. Gebhardt and R. Kruse. A comparative discussion of combination rules in numerical settings. Annual report, CEC–ESPRIT III BRA 6156 DRUMS II, 1993.

20. J. Gebhardt and R. Kruse. The context model — an integrating view of vagueness and uncertainty. *Int. Journal of Approximate Reasoning*, 9:283–314, 1993.

21. J. Gebhardt and R. Kruse. A new approach to semantic aspects of possibilistic reasoning. In M. Clarke, R. Kruse, and S. Moral, editors, *Symbolic and Quantitative*

Approaches to Reasoning and Uncertainty, Lecture Notes in Computer Science, 747, pages 151–160. Springer, Berlin, 1993.

22. J. Gebhardt and R. Kruse. On an information compression view of possibility theory. In *Proc. 3rd IEEE Int. Conf. on Fuzzy Systems,* pages 1285–1288, Orlando, 1994.

23. J. Gebhardt and R. Kruse. Learning possibilistic networks from data. In *Proc. 5th Int. Workshop on Artificial Intelligence and Statistics,* pages 233–244, Fort Lauderdale, 1995.

24. D. Geman. Random fields and inverse problems in imaging. In P. Hennequin, editor, *École d'Été de Probabilités de Saint-Flour XVIII — 1988, Lecture Notes in Mathematics, 1427.* 1990.

25. R.V.L. Hartley. Transmission of information. *The Bell Systems Technical Journal,* 7:535–563, 1928.

26. D. Heckerman. *Probabilistic Similarity Networks.* MIT Press, 1991.

27. J. Hertz, A. Krogh, and R. Palmer. *Introduction to the Theory of Neural Computation.* Addison Wesley, 1991.

28. K. Hestir, H.T. Nguyen, and G.S. Rogers. A random set formalism for evidential reasoning. In I.R. Goodman, M.M. Gupta, H.T. Nguyen, and G.S. Rogers, editors, *Conditional Logic in Expert Systems,* pages 209–344. North-Holland, 1991.

29. E. Hisdal. Conditional possibilities, independence, and noninteraction. *Fuzzy Sets and Systems,* 1:283–297, 1978.

30. S. Højsgaard and B. Thiesson. BIFROST – block rekursive models induced from relevant knowledge, observations, and statistical techniques. *Computational Statistics and Data Analysis,* 1994.

31. F.V. Jensen. *drHUGIN — A System for value of information in Bayesian Networks.* 1993.

32. M. Kearns. *The Computational Complexity of Machine Learning.* MIT Press, 1990.

33. R. Kruse, J. Gebhardt, and F. Klawonn. *Foundations of Fuzzy Systems.* Wiley, Chichester, 1994. (Translation of the book: Fuzzy Systeme, Series: Leitfäden und Monographien der Informatik, Teubner, Stuttgart, 1993).

34. S. Lauritzen, A. Dawid, B. Larsen, and H.G. Leimer. Independence properties of directed markov fields. *Networks,* 20:491–505, 1990.

35. S.L. Lauritzen and D.J. Spiegelhalter. Local computations with probabilities on graphical structures and their application to expert systems. *Journal of the Royal Stat. Soc., Series B,* 2(50):157–224, 1988.

36. S.L. Lauritzen, B. Thiesson, and D. Spiegelhalter. Diagnostic systems created by model selection methods — a case study. In *4th Int. Workshop on Artificial Intelligence and Statistics, January 3–6,* pages 93–105, Ft. Lauderdale, FL, 1993.

37. D. Maier. *The Theory of Relational Databases.* Computer Science Press, Rockville, MD, 1983.

38. H.T. Nguyen. On random sets and belief functions. *Journal of Mathematical Analysis and Applications,* 65:531–542, 1978.

39. J. Pearl. Fusion, propagation, and structuring in belief networks. *Artificial Intelligence,* 29:241–288, 1986.

40. J. Pearl. *Probabilistic Reasoning in Intelligent Systems: Networks of Plausible Inference (2nd edition).* Morgan Kaufmann, New York, 1992.

41. J. Pearl and A. Paz. Graphoids: A graph based logic for reasoning about relevance relations. In B.D. Boulay et al., editor, *Advances in Artificial Intelligence, 2,* pages 357–363. North Holland, Amsterdam, 1987.

42. J. Pearl and N. Wermuth. When can association graphs admit a causal interpretation (first report). In *Preliminary Papers of the 4th Int. Workshop on Artificial Intelligence and Statistics, January 3-6*, pages 141–150, Ft. Lauderdale, FL, 1993.

43. A. Saffiotti and E. Umkehrer. PULCINELLA: A general tool for propagating uncertainty in valuation networks. In B. D'Ambrosio, P. Smets, and P.P. Bonisonne, editors, *Proc. 7th Conf. on Uncertainty in Artificial Intelligence*, pages 323–331, San Mateo, 1991. Morgan Kaufmann.

44. R. Shachter. An ordered examination of influence diagrams. *Networks*, 20:535–563, 1990.

45. G. Shafer. *A Mathematical Theory of Evidence*. Princeton University Press, Princeton, 1976.

46. G. Shafer and P.P. Shenoy. Local computation in hypertrees. Working paper 201, School of Business, University of Kansas, Lawrence, 1988.

47. P.P. Shenoy. A valuation–based language for expert systems. *Int. Journal of Approximate Reasoning*, 3:383–411, 1989.

48. P.P. Shenoy. Conditional independence in valuation–based systems. Working Paper 236, School of Business, University of Kansas, Lawrence, KS, 1991.

49. P.P. Shenoy. Conditional independence in uncertainty theories. In D. Dubois, M.P. Wellman, B. D'Ambrosio, and P. Smets, editors, *Uncertainty in Artificial Intelligence: Proc. of the 8th Conference*, pages 284–291, San Mateo, CA, 1992. Morgan Kaufmann.

50. P.P. Shenoy. Valuation–based systems: A framework for managing uncertainty in expert systems. In L.A. Zadeh and J. Kacprzyk, editors, *Fuzzy Logic for the Management of Uncertainty*, pages 83–104. Wiley, New York, NY, 1992.

51. P.P. Shenoy and G.R. Shafer. Axioms for probability and belief–function propagation. In R.D. Shachter, T.S. Levitt, L.N. Kanal, and J.F. Lemmer, editors, *Uncertainty in Artificial Intelligence (4)*, pages 169–198. North–Holland, Amsterdam, 1990.

52. M. Singh and M. Valtorta. An algorithm for the construction of Bayesian network structures from data. In *Proc. 9th. Conf. on Uncertainty in Artificial Intelligence, Washington*, pages 259–265, 1993.

53. P. Smets and R. Kennes. The transferable belief model. *Artificial Intelligence*, 66:191–234, 1994.

54. J.Q. Smith. Influence diagrams for statistical modeling. *Annals of Statistics*, 17(2):654–672, 1989.

55. D. Spiegelhalter, A. Dawid, S. Lauritzen, and R. Cowell. Bayesian analysis in expert systems. *Statistical Science*, 8(3):219–283, 1993.

56. P. Spirtes, C. Glymour, and R. Scheines. *Causation, Prediction, and Search*, volume 81 of *Lecture Notes in Statistics*. Springer, 1993.

57. W. Spohn. Stochastic independence, causal independence, and shieldability. *Journal of Philosophical Logic*, 9:73–99, 1980.

58. W. Spohn. A general non-probabilistic theory of inductive reasoning. In R.D. Shachter, T.S. Levitt, L.N. Kanal, and J.F. Lemmer, editors, *Uncertainty in Artificial Intelligence*, pages 149–158. North Holland, Amsterdam, 1990.

59. V. Strassen. Meßfehler und Information. *Zeitschrift Wahrscheinlichkeitstheorie und verwandte Gebiete*, 2:273–305, 1964.

60. J.D. Ullman. *Principles of Database and Knowledge-Base Systems*, volume 1. Computer Science Press Inc., Rockville, Maryland, 1988.

61. L. Valiant. A theory of the learnable. *Communications of the ACM*, 27:1134–1142, 1984.

62. T. Verma and J. Pearl. Causal networks: Semantics and expressiveness. In R.D. Shachter, T.S. Levitt, L.N. Kanal, and J.F. Lemmer, editors, *Uncertainty in Artificial Intelligence*, pages 69–76. North Holland, Amsterdam, 1990.

63. T. Verma and J. Pearl. An algorithm for deciding if a set of observed independencies has a causal explanation. In *Proc. 8th Conf. on Uncertainty in Artificial Intelligence*, pages 323–330, 1992.

64. P.Z. Wang. From the fuzzy statistics to the falling random subsets. In P.P. Wang, editor, *Advances in Fuzzy Sets, Possibility and Applications*, pages 81–96. Plenum Press, New York, 1983.

65. J. Whittaker. *Graphical Models in Applied Multivariate Statistics*. John Wiley and Sons, 1990.

66. L.A. Zadeh. The concept of a linguistic variable and its application to approximate reasoning. *Information Sciences*, 9:43–80, 1975.

67. L.A. Zadeh. Fuzzy sets as a basis for a theory of possibility. *Fuzzy Sets and Systems*, 1:3–28, 1978.

Problem Decomposition and the Learning of Skills

Donald Michie*

University of Edinburgh
United Kingdom
E-Mail dm@aiai.ed.ac.uk

Abstract. One dimension of "divide and conquer" in problem solving concerns the domain and its subdomains. Humans learn the general structure of a domain while solving particular learning problems in it. Another dimension concerns the solver's goals and subgoals. Finding good decompositions is a major AI tactic both for defusing the combinatorial explosion and for ensuring a transparent end-product. In machine learning, pre-occupation with free-standing performance has led to comparative neglect of this resource, illustrated under the following headings. 1. Automatic manufacture of new attributes from primitives ("constructive induction"). 2. Machine learning within goal-subgoal hierarchies ("structured induction"). 3. Reconstruction of skills from human performance data ("behavioural cloning").

1 Introduction

Artificial Intelligence is the engineering science of concepts. We want machines to accept and use concepts from people. We want them to discover new concepts, and to communicate these back to people. We also want them to knit complex concepts together, and by combining observational data with pre-existing knowledge to build new theories of importance for science and technology.

At the lowest levels of machine-constructed theories, black boxes are acceptable. Above a certain level they are not. Reduction of complexity to transparently communicable theories demands more than simply following a symbolic paradigm. For non-trivial problems it usually requires structuring in some way or another, and in the present state of the art the intrusion (as purists might see it) of user interaction. But first I shall discuss a domain where interactive human brain-power reaps large rewards even from non-decompositional methods.

Concept Learning in Molecular Chemistry. In biomolecular modelling many important problems lie towards the simple end of the complexity scale, yet their solution is still beyond unaided human conjecture. Rewards from computer-aided discovery can be very high, for example in drug design. Following the development of efficient Inductive Logic Programming (ILP) algorithms [1], opportunities have multiplied. A recent co- development by members of the Programming

---

* Present address: 73-860 Shadow Mountain Drive, Unit 2, Palm Desert, CA 92260, USA.

Research Group, Oxford, and of the Imperial Cancer Research Fund, London, yielded significant advances based on (1) the expressive power of first order logic as a rule language, and (2) domain expert interaction in constructing "consensus rules" from induction products.

From existing biomolecular data it was required to extract theories able to suggest new compounds for trial syntheses. Rules must not only predict with good accuracy a specified biological activity but should also make sense to the scientists. The following case is taken from a summary of new applications of machine learning (ML) in structural molecular biology [2] and relates to the inhibition of E. coli dihydrofolate reductase by 2,4,-diamino-5-(substituted-benzyl) pyrimidines. Much previous study had previously been devoted to this problem using statistical and neural-net algorithms.

Here is a rule obtained by an ILP algorithm from a data-set describing 55 drugs for which results of tests for biological activity were available:

drug A is better than drug B if
drug A has a substitutent at position 3 with
hydrogen-bond donor = 0 and
p-acceptor = 0
and polarity > 0 and
size < 3 and
drug A has a substituent at position 4 and
drug B has no substituent at position 5.

In total 59 rules were found, from which seven consensus rules were formed manually by selecting the most commonly found features. These consensus rules were not only easier to understand than the automatically generated rules but in cross- validation their average predictivity was about 85%. This contrasted with about 67% for the products of stand-alone learners, whether ILP, neural net or regression. In contrast with these other learners ILP generated explicit forms that enabled both (a) formation of consensus rules and (b) a deepening of insight into the problem's stereochemistry. Sternberg and his co-workers summarize this approach to machine learning for scientific problems of this kind:

There is an interactive cycle between human analysis and machine learning. Initially traditional methods process the data and develop representations that characterize the system and rules describing the relationship between the components of the system. Next machine learning uses these representations to identify new, and hopefully more powerful and incisive, rules. Then human intervention is required for interpretation of the rules and the cycle can be repeated.

Purists will say "Very nice for the practical or even the commercial ends of scientific clients! Meanwhile we in ML have our own science to do in characterising and studying algorithms. For this, as chemists with new compounds, we have to isolate, analyse and test them in pure form, uncontaminated by human interaction."

This analogy makes sense only in the context of a certain phase of organic chemistry. As soon as biochemistry, and later molecular chemistry, started treading on its heels, the need to keep living cells away from the reagents gave place to the need to bring reagents and cells together. So with ML. We should be in the business of designing ML algorithms so that human brains, not Martian, can use the products. How else are we to gather data for further automation? In the biomolecular example, interactive development of the technique of consensus rules necessarily preceded consideration of how to mechanise it.

2 Categories of Problem Decomposition

Decompositional approaches are discussed in the following contexts:

- automatic manufacture of new attributes;
- machine learning within goal-subgoal hierarchies;
- reconstruction of skills from human performance data.

2.1 Attribute manufacture

Experienced statistical data analysts routinely augment the "given" set of independent variables by variously transforming and combining them. ML workers in general neither do this themselves nor incorporate such procedures into their algorithms. Yet attribute manufacture can make tractable to propositional learners problems that otherwise require the full machinery of ILP. SOAR's "chunking" (see [3] for overview) has something of this flavour as an aid to problem solving. My discussion here is of aids to learning. Two examples will be given, namely "KRK illegality" and "Michalski trains".

KRK Illegality Problem. Automatic discovery of the concept "position illegal" in the elementary chess end-game king and rook against king was studied as a bench-mark [4]. With only primitive attributes supplied, ILP outperformed decision-tree and rule learning algorithms. Performance of human learners was also tested. Michie and Bain [5] then re-attacked the problem using a decision-tree learner with an attribute-manufacture pre-process. Without it, learning was dismal as before. With it, highly accurate trees were generated.

We denote the king-rook-king chess endgame as KRK. There are about a quarter of a million ways of placing on the chess-board the three pieces: White king, White rook and Black king. Training sets consisted of examples represented simply as a vector of six integer-attributes, each drawn from the interval (1, 2, ..., 8). The attribute-vectors are interpretable as a sequence of three co-ordinate pairs specifying the locations on the board of, respectively, the White king, the White rook and the Black king. The two decision classes were "illegal" and "legal". The latter (negative examples) outnumbered the former (positive examples) in the ratio of about two to one. What follows is based on Michie and Bain's follow-up of the earlier study by Muggleton and co-workers.

The theory "KRK-illegal", derived from the laws of chess, can be expressed using the "negation as failure" convention, i.e. "legal" is the default class.

if the White rook and the Black king
  either occupy the same file and the white king is not directly between
  or occupy the same rank and the white king is not directly between
then illegal;
if the two kings
  either are vertically adjacent
  or are horizontally adjacent
  or are diagonally adjacent
then illegal;
if two pieces are on the same square
then illegal;
otherwise legal.

This is one possible formulation of the theory to be discovered, and a fragment of training data might look like this:

2 6 7 4 2 3 no
7 6 3 7 3 8 yes
3 6 1 2 6 3 no
4 8 3 2 4 7 yes
8 8 5 4 8 2 no

The first six symbols in each line represent the three co-ordinate pairs needed to specify the squares on the board occupied by the three pieces, and the seventh represents the decision class, with "yes" for "KRK-illegal" and "no" for its negation, "KRK-legal".

Faced with raw data in this form humans were unable to extract any meaningful patterns in several hours. But as a side-test (not previously reported) a professional data analyst, Dr Jane Mitchell, from the Strathclyde University Statistics Department was invited to tackle the problem. She was allowed whatever analytical methods or computational tools she cared to employ. After two days' intensive work she announced a complete, correct and concise formulation logically equivalent to the theory given above.

So this seemingly toy-sized task is interesting. It completely defeats untrained humans, but succumbs to a professional analyst using statistical but no ML aids. Moreover, decision-trees induced from training sets of size 700 scored no better than the 67% achievable by the trivial rule that always guesses "legal". The decision-tree learner was then equipped with 15 additional attributes manufactured as pairwise differences of the six primitives. The effect was spectacular. The same algorithm now constructed theories that correctly classified about 98% of new cases.

An ILP algorithm (CIGOL, see Muggleton et al., cited above) had earlier been trained on five sets of 40 positive and 60 negative cases. Of the resulting five theories, one scored as high as 91%. In terms of performance, the logically redundant addition to background knowledge had enabled decision-tree learning to do at least as well as ILP. Yet on the transparency criterion, decision trees showed up badly. Each was a bulky and opaque structure of some 40-50 nodes.

ILP-generated theories were short, clear and explicit, even though incomplete. It would be nice to see transparency combined with new attribute formation, as in the following case.

Extended Michalski trains problem. Michalski's classical Eastbound-versus- Westbound discrimination first appeared in a graphical representation [6]. Trains differ in such attributes as the number and shapes of cars and loads, types of roofs etc. Last year a public challenge was issued by Michie and colleagues [7] to induce Prolog rules from facts about trains. The Prolog fact

```
eastbound([c(1, bucket, short, not_double, none, 2 l(circle,1)),
           c(2, rectangle, long, not_double, none, 3, l(triangle, 1)),
           c(3, rectangle, short, not_double, peaked, 2, l(triangle, 1)),
           c(4, rectangle, long, not_double, none, 2, l(rectangle, 2))]]).
```

designates as eastbound a train with 4 cars, of which the first is bucket-shaped, short, single-walled, unroofed, and containing one circular load, the second is rectangular, long, etc. etc. A specimen rule in English looks like

If a train has a car with a peaked roof or a sequence of cars with the same load-shape that ends in a short car then Eastbound otherwise Westbound.

In "Trolog" (Prolog plus pre-supplied library of train-friendly predicates) the above rule reads:

```
eastbound(T):- has_car(T,C), arg(5,C,peaked);
               infront(T,C1,C2), short(C2), has_load0(C1,Shape),
               has_load0(C2,Shape).
```

The "size" of this rule is 23, determined by counting the number of distinct symbols, omitting comma, bracket and full-stop. Page and Srinivasan, in an Appendix to [7], give a formal rationale of this measure. Experiments in progress by Hayes Michie [8] show that it broadly correlates with two measures of "psychological complexity", namely (a) "perceived complexity" derived from subjective rankings of sets of rules and (b) the times taken by subjects to score sets of trains using different rules.

The main competition presented a set of twenty trains, ten Eastbound and ten Westbound. The winner was Bernhard Pfahringer of the Austrian Research Institute for Artificial Intelligence, with an ILP program that can find the smallest rule if this lies below a length limit. A "computational cliff" was encountered after size 17, but a marginally smaller theory, of size = 16, lurked in the training set for his program to discover. The "official" rule originally used to classify the 20 trains, was of size 19, as also the four runners-up . One of these came from Peter Turney of the National Research Council's Institute for Information Technology, Canada. His program RL-ICET [9, 10] is conceptually related to LINUS [11]. It makes repeated decision-tree inductions guided by cost-related parameters. A genetic algorithm repeatedly selects among parameter-sets and returns the "fittest" tree found, fitness here being inverse to size. He and Dr. Pfahringer then both tried a newly generated 12-versus-12 discrimination task. Pfahringer's program, now searching beyond its computational cliff, found a rule of size 20. Once again Turney's RL-ICET ran close with a rule of size 23. What ingredients could so boost decision-tree learning?

First a pre-processor translates the Prolog relations and predicates of the example set into feature vector format. Then each feature is assigned a cost based on the sizes of the corresponding fragment of Prolog code. Decision tree induction is iterated on the example set guided by weighting parameters bearing a relation, to be empirically determined, to sizes of attributes. They thus function as attribute-selection biases. Tree-generation is performed repeatedly using different candidate bias vectors taken from a pool evolved by Grefenstette's [12] GENESIS genetic algorithm. The latter searches a space of bias vectors for one that minimises the Trolog complexity of the resulting tree. An initial pool of 50 vectors was seeded with one that had as it elements Prolog sizes of attributes. The other 49 were set randomly. Mutation and recombination (mating) of bias vectors followed the usual lines of genetic algorithms. Now for attribute manufacture.

Each attribute vector representing a train, and hence each bias vector, comprises altogether 1199 elements, each attribute being truth-valued. From 28 initial predicates applying to cars in a train (e.g. ellipse(C) when the car C has an elliptical shape), a train attribute is defined according to whether the train has such a car. Next 378 attributes are formed as the unordered pairs from the original 28. Using the relation infront(T,C1,C2), 784 ordered pairs can be formed. For example, u_shaped_infront_peaked_roof has the value 1 when the train has a u-shaped car in front of a car with a peaked roof, and 0 otherwise. Finally 9 more train attributes are added such as train_4 which has the value 1 when the train has exactly four cars. Thus an attribute vector has $28+378+784+9 = 1199$ elements.

The rule language so defined is of course incomplete. But what I want to stress is that at first sight the size of the attribute set seems shockingly large. Yet relative to the pattern-memories used in human expert cognition it should seem shockingly small. The number of patterns stored in (largely subliminal) memory by a chess master comfortably exceeds 50,000. Yet complete specification of a chess position requires at most 32 co-ordinate-pairs expressible in a language of simple syntax using only eight primitives. Patterns, not board co-ordinates, are the building blocks of chess-master concepts. Moreover the intuitive store grows according to experience of different kinds of play.

This property of statistical adaptation is mirrored in the generic form of ICET (RL- ICET is "Relational Learning ICET"). Attributes can be declared as either "immediate" or "delayed", according to whether values are obtained at run time evaluation or by pre- evaluation. Under the train challenge's declarative rather than procedural measure of complexity it was rational to set RL-ICET's attributes to "delayed". Under the "immediate" option, the program would test each tree's fitness by actually running it over the training set, thus directly estimating its procedural complexity. The statistical properties of a domain sample determine the frequencies with which different parts of a rule are invoked. Hence without running the tree the same quantity can be estimated as the weighted mean costs associated with interior nodes (i.e. attribute calls). Only calls of attributes contribute to cost, so that weights are the relative probabilities during execution of traversing each given node. If the classification law remains constant but the statistical structure of the population changes, ICET will track these by picking differently from logically equivalent rules.

There is a complementary form of the problem, in which the logico-statistical structure of the domain remains fixed while the learner gains facility during successive trials. Biomolecular chemists become skilled in conjecturing new structure-activity relations for familiar classes of compounds. Familiarity grows with respect to logical as well as statistical regularities. Ways are needed for relational learning algorithms to add new patterns to their own background knowledge, allowing additions to persist from one discovery exercise to the next.

2.2 Structured Induction

The general notion of learning within a hierarchy was proposed as early as 1953 by Claude Shannon [13].

> Can we organize machines into a hierarchy of levels, as the brain appears to be organized, with the learning of the machine progressing up the hierarchy?

The example I shall examine illustrates the development of hierarchies of decision trees with backchaining links between the trees. The attribute invoked at each node of each tree can be either "primitive" or "procedural". The latter calls a lower-level concept also implemented as an induced tree. The method, termed "structured induction" by one of its originators, Alen Shapiro [14], can have spectacular effects on transparency. Shapiro demonstrated machine-mediated articulation of an elaborate chess concept subarticulately resident in every master player. He considered the 209,718 legal positions in which White has the move with king and pawn versus king and rook, with White's pawn on a7 threatening to queen immediately.

Without structuring, computer induction was still able to build a classifier directly from primitives, but in the form of a single unstructured decision-tree of 83 nodes, - an end-game theory for Martians. As a theory for humans it is useless. Concerning the desired human-type theory Shapiro noted that

1. no such representation had ever been constructed by human agency;
2. since the expertise is largely inaccessible to conscious review, no such representation, in the opinion of chess masters consulted, could ever be so constructed;
3. no representations (brain compatible or otherwise) could be constructed by known programming techniques other than by exhaustion of the domain;

4. because of the inaccessibility of expertise to conscious review ... the so-called "knowledge engineering" techniques of contemporary expert systems work would not be applicable;
5. in the absence of information about the structural features, conventional use of inductive learning techniques would be inadequate. Rules generated in this way might well be complete but not brain compatible.

By way of contrast to the black box decision tree, a structured theory was built interactively from the same vocabulary of 36 primitive attributes, supplemented with eight intermediate concepts named by the chess-master and individually implemented by computer induction. The machine was also responsible for rendering the whole into English. The top-level rule looks like this:

COMMENT:
This rule is used to decide if a White-to-move position of king and pawn (on a7) versus king and rook is won for White or not. Bracketed notes refer to the attribute-name associated with testing the corresponding condition.
END COMMENT.

Position is won for White if and only if
    the Black rook can be captured safely (primitive: rimmx)
    OR none of the following is true:
    there is a simple delay to White's queening the pawn (procedural: DQ)
    OR one or more Black pieces control the queening square (primitive: bxqsq)
    OR the WK is in stalemate (primitive: stlmt)
    OR there is a good delayed skewer threat (procedural: DS)

Each of the two procedural attributes called is similarly represented, and so on, spanning altogether four hierarchical levels.

During construction, the expert is shown positions and asked: "What properties of this case do you need to know in order to adjudicate it?" A list is made from his answers, and incremented by posing the same question for further selected cases. When the list of position-attributes has settled down, no further progress can be made on the given concept without machine aid. This is because once the half-dozen or so tests needed to classify a given case have been identified, the expert cannot give any further account that could be programmed of how he applies each attribute or of how he combines the results into a decision procedure. At this point computer induction takes over the task of articulation, returning to the above cycle as each given concept and sub-concept is induced.

When end-game specialists were allowed to interrogate this system, their impression was of contact with a sophisticated and resourceful mentality that exceeded their own grasp of this small domain at every level. Before concluding that structured induction is the only road to such transparency, mention should be made of a claim by B.R. Gaines [15] on behalf of his Exception Directed Acyclic Graphs as the basis for inducing from the same primitives a transparent solution to the same problem. The potential of the method is at an early stage of assessment.

Industrial impact. The technique of structured induction broadly escaped academic attention. Instead it found a world-wide niche in commercial applications. In industry and finance, numerous specific needs exist for knowledge-acquisition aids that allows tacit forms to be recovered and given explicit expression. Inaccessibility of intuitive expert know-how has been widely remarked. Sterling and Shapiro [16] give an account of their attempts to debrief an expert loan officer: "Our expert ... happily discussed the profiles of particular clients, and the outcome of their credit requests and loans, but was reluctant to generalize".

The induction engineer separately delegates each of the parts of the elicitation task: (i) the domain expert supplies or selects illustrative cases, (ii) machine learning generalizes them into decision trees. Large systems today can have a hundred or more small layered decision trees, comprising altogether thousands of rules. Early applications were reviewed in [17,18]. The flavour of contemporary use is well conveyed by snapshots of recent systems developed and installed by one small Swedish company. I am indebted to Mr Rudi Sillen, Director of Novacast AB, Ronneby, for permission to reproduce this information in an Appendix. References there to XpertRule denote a suite of structured induction development tools licensed from Attar Software, Leigh, UK.

A ten year track record now exists of accomplishments that are on any reckoning remarkable. So what factors inhibit ML research along this line? The most salient is that the methodology requires active availability of a domain specialist over long periods. When I was Technical Director of a company similar to Attar and Novacast we ordinarily put a clause into co-development contracts specifying an agreed number of hours per month of a domain specialist's time. Persuading a domain specialist to spend time in a software project is akin to persuading water to flow up-hill. It can be done, but needs pumping. In industry the pump is the contract. The specialist then does whatever the contract stipulates. Academic institutions cannot provide such pumps.

2.3 Behavioural cloning

Humans learn skilled real-time tasks partly by imitation. Successful beginnings have been made with ML to "clone" aspects of skilled behaviour from canned performance samples. Early success was recorded by Chambers and Michie [19] in 1969. They commented as follows concerning their pole-balancing task (they also studied their BOXES program under conditions of trial-and-error re-inforcement learning):

> On the face of it, it looks rather dull, since not much is involved beyond
> a passive transfer to the machine of experience acquired by the human.
> We might therefore think that a machine that has been educated in this
> way could not outperform its trainer when left to its own devices. This is
> a mistake. The human's performance is variable even within a given sit-
> uation, ... and one false step in a real-time task can be fatal. By contrast,
> the BOXES program which has accumulated for a given box [logically

defined "situation"] the sum total of the human's experience, will consistently apply, whenever it visits this box, whichever decision is indicated by the balance of this experience. Thus if the machine makes the right kind of summary for itself of even quite low-performance human efforts, this summary can be made the basis of a much higher-performance strategy - the human's errors being "averaged out".

In new work with Sammut [22] using a desktop flight simulator, a diversity of control actions was available, in contrast to the "push-left, push-right" repertoire of pole-balancing. A blackboard architecture was adopted within which each agent was inductively trained from selected traces of expert input-output behaviour. Successes and shortcomings of behavioural cloning have been reviewed by Urbancic and Bratko [20]. They discuss the following problem domains: pole-and-cart balancing [19, 21], flight-simulator control [22], telephone-line scheduling [23] and their own work on crane-simulator control. Their conclusions are:

- Successful clones have been induced using standard ML techniques in all four domains.
- The clean-up effect, whereby the clone surpasses its original, has been observed in all four domains.
- In all domains best clones were obtained when examples from a single human only were used.
- The present approach lacks robustness in that they do not guarantee inducing with high probability a successful clone from given data.
- Typically, the induced clones are not sufficiently robust with respect to changes in the control task.
- Although the clones do provide some insight into the control strategy, they in general lack conceptual structure that would clearly capture the causal relations in the domain and the goal structure of the control strategy.

The chief conclusion is that learning from exemplary performance requires more than mindless imitation. The point can be vividly illustrated with a program (Polecat for Windows Research Version, developed by Mr. John White) for interactively testing human subjects. The pole-and-cart task is elaborated to include a third action, OFF, in addition to LEFT and RIGHT. The leading performance-scoring term is the number of times in a set period that the simulated system can be piloted across the track's mid-line. From numerous performances by an expert, the package builds an arbitrarily large training set of exemplary snapshots. From these a "clone" is induced in the form of a decision tree. When tested at run time, performance on the screen can seem exasperating. The clone mimics the human exemplar by holding its modal position close to the mid-line, but differs in balancing the pole with more consistent accuracy (the clean-up effect). Hence errors and righting actions fail to carry the cart over the mid-line, so it scores poorly. How could it be so stupid? Of course, no-one has told the clone what else besides mimicry is the object of its exercise.

Current thinking centres on selective re-introduction of a cognitive level for goal setting and monitoring. Of considerable relevance are a number of essentially non-ML studies. Pearson, Huffman, Willis, Laird and Jones [24] worked with flight-simulator control (Cessna, on a Silicon Graphics workstation) at the University of Michigan. They made resourceful use of the SOAR architecture (see Newell [3]) while constructing skill models essentially by hand-crafting. Reported robustness to varied starting conditions is attributable, we believe, to the goal-directedness of their underlying architecture. Benson and Nilsson's [25] recent developments of the T-R formalism have demonstrated a particularly interesting integration of reactive control behaviour with hand-crafted goal-structures.

In this area too availability of domain specialists can be critical. For example, in behavioural cloning of piloting skills the closer the contact with professional pilots and flying instructors the better.

3 Human-Computer Learning

The crisis of unemployabilty in technically advanced nations has been aggravated by information technology's part in destabilising unskilled work. Yet research into intelligent uses of information technology to mend some of the damage is too long-term for most industrial and governmental sponsors. I see a role for studies of Human- Computer Learning, where agents of the two species interact in mutual enhancement of each other's knowledge-based skills.

With the idea that further advances might be directed towards trainability and self-trainability, the Human-Computer Learning Foundation, formed in 1994 by Rupert Macnee, Jean Hayes Michie and the author, was this year accepted as an educational charity by the UK Charities Commission. Mr Macnee lives in Los Angeles and is a documentary film maker. Ms. Hayes Michie is a cognitive psychologist. She and the author spend most of their research time in Palm Desert, California, in working relation with the Coachella campus of the University of California.

The Foundation's aim is to apply new advances in machine learning (ML) to computer-aided skill acquisition and self-instruction. Recent multimedia developments have found a growing market in home education. But the socially more sensitive area of skill training remains relatively untouched. The Board's intention is to attract sufficient benefactions to direct a significant flow of new work along this channel.

References

1. Muggleton, S. and Feng, C.: Efficient induction of logic programs. In Proc. First Conf. on Algorithmic Learning Theory (ed. S. Arikawa, S. Goto, S. Ohsuga and T. Yokomori, 1990), Tokyo: Japan. Soc. Art. Intell. pp. 368 - 381.
2. Sternberg, M.J.E., King, R.D., Lewis, R.A. and Muggleton,: S. Application of machine learning to structural molecular biology. Phil. Trans. R. Soc. Lond. B, 344 (1994) 365-371.

3. Newell, A.: A Unified Theory of Cognition. Boston, MA: Harvard University Press (1990).

4. Muggleton, S.H., Bain, M., Michie, D. and J. E. Hayes Michie.: An experimental comparison of human and machine learning formalisms. In Proc. Sixth Internat. Workshop on Machine Learning, (ed. A. Segre), Morgan Kaufman (1989) pp. 113-118.

5. Michie, D. and Bain, M. Machine acquisition of concepts from sample data.: In Artificial Intelligence and Intelligent Tutoring Systems, (eds. D. Kopec and R.B.Thompson), Ellis Horwood (1992) pp. 5-23.

6. Michalski, R.S. and Larson, J.B.: Inductive inference of VL decision rules. SIGART Newsletter, ACM, 63 (1977) 38-44.

7. Michie, D., Muggleton, S., Page, D. and Srinivasan., A.: To the International Computing Community: a New East-West Challenge (1994). Available as a Postscript file ml-chall.ps in URL ftp://ftp.comlab.ox.ac.uk/pub/Packages/ILP/trains.tar.Z. See also URL ftp://ftp.comlab.ox.ac.uk/pub/Packages/ILP/results.tar.Z.

8. Hayes Michie, J.E.: Comparisons of Human and Machine Assessments of Complexity. Unpublished typescript, available from Ms Hayes Michie, 73860 Shadow Mountain Drive, Apt 2, Palm Desert, CA 92260, USA.

9. Turney, P.: Low size-complexity Inductive Logic Programming: the East-West clallenge considered as a problem in cost-sensitive classification. Submitted to IJCAI-95 (1995).

10. Turney, P.: Cost-sensitive classification:empirical evaluation of a hybrid decision tree induction algorithm. Jour. AI. Research. In press.

11. Lavrac, N. and Dzeroski, S.: Inductive Logic Programming: Techniques and Applications. New York: Ellis Horwood (1994).

12. Grefestette, J J.: Optimization of control parameters for genetic algorithms. IEEE Trans. on Systems, Man and Cybernetics 16 (1986) 122-128

13. Shannon, C.E.: Computers and automata. Proc. I.R.E, 41 No. 10 (1953).

14. Shapiro, A.D.: Structured Induction in Expert Systems. Addison Wesley (1987).

15. Gaines, B.R.: Inducing Knowledge. Unpublished typescript. Available from Prof. Gaines at Knowledge Science Institute, University of Calgary, Alberta, Canada T2N 1N4. Email: gaines@cpsc.ucalgary.ca (1995).

16. Sterling, L. and Shapiro, E.: The Art of Prolog. Cambridge, MA: The MIT Press (1986).

17. Michie, D.: New commercial opportunities using information technology. In Knowledge-based Systems: Third Internat Congr (1989).

18. Michie, D.: Problems of machine-aided concept formation. In Applications of Expert Systems, Vol 2 (ed. J.R. Quinlan), Addison-Wesley (1989) pp. 310-333.

19. Chambers, R. A. and Michie, D.: Man-machine co-operation on a learning task. In Computer Graphics - Techniques and Applications (eds. R. D. Parslow, R. W. Prowse and R. E. Green), Plenum Press (1969) pp. 179 - 185.

20. Urbancic, T. and Bratko, I.: Reconstructing human skill with machine learning. In Proc. Europ. Conf. on AI (ECAI 94), Amsterdam (1994).

21. Michie, D., Bain, M. and Michie, J.E.: Cognitive models from subcognitive skills. In Knowledge-Based Systems in Industrial Control (eds. M. Grimble, J. McGhee and P. Mowforth), Stevenage, Peter Peregrinus (1990).

22. Sammut, C., Hurst, S., Kedzier, D. and Michie, D.: In Proc. Ninth Internat. Workshop on Machine Learning, Morgan Kaufmann (1992) pp. 385 - 393.

23. Kibira, D.: Developing an expert controller of a black box simulation of a telephone line using machine induction. Unpublished report, Sydney: AI Lab, Univ. of New South Wales (1993).

24. Pearson, D. J., Huffman, S. B., Willis, M. B., Laird, J. E., and Jones, R. M.: A symbolic solution to intelligent real-time control. In Robotics and Autonomous Systems, 11, Elsevier (1993) pp. 279 - 291.

25. Benson, S. and Nilsson, N.: Reacting, planning, and learning in an autonomous agent. In Machine Intelligence 14 (eds. K. Furukawa, D. Michie and S. Muggleton), Oxford: the Clarendon Press, (in press).

A Seven case studies from Novacast AB

A.1 Adaptive Thermal Analysis System

System task: To control the melting and treatment of cast iron alloys, based on the time-temperature curve of serial samples of the melt. Metallugically important parameters of the curve are available from a standard algorithm.

Approach: Numerous test melts were made and evaluated. The results were used as examples for an inductive system (XpertRule Analyser) to produce the predictive rules and also to discover new relations between parameters.

Field experience: Installed in a Swedish foundry since April 1994, engineers use the system first to optimise the process. Once optimised, the system verifies it and suggests corrections.

Measured benefits of use: Reduced scrap, higher yield, less consumption of energy and of additives. Saving of the order of US$ 50 per ton.

Primary client: The Swedish Foundry Association.

A.2 Metal Painting Guide

System task: To give diagnosis and advice on rust-prevention and final coating.

Approach: Structured induction using XpertRule of more than 200 linked modules from expert-supplied examples.

Field experience: In commercial use since 1993.

Primary client: Coatech AB in Sweden.

A.3 Credit Scoring

System task: To interact with a large database covering all Swedish companies to make assessments of credit-worthiness on demand.

Approach: Example cases were collected partly from the client's experienced experts and partly from credit history. The system was built in a concept-oriented way using NovaCast's NovaLogic machine-learning program.

Field experience: In daily use since 1989.

Primary client: Soliditet, Sweden's major credit scoring company.

A.4   Evaluating Military Units

System task: Evaluating military capabilities of units.
Approach: Within an XpertRule structure, combinations of factors were automatically generated for combat unit commanders to evaluate ("truth table" method of Validation- Directed Induction described in [18]). An expert evaluation system was built that surpassed traditional assessment methods.
Field experience: In use since 1992.
Measured benefits of use: Savings of the order of 10 million Swedish crowns per year.
Primary client: The Swedish Defence Material Administration.

A.5   VAT Advisor

System task: To guide administrators through the regulatory labyrinth of VAT tax calculations, and in particular to enable inexperienced assessors to make expert assessments.
Approach: Concept-oriented structured induction using XpertRule, resulting in more than 150 task-modules comprising about 3000 rules in all.
Field experience: In use at several sites since 1992.
Measured benefits of use: Large reductions in the long, complex and costly training in VAT assessment that had previously been needed.
Primary client: The Swedish company DIALOG.

A.6   Predicting recurrence of breast cancer

System task: To predict likelihood of recurrence within 5 years of surgery.
Approach: A database was available covering some 180 mastectomies and the patient's state 5 years later. Three methods of analysis were applied, namely multivariate statistics, neural nets and rule induction (XpertRule Analyser). Best results were obtained with rule induction.
Field experience: in use since 1993.
Measured benefits of use: System's predictive accuracy is about 80%. Medical specialists achieved 40%. They also preferred the inductively generated rules because they could read them and thus understand and validate them.
Primary client: Central Hospital in Karlstad, Sweden.

A.7   Reduction of nitrogen in waste water

System task: To reduce the content of chemically bonded nitrogen in the waste water from large cities by predicting outcomes and suggesting corrective measures.
Approach: A complex biological method is in use in which bacteria transform the nitrogen to gas. In co-operation with a leading specialists in water purification, a set of knowledge- based modules was developed, each simulating a step in the control sequence. Output from one module is used as an input parameter to

the next. Each module was built with XpertRule from expert-supplied examples using the "truth table" method mentioned in case A.4.

Field experience: In use since 1993 at the waste water purification plant in Ronneby, Sweden.

Measured benefits of use: In addition to its use for error-diagnosis and control, the system has proved to be a cost-effective training tool for new operators. They use it on a "what if" basis by simulating postulated situations and testing alternative actions.

Primary client: Ronneby local city authority.

Machine Learning in the World Wide Web

Tom M. Mitchell

School of Computer Science
Carnegie Mellon University
Pittsburgh, PA 15213, USA
Tom.Mitchell@cmu.edu

The flood of information available over the world wide web provides new opportunities for machine learning research. In software systems that find information for users, there is a role for learning the interests of individual users, and for learning how to locate different types of information. We describe two applications of machine learning to information finding, then suggest several directions for future research.

One task where learning can be useful is netnews reading. Although there are over 8000 electronic newsgroups, nobody reads more than a few. A newsreader that learned its user's interests could therefore help the user by locating appropriate articles within the thousands of unread newsgroups. NewsWeeder [Lang 1994] is one system with this goal. It employs a minimum description length approach to learn user ratings based on words occuring within the article.

A second task where learning is appropriate is helping user's locate desired information while browsing the world wide web. WebWatcher [Armstrong, et al. 95] is one system with this goal. It accompanies users as they browse the web, suggesting which hyperlinks to follow, and learning to give better advice based on the observed search trajectories of many users.

This talk will describe both of these systems, then consider a variety of basic machine learning research issues they raise. These include learning over extremely high dimensional spaces (i.e., text) with mostly irrelevant features, learning search control from observation and experimentation, combining supervised and unsupervised training data, and combining data obtained from many interrelated learning tasks (e.g., when learning the interests of many correlated users).

References

[Lang, 1994] Lang, K., NewsWeeder, 1994. Web URL http://anther.learning.cs.-cmu.edu/ifhome.html.

[Armstrong, et al., 1995] Armstrong, R., Frietag, D., Joachims, T., and Mitchell, T., WebWatcher: A learning apprentice for the world wide web, in *Proceedings of the 1995 AAAI Spring Symposium on Information Gathering from Heterogeneous, Distributed Environments*, March 1995. Also see Web URL http://www.-cs.cmu.edu:8001/afs/cs.cmu.edu/project/theo-6/web-agent/www/project-home.-html

Abstract Computer Models: Towards a New Method for Theorizing About Adaptive Agents

Stellan Ohlsson and James J. Jewett
Learning Research and Development Center
University of Pittsburgh

Abstract

After a brief flourish in the decade 1979-1989, the study of learning has once again stalled. The main method for theorizing about learning--symbolic computer simulation--is plagued by serious difficulties. *Abstract computer models*, i. e., models that capture the structural features of cognitive processes while ignoring their content, overcome those difficulties. An example of abstract modeling is discussed and a research agenda outlined.

1. A Promise Unfulfilled

During the decade 1979-1989, the newly invented techniques for implementing machine learning systems inspired a wave of theorizing about learning in general and skill acquisition in particular. An interesting variety of learning mechanisms were proposed, including rule generalization, rule discrimination, rule composition, chunking, subgoaling, procedure induction, proceduralization, strengthening and weakening, constraint-based error correction, redundancy elimination, genetic algorithms, analogical transfer and explanation-based learning (Anderson, 1981; Chipman & Meyrowitz, 1993; Holland, Holyoak, Nisbett & Thagard, 1986; Klahr, Langley & Neches, 1987; Kodratoff & Michalski, 1990; Shrager & Langley, 1990).

These hypotheses represent the first attempts at describing, at a fine level of detail, how adaptive agents alter themselves on the basis of experience. Although incomplete, the list nevertheless shows that *more hypotheses about the cognitive mechanisms underlying learning were invented in that decade than in the preceding century*, i. e., since Edward L. Thorndike and his contemporaries posed the explanation of learning as a central scientific problem in the 1890's.

In the mid-1980's, the stage was thus set for a productive research program aiming to invent more learning mechanisms, identify the properties of various mechanisms, derive their implications and use them to explain the behavior of particular adaptive agents. Instead, we now see scattered, isolated efforts at theory, surrounded by a cloud of unprincipled empirical studies that show no signs of crystallizing into a coherent body of knowledge. The production of new ideas about the mechanisms underlying learning has almost stopped and there is little work on analyzing and evaluating the hypotheses already proposed.[1] This impasse is caused, in part, by certain problems with symbolic machine learning systems as vehicles for theorizing.

2. Problems With Symbolic Models

We now have three decades of experience in building symbolic computer simulation models of cognitive processes. Several complexities and problems have appeared (Anderson, 1987; Frijda, 1967; Kieras, 1985; McCloskey, 1991; Neches, 1982; Ohlsson, 1988; Schneider, 1988; Young, 1985). These difficulties include the following:

Knowledge representation. A symbolic simulation model requires an explicit representation of the knowledge that the modeled agent is drawing upon. Such a knowledge base represents a large number of micro-hypotheses about what the modeled agent knows and how that knowledge is encoded. Those assumptions are, in principle, unverifiable. There are no empirical methods that deliver such fine grained information that we can ground the individual nodes and links in a knowledge base independently of each other. Hence, the knowledge base of a symbolic simulation model functions as a giant free parameter. Every process assumption can be made to generate a wide range of different behaviors by 'hacking the representation'. This introduces considerable fuzziness in interfacing such models with data.

Domain specificity. Because a symbolic model requires a knowledge base, its behavioral predictions are only valid for the corresponding task domain. To investigate the behavior of the model in a different domain, one has to implement a new knowledge base. Because knowledge is a major determinant of

---

[1] The work of John R. Anderson on the ACT theory (Anderson, 1993) and the work of the Soar group on the Soar theory (Newell, 1990) are the main exceptions to this generalization.

the model's behavior, its behavioral predictions may or may not hold up in the new domain. Hence, when a simulation model is claimed to explain a *general* empirical phenomenon (as opposed to a particular experimental result), it is difficult to evaluate the claim: How do we know what the model would do in another task domain? There is no principled way to identify what is general and what is task specific about the model's behavior.

Indeterminate referent. A symbolic model is a single entity, a particular cognitive agent. It has a particular knowledge base, a particular set of processes, particular parameter settings (e. g., activation levels), and so on. What is such a system a model *of*? Obviously, adaptive agents (e. g., people) differ at least slightly in their knowledge of a domain, as well as in their strategies for dealing with it; seldom if ever are two individuals exactly alike. But if all individuals differ from each other, then a simulation model can be a model of at most one of them.

One solution to this problem is to regard a simulation model as a model of the *average* individual. However, in the face of qualitative differences in knowledge or strategy, what is average? How does one take the average of two knowledge bases or two problem solving strategies? There is only one principled way to bridge the gap between the concretion of a symbolic computer program and the generality we desire in a learning theory: To include individual difference variables in the model, to systematically vary those variables and to verify that they cause the model to produce the range of behaviors observed empirically. However, it is difficult to vary a symbolic simulation model systematically.

Brittleness. Symbolic simulation models are no less brittle than other AI systems, i. e., they do not function well at the boundaries of their knowledge, they usually cannot be applied to new problems without extensive re-programming, and the effects of changes to either the knowledge base or the process assumptions are often unpredictable and sometimes disables the program entirely. If a change requires extensive reprogramming, it is difficult to describe in a principled way what changed and what remained the same. Hence, one cannot easily conduct experiments in which particular aspects of such a model are systematically varied.

Principles versus implementation. Symbolic simulation models always include a mixture of theoretically motivated code and what I call *convenience code*, i. e., code that had to be added to make the model run (Ohlsson, 1988). The behavior of the model, and hence its behavioral predictions, depend as

much on the convenience code as on the theoretically motivated code. Hence, it is difficult to know which predictions to
take seriously and which to dismiss as accidental consequences
of the particular implementation. The only principled solution
to this problem is to have a theoretical reason behind *every*
aspect of the code (Newell, 1990), a methodological dictum that
is hard to live by and which increases the amount of labor required to build a model.

Labor intensity. The first AI-based simulations of learning were small and simple (e. g., Anzai & Simon, 1979).
However, as the field shifted attention to real life tasks, the
complexity of our simulations increased to a point where the
implementation of a serious learning model requires several
man-years, perhaps even tens of man-years, of work. At the
end of that investment, the only product is a formalization of a
single point in the theory space, and the only benefit of having the model is that we can derive the behavioral predictions
at that point. This lack of proportion between initial investment and ultimate benefit is one reason why only one or two
research groups continue to build symbolic models of learning; those groups are already up and running, as it were, so
they can make progress through incremental improvements
on past achievements. However, there are few, if any, new
entrants into the field; the cost of entry is prohibitive.

In short, symbolic simulation models are not convenient
tools for theorizing about learning. The interaction between
domain specificity and labor intensity is lethal. At the end of
several years of work, the theoretician might have a formalization of single cell in the table of all mechanisms versus all
tasks. We need look no further for an explanation of why the
development of learning theory has stalled.

3. Abstract Computer Models

Continued progress in learning theory requires a theoretical
method that combines the abstraction, elegance and simplicity
of mathematical models with the flexibility and power of computational models. The solution that I am pursuing is called
abstract computer modeling. Abstract models are computer
programs and hence not limited by mathematical tractability,
but they are not AI systems and hence do not require domain
specific knowledge or complicated algorithms.

The key step that leads to abstract modeling is to turn a
common criticism of AI on its head: It is often said that computer programs are purely syntactic systems, i. e, they do not
understand the symbols they operate upon and the intended

meaning of those symbols has no impact on the system's behavior. Only the *structure* of the knowledge base and the associated processes are important.

The implication of this observation is that the content (i. e., the knowledge base) of an AI-based model is not needed to generate its behavioral predictions. Hence, the basic idea of abstract modeling is to take the content (knowledge) out of the model. The result is a computer program which mimics the structural properties of the corresponding AI system and *which therefore goes through the same number of steps,* i. e., which makes the same quantitative predictions.

This is not an entirely new idea. For example, within AI it has long been understood that one can compute the number of steps that a particular search algorithm requires to solve a problem, if one knows the length of the desired solution path and the branching factor of the search space, *without actually having to implement the system,* (e. g., Nilsson, 1971). We have taken this insight one step further by applying it to machine learning systems.

An abstract computer model is not an AI-program. It does not carry out the processes it models. An abstract model of problem solving does not solve problems and an abstract model of learning does not learn. Unlike AI models, abstract models do not satisfy the *sufficiency criterion* proposed by Newell, Shaw and Simon (1958, p. 151) as a touchstone for theories of cognition. An abstract model goes through certain motions and counts how many steps (of certain kinds) it takes to do so. For the study of adaptive systems, this is enough. As theoreticians, our task is to derive the behavioral consequences of our hypotheses with as little effort as possible, not to make computers intelligent.

An abstract computer model can be viewed as an abstraction of a particular symbolic model. For example, Rosenbloom (1986; see also Rosenbloom & Newell, 1987) used an abstract model to analyze certain aspects of the XAPS simulation model.[2] Similarly, our first abstract model was an abstraction of the HS simulation model (Ohlsson, 1993). From this point of view, an abstract model is a tool for analyzing the properties of an existing system.

---

[2]Rosenbloom (1986) called his abstract model a *meta-model,* to emphasize the relation between the abstract model and the AI system, XAPS, that it was abstracted from. Because we want to build abstract models for which there are no prior symbolic models, we find the term "abstract model" more descriptive.

However, this view is too limited. There is no need to limit abstract modeling to points in the theory space for which symbolic models have already been built. On the contrary, for purposes of studying adaptive agents we can *replace* symbolic models with abstract models.

The advantages of replacing symbolic models with abstract models are numerous. First, there is no need to implement and debug either a knowledge base or any AI algorithm. Implementing and debugging an abstract model can therefore be done in a few weeks, sometimes a few days. Second, an abstract model is not tied to a particular task, so its behavioral predictions are general. Third, an abstract model can easily be changed and manipulated.

In summary, one possible escape from the current impasse is to work with *abstract computer models*. Such models are not AI systems and hence do not suffer from the latters' problems and difficulties, but they are computer programs and hence escape from the constraints of mathematical tractability. Abstract models correspond to particular computational mechanisms in the sense of mimicking the structural features of those mechanisms. By going through the same motions as a symbolic model, an abstract model allows us to derive the behavioral predictions of the latter without implementing it. The ease with which abstract models can be built and manipulated encourages systematic search through the theory space and extensive exploration of parameter variations.

4. An Example of Abstract Modeling

Several different learning mechanisms have been modeled abstractly and a number of results derived (Ohlsson & Jewett, 1994). The purpose of this section is to present an illustrative example.

Like a symbolic model, an abstract model can be described as consisting of three components: a task environment, a performance module and one or more learning mechanisms. The main creative step in abstract modeling is to figure out how to represent change in knowledge without an explicit representation of the knowledge base.

4.1 An Abstract Task Environment

The central features of the environments in which adaptive behaviors occur are that (a) they require a *sequence* of actions, as opposed to a single action, and (b) there are *multiple options* at each point in that sequence, only some of which are correct in the sense of being on a path to the desired end state. These features imply that an environment can be conceptualized as a tree structure. Each situation corresponds to a node in the tree and an action that changes situation S_1 into situation S_2 corresponds to a link between nodes S_1 and S_2. This *situation tree* is a map of the task environment.[3]

Because we are abstracting from task content, the nodes and links in the tree structures that we use to model the environment are empty. Each node represents some situation but it contains no information as to *which* situation, i. e., which propositions are true with respect to the represented situation. Similarly, the actions are represented by links between the situations, but the links contain no information about which action is being represented; each link stands for some unspecified action. In short, the nodes are uninterpreted situations and the links are uninterpreted actions.

A situation tree has three additional features. We designate a randomly chosen leaf node as the goal. The fact that a particular node is the goal is modeled by putting the *label* "GOAL" on that node (rather than by writing down a propositional *description* of the goal situation, as in a symbolic model). Links which are on a path between the root node and the goal node are labeled "correct", the others are labeled "incorrect". In addition, each link is associated with a *strength*. Initially, all links have the same (arbitrarily chosen) strength value. (Nothing in the methodology forces equal initial strengths, but it is a natural starting state.)

4.2 Abstract Performance Module

To perform a task is to traverse the corresponding situation tree from the root to the goal. Each situation (node) presents the learner with the problem of deciding which option (link) to traverse. In our abstract models, performance is modeled as in Figure 1.

The program sketched in Figure 1 is simple. Nevertheless, it executes the same number of steps as an AI algorithm operating on a task-specific knowledge base. The abstract mechanism does not apply a strategy, execute operators or

---

[3]The situation tree obviously owes much to the concept of a *search space* or *problem space* (Newell & Simon, 1972). However, the problem space is an hypothesis about the mind. In contrast, the situation tree is a tool for describing the environment.

apply goal criteria, but it mimics the quantitative properties of a system that does perform those computations.

---

1. Check whether the current node is the goal node;
   a. if yes, exit with the relevant counter(s);
   b. if no, retrieve all outward-bound links (options).
2. Select one link probabilisticly, with the probability of link L a function of the strength associated with L.[4]
3. Make the node at the far end of that link the current node and update the step counter.
4. Check whether the step was correct or incorrect;
   a. if correct, go to 1;
   b. if incorrect, backup to the previous node and go to 2.

Figure 1. Pseudo-code for performance module.

We could derive predictions about steady state performance by running the performance model and study, e. g., how the number of steps required to complete a task (traverse a tree) varies with various parameters (e. g., tree size). However, the function of the performance model for present purposes is to serve as a platform for the learning mechanisms that we want to study.

4.3 A Model of Failure-Driven Learning

One plausible hypothesis about learning is that adaptive agents react to errors, expectation failures, negative feedback, or, in general, *negative outcomes* by revising the performance module in such a way as to avoid similar outcomes in the future. This hypothesis was explored in the (symbolic) HS model (Ohlsson, 1992, 1993, 1994; Ohlsson, Ernst & Rees, 1992; Ohlsson & Rees, 1991a, 1991b).

---

[4] The exact algorithm used is the following: Each strength value is multiplied with a random number between 0 and 1; the highest product wins. This algorithm gives a strong preference to the link with the highest strength. We are in the process of exploring alternative decision algorithms.

The HS model was based on an analysis of how a knowledge-based agent can detect and correct his or her own mistakes. In brief, the basic principles proposed were that (a) errors are caused by overly general rules which generate actions that are not appropriate or useful; (b) errors are detected by judging successive situations as either consistent or inconsistent with known constraints on 'good' situations; and (c) errors, once detected, are corrected by specializing the responsible rule in such a way that it will not be evoked in situations in which it causes errors; the particular specialization is determined by the learner's casual analysis of the error.

For example, consider a novice driver. (a) Driving on a two-lane highway, a novice driver is likely to have a general tendency to change into the left-hand lane whenever the vehicle in front is traveling too slowly. In its unrestricted form, this disposition is dangerous, because it will lead him or her to change lanes even when there is another car in the left-hand lane. (b) One possible outcome of such an error is screeching tires or irritated honkings from that other car. Even a novice driver knows that such signals indicate an error on his or her part. (c) The causal analysis is in this case obvious: The error arose because there was another car in the left-hand lane. Hence, the needed correction is to specialize the overly general disposition so that it is only evoked in situations in which the left-hand lane is empty.

Our efforts to derive the behavioral implications of the HS model illustrates the difficulties of symbolic modeling. The model was applied to three different, fairly small, task domains: counting, arithmetic and a particular skill in organic chemistry (see Ohlsson, 1993, for an overview of the three applications). Development of the knowledge base took over a year for each domain. Hence, providing minimal evidence for the generality of the learning mechanism took three years of work.

Furthermore, to derive the learning curve predicted by the HS model we ran a quantitative learning experiment in which the model learned a simple symbolic skill in chemistry: to construct Lewis structures (structural formulas) for particular molecules given their sum formulas. HS could learn this skill both by practicing repeatedly on a single molecule and by practicing a sequenced of different molecules. Figure 2 shows a typical result from repeated practice on a single molecule.

The simulation runs required to identify the learning curve of HS took several months to complete. To investigate how the curve is affected by various parameters, e. g., task complexity, we would have to run the simulation repeatedly for

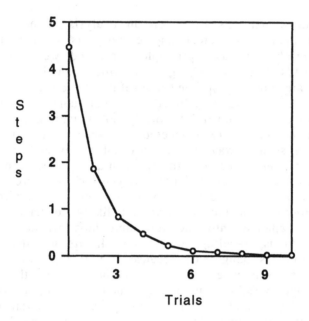

Figure 2. Learning curve for HS model.

each parameter value, making this seemingly simple analysis a multi-year enterprise.

Abstract representation. Abstract modeling provides a more convenient way to derive the implications of the basic hypotheses behind the HS model. The main creative step in constructing an abstract model is to represent the correction of faulty knowledge without an explicit representation of that knowledge. To a first approximation, the effect of detecting and correcting an error is that one avoids that error in the future. (Error correction might have other effects as well, but avoidance of the error is obviously central.) How do we represent this outcome in the abstract?

The effect of error correction is that the unsuccessful option will not be tried again. This effect can be modeled by *deleting the relevant link* from the situation tree. This operation has the same effect as constraining a knowledge structure so that it does not apply in a particular situation; the action generated by that knowledge structure will not be taken again. Similarly, to remove a link from a tree is to make the corresponding option unavailable for the decision making algorithm; but if the link is not considered during decision making, then it will not be selected and hence not traversed. The (abstract and simple) operation of deleting a link mimics the (content-full and complicated) process of correcting an error.

The abstract model that implements this learning mechanism works as shown in Figure 3 (the pseudo-code added to the performance module--see Figure 1--to model error correction is shown in bold faced font). This abstract model mimics the behavior of the symbolic HS model. To determine the learning curve produced by the version of failure-driven learning implemented in HS, we ran a series of simulation experiments with the abstract model.

---

1. Check whether the current node is the goal node;
   a. if yes, exit with the relevant counter(s);
   b. if no, retrieve all outward-bound links (options).
2. Select one link probabilisticly, with the probability of link L being proportional to the strength associated with L.
3. Make the node at the far end of that link the current node and update the step counter.
4. Check whether the step was correct or incorrect;
   a. if correct, go to 1;
   b. if incorrect, backup to the previous node, **remove the traversed link from the situation tree,** and go to 2.

Figure 3. Pseudo-code for error correction model.

Simulation experiments. Our goal was to make the experiments as similar as possible to empirical studies of skill acquisition. We used situation trees with a branching factor of 10 and a path length of 20. These trees represent the abstract structure of a task that requires 20 steps (actions) to solve and that present the performer with approximately 10 options in each step. Tasks that illustrate this level of complexity include proving a college-level algebra theorem, using a word processor to write a letter and cooking a dish from the classical French cuisine.

Each simulation experiment consists of running the model through a sequence of training trials, i. e., traversals of the situation tree. The model is started in the root node of the tree and cycles through the decision cycle until it reaches the goal node; it is then restarted in the root node; and so on. The training trials continue until mastery. The criterion for mastery is three consecutive error-free traversals of the situation tree.

We run several simulated subjects until criterion, as is standard procedure in experiments on learning. (Because the decision making module is probabilistic, successive runs are not identical.) In the explorations reported below, there were 20 simulated subjects in each simulation experiment.

Finally, we collect data on the behavior of the model, typically the number of steps (link traversals) required to traverse the tree. These numbers are averaged across simulated subjects for each trial. Hence, the procedure by which we construct learning curves corresponds closely to the empirical procedures used to construct the learning curves of human learners.

Selected results. We have performed extensive explorations of the abstract error correcting model (Ohlsson & Jewett, 1994). Figure 4 shows the basic result, plotted with logarithmic coordinates along the y-axis. The behavior of the model is a straight line in this type of plot. This is the hallmark of an *exponential* learning curve. The fit to the exponential is extremely good. Furthermore, the rate of learning is very high. The model requires less than 10 trials to reach criterion. (To judge the psychological plausibility of this achievement, remember that the task requires 20 steps and presents the learner with 10 options in each step.)

For comparison, Figure 5 shows the learning curve for the symbolic version of HS (see Figure 2) replotted in log-normal coordinates. Both the symbolic and the abstract models produce good approximations to straight lines in log-normal coordinates, indicating that both generate exponential (rather than power law) learning curves. The slopes of the two curves (as indicated by the exponents) are also comparable (.289 versus .314). Hence, the abstract model does indeed mimic the quantitative behavior of the symbolic model.

The amount of work required to derive the predicted learning curve with the abstract model was a mere fraction of what it took to make the corresponding derivation with the symbolic version of HS: a few days versus several months. The ease and speed with which the abstract model can be manipulated also enables us to carry out several other analyses that would be completely prohibitive with the symbolic model.

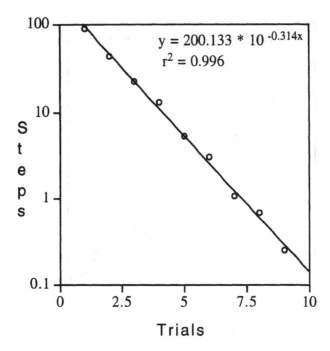

$$y = 200.133 * 10^{-0.314x}$$
$$r^2 = 0.996$$

Figure 4. Curve for failure-driven learning.

For example, one natural question is to what extent the learning curve predicted by failure-driven learning is robust across different task environments. Intuition suggests that the complexity of the task might affect the shape of the curve, because more difficult tasks ought to cause slower learning. To investigate this question, we have to perform a *sensitivity experiment* (Schneider, 1988) i. e., derive the learning curve again and again for different values of the relevant complexity parameters (i. e., branching factor and path length.

This 2-by-2 (path length by branching factor) experiment was carried out with the abstract model, with path lengths either 10 or 40 and branching factor either 3 and 17. Figure 6 shows the result. The four learning curves are straight lines in log-normal coordinates. Failure-driven learning is robustly exponential across levels of complexity. Furthermore, the four curves are almost parallel. Hence, manipulating either dimension of task complexity produces parametric displacement of the curve, but leaves its shape unaffected. The two dimensions do not interact. The exponential nature of failure-driven

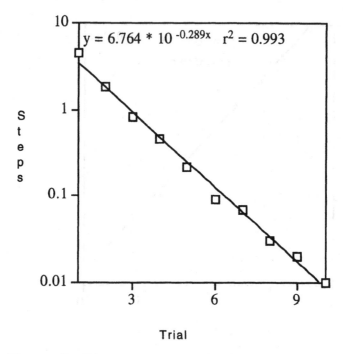

Figure 5. HS curve plotted in log-normal coordinates.

learning is robust across variations in task complexity (as measured by path length and branching factor).

A second natural question is how the efficiency of the learner affects the result. An alert learner has a greater probability of detecting and correcting an error. Intuitively, it is plausible that variation in learner efficiency affects the shape of the learning curve. This question is easily explored with the abstract model. The results presented so far were derived under the assumption that the learner catches and corrects every error he or she makes; let us call this 100% efficiency. Figure 8 shows the learning curve predicted under the alternative assumption that the learner has 50% efficiency, i. e., that he or she only detects or corrects every other error that he or she makes. Once again, we see that the learning curve is a straight line in log-normal coordinates. Hence, failure-driven learning is exponential across levels of learner efficiency.

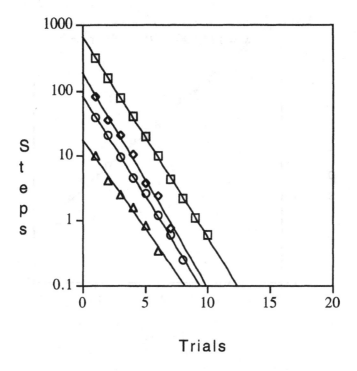

Figure 7. Effect of task complexity.

Discussion. Failure-driven learning appears to be robustly exponential across variations in both task and learner parameters. Empirical studies of skill acquisition (primarily in humans, but also in animals and social structures such as manufacturing plants) have shown that skill acquisition typically follows a power law, not an exponential curve (Lane, 1987; Newell & Rosenbloom, 1981). Hence, these simulations show that pure failure-driven learning does not predict the type of learning curve observed empirically. Contrary to the strong claims sometimes made for failure-driven leaning, people (and perhaps other adaptive agents as well) do not learn *solely* by reacting to their failures. (These results leave open the possibility that adaptive agents learn by some combination of error correction and one or more other learning mechanisms.)

The main point for present purposes is that the methodology of abstract modeling enables extensive exploration of the quantitative properties of particular learning mechanisms. The sensitivity experiments shown in Figures 7 and 8 would

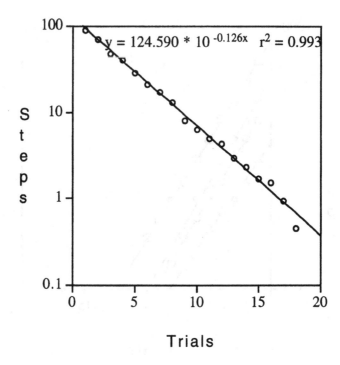

$$y = 124.590 * 10^{-0.126x} \quad r^2 = 0.993$$

Figure 8. Failure-driven learning with 50% efficiency.

have required at least one man-year of work each if carried out with a symbolic model, but they took only between two and three weeks with the abstract model.

5. Summary

The development of theories of skill acquisition has stalled. Although a rich and interesting variety of hypotheses about the cognitive mechanisms underlying learning emerged in the decade 1979-1989, little current work is devoted to the analysis and evaluation of those ideas and the production of new ideas has slowed down. To transform a set of hypothesized change mechanisms into a theory of adaptive agents we need to explore the properties of those mechanisms, derive their behavioral implications and use them to explain particular regularities in adaptive behavior.

Symbolic computer simulation are not convenient tools for such explorations. In particular, the combination of brittleness and labor intensity discourages experimentation and exploration. In addition, the task specificity that comes with dependence on a knowledge base makes it difficult to interpret a symbolic model. In particular, there is no principled way of deciding which behavioral predictions are general and which are task specific.

Abstract computer models avoid these difficulties by combining the abstraction, elegance and simplicity of mathematical models with the flexibility and power of computational models. An abstract model is a computer program, but it is not an AI system. Specifically, abstract models mimic the structural features (and hence the quantitative behavior) of symbolic models but without explicitly representing the content of the relevant knowledge base. Abstract models are orders of magnitude easier to design, implement, debug and run and hence encourage extensive exploration of the behavioral predictions of particular adaptive mechanisms.

The issues to be explored in future include the following. First, what types of learning curves are generated by other learning mechanisms (chunking, planning, strengthening, etc.)? Second, which, if any, of the learning mechanisms proposed to date correctly predicts some *set* of behavioral regularities (as opposed to a single regularity): forgetting, overlearning, the difference between distributed and massed practice, error distributions and so on? Third, we want to investigate more complex models of task environment. How are various learning mechanisms affected by, for example, multiple correct paths, non-uniform branching or random fluctuations in strengths? Fourth, how do learning mechanisms interact with individual difference variables? Can the mechanisms proposed to date account for so-called aptitude-treatment interactions?

Finally, a particularly important question is how learning mechanisms interact with each other in the production of adaptive behavior. Are learning curves and other regularities invariant over composition of learning mechanisms? If not, what are the effects of combining multiple learning mechanisms? In a multi-mechanism system, observable changes in behavior are not direct expressions of any one of the relevant mechanisms, but a composite result of their interactions. In other sciences, complex interactions between underlying causal mechanisms map onto observable system properties in complex ways. The mapping from genes to phenotypic traits or from molecules to macroscopic properties of substances are good examples. There is no reason to expect the mapping from cognitive mechanisms to observable behavior to be any simpler. We are currently exploring the consequences of composing error correction with other learning mechanisms.

Acknowledgment

Preparation of this manuscript was supported by Grant No. N00014-93-I-1013 from the Cognitive Science Program of the Office of Naval Research (ONR). No endorsement should be inferred. Approved for public release; distribution unlimited.

References

Anderson, J. R., (Ed.), (1981). *Cognitive skills and their acquisition*. Hillsdale, NJ: Erlbaum.

Anderson, J. R. (1987). Methodologies for studying human knowledge. *Behavioral and Brain Sciences, 10,* 467-505.

Anderson, J. R. (1993). *Rules of the mind*. Hillsdale, NJ: Erlbaum.

Anzai, Y., & Simon, H. A. (1979) The theory of learning by doing. *Psychological Review, 86,* 124-140.

Chipman, S., & Meyrowitz, A., (Eds.), (1993). *Foundations of knowledge acquisition: Cognitive models of complex learning*. Boston, MA: Kluwer.

Frijda, N. J. (1967). Problems of computer simulation. *Behavioral Science, 122,* 59-31.

Holland, J., Holyoak, K., Nisbett, R., & Thagard, P. (1986). *Induction: The processes of inference, learning, and discovery*. Cambridge, MA: MIT Press.

Kieras, D. E. (1985). The why, when, and how of cognitive simulation: A tutorial. *Behavior Research Methods, Instruments, and Computers, 17,* 279-285.

Klahr, D., Langley, P., & Neches, R., (Eds.), (1987). *Production system models of learning and development*. Cambridge, MA: MIT Press.

Kodratoff, Y., & Michalski, R. S., (Eds.), (1990). *Machine learning: An artificial intelligence approach* (Vol 4). San Mateo, CA: Kaufmann.

Lane, N. (1987). *Skill acquisition rates and patterns: Issues and training implications*. New York, NY: Springer-Verlag.

McCloskey, M. (1991). Networks and theories: The place of connectionism in cognitive science. *Psychological Science, 2,* 387-395.

Neches, R. T. (1982). Simulation systems for cognitive psychology. *Behavior Research Methods & Instrumentation, 14,* 77-91.

Newell, A. (1990). *Unified theories of cognition*. Cambridge, MA: Havard University Press.

Newell, A., & Rosenbloom, P. (1981). Mechanisms of skill acquisition and the law of practice. In J. Anderson, (Ed.), *Cognitive skills and their acquisition* (pp. 1-55). Hillsdale, NJ: Erlbaum.

Newell, A., Shaw, J. C., & Simon, H. A. (1958). Elements of a theory of problem solving. *Psychological Review, 65,* 151-166.

Newell, A., & Simon, H. (1972). *Human problem solving.* Englewood Cliffs, NJ: Prentice-Hall.

Nilsson, N. J. (1971). *Problem-solving methods in artificial intelligence.* New York, NY: McGraw-Hill.

Ohlsson, S. (1988). Computer simulation and its impact on educational research and practice. *International Journal of Educational Research, 12,* 5-34.

Ohlsson, S. (1992). Artificial instruction: A method for relating learning theory to instructional design. In M. Jones & P. H. Winne, (Eds.), *Adaptive learning environments: Foundations and frontiers* (pp. 55-83). Berlin, Germany: Springer-Verlag.

Ohlsson, S. (1993). The interaction between knowlede and practice in the acquisition of cognitive skills. In S. Chipman and A. L. Meyrowitz, (Eds.), *Foundations of knowledge acquisition: Cognitive models of complex learning* (pp. 147-208). Boston, MA: Kluwer.

Ohlsson, S. (1994, February). *Learning from performance errors* (Technical Report, KUL-94-02). Pittsburgh, PA: University of Pittsburgh.

Ohlsson, S., Ernst, A. M., & Rees, E. (1992). The cognitive complexity of doing and learning arithmetic. *Journal of Research in Mathematics Eduation, 23*(5), 441-467.

Ohlsson, S., & Jewett, J. J. (1994, December). *Abstract models of learning from success and failure* (Technical Report). Pittsburgh, PA: University of Pittsburgh.

Ohlsson, S., & Rees, E. (1991a). The function of conceptual understanding in the learning of arithmetic procedures. *Cognition and Instruction, 8,* 103-179.

Ohlsson, S., & Rees, E. (1991b). Adaptive search through constraint violation. *Journal of Experimental and Theoretical Artificial Intelligence, 3,* 33-42.

Rosenbloom, P. (1986). The chunking of goal hierarchies. A model of practice and stimulus-response compatibility. In J. Laird, P. Rosenbloom, & A. Newell, *Universal subgoaling and chunking: The automatic generation and learning of goal hierarchies* (pp. 135-1282). Boston, MA: Kluwer.

Rosenbloom, P., & Newell, A. (1987). Learning by chunking: A production system model of practice. In D. Klahr, P. Langley,

& R. Neches, (Eds.), *Production system models of learning and development* (pp. 221-286). Cambridge, MA: MIT Press.

Schneider, W. (1988). Sensitivity analysis in connectionist modeling. *Behavior Research and Methods, Instruments, & Computers, 20,* 282-288.

Shrager, J., & Langley, P., (Eds.), (1990). *Computational models of scientific discovery and theory formation.* San Mateo, CA: Kaufmann.

Young, S. R. (1985). Programming simulations of cognitive processes: An example of building macrostructures. *Behavior Research Methods, Instruments, and Computers, 17,* 286-293.

Young, R., & O'Shea, T. (1981). Errors in children's subtraction. *Cognitive Science, 5,* 153-177.

Part II: Papers

Learning Abstract Planning Cases

Ralph Bergmann and Wolfgang Wilke

University of Kaiserslautern,
Dept. of Computer Science,
P.O.-Box 3049, D-67653 Kaiserslautern, Germany
E-Mail: {bergmann,wilke}@informatik.uni-kl.de

Abstract. In this paper, we propose the PARIS approach for improving complex problem solving by learning from previous cases. In this approach, *abstract planning cases* are learned from given concrete cases. For this purpose, we have developed a new abstraction methodology that allows to completely *change the representation language* of a planning case, when the concrete and abstract languages are given by the user. Furthermore, we present a learning algorithm which is correct and complete with respect to the introduced model. An empirical study in the domain of process planning in mechanical engineering shows significant improvements in planning efficiency through learning abstract cases while an explanation-based learning method only causes a very slight improvement.

1 Introduction

Improving complex problem solving (i.e. planning, scheduling, design, or model-based diagnosis) by reusing past problem solving experience is one of the major topics addressed by machine learning research. Although a lot of methods for systematically solving complex problems are known from the literature on search, e.g. [20, 22] and planning [12, 38, 39, 45, 46, 26] most of them are intractable for solving problems in real-world applications due to basic search oriented nature of the algorithms. Learning from past experience promises to automatically acquire knowledge, useful to guide problem solvers so that they can improve their efficiency and competence. Most prominent are methods like explanation-based learning [33, 9, 37, 29, 31, 40, 10, 32, 23, 17] and analogical or case-based reasoning [7, 16, 42, 41]. While in explanation-based learning a control rule or a schema is *generalized* from an example problem solving trace, case-based approaches store detailed problem solving cases, index them appropriately and reuse and modify the cases according to the new problem to be solved.

In this paper we propose an alternative approach to improve complex problem solving. Instead of using learning methods which are based on *generalization*, we present a learning approach which computes *abstractions* of planning cases. As already pointed out by Michalski and Kodratoff [28, 27] abstraction has to be clearly distinguished from generalization. While generalization transforms a description along a set-superset dimension, abstraction transforms a description along a level-of-detail dimension. In general, abstraction requires *changing the complete representation language* while generalization usually maintains the representation language and introduces new variables for several objects to be generalized.

As the main contribution of this paper, we present an *abstraction methodology* and a related *learning algorithm* in which *abstract cases* are automatically derived from given concrete planning cases. Based on a given *concrete and abstract language* together with a *generic abstraction theory*, this learning approach allows to change the whole representation of a case from a concrete to abstract. Abstract cases learned from several concrete cases are then organized in a *casebase* for efficient retrieval during novel problem solving. This approach is realized in PARIS (**P**lan **A**bstraction and **R**efinement in an **I**ntegrated **S**ystem), which is fully implemented. PARIS is an integrated architecture for learning an problem solving [36] in which besides the abstraction mechanism described in this paper also an explanation-based approach is included. This allows to comprehensively investigate the different nature of abstraction and generalization as well as their integration.

The presentation of this approach is organized as follows. The next section describes the basic idea behind case abstraction and introduces the architecture of the PARIS system. The following three sections of the paper formalize the abstraction approach. After introducing the basic terminology, section 4 defines a new formal model of case abstraction. Section 5 gives a detailed description of a correct and complete learning algorithm for case abstraction. An experimental evaluation of the presented approach in a real-world domain is given in section 6. Finally, we discuss the presented approach in relation to similar work in the field.

2 Motivation: Case Abstraction and Refinement

This section wants to motivate the approach of learning abstract cases. The general approach is sketched and demonstrated by a real-world example. Furthermore, the PARIS architecture which realizes the presented approach is introduced.

2.1 Improving Problem Solving

Our main goal of learning is to improve the efficiency of a problem solver. We rely on the largely accepted view of problem solving which can be described as the task of transforming a given initial state into a given goal state by a sequence of available operators [34, 12, 8, 29, 41]. Thereby, initial state and goal state together constitute the problem description while the sequence of operators (plan) is the aspired solution. A definition of a problem solving domain usually consists of a description of the representation of the states which can occur during problem solving (usually a set of first order sentences) and a description of the available operators. An operator is usually described as a function which maps a certain starting state into a successor state, if certain conditions on the starting state hold. Efficiency is one of the major problems of this kind of problem solving because usually large search spaces need to be searched until a solution can be found.

2.2 The Basic Idea

Unlike well-known methods for improving problem solvers such as explanation-based learning [29, 31, 10, 32, 17] and analogical or case-based reasoning [7, 16, 42, 41] we propose an abstraction approach.

While the main goal of generalization is to extend the set of objects to which a certain piece of knowledge relates to, abstraction reduces the level of detail of a piece of knowledge. Unlike generalization, abstraction usually requires changing the representation language of an example or case [28, 15, 27] during learning. Several distinct concrete level objects need to be grouped into a smaller set of objects (out of the new representation language) at the abstract level. Abstraction must drop certain details of a description which are not useful for the kind of reasoning aspired. However, the most important relations between the concrete objects at the abstract level must be maintained. The advantage of abstraction is that it allows to simplify the representation and consequently speeds-up a reasoning process. Irrelevant details must not be considered anymore.

Our approach deals with the abstraction of planning cases. Thereby, a case consists of a problem description (initial state and goal state) and a related solution (operator sequence). The goal of abstraction is to reduce the level of detail of the problem description and solution in a consistent manner, i.e. the abstract solution must sill be a solution to the abstracted problem.

As a prerequisite, our approach requires that the abstract language and the concrete language are given by a domain expert. The abstract language itself is not constructed by the learning approach. This has the additional advantage that abstract cases are expressed in a language that the user is familiar with. Consequently, understandability and explainability, which are always important issues when applying a system, can be achieved much easier.

During a *learning phase*, a set of abstract cases is generated from each available concrete case. Different abstract cases may be situated at different levels of abstraction or may be abstractions according to different aspects. Usually, several concrete cases may share the same abstractions. The set of all abstract cases is the organized in a *case-base*.

When a new problem must be solved, the *problem solving phase* is entered. During this phase, the case base is searched until an abstract case is found which contains an abstract problem description which is an abstraction of the current concrete problem at hand. During further problem solving, the abstract solution (abstract plan) found in the retrieved abstract case must be refined (specialized) to become a solution to the current problem. During this process, this abstract solution serves as a *decomposition* of the original concrete problem into several smaller sub-problems, i.e. the sub-problems of refining the abstract steps. The sum of these sub-problems can usually be solved much more efficiently than the original problem as a whole [21, 19]. This effect leads to the desired overall improvement of problem solving.

2.3 A Real-World Example

To enhance the understanding of the following sections, we present an example now. This example is a simplification of the real-world domain of process planning in mechanical engineering.

Domain Description. As a real-world example domain we have selected a sub-task from the field of process planning in mechanical engineering.[1] The goal is to generate a process plan for the production of a rotary-symmetric workpiece on a lathe. The problem description contains the complete specification (especially the geometry) of the desired workpiece (goal state) together with a specification of the piece of raw material (called mold) it has to be produced from (initial state). Rotary parts are manufactured by putting the mold into the fixture (chucking) of a lathe. The chucking fixture, together with the attached mold is then rotated with the longitudinal axis of the mold as rotation center. While the mold is rotated, a cutting tool moves along some contour and thereby removes certain parts of the mold until the desired goal workpiece is reached. Within this process, it is very hard to determine in which sequence the specific parts of the workpiece can be removed and which cutting tools must be used therefor. These decisions are very much influenced by the specific geometric shape of the workpiece.

A Case. In Figure 1, case C_1 shows an example of a rotary-symmetric workpiece which has to be manufactured out of a cylindrical mold.[2] The left side of the picture of case C_1 shows the drawing of the inital state (outer cylindrical form) together with the goal state (inner contour). The representation of this drawing contains the exact geometrical specification of each element of the contour. Several areas of this contour are named by the indicated coordinates (e.g. #2, #2) for further reference. The right side of the case specifies the concrete plan which solves the problem. The solution plan consists of a sequence of 7 steps. In the first step, the workpiece (cylindrical mold) must be chucked at its left side. Then a cutting tool must be selected which can be used to cut the area specified by (#2, #2) from the workpiece in the next step. In step 4, a different tool must be selected which allows to process the two small groves named (#1, #2) and (#1, #3). These groves are removed in step 5 and 6. Finally, the workpiece must be unchucked.

---

[1] This domain was adapted from the CAPLAN-System [35], developed at the University of Kaiserslautern.

[2] Note, that this figure shows a 2-dimensional drawing of the 3-dimensional workpiece.

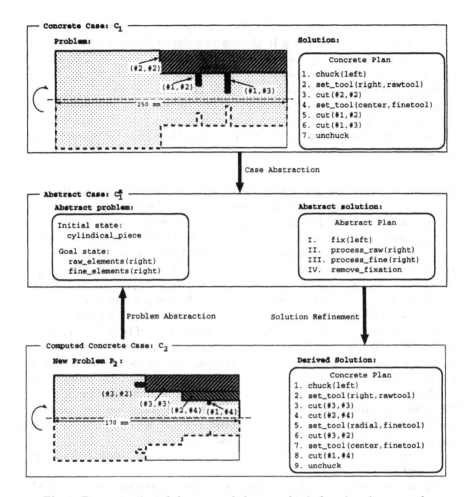

Fig. 1. Demonstration of the approach for a mechanical engineering example

Case Abstraction. The demonstrate the abstraction approach, we assume that case C_1 is available for learning. Case C_1^a shows an abstraction which we may want to learn from C_1. The left side of this case shows a problem description with a reduced level of detail. The exact geometrical specification of the workpiece is omitted and replaced by qualitative description. The workpiece is divided into a left and a right side, and only raw and fine processing elements are distinguished. The right side of the description of case C_1^a shows the abstracted plan which only consists of 4 abstract steps. The workpiece must be fixed at its left side, the raw parts on the right side must be processed, the fine parts on the right side must be processed, and finally the fixation must be removed. By this abstraction process, the concrete step 1 is turned into the abstract step I, the concrete steps 2 and 3 are turned into the abstract step II, the concrete steps 4,5, and 6 are abstracted towards step III, and step 7 is turned into the abstract step IV. Please note that in order to achieve the abstraction including a change of the representation language, the abstract language itself must be given in addition to the concrete language. In this example, the abstract language specifies how an abstract state can be described (e.g. my a term such as raw-elements(right)) and what abstract operators are available (e.g. process-raw) and how those abstract operators are specified.

Problem Solving The learned abstract case C_1^a can be used to solve the new problem P_2 shown in the bottom of Figure 1. Although this problem is completely different at the concrete level from the problem in case C_1, it is identical at the abstract level. Both pieces have to be manufacture from a cylindrical mold even if the dimensions of the mold are quite different. Both goal pieces contain raw and fine elements on the right side of the workpiece. However, the detailed shape of those elements is completely different. Since the abstract problem as stated in the abstract cases C_1^a matches the abstraction of the new problem P_2 completely, the abstract solution from C_1^a can be used to solve the concrete problem. This abstract solution determines already the overall structure of the solution plan to be computed. Instead of solving the complete problem as a whole, the problem solver can now solve the four subproblems separately, i.e. determine a fixation, determine how to process the raw parts of the piece, determine how to process the fine parts of the piece, and finally determine how to remove the fixation. These four subproblems can be solved much more efficiently than the complete problem as a whole. For solving P_2, the abstract step II must be refined towards a sequence of the three concrete steps 2,3, and 4 as shown in the bottom of Figure 1. The abstract step III must be refined to a sequence of the four concrete steps 5,6,7, and 8.

Please note that except for the first two steps and the last step, the resulting concrete solution to problem P_2 is completely different from the solution contained in case C_1. However, an abstract case is still very helpful to find the new solution to the problem. Explanation-based or case-based approaches would not be able to learn knowledge from case C_1 to solve the problem P_2, because they cannot change the representation language appropriately. Neither a useful generalization can be derived nor can the case be reused directly.

2.4   The PARIS Architecture

PARIS (Plan Abstraction and Refinement in an Integrated System) is a fully implemented system for learning and problem solving which realizes the sketched approach to case abstraction. Figure 2 shows an overview of the whole system and its components. Besides case abstraction and refinement, PARIS also includes an explanation-based approach for generalizing cases during learning and for specializing them during problem solving. Furthermore, the system includes several indexing and retrieval mechanisms for organizing and accessing the case-base of abstract cases, ranging from simple sequential search, via hierarchical clustering up to a sophisticated approach for balancing a hierarchy of abstract cases according to the statistic distribution of the cases within the problem space. This also includes methods for evaluating different abstract cases according to their ability to improve problem solving. More details on the generalization procedure can be found in [1], while the indexing and evaluation mechanisms are reported in [5, 44]. The whole multi-strategy system including the various interactions of the described components will be the topic of a forthcoming article, while first ideas can already be found [2, 4]. However, as the target of this paper we will concentrate on the core of PARIS, namely the abstraction approach. A detailed presentation of the related refinement approach can be found in [6].

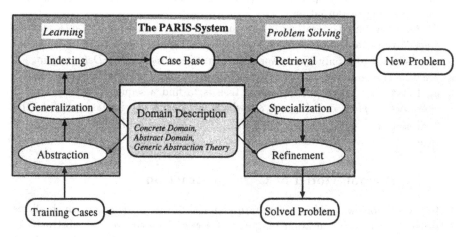

Fig. 2. The Components of the PARIS-System

3 Basic terminology

In this section we want to introduce the basic formal terminology followed throughout the rest of this paper. Following a STRIPS-oriented representation [12], the domain of problem solving $\mathcal{D} = \langle \mathcal{L}, \mathcal{E}, \mathcal{O}, \mathcal{R} \rangle$ is described by a language $\mathcal{L}$, a set of essential atomic sentences [24] $\mathcal{E}$ of $\mathcal{L}$, a set of operators $\mathcal{O}$ with related descriptions, and additionally, a set of Horn clauses $\mathcal{R}$ out of $\mathcal{L}$. A state $s \in \mathcal{S}$ describes the dynamic part of a situation in a domain and consists of a finite subset of ground instances of essential sentences of $\mathcal{E}$. With the symbol $\mathcal{S}$, we denote the set of all possible states descriptions in a domain, which is defined as $\mathcal{S} = 2^{\mathcal{E}^*}$, with $\mathcal{E}^* = \{e\sigma | e \in \mathcal{E} \text{ and } \sigma \text{ is a substitution such that } e\sigma \text{ is ground}\}$. In addition, the Horn clauses $\mathcal{R}$ allow to represent static properties which are

true in all situations. These Horn clauses must not contain an essential sentence
in the head of a clause.

An operator $o(x_1, \ldots, x_n) \in \mathcal{O}$ is described by a triple $\langle Pre_o, Add_o, Del_o \rangle$,
where the precondition Pre_o is a conjunction of atoms of $\mathcal{L}$, and the add-list
Add_o and the delete-list Del_o are finite sets of (possibly instantiated) essential
sentences of $\mathcal{E}$. Furthermore, the variables occuring in the operator descriptions
must follow the following restrictions: $\{x_1, \ldots, x_n\} \supseteq Var(Pre_o) \supseteq Var(Del_o)$
and $\{x_1, \ldots, x_n\} \supseteq Var(Add_o)$.[3]

An *instantiated* operator is an expression of the form $o(t_1, \ldots, t_n)$, with t_i
being ground terms of $\mathcal{L}$. For notational convenience, we define the *instantiated
precondition* as well as the *instantiated add-list* and *delete-list* for an instantiated
operator as follows: $Pre_{o(t_1, \ldots, t_n)} := Pre_o \sigma$, $Add_{o(t_1, \ldots, t_n)} := \{a\,\sigma | a \in Add_o\}$,
$Del_{o(t_1, \ldots, t_n)} := \{d\,\sigma | d \in Del_o\}$, with $\langle Pre_o, Add_o, Del_o \rangle$ is the description of
the (uninstantiated) operator $o(x_1, \ldots, x_n)$, and $\sigma = \{x_1/t_1, \ldots, x_n/t_n\}$ the
corresponding instantiation.

An instantiated operator o is *applicable* in a state s if and only if $s \cup \mathcal{R} \vdash Pre_o$
holds.[4] An instantiated operator o transforms a state s_1 into a state s_2 (we write:
$s_1 \xrightarrow{o} s_2$) if and only if o is applicable in s_1 and $s_2 = (s_1 \setminus Del_o) \cup Add_o$. A
problem description $p = \langle s_I, s_G \rangle$ consists of an initial state s_I together with a
final state s_G. The problem solving task is to find a sequence of instantiated
operators (a *plan*) $\bar{o} = (o_1, \ldots, o_l)$ which transforms the initial state into the
final state $(s_I \xrightarrow{o_1} \cdots \xrightarrow{o_l} s_G)$. A *case* $C = \langle p, \bar{o} \rangle$ is a problem description p
together with a plan $\bar{o}$ that solves p.

4   A Formal Model of Case Abstraction

In this section, we present a new formal model of case abstraction which allows
to change the representation language of a case from concrete to abstract. As
already stated, we assume, that in addition to the concrete language, the abstract
language is supplied by a domain expert. Following the introduced formalism,
we assume that the concrete level of problem solving is defined by a *concrete
problem solving domain* $\mathcal{D}_c = \langle \mathcal{L}_c, \mathcal{E}_c, \mathcal{O}_c, \mathcal{R}_c \rangle$ and the abstract level of (case-
based) problem solving is represented by an *abstract problem solving domain*
$\mathcal{D}_a = \langle \mathcal{L}_a, \mathcal{E}_a, \mathcal{O}_a, \mathcal{R}_a \rangle$. In the remainder of this paper, states and operators
from the concrete domain are denoted by s^c and o^c, respectively, while states
and operators from the abstract domain are denoted by s^a and o^a, respectively.
The problem of case abstraction can now be described as transforming a case
from the concrete domain $\mathcal{D}_c$ into a case in the abstract domain $\mathcal{D}_a$ (see Figure
3). This transformation will now be formally decomposed into two independent
mappings: a *state abstraction mapping* α, and a *sequence abstraction mapping* β
[3].

---

[3] These restrictions can however be relaxed such that $\{x_1, \ldots, x_n\} \supseteq Var(Pre_o)$ is
not required. But the introduced restriction simplifies the subsequent presentation.

[4] In the following, we will simply omit the parameters of operators and instantiated
operators in case they are unambiguous or not relevant.

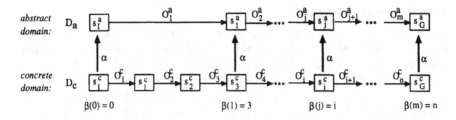

Fig. 3. General Idea of Abstraction

4.1 State Abstraction

A state abstraction mapping translates states of the concrete world into the abstract world. For this translation, we require additional domain knowledge about how an abstract state description relates to a concrete state description. We want to assume that this kind of knowledge can be provided in terms of a domain specific *generic abstraction theory* $\mathcal{A}$ [14]. In our model of case abstraction, such a generic abstraction theory defines each essential sentence $E_a \in \mathcal{E}_a$ in terms of the concrete domain by a set of horn-rules of the form $e_a \leftarrow a_1, \ldots, a_k$, where $e_a = E_a\sigma$ for a substitution σ and a_i are atoms out of $\mathcal{L}_c$.

Based on such a generic abstraction theory, we can restrict the set of all possible state abstraction mappings to mappings that are deductively justified by the generic abstraction theory:

Definition 1 (Deductively Justified State Abstraction Mapping)
A deductively justified state abstraction mapping which is based on a generic abstraction theory $\mathcal{A}$, is a mapping $\alpha : \mathcal{S}_c \to \mathcal{S}_a$ for which the following conditions hold:

- *if $\phi \in \alpha(s^c)$ then $s^c \cup \mathcal{R}_c \cup \mathcal{A} \vdash \phi$ and*
- *if $\phi \in \alpha(s^c)$ then for all $\tilde{s}^c$ such that $\tilde{s}^c \cup \mathcal{R}_c \cup \mathcal{A} \vdash \phi$ holds, $\phi \in \alpha(\tilde{s}^c)$ is also fulfilled.*

In this definition, the first conditions assures that every abstract sentence reached by the mapping is justified by the abstraction theory. Additionally, the second requirement guarantees that if an abstract sentence is considered in the abstraction of one state, it is also considered in the abstraction of all other states. Please note that a deductively justified state abstraction mapping can be completely induced, with respect to a generic abstraction theory, by a set $\alpha^* \subseteq \mathcal{E}_a^*$ as follows: $\alpha(s^c) := \{\phi \in \alpha^* | s^c \cup \mathcal{R}_c \cup \mathcal{A} \vdash \phi\}$.

To summarize, the state abstraction mapping transforms a concrete state description into an abstract state description and thereby changes the representation of a state from concrete to abstract.

4.2 Sequence Abstraction

The solution to a problem consists of a sequence of operators and a corresponding sequence of states. To relate an abstract solution to a concrete solution, the relationship between the abstract states (or operators) and the concrete states (or operators) must be captured. Thereby, each abstract state must have a corresponding concrete state, but not every concrete state must have an associated abstract state. To select those states of the concrete problem solution that have a related abstract state, the sequence abstraction mapping is defined as follows:

Definition 2 (Sequence Abstraction Mapping) *A sequence abstraction mapping $\beta : \mathbb{N} \to \mathbb{N}$ relates an abstract state sequence $(s_0^a, \ldots, s_m^a)$ to a concrete state sequence $(s_0^c, \ldots, s_n^c)$ by mapping the indices $j \in \{1, \ldots, m\}$ of the abstract states s_j^a into the indices $i \in \{1, \ldots, n\}$ of the concrete states s_i^c, such that the following properties hold:*

- *$\beta(0) = 0$ and $\beta(m) = n$: The initial state and the goal state of the abstract sequence must correspond to the initial and goal state of the respective concrete state sequence.*
- *$\beta(u) < \beta(v)$ if and only if $u < v$: The order of the states defined through the concrete state sequence must be maintained for the abstract state sequence.*

Note that the defined sequence abstraction mapping formally maps indices from the abstract domain into the concrete domain. However, an abstraction mapping should better map indices from the concrete domain to indices in the abstract domain such as the inverse mapping β^{-1} does. But such a mapping is more inconvenient to handle formally, since the range of definition of β^{-1} must always be considered. Therefore, we stick to presented definition.

4.3 Case Abstraction

Based on the two introduced abstraction functions, our intuition of case abstraction is captured in the following definition.

Definition 3 (Case Abstraction) *A case $C_a = \langle (s_0^a, s_m^a), (o_1^a, \ldots, o_m^a) \rangle$ is an abstraction of a case $C_c = \langle (s_0^c, s_n^c), (o_1^c, \ldots, o_n^c) \rangle$ with respect to the domain descriptions $(\mathcal{D}_a, \mathcal{D}_c)$ if $s_{i-1}^c \xrightarrow{o_i^c} s_i^c$ for all $i \in \{1, \ldots, n\}$ and $s_{j-1}^a \xrightarrow{o_j^a} s_j^a$ for all $j \in \{1, \ldots, m\}$ and if there exists a state abstraction mapping α and a sequence abstraction mapping β, such that: $s_j^a = \alpha(s_{\beta(j)}^c)$ for all $j \in \{0, \ldots, m\}$*

This definition of case abstraction is demonstrated in Figure 3. The concrete space shows the sequence of n operations together with the resulting state sequence. Selected states are mapped by the α into states of the abstract space. The mapping β maps the indices of the abstract states back to the corresponding concrete states.

In [6] we have discussed the generality of presented case abstraction methodology. We formally showed that hierarchies of abstraction spaces as well as abstractions with respect to different aspects can be represented using the presented methodology.

5 Computing Case Abstractions

Now we present the PABS-algorithm [3, 43] for automatically learning a set of abstract cases from a given concrete case. Thereby, we assume that a concrete domain $\mathcal{D}_c$ and an abstract domain $\mathcal{D}_a$ are given together with a generic abstraction theory $\mathcal{A}$.

Roughly speaking, the algorithm consists of four separate phases or sub-procedures. In the first sub-procedure, the sequence of concrete states which results from the execution of the concrete solution is computed. The second sub-procedure derives for each concrete state all possible abstract essential sentences justified by the generic abstraction theory. In the subsequent procedure, a graph of all applicable abstract operators is constructed, in which each edge leads from an abstract state to an abstract successor state. Finally, all consistent paths, starting at the abstract initial state and leading to the final abstract state are determined. Each of these paths represents a case which is an abstraction of the concrete case. In the following, we will present these phases in more detail. We presuppose a procedure for determining whether a conjunctive sentence in some language is a consequence of a set of clauses. More precisely, we assume a SLD-refutation procedure [25] which is given a set of clauses (a logic program) C together with conjunctive sentence G (a goal clause). The refutation procedure determines a set of answer substitutions Ω such that $C \vdash G\sigma$ for all $\sigma \in \Omega$. This set of answer substitutions is empty if $C \vdash G\sigma$ does not hold. We also require the derivation tree in addition to the answer substitutions. Then we write $\Pi = \mathrm{SLD}(C, G)$ and assume, that Π is a set of pairs (σ, τ), where σ is an answer substitution and τ is a derivation of $C \vdash G\sigma$.

5.1 Phase-I: Computing the Concrete State Sequence

As input to the case abstraction algorithm, we assume a concrete case $C_c = \langle (s_I^c, s_G^c), (o_1^c, \ldots, o_n^c) \rangle$. Note that $(o_1^c, \ldots, o_n^c)$ is a sequence of $instantiated$ operators. In the first phase, the state sequence which results from the simulation of problem solution is computed as follows:

Algorithm 1 (Phase-I: Computing the concrete state sequence)
$s_0^c := s_I^c$
for $i := 1$ **to** n **do**
   if $\mathrm{SLD}(s_{i-1}^c \cup \mathcal{R}_c, Pre_{o_i^c}) = \emptyset$ **then** $STOP$ *"Failure: Operator not applicable"*
   $s_i^c := (s_{i-1}^c \setminus Del_{o_i^c}) \cup Add_{o_i^c}$
   end
if $s_G^c \not\subseteq s_n^c$ **then** $STOP$ *"Failure: Goal state not reached"*

By this algorithm, the states s_i^c are computed such that $s_{i-1}^c \xrightarrow{o_i^c} s_i^c$ holds for all $i \in \{1, \ldots, n\}$. If a failure occurs, the plan is not correct and the case is rejected.

5.2 Phase-II: Deriving Abstract Essential Sentences

Using the derived concrete state sequence as input, the following algorithm computes a sequence of abstract state descriptions (s_i^a) by applying the generic abstraction theory separately on each concrete state.

Algorithm 2 (Phase-II: State abstraction)
for $i := 0$ **to** n **do**
  $s_i^a := \emptyset$
  for each $E \in \mathcal{E}_a$ **do**
    $\Omega := \mathrm{SLD}(s_i^c \cup \mathcal{R}_c \cup \mathcal{A}, E)$
    for each $\sigma \in \Omega$ **do**
      $s_i^a := s_i^a \cup \{E\,\sigma\}$
    end
  end
end

Within the introduced model of case abstraction, we have now computed a superset for the outcome of possible state abstraction mappings. Each deductively justified state abstraction mapping α is restricted by $\alpha(s_i^c) \subseteq s_i^a = \{e \in S_a | s_i^c \cup \mathcal{R}_c \cup \mathcal{A} \vdash e\}$ for all $i \in \{1, \ldots, n\}$. Consequently, we have determined all abstract sentences that an abstract case might require.

Fig. 4. An example of abstract states computed in phase-II. The abstract essential sentences are abbreviated as follows: *cylindr* = *cylindrical_piece*, *raw_el(r)* = *raw_elements(right)*, *fine_el(r)* = *fine_elements(right)*, *fixed(l)* = *fixed_piece(left)*.

Figure 4 gives an example of the 8 abstract states s_i^a computed during the abstraction of case C^1 shown in Figure 1. The abstract sentences used in these cases are a subset of the abstract sentences that occur in the abstract problem solving domain D_a and which are defined in terms of the concrete sentences by the generic abstraction theory provided by the user.

5.3 Phase-III: Computing Possible Abstract State Transitions

In the next phase of the algorithm, we search for instantiated abstract operators which can transform an abstract state $\tilde{s}_i^a \subseteq s_i^a$ into a subsequent abstract state $\tilde{s}_j^a \subseteq s_j^a$ $(i < j)$. Therefore, the preconditions of the instantiated operator must at least be fulfilled in the state $\tilde{s}_i^a$ and consequently in also s_i^a. Furthermore, all added effects of the operator must be true in $\tilde{s}_j^a$ and consequently also in s_j^a.

Algorithm 3 (Phase-III: Abstract state transitions)

$G := \emptyset$
for $i := 0$ **to** $n - 1$ **do**
  for $j := i + 1$ **to** n **do**
    for each $o(x_1, \ldots, x_u) \in \mathcal{O}_a$ **do**
      let $\langle Pre_o, Del_o, Add_o \rangle$ *be the description of* $o(x_1, \ldots, x_u)$
      $\Pi := \mathrm{SLD}(s_i^a \cup \mathcal{R}_a, Pre_o)$
      for each $\langle \sigma, \tau \rangle \in \Pi$ **do**
        let $Add_o' = \{a\sigma | a \in Add_a\}$
        (* Compute all possible instantiations *)
        (* of added sentences which hold in s_j^a *)
        $M := \{\lambda\}$ *with* $\lambda = \emptyset$ *is the empty substitution.*
        (* M is the set of possible substitutions *)
        (* initially the empty substitution *)
        for each $a \in Add_o'$ **do**
          $M' := \emptyset$
          for each $\theta \in M$ **do**
            for each $e \in s_j^a$ **do**
              if *there is a substitution* ρ *such that* $a\theta\rho = e$ **then** $M' := M' \cup \{\theta\rho\}$
            end
          end
          $M := M'$
        end
        (* Now, M contains the set of all possible substitutions *)
        (* such that all added sentences are contained in s_j^a *)
        for each $\theta \in M$ **do**
          $G := G \cup \{\langle i, j, o(x_1, \ldots, x_u)\sigma\theta, \tau \rangle\}$
        end
      end
    end
  end
end

The set of all possible operator transitions are collected as directed edges of a graph which vertexes represent the abstract states. In the algorithm, the set G of edges of the acyclic directed graph is constructed. For each pair of states (s_i^a, s_j^a) with $i < j$ it is checked, whether there exists an operator $o(x_1, \ldots, x_u)\sigma$ which is applicable in s_i^a. For this purpose, the SLD-refutation procedure computes the set of all possible answer substitutions σ such that the precondition of the operator is fulfilled in s_i^a. The derivation τ which belongs to each answer substitution is stored together with the operator in the graph since it is required for the next phase of case abstraction. This derivation is an "and-tree" where each inner-node reflects the resolution of a goal literal with the head of a clause and each leaf-node represents the resolution with a fact. Note that for proving the precondition of an abstract operator, the inner nodes of the tree always refer to clauses of the Horn rule set $\mathcal{R}_a$, while the leave-nodes represent facts stated in $\mathcal{R}_a$ or essential sentences contained in s_i^a. Then, each answer substitution σ is applied to the add-list of the operator, leading to a partially instantiated add-list Add_o'. Note that there can still be variables in Add_o' because the operator may contain variables which are not contained in its precondition but may occur in the add-list. Therefore, the set M of all possible substitutions θ is incrementally constructed such that $a\theta \in s_{aj}$ holds for all $a \in Add_o'$. The completely instantiated operator derived thereby is finally included as a directed edge (from i to j) in the graph G.

By the algorithm it is guaranteed that each (instantiated) operator which leads from s_i^a to s_j^a is applicable in s_i^a and that all essential sentences added by this operator are contained in s_j^a. Furthermore, if we claim that the applied SLD-refutation procedure is complete (it always finds all answer substitutions), then every instantiated operator which is applicable in s_i^a such that all essential sentences added by this operator are contained in s_j^a is also contained in the graph. From this follows immediately that if $\alpha(s_{\beta(i-1)}^c) \xrightarrow{o_i^a} \alpha(s_{\beta(i)}^c)$ holds for an arbitrary deductively justified state abstraction mapping α and a sequence abstraction mapping β, then $\langle \beta(i-1), \beta(i), o_i^a, \tau \rangle \in G$.

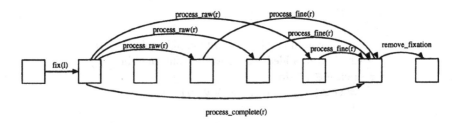

Fig. 5. An example of a transition graph computed in phase-III. The operator- parameters l and r abbreviate *left* and *right*, respectively.

Figure 5 gives an example of the graph G computed in phase-III during the abstraction of case C^1 shown in Figure 1. The lables at the edges denote the respective instantiated operators that are determined by the algorithm.

5.4 Phase-IV: Determining Sound Paths

Based on the state abstractions s_i^a derived in phase-II and on the graph G computed in the previous phase, phase-IV selects a set of sound paths from the initial abstract state to the final abstract state. During the construction of each path, a set of significant abstract sentences α^* and a sequence abstraction mapping β are also determined. While the construction of the sequence abstraction mapping is obvious, the set α^* represents the image of a state abstraction mapping α and thereby determines the set of sentences that have to be reached in order to assure the applicability of the constructed operator sequence. Note that from α^* the state abstraction mapping α can be directly determined as follows: $\alpha(s_i^c) = \{e \in \alpha^* | s_i^c \cup \mathcal{R}_c \cup \mathcal{A} \vdash e\}$.

The idea of the algorithm is to start with an empty path. In each iteration of the algorithm, one path is extended by an operator from G. In this operator, new essential sentences α' may occur in the proof of the precondition or as added effects. The path constructed so far must still be consistent according to the extension of the state description and, in addition, the new operator must transform the sentences of α^* correctly.

Algorithm 4 (Phase-IV: Searching sound paths)
$Paths := \{\langle (), \emptyset, (\beta(0) = 0) \rangle\}$
while *it exists* $\langle (o_1^a, \ldots, o_k^a), \alpha^*, \beta \rangle \in Paths$ *with* $\beta(k) < n$ **do**
   $Paths := Paths \setminus \langle (o_1^a, \ldots, o_k^a), \alpha^*, \beta \rangle$
   for each $\langle i, j, o^a, \tau \rangle \in G$ *with* $i = \beta(k)$ **do**
      let $\tau_\mathcal{E}$ *be the set of essential sentences contained in the derivation* τ
      let $\alpha' = \tau_\mathcal{E} \cup Add_{o^a} \cup \alpha^*$
      if for all $\nu \in \{1, \ldots, k\}$ *holds:*

$$(s_{\beta(\nu-1)}^a \cap \alpha') \xrightarrow{o_\nu^a} (s_{\beta(\nu)}^a \cap \alpha') \text{ and}$$
$$(s_{\beta(k)}^a \cap \alpha') \xrightarrow{o^a} (s_j^a \cap \alpha') \text{ then}$$
           $Paths := Paths \cup \{\langle (o_1^a, \ldots, o_k^a, o^a), \alpha', \beta \cup \{\beta(k+1) = j\}\rangle \}$
   end
   end
$Cases_{Abs} := \emptyset$
for each $\langle (o_1^a, \ldots, o_k^a), \alpha^*, \beta \rangle \in Paths$ *with* $\beta(k) = n$ **do**
   $Cases_{Abs} := Cases_{Abs} \cup \{\langle (s_0^a \cap \alpha^*, s_n^a \cap \alpha^*), (o_1^a, \ldots, o_k^a)\rangle\}$
   end
return $Cases_{Abs}$

As a result, phase-IV returns all cases that are abstractions of the given concrete input case, with respect to concrete and abstract domain definitions and the generic abstraction theory. Depending on the domain theory, more than a single abstract case will be learned from one concrete case.

For the abstraction of case C^1, the algorithm determines four consistent paths from the initial abstract state to the final abstract state. Three of these paths lead to one abstract case, namely the abstract case C_1^a which had been already shown in Figure 1. The fourth path leads to a different abstract case which consists of the abstract operator sequence `fix(left)`, `process_complete(right)`, `remove_fixation`. This abstract cases differs from the other in that it is more abstract. The operator `process_complete` is an operator which completely processes one side of the workpiece, including raw and fine elements. This abstract cases is also valuable in situations in which no fine elements need to be processed for solving a problem.

5.5 Correctness, Completeness, and Complexity of the Algorithm

In [6] we have shown the strong connection between the formal model of case abstraction and the presented algorithm. We have proven that the algorithm is *correct*, that is every abstract case computed by the PABS algorithm is a case abstraction according to the introduced model. If the SLD-refutation procedure applied in PABS is *complete*, than every case which is an abstraction according to definition 3 is computed by PABS.

The complexity of the algorithm is mainly determined by the phases III and IV. The overall complexity of the complete PABS-algorithm is $O(n \cdot 2^{(n-1)})$ where n is the length of the concrete level plan. The exponential factor comes from possibly exponential number of paths in a directed acyclic graph with n nodes if every state is connected to every successor state. However, such a graph is really unrealistic in real applications. In particular, this worst-case complexity did not lead to a problem in our application domain.

6 Empirical Evaluation and Results

In this section, we want to present the results of an empirical study of the presented approach in the domain of mechanical engineering, introduced in section 2. This evaluation was performed with the fully implemented PARIS-system using the described abstraction component and the explanation-based plan generalization component (not described in this paper) separately for comparison. The problem solver is a depth-first iterative-deepening search procedure [20].

6.1 Experimental Setting

We have randomly generated a case base of 100 planning cases. From the 100 available cases, we have randomly chosen 10 training sets of 5 cases and 10 training sets of 10 cases. These training sets are selected independently from each other. For each training set, a related testing set is determined by choosing those of the 100 cases which are not used for training. By this procedure, training set and test set are completely independent. We trained PARIS with each of the training sets separately and measured the time for problem solving on the related testing sets. The time for *learning* a set of abstract cases from one concrete cases is between 30 and 180 seconds in our domain, depending on the length of the plan in the concrete cases. For *problem solving*, a time-bound of 200 CPU seconds was used for each problem. If the problem could not be solved within this time limit, the problem solver was aborted and the problem remained unsolved. The number of unsolved problems was also evaluated. For each training/testing set, PARIS was run in three different modes: a) using the abstraction approach, b) using the explanation-based generalization approach, and c) without any learning.

6.2 Results

Table 1 shows the average number of solved problems for the training sets of the two different sizes and the different modes of PARIS. These average numbers are computed from the 10 training and testing sets for each size. We can see that learning explanation-based generalizations slightly improves problem solving through a slightly increased number of solved problems that could be solved. Learning abstractions, however, leads to really significant improvements in the number of problems which could be solved and drastically outperforms the generalization approach.

Table 1. Percentage of solved problems after different training sets

Size of training sets (cases)	Percentage of Solved Problems		
	Abstraction	Generalization	No Learning
5	83	37	29
10	86	37	29

A similar result can be found when examining the average time for solving a problem. Table 2 shows the average problem solving time for the different training sets in the three different modes of PARIS. Here, we can also see only a slight speed-up caused by learning generalizations but a much more significant speedup when the proposed abstraction approach is used.

Table 2. Problem solving time after different training sets

Size of training sets (cases)	Average problem solving time (sec.)		
	Abstraction	Generalization	No Learning
5	59	142	156
10	56	141	156

Additionally, all of the above mentioned speedup results were analyzed with the maximally conservative sign test as proposed in [11]. When using abstraction, it turned out that 19 of the 20 training sets lead to highly significant speedups ($p < 0.0005$) of problem solving. Only one training set caused a significant speedup result for $p < 0.075$. Altogether, the reported experiment showed that even a small number of training cases (i.e. 5% and 10%) can already lead to strong improvements on problem solving in our domain.

Additionally, we made comparisons with ALPINE [18] which is part of PRO-DIGY [31] and automatically generates abstractions by dropping conditions. It maintained. Otherwise, our abstraction approach would not work either. For the construction of a planning system, the concrete world descriptions must be acquired anyway, since they are the 'language' of the problem description (essential sentences) and the problem solution (operators). An appropriate abstract world and a generic abstraction theory must be acquired additionally. We feel that this is indeed the price we have to pay to make problem solving more tractable by learning in certain practical situations.

7.2 Related Work

Theory of Abstraction. Within Giunchiglia and Walsh's [15] theory of abstraction, the PARIS approach can be classified as follows: The formal system of the ground space Σ_1 is given by the concrete problem solving domain $\mathcal{D}_c$, and the abstract formal system Σ_2 is given by the language of the abstract problem solving domain $\mathcal{D}_a$. However, the operators of $\mathcal{D}_a$ are not turned into axioms of Σ_2. Instead, the abstract cases build the axioms of Σ_2. Moreover, the generic abstraction theory $\mathcal{A}$ defines the abstraction mapping $f : \Sigma_1 \Rightarrow \Sigma_2$. Within this framework, we can view PARIS as a system which learns useful axioms of the abstract system, by composing several smaller elementary axioms (the operators). However, to prove a formula (the existence of a solution) in the abstract system, exactly one axiom (case) is selected. So the deductive machinery of the abstract system is restricted with respect to the ground space. Depending on the learned abstract cases, the abstractions of PARIS are either theory decreasing (TD) or theory increasing (TI). If the case-base of abstract cases is completely empty, then no domain axiom is available and the resulting abstractions are consequently TD. But if the case-base contains the maximally abstract case $\langle(true, true)(nop)\rangle$[5] then this case can be applied to every concrete problem and the resulting abstraction is consequently TI. Even if this maximally abstract case does not improve problem solving, it should be always included into the case-base to ensure the TI property, that is not losing completeness.

Skeletal Plans. The PARIS approach was inspired by the idea of skeletal plans [13]. A abstract cases can be seen as a skeletal plan, and our learning algorithm is a means to learn skeletal plans automatically out of concrete plans. Even if the idea of skeletal plans is intuitively very appealing, to our knowledge, this paper contains the first comprehensive experimental support of usefulness of planning with skeletal plans. Since we have shown that skeletal plans can be acquired automatically, this planning method can be applied more easily.

ALPINE. ALPINE [19, 18] automatically learns hierarchies of abstraction spaces from a given domain description or from a domain description together with a planning problem. ALPINE relies on abstraction by dropping sentences.

---

[5] *nop* is the 'no operation' operator which is always applicable and does not change the abstract state.

turned out that for our domain, ALPINE was not able to improve problem solving at all because no useful abstractions could be built by dropping sentences as performed by ALPINE (see [6] for details).

7 Discussion

7.1 Conclusion

In this paper, we have presented a new approach to improving problem solving through reasoning from abstract cases. A methodology for abstracting planning cases and a sound and complete learning algorithm has been presented. An empirical evaluation in a real-world domain shows significant efficiency improvements of the problem solver while an explanation-based generalization approach leads to much slighter improvements.

Even if we have shown an advantage of abstraction over generalization in one specific application example, we clearly do not want to claim that abstraction is always better than generalization. In particular, explanation-based generalization has already proven useful in a couple of domains [29, 10, 40, 17]. However, the reason why it works so poorly in our domain is twofold. First of all, the representation of our domain requires a very detailed and complex representation of operators and states. Typically, a single concrete level state is described by over 200 ground facts. Moreover, the operator descriptions contain a large set of different preconditions. The well-known methods for explanation-based generalization of plans lead to rules or schemas which contain a very large set of conjunctively combined preconditions. This causes very high matching costs to determine the applicability of a rule or schema, because in the worst case the matching costs are exponential in the number (not on their size) of conditions. In our domain, these matching costs mostly exceed the savings caused by the application of the rules. Consequently, no overall speedup occurs. This problem is very much related to the utility-problem [30]. Our abstraction approach reduces the required level of detail in the descriptions that have to be matched to determine the applicability of an abstract case. Consequently, the matching process at the abstract level is much more efficient. However, the reused abstract plans must still be refined to come to a concrete solution, so that the potential speedup is obviously smaller than when reusing a concrete solution as in an explanation-based approach. But the key to success is that the matching costs at the abstract level are much smaller than the gain in efficiency.

The second reason for the advantage of abstraction over generalization in our domain is caused by the high flexibility of reusing abstract solutions. As already shown in section 2.3, an abstract case can be reused in a situation in which the concrete case or even a generalization of it is of no use. In particular if only a small number of cases is available for training, this flexibility is of high value.

Nevertheless, the availability of an adequate abstract domain theory is crucial to the success of the approach. This theory must allow to significantly simplify the representation of a case while the most important solution properties can be

However, this enables ALPINE to generate abstraction hierarchies automatically. For the stronger abstraction framework we follow in PARIS, the automatic generation of abstraction hierarchies (or abstract domain descriptions) does not seem to be realistic due to the large (infinite) space of possible abstract spaces. To use our powerful abstraction methodology, we feel that we have to pay the price of losing the ability to automatically construct an abstraction hierarchy.

Acknowledgements

The authors want to thank Agnar Aamodt, Jaime Carbonell, Manuela Veloso, as well as Michael M. Richter and all members of our research group for helpful discussions and for remarks on earlier versions of this paper. We particularly appreciate the comments of the anonymous ECML reviewers. This research was partially funded by the Commission of the European Communities (ESPRIT contract P6322, the INRECA project). The partners of INRECA are AcknoSoft (prime contractor, France), tecInno (Germany), Irish Medical Systems (Ireland) and the University of Kaiserslautern (Germany).

References

1. R. Bergmann. Knowledge acquisition by generating skeletal plans. In F. Schmalhofer, G. Strube, and Th. Wetter, editors, *Contemporary Knowledge Engineering and Cognition*, pages 125–133, Heidelberg, 1992. Springer.
2. R. Bergmann. Learning abstract plans to speed up hierarchical planning. In P. Tadepalli, editor, *Proceedings of the ML92 Workshop on Knowledge Compilation and Speedup Learning*. University of Aberdeen, Scotland, 1992.
3. R. Bergmann. Learning plan abstractions. In H.J. Ohlbach, editor, *GWAI-92 16th German Workshop on Artificial Intelligence*, volume 671 of *Springer Lecture Notes on AI*, pages 187–198, 1992.
4. R. Bergmann. Integrating abstraction, explanation-based learning from multiple examples and hierarchical clustering with a performance component for planning. In Enric Plaza, editor, *Proceedings of the ECML-93 Workshop on Integrated Learning Architectures (ILA-93)*, Vienna, Austria, 1993.
5. R. Bergmann and W. Wilke. Inkrementelles Lernen von Abstraktionshierarchien aus maschinell abstrahierten Plänen. In *Proceedings of the German GI Workshop on Machine Learning*. University of Karlsruhe, 1993.
6. R. Bergmann and W. Wilke. Building and refining abstract planning cases by change of representation language. Technical report, University of Kaiserslautern,, 1994.
7. J. G. Carbonell. Derivational analogy: A theory of reconstructive problem solving and expertise aquisition. In R. S. Michalski, J. G. Carbonell, and T. M. Mitchell, editors, *Machine learning: An artificial intelligence approach*, volume 2, chapter 14, pages 371–392. Morgan Kaufmann, Los Altos, CA, 1986.
8. D. Chapman. Planning for conjunctive goals. *Artificial Intelligence*, 32:333–377, 1987.
9. G. DeJong and R. Mooney. Explanation-based learning: An alternative view. *Machine Learning*, 1(2):145–176, 1986.
10. O. Etzioni. A structural theory of explanation-based learning. *Artificial Intelligence*, 60:93–139, 1993.

11. O. Etzioni and R. Etzioni. Statistical methods for analyzing speedup learning. *Machine Learning*, 14:333–347, 1994.

12. R. E. Fikes and N. J. Nilsson. Strips: A new approach to the application of theorem proving to problem solving. *Artificial Intelligence*, 2:189–208, 1971.

13. P. E. Friedland and Y. Iwasaki. The concept and implementation of skeletal plans. *Journal of Automated Reasoning*, 1(2):161–208, 1985.

14. A. Giordana, D. Roverso, and L. Saitta. Abstracting background knowledge for concept learning. In Y. Kodratoff, editor, *Lecture Notes in Artificial Intelligence: Machine Learning-EWSL-91*, pages 1–13, Berlin, 1991. Springer.

15. F. Giunchiglia and T. Walsh. A theory of abstraction. *Artificial Intelligence*, 57:323–389, 1992.

16. S. Kambhampati and J. A. Hendler. A validation-structure-based theory of plan modification and reuse. *Artificial Intelligence*, 55:193–258, 1992.

17. S. Kambhampati and S. Kedar. A unified framework for explanation-based generalization of partially ordered partially instantiated plans. *Artificial Intelligence*, 67:29–70, 1994.

18. C. Knoblock. Automatically generating abstractions for planning. *Artificial Intelligence*, 68:243–302, 1994.

19. C. A. Knoblock. A theory of abstraction for hierachical planning. In *Proceedings of the Workshop on Change of Representation and Inductive Bias*, pages 81–104, Boston, MA, 1989. Kluwer.

20. R. E. Korf. Depth-first iterative-deepening: An optimal admissible tree search. *Artifical Intelligence*, 27:97–109, 1985.

21. R. E. Korf. Planning as search: A quantitative approach. *Artifical Intelligence*, 33:65–88, 1987.

22. R. E. Korf. Linear-space best-first search. *Artifical Intelligence*, 62:41–78, 1993.

23. P. Langley and J.A. Allen. A unified framework for planning and learning. In S. Minton, editor, *Machine Learning Methods for Planning*, chapter 10, pages 317–350. Morgan Kaufmann, 1993.

24. V. Lifschitz. On the semantics of strips. In *Reasoning about Actions and Plans: Proceedings of the 1986 Workshop*, pages 1–9, Timberline, Oregon, 1987.

25. J.W. Lloyd. *Foundations of Logic Programming*. Springer, 1984.

26. D. McAllester and D. Rosenblitt. Systematic nonlinear planning. In *Proceedings of the 9th National Conference on Artificial Intelligence*, pages 634–639, 1991.

27. R. Michalski. Inferential theory of learning as a conceptual basis for multistrategy learning. In R. Michalski and G. Tecuci, editors, *Machine Learning: A Multistrategy Approach*, number 11, chapter 1, pages 3–62. Morgan Kaufmann, 1994.

28. R. S. Michalski and Y. Kodratoff. Research in machine learning: Recent progress, classification of methods, and future directions. In Y. Kodratoff and R. S. Michalski, editors, *Machine learning: An artificial intelligence approach*, volume 3, chapter 1, pages 3–30. Morgan Kaufmann, San Mateo, CA, 1990.

29. S. Minton. *Learning Search Control Knowledge: An Explanation-Based Approach*. Kluwer, Boston, MA, 1988.

30. S. Minton. Quantitativ results concerning the utility of explanation-based learning. *Artifical Intelligence*, 42:363–391, 1990.

31. S. Minton, J. G. Carbonell, C.A. Knoblock, D. R. Kuokka, O. Etzioni, and Y. Gil. Explanation-based learning: A problem solving perspective. *Artificial Intelligence*, 40:63–118, 1989.

32. S. Minton and M. Zweben. Learning, planning and scheduling: An overview. In S. Minton, editor, *Machine Learning Methods for Planning*, chapter 1, pages 1–30. Morgan Kaufmann, 1993.

33. T. M. Mitchell, R. M. Keller, and S. T. Kedar-Cabelli. Explanation-based generalization: A unifying view. *Machine Learning*, 1(1):47–80, 1986.

34. A. Newell and H. Simon. *Human Problem Solving*. Prentice-Hall Englewood Cliffs, NJ, 1972.

35. J. Paulokat and S. Wess. Planning for machining workpieces with a partial-order, nonlinear planner. In *AAAI-Fall Symposium on Planning and Learning: On to Real Applications*, 1994.

36. E. Plaza, A. Aamodt, A. Ram, W. VandeVelde, and M. vanSommeren. Integrated learning architectures. In B. Brazdil, editor, *European Conference on Machine Learning: ECML-93*, volume 667 of *Lecture Notes in Artificial Intelligence*, pages 429–441, Berlin, 1993. Springer.

37. P.S. Rosenbloom and J.E. Laird. Mapping explanation-based learning onto SOAR. In *Proceedings National Conference on Artificial Intelligence*, volume 2, Philadelphia, PA, August 1986.

38. E.D. Sacerdoti. Planning in a hierarchy of abstraction spaces. *Artificial Intelligence*, 5:115–135, 1974.

39. E.D. Sacerdoti. *A Structure for Plans and Behavior*, volume 5. American-Elsevier, New York,, 1977.

40. J.W. Shavlik and P. O'Rorke. Empirically evluation ebl. In *Investigating Explanation-Based Learning*, volume 5, chapter 7, pages 222–294. Kluwer Academic Publishers, 1993.

41. M. M. Veloso. PRODIGY/ANALOGY: Analogical reasoning in general problem solving. In M.M. Richer, S. Wess, K.D. Althoff, and F. Maurer, editors, *Topics in Case-Based Reasoning*, pages 33–52. Lecture Notes in AI, Vol. 837, Springer, 1994.

42. M. M. Veloso and J. G. Carbonell. Towards scaling up machine learning: A case study with derivational analogy in PRODIGY. In Steven Minton, editor, *Machine Learning Methods for Planning*, chapter 8, pages 233–272. Morgan Kaufmann, 1993.

43. W. Wilke. Entwurf und Implementierung eines Algorithmus zum wissensintensiven Lernen von Planabstraktionen nach der PABS-Methode. Projektarbeit, Universität Kaiserslautern, 1993.

44. W. Wilke. Entwurf, Implementierung und experimentelle Bewertung von Auswahlverfahren für abstrakte Pläne im fallbasierten Planungssystem PARIS. Master's thesis, University of Kaiserslautern, Germany, 1994.

45. D. Wilkins. Domain-independent planning: Representation and plan generation. *Artificial Intelligence*, 22:269–301, 1984.

46. Q. Yang and J.D. Tenenberg. Abtweak: Abstracting a nonlinear, least commitment planner. In *Proceedings of the 8th National Conference on Aritificial Intelligence*, pages 204–209, Boston, MA, 1990.

The Role of Prototypicality in Exemplar-Based Learning

Yoram Biberman

Department of Mathematics and Computer Science
Ben-Gurion University of the Negev
P.O.B. 653, 84105 Beer-Sheva, Israel
e-mail: yoramb@cs.bgu.ac.il, phone: 972-2-437-244, fax: 972-7-472909

keywords: Concept learning, Exemplar-Based Learning, Prototypes.

Abstract. This paper examines the role of prototypicality in exemplar-based concept learning methods. It proposes two approaches to prototypicality: a shared-properties approach, and a similarity-based approach, and suggests measures that implement the different approaches. The proposed measures are tested in a set of experiments. The results of the experiments show that prototypicality serves as a good storing filter in storage reduction algorithms; combining it in algorithms that store all the training set does not improve significantly the accuracy of the algorithm. Finally, prototypicality is a useful notion only in a subset of the domains; a preliminary examination of those domains and their characteristics is proposed.

1   Background and Motivation

Human concept learning is studied intensively for about seventy years. In its early days the research concentrated about *logical concepts* defined by a set of conditions. Logical concepts have the property that any given object either belongs to the concept or not, and all members of a concept represent it equally, or belong to it to the same extent (e.g., 'prime number', as each number is either prime or not, and no number is 'more prime' than another; 'grandmother' can be defined as the mother of a parent, and any grandmother is as good exemplar of this concept as any other). Logical concepts are thus *unstructured*.

During the last three decades it is argued that *natural concepts*, occurring in everyday life, are totally different from logical concepts, cannot be defined by a set of necessary and sufficient conditions, and are structured. The first to propose this idea was Wittgenstein [18] who asked "how would you define the concept of *game*?" He claimed that this concept contains a large variety of objects; each game is similar to some other games in some of its properties, but there are no properties common to all of them. Wittgenstein concluded that natural concepts, like games, can not be defined by rules. He suggested that members of a natural concept share *a family resemblance:* each member of the concept is similar to *few* other members of its concept, or shares *few* properties with *some* other members of its concept, the member need not be similar to *all* other members of its concept.

In line with this argument, Rosch and Mervis [15] claim that natural concepts are represented in our mind by *an image* of the *prototype* of the concept. The prototype is an object that belongs to the concept, and represents it best.

Rosch further argues that prototypicality is a graded property, i.e., members of a concept can be rated according to the extent that they represent the concept. Thus, Rosch suggests that natural concepts are *structured:* different members have different status in them, and prototypicality may serve as a measure of membership in a concept. She writes:

> "The basic hypothesis was that members of a category come to be viewed as prototypical of the category as a whole in proportion to the extent that they bear a family resemblance to (have attributes which overlap those of other members of) the category. Conversely, items viewed prototypical of one category will be those with least family resemblance to or membership in other categories. In natural categories of concrete objects, the two aspects of family resemblance should coincide rather than conflict." ([15], p. 575)

Thus Rosch suggests that the rated prototypicality of an item is affected by two factors: The number of properties it shares with other members of its concept, and the number of properties it shares with members of contrasting concepts. We term the first factor *focality*, and the second *peripherality*. Rosch argues that in a natural concept the two measures correlate.

The notion of prototypicality is now considered central to theories of human categorization. Many findings concerning phenomenon about human concept learning are explained in terms of prototypicality. For example, Rosch showed that children first learn to classify prototypical members of a category, their ability to classify peripheral members develops only later [14]. Posner and Keele [11] found that more prototypical members of a category are classified faster and more accurately, and are better remembered.

In modern machine learning prototypicality does not have such a central status. Rendell [13] adopts a classic definition of prototypicality, he proposes that *the* prototype of a concept is the centroid of a ball in an Euclidean space. In STAGGER [17] the prototypicality of an object is the extent that it satisfies the necessary and sufficient conditions for membership in the concept. In ID3 [12] the prototypicality of an example may be obtained by considering its depth as a leaf of a decision tree. In AQ15 [8] one can infer the prototypicality of an object from the rule that captures it (if a concept is defined by a set of rules, then a rule that covers more members of the concept is considered more prototypical). A similar approach is held by Bergadano et al. [4] in the POSEIDON system, where they suggest that a *Base Concept Representation* should capture the prototypical members of each concept; the exceptional cases would be identified by an *Inferential Concept Interpretation* process. STAGGER, AQ15, POSEIDON and ID3 relate to prototypicality but do not rely on it: the prototypicality of the objects can be inferred but is not used in the learning or classification process.

In PROTOS [10], EACH [16] and PEBLS [6] the prototypicality of an object O refers to the system's 'confidence' in O as a reliable representative of its class. O is considered a good representative of its concept to the extent that if the system uses O in order to classify unseen objects (using a nearest neighbour, or similar, classification method) then the system predictions would be relatively accurate. The weight of an exemplar E in EACH and PEBLS, which can be seen as its prototypicality, is the quotient between number of objects E correctly classifies (using a nearest neighbour classification rule), and the total number of objects E classifies. A similar approach is held by PROTOS.

As prototypicality bears so much importance in human categorization we might expect that it would also be useful in machine learning. Therefore in the sequel I propose and examine two computational models of prototypicality. The examination shows that while some usages of prototypicality in exemplar-based concept learning improves the accuracy of the learning algorithm other usages degrade the accuracy.

The next section presents the intuitions that led to the two prototypicality measures that are presented in sections 3 and 4. Sections 5.2 and 5.3 presents experiments that were conducted with the proposed measures. The measures were combined in algorithms that store all the training set (Sec. 5.2), and in these algorithms they did not cause an improvement in the accuracy of the algorithm; they were also embedded in storage-reduction algorithms (Sec. 5.3), and in these algorithms they served as a successful storage filters: When the more prototypical items from each concept are stored the accuracy of the algorithm is better than when other criterions for storing exemplars are applied.

2 Intuition

Following Rosch I suggest that an object is considered *prototypical* in a concept if it is *focal* and not *peripheral*, where focality relates to the extent that the object represents the concept under discussion, and peripherality describes the extent that it represents other concepts.

Two alternative approaches to prototypicality are examined. The first is termed *the shared-properties approach*; it is derived from Rosch's theory. Rosch suggests that the focality of an object is determined by the number of properties it shares with other members of its concept; thus if a concept C_1 contains seven members, which in some feature f have the following values $\{a, a, a, a, b, b, b\}$ then the focality of the value a in C_1 is greater than that of b. Consider now another concept C_2 with the following set of values in f: $\{a, a, a, a, x, y, z\}$; I suggest that while in C_2 a is the *only* 'representative' value, in C_1 a is the *best* representative, but there is another value that also serves as a good representative of the category; therefore, the focality of a in C_2 is greater than its focality in C_1. Thus, the focality of a value v in a category C is determined by two factor: (a) the prevalence of v in C, (b) the prevalence of other values $u \neq v$ in C.

Another, more subtle, point in Rosch's theory that was adopted by the shared-properties based prototypicality measure is that prototypicality is not a gestalt property of the object as a whole, but may be expressed as a function of its distinct features. Therefore, the focality of an object is defined as the the sum of the focality of its features.

. The peripherality of an object is defined as its focality among members of contrasting concepts; the prototypicality of an object is the difference between its focality and its peripherality.

Neumann [9] proposed a concept acquisition model that argue that humans, during the learning phase, count the frequency of each feature in each concept (e.g., red occurs half of the times among members of C). During the test phase, probe items that are described by more frequent features are classified more easily. Thus Neumann's model also relys on feature counting processes.

An alternative approach to prototypicality, one that emerges from Wittgenstein's ideas, relies more directly on similarity evaluations. I denote this approach *the similarity-based approach*. We may suggest that the focality of an object should be defined as its average similarity to other members of its concept, the peripherality of an object is its similarity to members of contrasting concepts, and, like in the previous approach, the prototypicality of an object is the difference between its focality and its peripherality. Two variants of this approach are also tested.

The two approaches are not independent, as if an object shares many properties with other members of its concept, it is, generally, also similar to many other object as well; yet there are also differences between the two definitions, for example an object might be highly similar to few other objects, but not share many properties with many other members of its concept.

The next section presents the shared-properties approach to prototypicality, the section afterward presents the alternative, similarity-based approach to prototypicality.

3 The Shared-Properties Approach to Prototypicality

During the learning process the teachers supply examples of different concepts (assume that a positive example of a certain concept is a negative example for the other concepts). Let $\{E_1, ..., E_m\}$ be a set of m examples that represent a concept C. Each example $E_i = (v_{i1}, ..., v_{in})$ is a vector of n values, where each value represents a feature, and is taken from a nominal scale domain. For each E_i in C we define its focality, peripherality, prototypicality.

Denote by C_f the set of values in the feature f occurring in members of the concept C. Denote by $num(v, C_f)$ the number of examples that belong to C and share the value v in the feature f.

3.1 The Focality Measure

The focality of an example in a concept reflects the extent that this example is a good representative of the concept as it shares many features with other members of the concept. The focality of an example E in a concept C is a sum of the focalities of its features, $Foc_{ex}(E, C) = \sum_{j=1}^{n} foc_{val}(v_j, C)$; (the same holds for the other two measures as well, therefore in the sequel we concentrate upon focality/peripherality/prototypicality of a value. In most cases C is understood from the context, and is, therefore, omitted from the notation).

The focality of a value v in a feature f in a concept C reflects the extent that v represents C_f; it is influenced by two factors: (a) the extent that v is frequent in C: (b) the extent that other values represent C, or are frequent in C:

To combine the above two factors we may define the focality of v in C_f to be:

$$foc_{val}(v, C_f) = num^2(v, C_f) - \sum_{v_i \neq v} num^2(v_i, C_f) \; .$$

The first factor in the above definition reflects the prevalence of v in C, the second factor reflects the prevalence of other values. To normalize the above measure to the range $[0..1]$ we actually define it to be:

$$foc_{val}(v, C_f) = \frac{num^2(v, C_f) - \sum_{v_i \neq v} num^2(v_i, C_f)}{2 \sum_{v_j} num^2(v_j, C_f)} + 0.5 \; .$$

For example, the focality of b in $\{b, b, b, b, a, a, a\}$ is $(4^2 - 3^2)/(2 \cdot (4^2 + 3^2)) + 0.5 = .64$, while the focality of b in $\{b, b, b, b, x, y, z\}$ is $(4^2 - (1^2 + 1^2 + 1^2))/(2 \cdot (4^2 + 1^2 + 1^2 + 1^2)) + 0.5 = .84$.

The focality measure is a continuous necessity condition: A normal necessity condition is Boolean— an object either satisfies the condition or not, and if it does not then it is not considered member of the concept. Above it was argued that Boolean conditions are not suited for natural concepts that lack sharp boundaries; here the Boolean condition is relaxed to a continuous measure: the measure gets the extreme values 0 and 1 when a normal necessity condition can be applied, i.e. when there is a single value that can serve as a necessity membership condition; the measure gets intermediate values in cases where some values are more prevalent than others, in these cases the measure is larger for the more prevalent values; for example: $foc_{val}(a, \{a, a, a, b\}) > foc_{val}(a, \{a, a, b, b\})$ as in the left concept a is 'a more necessary value for membership in the concept' in the sense that there are less non-a members of this concept, which means that in order to be a member of the concept, an example should have an a in this feature.

3.2 The Peripherality and Prototypicality Measures

The peripherality of a value v in C_f reflects the extent that v is frequent among examples of other concepts: the more frequent v is outside C, the more peripheral it is in C. Denote by $\overline{C}$ the set of examples that do not belong to the concept C. The peripherality is dual to the focality and it is defined to be the focality in $\overline{C}$:

$$per_{val}(v, C_f) = foc_{val}(v, \overline{C}_f).$$

The prototypicality of a value v in C_f reflects the extent that v is frequent among members of C and is infrequent in $\overline{C}$, while taking into consideration the extent that other values have this property; in other words, the prototypicality of v is the extent that v and only v characterizes C and only C. The prototypicality is define to be:

$$proto_{\text{val}}(v, C_f) = foc_{\text{val}}(v, C_f) - per_{\text{val}}(v, C_f).$$

Both the focality and peripherality measures are in the range $[0..1]$, therefore the prototypicality measure is in the range $[-1..1]$. A larger value in each measure evidences that the example has more of this property; that is, if the focality of an example E_1 is larger than the focality of E_2 in a concept C, then it evidences that the properties (or features) of E_1 are more prevalent in C then the properties of E_2; if the prototypicality of E_1 is larger than that of E_2 it indicates that E_1 is a better representative of C as its properties are more prevalent in C, and less prevalent in concepts contrasting with C. If the prototypicality of E is less than zero it indicates that E represents $\overline{C}$ better than it represents C.

This section presented a prototypicality measure that originates from the shared-properties approach. The next section presents two alternative prototypicality measures that originate from the similarity based approach.

4 The Similarity-Based Approach to Prototypicality

The similarity-based approach to prototypicality defines prototypicality by means of similarity. Two variants of this approach are tested. The first variant defines the focality of an exemplar E that belongs to a concept C as the average similarity between E and *all* other members of C, the peripherality of E is defined as the average similarity between E and *all* members of $\overline{C}$. Formally expressed, let $E_1, ..., E_m$ be the members of C, $E'_1, ..., E'_k$ be the exemplars that do not belong to C; denote by $Sim(E_j, E_j)$ the similarity between the examples E_i, E_j. The focality of E in C is:

$$Foc_{\text{ex}}(E, C) = \sum_{i=1}^{m} Sim(E, E_i)/m \quad .$$

The peripherality E in C is defined as:

$$Per_{\text{ex}}(E, C) = \sum_{i=1}^{k} Sim(E, E'_i)/k \quad .$$

The second variant of the similarity-based approach defines the focality of E as the average similarity between E and the three members of C that are most similar to it; peripherality is, accordingly, defined as the average similarity between E and the three objects in $\overline{C}$ that are most similar to E. In both variants the prototypicality of E is the difference between its focality and peripherality.

Two considerations led me to try the second variant as well: (a) If a concept is composed of two or more homogeneous and distinct clusters that are dissimilar one from the other (e.g., in a xor like configuration) then the second definition might be more successful than the first one. (b) In the context of exemplar-based learning, prototypicality generally serves as a 'utility measure' over the exemplars, that is, it should evidence how useful and accurate an exemplar is as a classifier of probe items in the context of a k nearest neighbour, or similar, classification method. For this usage, similarity to items that are distant from E is not important, only the near neighbours of E: whether they belong to C or to contrasting concepts is relevant.

The rest of the paper presents the experiments that were conducted with the proposed prototypicality measures, and discusses their results.

5 Experimental Results and Discussion

Two main sets of experiments or comparisons were performed with the proposed prototypicality measures: The first set involved exemplar-based learning methods that store, and use during in the test phase, all the training set, the second set of experiments involves storage reduction algorithms, i.e., algorithms that store, and use during the test phase, only a subset of the training examples. It turns out that: (a) combining prototypicality measures in algorithms of the first kind does not improve their accuracy; (b) prototypicality measures serve as successful 'storing filters' [7] in storage reduction methods, that is, by storing the more prototypical members of each concept, the algorithm would achieve best results.

I shall first describe the negative results, which I find no less interesting. I would like to suggest that these negative results raise substantial questions concerning the role of prototypicality (at least) in computerized learning systems, and concerning the relation between human categorization and computerized models.

5.1 The Examples that were Used in the Experiments

This section overviews the domains that were used in the experiments, and their main properties.

The examples that were used were obtained from the repository of machine learning databases cited in the University of California, Irvine (UCI). As this paper concentrates upon examples that are described by nominal domain features only databases that satisfy this condition are used. On the other hand almost all nominal valued databases are examined; thus we may argue that the set of domains that is used is representative of the set of domains used in machine learning. Figure 1 presents a statistical overview of the examples.

Three of the databases that are used in the following experiments are good examples of domains that contain natural concepts: (a) The 'Zoo' domain contains different kinds of animals. (b) The 'LED display' example can be described as an 'artificial natural concept': It is artificial on the one hand, as it is produced by a computer program, but it has many characteristics of natural concepts on the other hand; it also resembles the kind of concepts psychologists use in their laboratory experiments that aim to investigate human categorization in natural domains. (c) 'Hayes-Roth and Hayes-Roth (1977)' is an example of a database that was borrowed from such experiments. The characterization of other concepts is less obvious, at least for someone who is not expert in these fields.

The domains that were used in the experiments

Domain #	Domain	Number of examples	Number of predicting attributes	Number of values in attribute	Number of concepts	Frequency of most frequent concept (%)	Missing values
1	1984 U.S. Congressional voting	435	16	2	2	61	y
2	LED display	500	7	2	10	10	n
3	LED display + 17 irrelevant attributes	500	24	2	10	10	n
4	Tic-Tac-Toe endgame	958	9	3	2	65	n
5	Standardized audiology	226	69	2	24	48	y
6	Lung cancer data	32	56	3	3	41	y
7	E. coli promoter gene sequences (DNA)	106	57	4	2	50	n
8	Primate splice-junction gene sequences (DNA)	1200	60	4	3	50	n
9	Zoo	101	16	2	7	41	n
10	Hayes-Roth & Hayes-Roth (1977)	160	4	4	3	41	n

Fig. 1. A statistic overview of the examples.

5.2 Prototypicality in algorithms that store all the training set

The proposed prototypicality measures were added to a basic Nearest Neighbour (NN) classifier that bases its predictions over a single exemplar–the one that is most similar to the probe, and to a classifier that bases its predictions over a set of three exemplars. The following subsections presents these experiments, and their results.

1-NN Classifiers The most common, and probably basic, exemplar-based learning method is the IB1 algorithm [2] that bases its classification of a probe over its similarity to a single exemplar—the one that is most similar to the probe, i.e. its Nearest Neighbour (NN). This algorithm works as follows:

– *During the learning phase:* Store all the exemplars the teacher supplies as they are without any processing.

– *During the test phase:* In order to classify a probe object P— Evaluate the similarity between P and all the stored exemplars, and predict that P belongs to the same concept as the exemplar that is most similar to it.

We could expect that if the algorithm in addition to evaluating the similarity between P and each stored exemplar E_i, would also consider the prototypicality of E_i in its concept, it would be more accurate. Therefore we may propose the following Proto-IB1 algorithm:

– *During the learning phase:* Store all the exemplars the teacher supplies. For each exemplar compute its prototypicality.
– *During the test phase:* In order to classify a probe object P— For each stored exemplar E_i, compute $Sim(P, E_i) \cdot Proto(E_i)$ (where $Sim(P, E_i)$ denotes the similarity between P and E_i, and $Proto(E_i)$ denotes the prototypicality of E_i in its concept), and predict that P belongs to the same concept as the exemplar for which this term is maximal.

A comparison between these two algorithms is depicted in Fig. 2. The indices in first line of the figure relates to the domains from Fig. 1. The second line presents the accuracy of a basic IB1 algorithm. (All the algorithms that are examined in this experiment utilize the Context-Similarity measure [5].) The third line presents the classification rate of a Proto-IB1 algorithm that uses the shared-properties based definition of prototypicality. The last two lines depict the accuracies of variants of Proto-IB1 that use the similarity-based definition of prototypicality: In the fourth line prototypicality of an exemplar E that belongs to a concept C is defined as the average similarity between E and its three nearest neighbours in C, versus its three nearest neighbours outside C. In the fifth line the prototypicality of E is defined as the average similarity to all other members of its concept, versus to all the objects that belong to contrasting concepts. Each entry in the table is a result of averaging over 50 runs.

Few conclusions can be drawn from a comparison between the accuracies of the four classifiers. Probably the most notable one is that in seven out of the ten domains that were examined, the basic IB1 algorithm performs best. In three domains the Proto-IB1 algorithms were more successful, two out of these domains are the artificial examples: 'LED display' and 'Hayes Roth & Hayes Roth (1977)'. These domains were proposed by researchers that synthesized them on the basis of their assumptions concerning the structure of prevalent natural domains. (cf. [1,3] concerning performing experiments, and synthesizing artificial domains.) It should be said that the assumptions their inventors held are widely accepted among researchers in cognitive psychology. In both these domains concepts are composed of 'ideal' prototypes and other examples that are distortions of the prototypes. The finding that in them the prototypicality-based algorithms perform well evidence that the proposed definitions of prototypicality are valid– if the concepts are truly composed of ideal prototypes and other objects with graded degrees of prototypicality then using the proposed prototypicality measures improves the accuracy. The finding that even in these two domains the accuracy of the three different Proto-IB1 algorithms is not always similar evidences that

Average classification accuracy
of 1-NN algorithms

Domain #	1	2	3	4	5	6	7	8	9	10
IB1	93	60	64	57	81	44	77	78	96	95
Proto-IB1 (shared properties)	89	70	62	49	69	48	57	69	94	94
Proto-IB1 (similarity to 3 vs. 3 objects)	92	54	60	49	81	51	74	78	94	96
Proto-IB1 (similarity to all objects)	89	61	52	46	23	49	50	48	88	25

Fig. 2. The accuracy of four classifiers that base their classification on a single exemplar. 'IB1' is the basic nearest neighbour algorithm, 'Proto-IB1 (shared properties)' refer to the variant of Proto-IB1 that utilizes the shared-properties based definition of prototypicality, 'Proto-IB1 (similarity to 3 vs. 3 objects)' refer to a variant of Proto-IB1 that utilizes a similarity-based definition of prototypicality, but examines the similarity to only three other objects within the exemplar's concept versus to three other objects from contrasting concepts, 'Proto-IB1 (similarity to all objects)' is the variant that examines the similarity to all other objects when evaluating the prototypicality of an object.

even in domains that are composed of structured concepts (that are composed of prototypes), the way to capture this structure may differ. In this experiment the most successful prototypicality measure is the one that bases its evaluation over similarity to '3 vs. 3' objects. The fact that this definition is far more successful than the similarity-based definition that relies over similarity to all the exemplar hints that most of the concepts in our domains are not composed of a single distinct cluster. Finally, and what I find as the most interesting result, the fact that in seven out of the eight real life domains the prototypicality-based classifiers were less accurate than the basic IB1 algorithm raise a question whether the common assumption that natural concepts are structured and contain prototypes is valid, or, if we rephrase the question in a more positive manner: what is the role of prototypes and prototypicality in natural domains? Do they have different role in human learning than in computerized one?

The Family Resemblance Measure and 3-NN Classifiers In a slightly different experiment I compared algorithms that base their classification of a probe item not over its similarity to a single exemplar, but over its three nearest neighbours. The basic 3-NN classifier works as follows:

- *During the learning phase:* Store all the exemplars the teacher supplies as they are.
- *During the test phase:* In order to classify a probe object P— Evaluate the similarity between P and all the stored exemplars. Let S be the set of three exemplars that are most similar to P. If at least two members of S belong to the same concepts C, then predict that P also belongs to this concept, otherwise predict the P belongs to the same concept as its nearest neighbour.

The basic 3-NN algorithm is compared with a version that bases its predictions over three exemplars from each concept, and also weights the prototypicality of the stored exemplars. The measure that is used is termed *family resemblance (fare)*. The family resemblance between a probe object P and a concept C that is represented by the exemplars $\{E_1, ..., E_m\}$ is define as follows

$$fare(P, C) = \sum_{i=1}^{3} Sim(P, E'_i) \cdot Proto(E'_i)/3 \ ,$$

where E'_i belongs to C, and the summation goes over the three exemplars in C that maximize $Sim(P, E'_i) \cdot Proto(E'_i)$.

The *fare* based algorithm that is examined is termed *a family resemblance classifier*. It operates as follows:

- *During the learning phase:* Store all the exemplars the teacher supplies. For each exemplar compute its prototypicality.
- *During the test phase:*
  In order to classify a probe object P do:
  For each concept C_i compute $fare(P, C_i)$.
  Predict that P belongs to the concept for which $fare(P, C_i)$ is maximal.

The results of the comparison between the basic 3-NN algorithm and the family resemblance classifiers are depicted in Fig. 3.

Average classification accuracy of 3-NN algorithms

Domain #	1	2	3	4	5	6	7	8	9	10
3-NN classifier	94	64	71	56	81	49	76	78	93	96
fare-3 (shared properties)	90	69	65	49	50	49	55	69	93	96
fare-3 (similarity to 3 vs. 3 objects)	92	59	65	48	81	52	74	78	95	89

Fig. 3. The accuracy of three classifiers that base their classification on three exemplars. '3-NN classifier' is the basic three-nearest-neighbour algorithm, 'fare-3 (shared properties)' refer to the family resemblance classifier that utilizes the shared-properties based definition of prototypicality, 'fare-3 (similarity to 3 vs. 3 objects)' refer to a variant of the family resemblance classifier that utilizes the similarity-based definition of prototypicality.

The first finding that emerges from Fig. 3, and that is consistent with the previous experiment, is that in four domains the basic 3-NN algorithm is more accurate than the prototypicality-based methods, while in three domains the prototypicality-based algorithms (as a group) are most successful.

As can be seen from Fig. 3, again, the prototypicality-based algorithms are successful on the two artificial domains: 'LED display' and the 'Hayes-roth &

Hayes-Roth (1977)'. A third domain in which these algorithms are accurate is the 'Zoo' domain. Thus we may say that the prototypicality-based classifiers are successful in domains that are composed of structured concepts, that contain more and less prototypical members. But, from the results of the two experiments we may also conclude that many concepts do not have this desired(?) structure. A clear example is the 'Tic-Tac-Toe endgame' domain. Each example in this domain represents a possible board configuration at the end of a 'Tic-Tac-Toe' game. The examples are divided into two concepts: 'a win for player ×' or not. This domain is not structured, and contains no prototypes: there is no 'prototypical winning configuration', each 'winning configuration' is as good as any other one, by changing a single attribute we may turn each 'winning configuration' into a non winning one, that is we may move the example from one concept to the other. Other domains are more difficult to analyze: For example in the '1984 U.S. congressional voting' domain we may wonder are there prototypical 'Democrat members'? Can we infer from the results of the experiment that the answer to this question is negative, or maybe we have to invoke another definition of prototypicality in order to reveal the structure that does exist in this domain? Databases #5 and #6 represent diseases, while domains #7 and #8 are taken from the molecular biology, we may prematurely speculate that in the first area prototypicality-based methods are relatively successful, while in the latter they are not. A more cautious conclusion would be that different domains have different properties, that could be used by a learning algorithm, if and when these properties would be better explored.

5.3 Prototypicality in Storage-Reduction algorithms

In the previous section prototypicality was used as a kind of weighting over the exemplars in algorithms that store, and use during the test phase, all the training set. There are situations in which we need to store only a subset of the training set; in such situations the algorithm needs to decide which exemplars would be stored, and which would be discarded. Different authors have proposed different storing criterions ([2,19]). Here I would like to suggest the following storing criterion: From each concept C, store the $f(C)$ most prototypical exemplars (where $f(C)$ is determined by some constraints).

The proposed storing criterion was tested, by comparing it with three other storage-reduction algorithms: IB2, IB3 [2], and TIBL [19]. The comparison was done in the following way: The IB2 and TIBL algorithms were executed on a given training set and test set; the number of exemplars they stored from each concept, and their accuracy was recorded; then the prototypicality-based algorithm was ran on the same dataset, the algorithm stored from each concept the same number of exemplars as IB2 (or as TIBL) did, and its accuracy was measured. All the algorithms used during the test phase the same classification method: the nearest-neighbour, and stored the same number of exemplars, they differ in their storing criterion.

The results of the comparisons are depicted in Fig.4, 5.

Average classification accuracy
IB2, IB3, Proto-IB2

Domain #	1	2	3	4	5	6	7	8	9	10
IB2	.66	.55	.42	.53	.65	.39	.68	.63	.92	.68
IB3	.90	.58	.41	.65	.69	.40	.69	.65	.90	.75
Proto-IB2	.84	.67	.68	.47	.77	.42	.76	.77	.90	.96

Fig. 4. The accuracy of three storage reduction algorithms: IB2, IB3 and Proto-IB2. The latter stores from each concept the same amount of exemplars as IB2 does, but picks the most prototypical objects.

Average classification accuracy
TIBL, Proto-TIBL

Domain #	1	2	3	4	5	6	7	8	9	10
TIBL	.88	.44	.26	.50	.70	.29	.50	.57	.87	.89
Proto-TIBL	.59	.59	.65	.47	.81	.46	.73	.77	.91	.96

Fig. 5.

If we compare the prototypicality-based algorithm with IB2, IB3, TIBL we notice that it is more accurate than IB2 in nine out of the ten domains, more accurate than IB3 in seven domains (but it also generally stores more exemplars than IB3), and more accurate than TIBL in eight domains.

Looking at the domains in which Proto-IB2 is less accurate reveals that in the '1984 U.S. congressional voting' domain, and in the 'Tic-Tac-toe endgame' one Proto-IB2 and Proto-TIBL are less successful than IB3 and TIBL. The latter domain was discussed earlier, and the failure of the prototypicality-based algorithm in it was expected, and is understood; concerning the former domain, it is a wonder to me why on this domain prototypicality fails; I wonder whether an expert in the American political system could foresee this result; and more generally, should it be possible for an expert in a field to foresee whether a prototypicality-based algorithm would be successful on a given domain.

The results clearly evidence that storing the more prototypical exemplars is a relatively successful storing criterion. It is 'relatively' successful in the sense that it truly produces better results than other storing filters; yet, the accuracies of Proto-IB2 or Proto-TIBL are generally inferior to those of the basic IB1 algorithm; thus, at least theoretically, it is possible to achieve even better accuracies than those achieved by Proto-IB2, Proto-TIBL—If the storage reduction algorithm would store all the exemplars that are used for the classification of probe objects by IB1 then it would achieve the same accuracy as IB1 does.

6 Conclusion

This paper examines the role of prototypicality in exemplar-based concept learning methods. It proposes two approaches to prototypicality, and suggests measures that implement the different approaches. The proposed measures were

tested in a set of experiments. The results of the experiments show that prototypicality serves as a good storing filter in storage reduction algorithms, combining it in algorithms that store all the training set does not cause a meaningful
improvement in the accuracy of the algorithm. It was also found that the relative accuracy of an algorithm that utilizes prototypicality varies across domains:
while in some domains (e.g. the 'LED display' one) it improves the performance,
in other domains (e.g., the 'Tic-Tac-Toe endgame') it even degrade the accuracy. While in some of the domains this result is understood, in other its reasons
are not clear enough and require further examination. Future research should
also address questions like: how can a prototypicality measure be combined in a
learning algorithm, what is the similarity and difference between the way humans
utilize prototypicality versus the manner computers (should) do it.

References

1. D. W. Aha. Generalizing from case studies: A case study. In *Proc. of the 8th int. workshop on machine learning*, pages 1–10. Morgan Kaufmann, 1991.
2. D. W. Aha, D. Kibler, and M. K. Albert. Instance-based learning algorithms. *Machine Learning*, 6:37–66, 1991.
3. J. R. Anderson and M. Matessa. Explorations of an incremental, Bayesian algorithm for categorization. *Machine Learning*, 9:275–308, 1992.
4. F. Bergadano, S. Matwin, R. S. Michalski, and J. Zhang. Learning two-tiered descriptions of flexible concepts: The POSEIDON system. *Machine Learning*, 8:5–43, 1992.
5. Y. Biberman. A context similarity measure. In *Proc. of the 7'th European Conf. on Machine Learning*, pages 49–63. Springer-Verlag, 1994.
6. S. Cost and S. Salzberg. A weighted nearest neighbor algorithm for learning with symbolic features. *Machine Learning*, 10:57–78, 1993.
7. S. Markovitch and P. D. Scott. Information filters and their implementation in the syllog system. In *Proc. of the 6th int. workshop on machine learning*, pages 404–407. Morgan Kaufmann, 1989.
8. R. S. Michalski, I. Mozetic, J. Hong, and N. Lavrac. The multi-purpose incremental system AQ15 and its testing application to three medical domains. In *Proc. of the American Association for AI Conference*, Philadelphia, 1986.
9. P. G. Neumann. An attribute frequency model for the abstraction of prototypes. *Memory and Cognition*, 2:241–248, 1974.
10. B. W. Porter, R. Bareiss, and R. C. Holte. Concept learning and heuristic classification in weak-theory domains. *Artificial Intelligence*, 45:229–263, 1990.
11. M. I. Posner and S. W. Keele. Retention of abstract ideas. *Journal of Experimental Psychology*, 83:304–308, 1970.
12. J. R. Quinlan. Induction of decision trees. *Machine Learning*, 1(1):81–106, 1986.
13. L. Rendell. A general framework for induction and a study of selective induction. *Machine Learning*, 1:177–226, 1986.
14. E. Rosch. On the internal structure of perceptual and semantic categories. In T. E. Moore, editor, *Cognitive development and the acquisition of language*. Academic Press, 1973.
15. E. Rosch and C. B. Mervis. Family resemblance studies in the internal structures of categories. *Cognitive Psychology*, 7:573–605, 1974.

16. S. L. Salzberg. *Learning with nested generalized exemplars*. Kluwer Academic Publishers, Norwell: MA, 1990.

17. J. C. Schlimmer and R. H. Granger. Incremental learning from noisy data. *Machine Learning*, 1(1):317–354, 1986.

18. L. Wittgenstein. *Philosophical investigations*. Macmillan, New York, 1953.

19. J. Zhang. Selecting typical instances in instance-based learning. In *Proc. of the 9th intl. conf. on machine learning*, pages 470–479. Morgan Kaufmann, 1992.

Specialization of Recursive Predicates

Henrik Boström

Dept. of Computer and Systems Sciences
Stockholm Univer sity
Electrum 230, 164 40 Kista, Sweden
henke@dsv.su.se
fax: +46 8 703 90 25 tel: +46 8 16 16 16

Abstract. When specializing a recursive predicate in order to exclude a set of negative examples without excluding a set of positive examples, it may not be possible to specialize or remove any of the clauses in a refutation of a negative example without excluding any positive examples. A previously proposed solution to this problem is to apply program transformation in order to obtain non-recursive target predicates from recursive ones. However, the application of this method prevents recursive specializations from being found. In this work, we present the algorithm SPECTRE II which is not limited to specializing non-recursive predicates. The key idea upon which the algorithm is based is that it is not enough to specialize or remove clauses in refutations of negative examples in order to obtain correct specializations, but it is sometimes necessary to specialize clauses that appear only in refutations of positive examples. In contrast to its predecessor SPECTRE, the new algorithm is not limited to specializing clauses defining one predicate only, but may specialize clauses defining multiple predicates. Furthermore, the positive and negative examples are no longer required to be instances of the same predicate. It is proven that the algorithm produces a correct specialization when all positive examples are logical consequences of the original program, there is a finite number of derivations of positive and negative examples and when no positive and negative examples have the same sequence of input clauses in their refutations.

1 Introduction

The search for an inductive hypothesis can be performed either top-down, i.e. from an overly general hypothesis to a more specific, or bottom-up, i.e. from an overly specific hypothesis to a more general. In the field of inductive logic programming, the top-down search for an inductive hypothesis has been performed by using various specialization techniques, such as clause removal, addition of literals and goal reduction [13, 2, 9, 12, 11, 4, 15, 5, 10, 16, 3]. In this work, it is assumed that the overly general hypothesis is given as a logic program.

In [3], the algorithm SPECTRE is presented, which specializes logic programs by applying the transformation rule *unfolding* [14] together with clause removal. One limitation of the algorithm is that it assumes the target predicate to be non-recursive. The reason for this is that when excluding a negative example of a recursive predicate, it may not be possible to specialize or remove any of the clauses in the refutation of the example without excluding a positive example. It should be noted that this is a general problem that is not limited to a particular type of specialization operator, but applies to all specialization techniques that exclude negative examples by specializing or removing clauses in their refutations. A solution to this problem that has been proposed in [3] is to apply the transformation rules *definition*, *unfolding* and *folding* [14] in order to obtain non-recursive target predicates from recursive ones. The draw-back of applying this transformation technique is that recursive specializations can not be obtained, which means that many desired specializations can not be found.

In this work, we present the algorithm SPECTRE II which is not limited to specializing non-recursive predicates. The key idea upon which the algorithm is based is that it is not enough to specialize or remove clauses in refutations of negative examples in order to obtain correct specializations, but it is sometimes necessary to specialize clauses that appear only in refutations of positive examples. In contrast to SPECTRE, the new algorithm is not limited to specializing clauses defining one predicate, but may specialize clauses defining multiple predicates. Furthermore, the positive and negative examples are no longer required to be instances of the same predicate.

In the next section we give a formal definition of the specialization problem, and we also give definitions of the three transformation rules according to [14]. In section three, we exemplify the limitation of SPECTRE, and in section four, we present SPECTRE II, which overcomes this limitation. We also prove that the algorithm produces correct specializations (under some assumptions). In section five, we present some experimental results and in section six we discuss related work. Finally, in section seven we give concluding remarks and point out problems for future research. In the following, we assume the reader to be familiar with the standard terminology in logic programming [8].

2 Preliminaries

We first give a formal definition of the specialization problem that is studied, and then define the three transformation rules that are used in this work.

2.1 The Specialization Problem

The problem of specializing a logic program (definite program) w.r.t. positive and negative examples can be stated as follows:

Given: a definite program P and two disjoint sets of ground atoms E^+ and E^- (positive and negative examples).
Find: a definite program P', called a *correct specialization* of P w.r.t. E^+ and E^- such that $M_{P'} \subseteq M_P$, $E^+ \subseteq M_{P'}$ and $M_{P'} \cap E^- = \emptyset$[1]

---

[1] M_P denotes the least Herbrand model of P.

2.2 Transformation Rules

The following rules for transformation of a definite program (below referred to as P) are taken from [14], where formal definitions can be found as well as proofs of their meaning preserving properties.

Rule 1. Definition
Add to P a clause C of the form $p(x_1, \ldots, x_n) \leftarrow A_1, \ldots, A_m$ where p is a predicate symbol not appearing in P, $x_1, \ldots, x_n$ are distinct variables and $A_1, \ldots, A_m$ are literals whose predicate symbols all appear in P.

Rule 2. Unfolding
Let C be a clause in P, A a literal in its body and $C_1, \ldots, C_n$ be all clauses in P whose heads are unifiable with A. Let $C'_i (1 \leq i \leq n)$ be the result of resolving C with C_i upon A. Then replace C with $C'_1, \ldots, C'_n$.

Rule 3. Folding
Let C be a clause in P of the form $A \leftarrow A_1, \ldots, A_{i+1}, \ldots, A_{i+m}, \ldots, A_n$ and C_1 be a clause that previously have been introduced by the rule of definition of the form $B \leftarrow B_1, \ldots, B_m$. If there is a substitution θ such that $A_{i+1}, \ldots, A_{i+m} = B_1, \ldots, B_m \theta$ where θ substitutes distinct variables for the internal variables of C_1 and moreover those variables do not occur in $A, A_1, \ldots, A_i$ or $A_{i+m+1}, \ldots, A_n$, then replace C by the clause $A \leftarrow A_1, \ldots, A_i, B\theta, A_{i+m+1}, \ldots, A_n$.

3 Applying SPECTRE to Recursive Predicates

The algorithm SPECTRE [3] specializes logic programs with respect to positive and negative examples by applying unfolding together with clause removal. This is done in the following way. As long as there is a clause in the program that *covers* (i.e. is used as the first input clause in the refutation of) a negative example, it is checked whether it covers any positive examples or not. If the clause covers any positive examples, then it is unfolded, otherwise it is removed. SPECTRE is not guaranteed to obtain correct specializations when specializing recursive target predicates. For example, assume that the following definition of the predicate odd(X) is given:

```
odd(0).
odd(s(X)):- odd(X).
```

together with the following positive and negative examples:

$E^+ = \{$ odd(s(0)), odd(s(s(s(0)))), odd(s(s(s(s(s(0)))))) $\}$
$E^- = \{$ odd(0), odd(s(s(0))), odd(s(s(s(s(0))))) $\}$

Then the only clause that is used in the refutation of the first negative example is the first clause in the definition. Clearly, this clause cannot be removed or specialized without excluding the positive examples, since it is used in their refutations. Thus it is not enough to consider removing or specializing clauses in refutations of negative examples in order to obtain correct specializations.

In order to avoid the problem with recursive predicates in SPECTRE, it is assumed that recursive target predicates are transformed into equivalent non-recursive definitions in the following way.

Let T be the recursive target predicate. Then introduce a new predicate T' by adding a clause $T' \leftarrow T$, where the arguments of T' are all variables in T (*definition*). Unfold upon T in the clause, and replace each instance $T\theta$ in the bodies of the clauses defining T and T' (directly or indirectly) with $T'\theta$ (*folding*). Then an equivalent definition of T has been obtained which is non-recursive.

For example, a non-recursive definition of **odd(X)** would then be:

```
odd(0).
odd(s(X)):- rec_odd(X).
rec_odd(0).
rec_odd(s(X)):- rec_odd(X).
```

It should be noted that although it is always possible to avoid the problem with recursive target predicates, there are cases when SPECTRE is unable to find the desired specialization. For example, assume that we are given the above non-recursive definition of **odd(X)** together with the examples above. Then the specialization produced by SPECTRE will exclude the negative examples only (i.e. a maximally general specialization is obtained):

```
odd(s(0)).
odd(s(s(s(0)))).
odd(s(s(s(s(s(X)))))):- rec_odd(X).
rec_odd(0).
rec_odd(s(X)):- rec_odd(X).
```

Removing the third element from E^+ results in a specialization which includes the positive examples only (i.e. a maximally specific specialization is obtained).

4 Specializing Recursive Predicates

In this section we present the algorithm SPECTRE II, which overcomes SPECTRE's inability to produce recursive specializations. We first describe the algorithm, and then illustrate it by some examples. Finally, we prove that the algorithm produces correct specializations.

4.1 SPECTRE II

Like SPECTRE, SPECTRE II specializes logic programs by using unfolding and clause removal. The major difference between the algorithms is that while SPEC-TRE only applies unfolding upon clauses that appear first in refutations of both positive and negative examples, SPECTRE II may apply unfolding upon any clause that is used in a refutation of a positive example. This means that in contrast to SPECTRE, SPECTRE II is not limited to specializing clauses that are used in refutations of negative examples and to specializing clauses that define the target predicate only.

The algorithm works in two steps. First, as long as there is a refutation of a negative example, such that all input clauses are used in refutations of positive examples, a literal in an input clause is unfolded. Second, for each refutation of a negative example, one input clause that is not used in any refutation of a positive example is removed. It is not defined by the algorithm how to make the choices of which literal to unfold upon and which clause to remove. As will be shown in section 4.3, these choices can be made arbitrarily without affecting the correctness of the algorithm. However, they are crucial to the performance of the algorithm, since the generality of the resulting specialization is dependent on them. This will be further discussed in section five. A formal description of the algorithm SPECTRE II is given below.

Algorithm SPECTRE II

Input: a definite program P and two sets of ground atoms E^+ and E^-.
Output: a correct specialization P' of P w.r.t. E^+ and E^-.

LET $P' = P$.
WHILE there is an SLD-refutation of $P' \cup \{\leftarrow e^-\}$, for some $e^- \in E^-$,
such that each input clause C_i is used in an SLD-refutation of $P' \cup \{\leftarrow e_i^+\}$,
where $e_i^+ \in E^+$ DO
    Let C be a non-unit input clause in an SLD-refutation of $P' \cup \{\leftarrow e^+\}$,
    where $e^+ \in E^+$.
    Unfold upon a literal in C.

FOR each $e^- \in E^-$ DO
    Remove an input clause in each SLD-refutation of $P' \cup \{\leftarrow e^-\}$, that
    does not appear in any SLD-refutation of $P' \cup \{\leftarrow e^+\}$, where $e^+ \in E^+$.

4.2 Examples

Assume that the following definition of the predicate odd(X) is given as input to SPECTRE II:

    (c_1) odd(0).
    (c_2) odd(s(X)):- odd(X).

together with the following positive and negative examples:

$E^+ = \{\ odd(s(0)),\ odd(s(s(s(0)))),\ odd(s(s(s(s(s(0))))))\}$
$E^- = \{\ odd(0),\ odd(s(s(0))),\ odd(s(s(s(s(0)))))\ \}$

Then there is a negative example (e.g. $odd(0)$) for which all clauses in the refutation appear in refutations of positive examples. Let c_2 be the selected clause, and unfolding upon the literal in its body results in the following program:

(c_1) $odd(0)$.
(c_3) $odd(s(0))$.
(c_4) $odd(s(s(X))):-$ $odd(X)$.

Then there is no negative example for which all clauses in the refutation appear in refutations of positive examples, and thus the condition for the while-loop is false. Then for each refutation of a negative example, a clause that does not appear in a refutation of a positive example is removed (in this case the clause c_1 is removed for each refutation of the negative examples). Thus the resulting specialization produced by SPECTRE II is:

(c_3) $odd(s(0))$.
(c_4) $odd(s(s(X))):-$ $odd(X)$.

To see how SPECTRE II works when specializing multiple predicates, consider the following program and examples:

```
p(a).
p(f(X)):- q(X).
q(b).
q(g(X)):- p(X).
```

$E^+ = \{\ p(f(b)),\ q(g(a))\}$
$E^- = \{\ p(a),\ q(b)\}$

Note that although a correct specialization can be obtained for each predicate by simply removing the input clause in the refutation of the negative example, a correct specialization w.r.t. both predicates can not be obtained in this way. However, SPECTRE II produces a correct specialization in the following way.

After the first step in the algorithm, in which unfolding is applied twice, the following program is obtained:

```
p(a).
p(f(b)).
p(f(g(X))):- p(X).
q(b).
q(g(a)).
q(g(f(X))):- q(X).
```

In the final step of the algorithm, two clauses are removed resulting in the following correct specialization:

```
p(f(b)).
p(f(g(X))):- p(X).
q(g(a)).
q(g(f(X))):- q(X).
```

4.3 Correctness of SPECTRE II

In this section we prove that SPECTRE II produces a correct specialization in a finite number of steps when all positive examples are logical consequences of the original program, there is a finite number of derivations of positive and negative examples (i.e. the program terminates for all examples) and there is no positive and negative examples that have the same sequence of input clauses in their refutations.

We first prove a lemma that states that under these assumptions, each refutation of a negative example will after a finite number of applications of unfolding have an input clause that is not used in any refutation of a positive example.

Lemma

Let E^+ and E^- be two sets of ground atoms and P be a definite program, such that the number of SLD-derivations of $P \cup \{\leftarrow e\}$ are finite for all $e \in E^+ \cup E^-$, and there is no $e^+ \in E^+$ and $e^- \in E^-$ such that the same sequence of input clauses is used both in an SLD-refutation of $P \cup \{\leftarrow e^+\}$ and in an SLD-refutation of $P \cup \{\leftarrow e^-\}$. Let $P'' = P$. Then after a finite number of arbitrary applications of unfolding upon clauses in P'' that are input clauses in SLD-refutations of $P'' \cup \{\leftarrow e^+\}$, where $e^+ \in E^+$, each SLD-refutation of $P'' \cup \{\leftarrow e^-\}$, for all $e^- \in E^-$, has an input clause that is not used in any SLD-refutation of $P'' \cup \{\leftarrow e^+\}$, for all $e^+ \in E^+$.

Proof: Since the length of at least one SLD-refutation of $P'' \cup \{\leftarrow e^+\}$, where $e^+ \in E^+$ decreases when applying unfolding, and the number of SLD-refutations does not increase (proven in [6]), all input clauses in SLD-refutations of $P'' \cup \{\leftarrow e^+\}$, for all $e^+ \in E^+$ will be unit clauses after a finite number of applications of unfolding. All SLD-refutations of $P'' \cup \{\leftarrow e^-\}$ of length > 1, where $e^- \in E^-$ have at least one non-unit input clause and thus have at least one clause that is not used as an input clause in any SLD-refutation of $P'' \cup \{\leftarrow e^+\}$, for all $e^+ \in E^+$. Thus it suffices to show that no unit input clause in an SLD-refutation of $P'' \cup \{\leftarrow e^-\}$ of length $= 1$, where $e^- \in E^-$ is used in an SLD-refutation of $P'' \cup \{\leftarrow e^+\}$, where $e^+ \in E^+$. Let C be a unit clause in P'', such that $C \times \{\leftarrow e^-\}^2 = \square$, for some $e^- \in E^-$ and $C = C_1 \times \ldots \times C_n$, where each C_i is a variant of a clause in P. Then there is an SLD-refutation of $P \cup \{\leftarrow e^-\}$ with input clauses $C_1, \ldots, C_n$, since $C_1 \times \ldots \times C_n \times \{\leftarrow e^-\} = \square$. Assume

_____
[2] $C \times D$ denotes the resolvent of C and D.

that there is some $e^+ \in E_i^+$ such that $C \times \{\leftarrow e^+\} = \Box$. Then it follows that there is an SLD-refutation of $P \cup \{\leftarrow e^+\}$, with input clauses $C_1, \ldots, C_n$, since $C_1 \times \ldots \times C_n \times \{\leftarrow e^+\} = \Box$. This contradicts the assumption that no $e^+ \in E^+$ and $e^- \in E^-$ have the same sequence of input clauses in their SLD-refutations. $\Box$

Using this lemma, we can now prove that SPECTRE II produces a correct specialization under the above assumptions.

Theorem
Let the input to SPECTRE II be two sets of ground atoms E^+ and E^- and a definite program P, such that $E^+ \subseteq M_P$, the number of SLD-derivations of $P \cup \{\leftarrow e\}$ are finite for all $e \in E^+ \cup E^-$ and there is no $e^+ \in E^+$ and $e^- \in E_i^-$ such that the same sequence of input clauses is used both in an SLD-refutation of $P \cup \{\leftarrow e^+\}$ and in an SLD-refutation of $P \cup \{\leftarrow e^-\}$. Then the algorithm produces a correct specialization P' of P w.r.t. E^+ and E_i^-.

Proof: According to the lemma, the while-loop in the algorithm terminates after a finite number of steps resulting in a program P'', such that each SLD-refutation of $P'' \cup \{\leftarrow e^-\}$, for all $e^- \in E_i^-$ has an input clause that is not used in any SLD-refutation of $P'' \cup \{\leftarrow e^+\}$, for all $e^+ \in E_i^+$. Then $P' = P'' \setminus R$, where R is the set of clauses removed in the last step of the algorithm. Since one input clause is removed for each SLD-refutation of $P'' \cup \{\leftarrow e^-\}$, for all $e^- \in E_i^-$ it follows that there is no SLD-refutation of $P' \cup \{\leftarrow e^-\}$, for any $e^- \in E_i^-$ Thus $M_{P'} \cap E^- = \emptyset$. Since $M_P = M_{P''}$ and thus $E^+ \subseteq M_{P''}$ and since none of the clauses in R is used as an input clause in an SLD-refutation of $P'' \cup \{\leftarrow e^+\}$, for any $e^+ \in E_i^+$ it follows that $E^+ \subseteq M_{P'}$. Since $M_P = M_{P''} \supseteq M_{P'}$, it follows that P' is a correct specialization of P w.r.t. E^+ and E_i^- $\Box$

The condition that no refutations of positive and negative examples should have the same sequence of input clauses can be relaxed by slightly altering the algorithm in the following way. Instead of considering all refutations of the positive examples, only a subset needs to be considered such that each positive example has at least one refutation in the subset. Then by guaranteeing that no refutation in the subset has a sequence of input clauses in common with any refutation of a negative example, the condition can be relaxed to require only that for each positive example there is at least one refutation that does not have the same sequence of input clauses as any refutation of a negative example. This altered version of the algorithm allows that many correct specializations can be found, which can not be found by the algorithm in its original formulation.

5 Experimental Results

The choices of which literal to unfold upon and which clauses to remove when applying SPECTRE II determine the generality of the resulting specialization. Moreover, when applying the altered version of the algorithm, the selection of which refutations to consider for the positive examples are of crucial importance for the result. In the current implementation of the algorithm, these choices are made in order to minimize the number of applications of unfolding. However, since it is computationally expensive to find the optimal choices, the following approximations are used.

When selecting one of the refutations of a positive example, a refutation that already has been selected is preferred. If no such refutation exists, a refutation that does not subsume a refutation of a negative example is preferred. The motivation for this heuristic is that it is presumably easier to exclude the refutation of a negative example if it is not included in a refutation of a positive example.

When selecting a (non-unit) clause to apply unfolding upon, the only refutations of negative examples that are considered are those for which all clauses are used in refutations of positive examples. A clause is preferred that appears first in one of these refutations, if no other clause in the same refutation is first in one of the other refutations. If no such clause exists, a non-unit clause that appears first in a refutation of a negative example is preferred. Finally, if there is no such clause, a non-unit clause that appears first in a refutation of a positive example is preferred. The motivation for this heuristic is that it is presumably easier to find a correct specialization by first excluding the refutations which only involves one clause that is first in a refutation of a negative example, than starting with refutations that contain several such clauses.

The leftmost (unfoldable) literal is always selected, and all clauses defining the target predicate that are not used as input clauses in any refutations of positive examples are removed.

In order to test the performance of the algorithm together with the above heuristics, an experiment is performed using the following program as input, where the predicate target(X,Y,Z) can be specialized into various list handling predicates:

```
target(X,Y,Z):- comp(X,Y,Z).
target(X1,Y1,Z1):-
        new_lists(X1,Y1,Z1,X2,Y2,Z2), target(X2,Y2,Z2).

comp(X,Y,Z):-
        eq_or_neq(X,Y), eq_or_neq(X,Z), eq_or_neq(Y,Z),
        list(X), list(Y), list(Z).

eq_or_neq(E,E).
eq_or_neq(E1,E2):- E1\==E2.
```

```
list([]).
list([_|_]).

new_lists([E|X],Y,[E|Z],X,Y,Z):- check(E,Y).
new_lists([E|X],Y,Z,X,Y,Z):- check(E,Y).

check(E,_).
check(E,X):- member(E,X).
check(E,X):- not_member(E,X).


member(X,[X|_]).
member(X,[_|L]):- member(X,L).

not_member(X,[]).
not_member(X,[Y|L]):- X\==Y,not_member(X,L).
```

The examples used in this experiment are all instances of target(X,Y,Z), where the variables are replaced by lists of length ≤ 2, containing the constants a, b and c (i.e. 2197 instances). When the examples are classified using the predicate append(X,Y,Z) (resulting in that 34 of the instances are positive), and given as input to SPECTRE II, the following program is produced in 54.6+6.8 seconds:[3]

```
target([],[],[]):-
        list([]),list([]).
target([A|B],[],[A|B]):-
        [A|B]\==[], []\==[A|B], list([A|B]).
target([],A,A):-
        []\==A, []\==A, list(A), list(A).
target([B|C],D,[B|A]):-
        check(B,D), target(C,D,A).
```

It can be seen that the resulting program is in fact equivalent to the definition of append(X,Y,Z), although it contains a redundant clause and some redundant literals.

When the examples are classified using the predicate intersection(X,Y,Z) (resulting in that 169 of the instances are positive), and given as input to SPEC-TRE II, the following (correct) program is produced in 49.6+5.8 seconds:

---

[3] The algorithm was implemented in SICStus Prolog 2.1 on a Sun SPARCstation 5. The first number shows the time taken to find all refutations, and the second number shows the time taken to find a correct specialization, given the refutations.

```
target(A,A,A):-
        eq_or_neq(A,A), list(A), list(A), list(A).
target([],A,[]):-
        []\==A, A\==[], list(A), list([]).
target([A|B],[],[]) :-
        [A|B]\==[], [A|B]\==[], list([]).
target([B|C],D,[B|A]) :-
        member(B,D), target(C,D,A).
target([A|B],C,D):-
        not_member(A,C), target(B,C,D).
```

When the examples are classified using the predicate difference(X,Y,Z) (resulting in that 169 of the instances are positive), and given as input to SPEC-TRE II, the following (correct) program is produced in 50.8+8.3 seconds:

```
target([],[],[]):-
        list([]), list([]).
target([A|B],[A|B],[]):-
        [A|B]\==[], [A|B]\==[].
target([],A,[]):-
        []\==A, A\==[], list(A), list([]).
target([A|B],[],[A|B]):-
        [A|B]\==[], []\==[A|B], list([A|B]).
target([B|C],D,[B|A]):-
        not_member(B,D), target(C, D, A).
target([A|B],C,D):-
        member(A,C), target(B, C, D).
```

The following experiment illustrates how the computation time grows with the number of examples given as input to the algorithm. The entire example set is randomly split into two halves, where one half is used for training and the other for testing. The number of examples in the training sets that are given as input to the algorithm is varied, representing 1%, 5%, 10%, 20%, 30%, 40% and 50% of the entire example set, where the last subset corresponds to the entire set of training examples and a greater subset always includes a smaller. Each experiment is iterated 50 times and the mean time to find a correct specialization for the given examples is presented in Fig 1. It can be seen that the computation time grows linearly with the number of examples. In Fig 2, the accuracy of the produced hypothesis on the test examples is presented. The accuracy is above 99% for all three example sets, when using 20% of the examples as input to SPECTRE II.

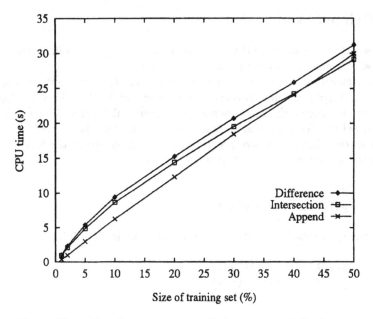

Fig. 1. Time taken for SPECTRE II to find correct specializations.

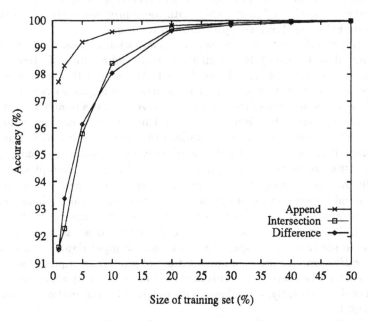

Fig. 2. Accuracy of the resulting specializations on the test examples.

6 Related Work

In this section, we discuss other specialization techniques, and in particular how they work when specializing recursive predicates.

In contrast to SPECTRE II, the techniques in [7, 1] attempt to minimally specialize logic programs. However, as pointed out in [16], the specializations produced by these techniques are not always minimal. That is the case when the specialized predicate appears in bodies of clauses, and this is true in particular when specializing a recursive predicate. For example, given the following program and the negative example p(a,a):

```
p(X,X).
p(f(X),g(Y)):- p(X,Y).
```

Then the specialization produced by the technique in [1] will be:

```
p(X,X):- not(p1(X)).
p(f(X),g(Y)):- p(X,Y).
p1(a).
```

Note that not only is the negative example excluded, but also p(f(a),g(a)), p(f(f(a)),g(g(a))), ..., and thus the resulting specialization is certainly not minimal. However, this problem can be solved by applying the same transformation technique as was presented in section three, namely define a new predicate to be equivalent to the target predicate and then replace each occurence of the original predicate in bodies of clauses with the appropriate instances of the new predicate before applying the specialization technique.

In [16] a technique for incremental specialization is presented, called MBR (Minimal Base Revision). It uses clause removal and addition of literals to prevent negative examples from being derived. The aim of this technique is not to specialize a program with respect to positive and negative examples, but to make a minimal revision of the program in the sense that a minimal set of clause applications is prevented from being used. This should be contrasted to SPEC-TRE II, which may produce specializations that are not minimal in this sense. Another difference is that the only clauses that are considered for being specialized by MBR are those appearing in refutations of negative examples, since this is sufficient when specializing a program with respect to negative examples only.

The only specialization operator that is used in [9, 15] is clause removal. These approaches are limited to removing clauses that appear in the original program that is to be specialized. As a consequence, these approaches will not be able to produce correct specializations when all input clauses in a refutation of a negative example are used in refutations of positive examples. However, the condition for when correct specializations can be obtained by clause removal can be relaxed significantly, if combined with program transformation, as shown by SPECTRE II.

In [13, 2, 12, 11, 10], clauses are specialized by adding literals to their bodies.

The literals considered for being added are in these approaches restricted to those whose predicate symbols are defined in the original program. Various restrictions are also put on the variables in the literals (e.g. at least one of the variables should appear elsewhere in the clause [12]). It should be noted that literal addition is in general not sufficient to obtain correct specializations of logic programs. Consider again the program defining the predicate odd(X):

```
odd(0).
odd(s(X)):- odd(X).
```

The only way to exclude the negative example odd(0) by literal addition is to add a false literal to the body of the first clause. But the resulting specialization will not be correct if there are any positive examples, since these are excluded as well.

A number of previous specialization techniques use goal reduction to specialize clauses (ML-SMART [2], ANA-EBL [4], FOCL [11], GRENDEL [5], FOCL-FRONTIER [10]). One major difference between SPECTRE II and these techniques is the way in which the search for a specialization is performed. The algorithms ANA-EBL, FOCL, GRENDEL and FOCL-FRONTIER, like MIS [13] and FOIL [12], use covering methods for finding correct specializations, i.e. the resulting definition is found by repeatedly specializing an overly general definition and for each repetition adding a clause to the resulting definition. This contrasts to SPECTRE II and ML-SMART, which do not specialize the same definition more than once. The most important difference is however, that the previous techniques specialize only one predicate at a time in contrast to SPECTRE II, which may specialize multiple predicates. In section 4.2 it was shown that this capability can be crucial in order to obtain correct specialization w.r.t. multiple predicates.

7   Concluding Remarks

We have presented the algorithm SPECTRE II, which is based on the observation that in order to obtain correct specializations of recursive predicates it is not in general sufficient to specialize clauses that are used in refutations of negative examples, but it is sometimes necessary to specialize clauses that are used in refutations of positive examples only. The main properties of the algorithm are the ability to produce recursive specializations and to revise multiple predicates. In contrast to its predecessor SPECTRE, the algorithm does not require the examples to be instances of the same predicate.

The main problem for future research is to develop more sophisticated heuristics than what is used in the current implementation of the algorithm, i.e. heuristics for how to select which refutations of positive examples to consider and what literals to apply unfolding upon. Other directions for future research are to investigate how to handle cases when all refutations of a positive example have the same sequences of input clauses as refutations of negative examples, and when some positive examples are not included in the meaning of the original program.

Acknowledgements

This work has been supported by the European Community ESPRIT BRA 6020 ILP (Inductive Logic Programming). Thanks to the anonymous reviewers and Robert Engels for comments and suggestions for improvement on the article.

References

1. Bain M. and Muggleton S., "Non-Monotonic Learning", in Muggleton S. (ed.), *Inductive Logic Programming*, Academic Press, London (1992) 145–161
2. Bergadano F. and Giordana A., "A Knowledge Intensive Approach to Concept Induction", *Proceedings of the Fifth International Conference on Machine Learning*, Morgan Kaufmann, CA (1988) 305–317
3. Boström H. and Idestam-Almquist P., "Specialization of Logic Programs by Pruning SLD-Trees", *Proceedings of the 4th International Workshop on Inductive Logic Programming*, volume 237 of *GMD-Studien, Gesellschaft für Mathematik und Datenverarbeitung MBH* (1994) 31–48
4. Cohen W. W., "The Generality of Overgenerality", *Machine Learning: Proceedings of the Eighth International Workshop*, Morgan Kaufmann (1991) 490–494
5. Cohen W. W., "Compiling Prior Knowledge Into an Explicit Bias", *Machine Learning: Proceedings of the Ninth International Workshop*, Morgan Kaufmann (1992) 102–110
6. Kanamori T. and Kawamura T., "Preservation of Stronger Equivalence in Unfold/Fold Logic Program Transformation (II)", ICOT Technical Report TR-403, Japan (1988)
7. Ling C. X., "Non-Monotonic Specialization", *Proceedings of International Workshop on Inductive Logic Programming*, Portugal (1991) 59–68
8. Lloyd J. W., *Foundations of Logic Programming*, (2nd edition), Springer-Verlag (1987)
9. Ourston D. and Mooney R. J., "Changing the Rules: A Comprehensive Approach to Theory Refinement", *Proceedings of the Eighth National Conference on Artificial Intelligence*, MIT Press (1990) 815–820
10. Pazzani M. and Brunk C., "Finding Accurate Frontiers: A Knowledge-Intensive Approach to Relational Learning", *Proceedings of the Eleventh National Conference on Artificial Intelligence*, Morgan Kaufmann (1993) 328–334
11. Pazzani M., Brunk C. and Silverstein G., "A Knowledge-Intensive Approach to Learning Relational Concepts", *Machine Learning: Proceedings of the Eighth International Workshop*, Morgan Kaufmann (1991) 432–436
12. Quinlan J. R., "Learning Logical Definitions from Relations", *Machine Learning* 5 (1990) 239–266
13. Shapiro E. Y., *Algorithmic Program Debugging*, MIT Press (1983)
14. Tamaki H. and Sato T., "Unfold/Fold Transformations of Logic Programs", *Proceedings of the Second International Logic Programming Conference*, Uppsala University, Uppsala, Sweden (1984) 127–138
15. Wogulis J., "Revising Relational Domain Theories", *Machine Learning: Proceedings of the Eighth International Workshop*, Morgan Kaufmann (1991) 462–466
16. Wrobel S., "On the Proper Definition of Minimality in Specialization and Theory Revision", *Proceedings of the European Conference on Machine Learning*, Springer-Verlag (1993) 65–82

A Distributed Genetic Algorithm Improving the Generalization Behavior of Neural Networks

Jürgen Branke, Udo Kohlmorgen, Hartmut Schmeck

Institut für Angewandte Informatik
und Formale Beschreibungsverfahren
Universität Karlsruhe (TH), 76128 Karlsruhe, Germany
{Branke|Kohlmorgen|Schmeck}@aifb.uni-karlsruhe.de

Abstract. Artificial neural networks sometimes generalize poorly to unknown inputs, if they have been trained perfectly on relatively small training sets using standard learning algorithms like e.g. backpropagation. In this paper a distributed genetic algorithm is designed and used to improve the network's generalization capabilities by reducing the number of different weights in the neural network.

1 Introduction

A difficult and challenging problem in training artificial neural networks is to ensure that they will generalize well to cases they have not been trained on. This is especially true, if the number of training patterns is small compared to the number of independent weights in the network.

Some theoretical results (see Section 2) suggest that networks with few degrees of freedom can be expected to generalize better than those with many degrees of freedom. On the other hand, the network has to be complex enough to be able to represent the training set correctly. To determine an appropriate degree of complexity, several approaches have been suggested that start with training a larger than necessary network and then reduce the complexity e.g. by removing edges or nodes ("pruning" [Ree93]) or by minimizing the number of independent weights ("weight sharing"). Although weight sharing has been used successfully in some applications [CDS89, LeCu89, LWH90, NoHi92], it is not very popular, since it is difficult to decide

- which connections are to be grouped together
- how many groups of connections are needed and
- which weight shall be assigned to each group of connections.

Nowlan and Hinton [NoHi92] developed a method that clusters the weights automatically during the training. The basic idea behind this algorithm is to model the distribution of weight values as a mixture of multiple gaussians. Each gaussian that takes responsibility for a subset of the weights will squeeze those weights together when the variance of the gaussians is shrunk during the process.

In this paper, we report on some experimental results of a different approach to the introduction of weight sharing:

After a network has been trained perfectly on a specific set of training patterns (e.g. by backpropagation), a distributed genetic algorithm is used to find a minimal number of different weights without affecting the network's performance on the training set significantly. As expected, this improves the network's performance on a separate test set, i.e. it's generalization ability.

The algorithm is executed on a transputer network. It uses several subpopulations which exchange their best individuals from time to time, but - different from other approaches - the migration does not take place after a predetermined number of generations but after the subpopulations have reached some pre specified performance level.

The problem chosen for testing this approach is the shift-detection-problem that has already been used by Nowlan and Hinton [NoHi92] to compare simple backpropagation, cross-validation, weight decay and soft weight sharing.

The outline of the paper is as follows:

In Section 2, we present some theoretical evidence as to why weight sharing might improve the generalization behavior of neural networks. The main parts of the genetic algorithm are presented in Section 3, followed by a description of the parallelization strategy in Section 4.

Empirical results are reported in Section 5, followed by a summary and some concluding remarks.

2 Generalization and Weight Sharing

Artificial neural networks have two basic qualities:

- They can reproduce a set of input-output pairs after having been trained on them.
- They can find some regularities in the training data and use them to generalize to inputs they have not been trained on.

The far more interesting quality definitely is the generalization capability, i.e. the ability that the network produces the desired output given previously unseen input data. This quality can be estimated by measuring the network's performance on a test set disjoint to the training set.

But whereas there exist more or less efficient methods to train a network, it is practically unknown how to build a network that generalizes in the desired way.

An example may illustrate the difficulty: the shift detection problem used in this paper (s. Section 5) has 2048 possible binary input patterns and one binary output, i.e. there exist 2^{2048} theoretically possible "rules", each characterized by a distinct truth table. Training the net on 100 training patterns fixes 100 rows of this table, such that 2^{1948} rules remain which are consistent with the training set. And we are interested in just one of those rules.

One reason that a network ever has the chance to actually find that rule is that, on one hand, rules in the real world are usually rather simple and, on the other hand, neural nets, depending on their degree of complexity, can only encode rules of a limited complexity.

Intuitively, it would be advantageous to have networks of minimal complexity (such that they can only represent a small fraction of the theoretically possible rules) being complex enough though, to actually represent the desired rule.

The same idea can be illustrated by an analogy to curve fitting (cf. Figure 1). There, excess parameters result in overfitting. The best interpolation and extrapolation results are obtained with a curve of minimum degree that still represents the "training set" satisfactorily.

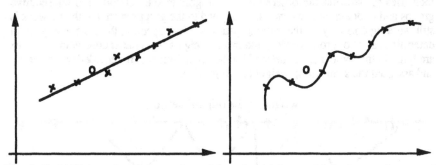

Fig. 1: (Left) Fitting a low-degree polynomial on the training set (x) focuses on the general trend and leads to good interpolation (o) results. (Right) Too many degrees of freedom lead to overfitting and bad generalization (o).

Weight sharing is one way to reduce the network's complexity or degrees of freedom and so seems to be a reasonable approach if one tries to improve the generalization behavior of neural networks.

Apart from this more intuitive reasoning for minimum complexity networks, there exists some theory supporting the use of weight sharing:

The worst case analysis by Vapnik and Chervonenkis [VaCh71] bounds the probability for bad (undesired) generalization dependent on the number of training examples and the complexity of the network. Unfortunately, except for very simple problems, it is hard to exactly determine the VC-dimension, a measure for the network's complexity. Instead, very often the number of independent weights is used as an approximation. For a good introduction to this theory, the reader is referred to [Abu-M89].

Another useful theory in this context is the minimum description length (MDL) principle by Rissanen [Riss78] which states that in the mean, the shortest description of a given sequence of data is the statistical process that generated the data. Therefore networks which can be described with less information are more likely to model the underlying process and also to generalize better. As a network with many equal weights can be described more compact than a network with all the weights independent from each other, this also supports the concept of weight sharing.

3   Description of the Genetic Algorithm

Genetic algorithms copy nature by using recombination, mutation, and selection of the fittest in their search for good solutions to optimization problems. For an introduction into genetic algorithms and for some justification for their use, the reader is referred to the literature, for example to the books of Goldberg or Michalewicz [Gol89, Mic94].

3.1 General Idea

Our genetic algorithm starts from a neural network which has been trained perfectly[1] by backpropagation (although any other training method would be acceptable, too). It then tries to partition the ordered set of weights in the network into consecutive groups and to determine new weights assigned to the groups such that the network is still working correctly on the training patterns. More specific, the genetic algorithm determines a set of group borders and group weights. All connections who's weights are lying in the same interval defined by the group borders are regarded as one group and assigned the same group weight (see Figure 2).

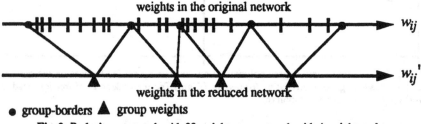

weights in the original network

w_{ij}

w_{ij}'

weights in the reduced network

● group-borders ▲ group weights

Fig. 2: Reducing a network with 20 weights to a network with 4 weights only.

One may note that the search space in this concept is more or less restricted to the neighborhood of the original trained network. The advantage here is that the search space is small and much information of the original network is preserved. The disadvantage is that many of the best possible solutions may lie outside the search space and will never be found. An alternative model that does not have this limitation is a current target of research at our institute.

3.2 Representation and Evaluation

As genetic representation for the individuals, an ascending sequence of group borders and group weights is chosen, forming a blueprint according to which the reduced network may be built (Fig. 3). As it is not known in advance how many groups are necessary, these strings may be of varying length.

To additionally allow the algorithm to completely prune small excess connections, a minimum group weight of 0.0 is implicitly assumed. All connections with an original weight smaller than the smallest group border receive the weight 0.0 and are thereby practically pruned (see dashed connection in Fig. 3).

---

[1] Perfectly here means that the network is capable of correctly classifying 100% of the training data. Outputs are between -1.0 and +1.0. Any output > 0.5 matches 1.0, any output < -0.5 matches -1.0, i.e. the output is considered correct, if it deviates from the desired output by less than 0.5. Outputs between -0.5 and +0.5 are alway considered incorrect.

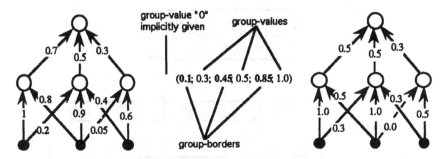

Fig. 3: Transformation of the original network (left) to the reduced network (right) according to the genetic string (middle).

The problem when evaluating the individuals is that it is not possible to measure the generalization capability directly. Thus, following the reasoning of Section 2, a good strategy may be to search for a network that performs well on the training set (i.e. the set the original net was trained on) while having a minimum number of different weights.

The performance on the training set is determined by building the corresponding reduced network and calculating e.g. the mean squared error. The preference for shorter strings (i.e. a smaller number of different weights) might be included by adding an additional term that penalizes string length. However it could be difficult to find a suitable weighting factor. As an alternative, in our implementation a biased crossover operator is used that occasionally reduces the length of a string (see below). Also, the novel distribution strategy (described in Section 4) contributes to the search for shorter strings.

3.3 Selection, Crossover, and Mutation

For production of offspring parents are selected according to roulette wheel selection, i.e. an individual's chance to get selected depends on its relative performance within the population. For recombination of selected parents a single point crossover operator with repair function is used. As crossover point, a position smaller than the length of the shorter parent string is randomly chosen. Whenever the resulting strings are not valid (their values not in ascending order), pairs of values (one group value and one group border) are cut out until the remaining string becomes valid. An example is given in Figure 4.

This crossover operator

- produces valid offspring only
- occasionally introduces shorter strings into the population, i.e. it has a built-in bias towards shorter strings (as desired)
- preserves information from the parents, as group values are mapped to group values and group borders to group borders.

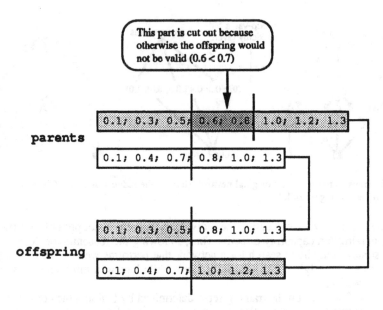

Fig. 4: The crossover operator.

After crossover, each offspring undergoes mutation. Each of the string's positions is subject to mutation with some fixed probability. If a position is chosen for mutation, it is first decided with equal probability whether the value on that position is to be increased or decreased. A new value is then chosen with uniform probability between the old value and the value at the next position to the right or to the left, respectively (see Figure 5). In this way the mutation operator will produce valid strings only.

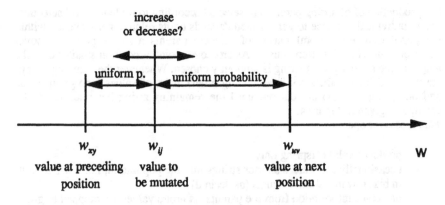

Fig. 5: The mutation operator.

The offspring competes with the individuals of the old population for survival to the next generation. The biggest advantage of this method is that the best individuals found so far will always survive and the average performance of the population is increasing monotonically. On the other hand, this bears the risk of drifting towards a uniform population where all individuals are more or less the same.

This risk has been reduced by using large populations and high mutation probabilities.

4 Distribution Strategy

Genetic algorithms are highly parallel by nature. Crossover, mutation and evaluation of different individuals can easily be performed in parallel on different processors. The major bottleneck for parallelization is the selection procedure which needs global information to determine the *relative* performances.

A straightforward parallelization strategy is the so-called farming approach (see e.g. [DMM91]) where a master (farmer) process keeps the global information in form of the entire population, selects the mating partners and distributes those to the processor farm for crossover, mutation and evaluation. The offspring is then returned to the farmer and inserted into the population (Figure 6).

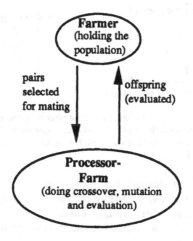

Fig. 6: The Farming Approach.

Although evaluation usually is the most time consuming step, it is obvious that there is a significant communication overhead in this model.

An alternative could be to renounce global information and to distribute the population among several processors, such that every processor runs its own genetic algorithm on a subpopulation. The resulting *distributed* algorithm is different from the original sequential algorithm, since selection is done locally with respect to the subpopulation only.

This avoids the large communication overhead. Also, by developing the different subpopulations in more or less separate "niches", it very often maintains a larger diversity and avoids premature convergence to a local minimum. A disadvantage, though, is that global information gets lost. This might lead to the processing of *locally* fit individuals which, according to a *global* criterion, would be discarded.

We have chosen an intermediate course insofar as several subpopulations are used, each owning a processor farm (cf. Fig. 8). Occasionally, the subpopulations are allowed to exchange copies of their best individuals with neighboring subpopulations (this is also known as *swapping* or *migration*). In this way, the communication overhead is reduced while at the same time the subpopulations share some information.

One problem has been observed with this approach ([WhSt90]): Since the subpopulations evolve at different paces (see Fig. 7) and the migration takes place after some fixed number of generations, it may happen that very 'strong' individuals from a far evolved subpopulation are sent to a 'weak' subpopulation. Also 'weak' individuals could be sent to a 'stronger' subpopulation. In the first case, the immigrated 'strong' individuals may soon dominate the subpopulation, in the latter case, the 'weak' individuals will have no influence on the 'strong' subpopulation and will not enrich its gene base.

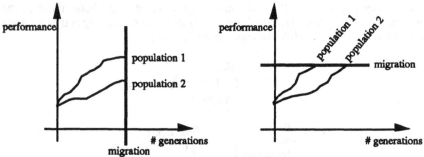

Fig. 7: (Left) If migration takes place after a fixed number of generations, individuals from a far evolved population may soon dominate the weaker population. (Right) If migration is to take place after the populations reached some performance level, different populations will need different times to finish.

None of these cases is desired. In order to avoid the effects, Whitley and Starkweather [WhSt90] suggest to always use rank based selection schemes[2] that level out the strong differences between individuals.

In this paper, however, a new migration strategy is suggested that allows arbitrary selection schemes.

The basic idea is to perform the migration after the subpopulations have reached some pre specified performance level instead of after a fixed number of generations. A performance measure that has proven successful is for example the average performance over all individuals in the subpopulation. In this way it is assured that the exchanging subpopulations are approximately comparable in performance.

But a new problem arises, namely that the subpopulations will need different times to reach this performance level and thus some populations will have to wait for others. In order to be able to take full advantage of all the available processors anyway, the possibility to lend processors is introduced:

---

[2] For a comparison of several selection schemes see for example [Han94], [Bäck94] or [GoDe90].

A farmer (holding one subpopulation) that has reached the performance level may lend its processor farm to still working neighboring subpopulations. The receiving farmer integrates those processors into his farm and may thus process more individuals during the same period of time. As a result, the 'slower' subpopulation usually catches up fairly quickly. When the slower subpopulation reaches the performance level as well[3], it returns the processors to its owner.

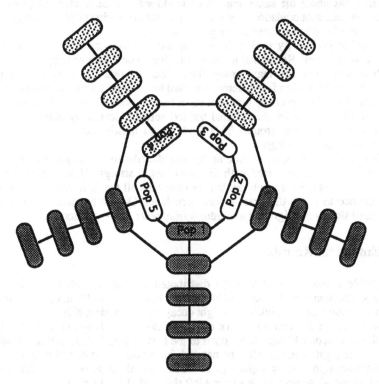

Fig. 8: Hardware topology for 5 subpopulations and 25 processors. The populations 2, 3 and 5 have already reached the performance level and loaned their processor farms to populations 1 and 4.

To realize this algorithm on a 64 transputer-supercluster, a double-ring structure was adopted as shown in Figure 8. The inner ring serves for communication between the farmer processes and for migration. The outer ring is used to integrate borrowed processors. In the simulations described later, 5 populations and 60 processors were used.

---

[3] To make sure that one subpopulation does not block the entire process forever, a maximum number of generations can be specified. If that many generations have elapsed, the migration process is performed no matter what the populations' performances are.

There are some additional features of the algorithm that make it distinct from standard genetic algorithms and that are especially adapted to the hardware topology.

One is that the number of offspring created during one generation depends on the number of processors in the farm. Each processor is assigned one pair (which could also be 2 or 3 if fewer processors were available) of individuals, performs crossover, mutation and evaluation, and returns one pair of offspring. This guarantees that each processor has about the same amount of workload. As the number of processors available to one subpopulation may vary (due to the borrowing of processors) so may the number of children created in one generation.

A further peculiarity is that the subpopulations were used to level out some 'starting inequalities'. Recall that the algorithm has to deal with genotypes of varying length, depending on how many groups the individual represents. The task is to find a short string (representing few different weights) that still performs reasonably well on the training set. However, by pure statistics, random individuals with many groups are more likely to model the original trained network accurately than are random individuals with fewer groups. This leads to an unfair and undesired 'starting advantage' for longer strings.

This problem is easily overcome by our distribution strategy: The different subpopulations are initialized with different length strings. Therefore, due to the migration strategy, all the subpopulations (and thus all the different length strings) get a chance to reach the first performance level. Only after that competition is introduced slowly by migrating individuals from other subpopulations.

5 Empirical Results

The problem chosen for testing our distributed genetic algorithm was the shift-detection-problem already used by Nowlan and Hinton [NoHi92] to compare simple backpropagation, cross-validation, weight decay and soft weight sharing:

The inputs to the neural network consist of 20-bit words (-1/+1 representation) such that the second 10 bits correspond to the first 10 bits, but are circularly shifted either to the right or to the left. The network has to detect the direction of the shift. The learning algorithm is applied to a neural network as shown in Figure 9. The desired output of the network is +1 for a left shift and -1 for a right shift.

Out of the 2048 possible patterns, 100 were chosen randomly as training data (and used for the training with backpropagation and for the evaluation in the genetic algorithm). 1300 were used to test the generalization capabilities of the original trained and of the reduced network. The training set was deliberately chosen to be very small to make generalization more difficult.

First, the network was trained until it correctly[4] classified 100% of the training data. 10 runs were performed to determine an average percentage of correct answers on the test set of 79%. Then, one network with approximately average performance (78.3% correct answers on the test set) was chosen and reduced by the proposed genetic algorithm using five subpopulations of 100 individuals each.

---

[4] Correctly again means a deviation from the desired output by less than 0.5.

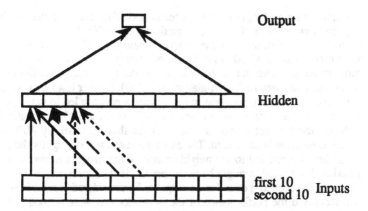

Fig. 9: Shift-detection network used for simulations. Each hidden unit is connected to 8 input units: 4 from the first block of 10 inputs and the corresponding 4 from the second block of 10 inputs. The solid, dashed and dotted lines indicate the group of input units connected to the first, second and third hidden unit, respectively. The output unit is connected to all hidden units. The bias unit is connected to all hidden units and the output unit but omitted in the illustration for clarity (cf. [NoHi92]).

Again, 10 runs were performed with different initial random populations. An average of 84.2% correct answers on the test set was measured which represents a significant improvement (p > 99%). The number of correct answers on the training set decreased slightly to 99.2%.

The final performance level was found after an average of 90 generations[5]. At this stage, the best individuals used 7 or 9 groups of weights.

Table 1 shows a typical result and compares the weight values of the original network with the new values of the reduced network. Although already the original network was not fully connected (101 instead of 211 possible connections), the genetic algorithm pruned another quarter of the connections. It reduced the number of different weights from 101 to only 7 and increased the percentage of correct answers on the test set from 78.3% to 85.2%.

Further test executions with different parameter settings showed that

- the algorithm works best with a high mutation probability (about 10% per real value) but is very robust to changes between 5% and 50%. That is, it still finds equivalent solutions, although it usually takes longer to get them.
- the number of processors available has almost no effect on the solutions found, however, when using half the number of processors it takes approximately twice the time to find the solution.
- compared to the same algorithm using one big population instead of five medium sized subpopulations, the distributed algorithm was able to sustain

---

[5] With the proposed algorithm, not every subpopulation performs the same number of generations. Here, and at all other places in this paper, the maximum over all subpopulations is given.

diversity in string length over a longer period. The results of the distributed algorithm were better, though not significantly (p > 70%).

- running the algorithm with the proposed new migration strategy and with migration after a fixed number of generations showed no significant differences. One reason may be that the number of exchanged individuals (2) was small compared to the population size (100). Further tests are necessary.

- using the test set for evaluation in the genetic algorithm led to networks with 96% correct answers on the training set (still used for backpropagation) and 92% on the test set (used for the GA). In this net, usually 40% of the connections have been pruned. The experiment shows how tightly the genetic algorithm is restricted to the neighborhood of the original network and that relaxing the restriction might be necessary to yield better results.

- changing the accepted error for an output to be considered correct from 0.5 to 0.3 decreased the performance of the networks that were trained purely by backpropagation to an average of 74.9% correct answers on the test set. However, running the GA on those nets improved the result again to 84.1%, or approximately to the same performance as with the earlier notion of correctness.

  Training with backpropagation until the net perfectly classified the training data with the 0.3 limit, but allowing 0.5 for the GA yielded an average of 87.1% correct answers on the test set and 99.9% on the training set. This indicates that it might be possible to further improve the results by using better trained original networks and that the GA will improve the results, no matter how well the original network was trained.

The complete experimental results are documented in [Br94].

The observation that the group weights are often very close to the group borders (cf. Table 1) suggests that the performance might be further improved by relaxing the constraints on the group weights, which always have to lie between group borders due to the chosen representation.

Recent experiments with a representation where the group weights may lie anywhere between the preceding and next group weight (not group border) improved the performance of the same original network to an average of 89.2% correct classification on the test set and perfect score on the training set. Using a longer trained original network (see last point above) and this less constraint representation even yielded an average of 90.8% classification accuracy on the test set with relatively low standard deviation (0.85).

When trying to compare the results of this paper to the results reported by Nowlan and Hinton [NoHi92] on the same test problem, the genetic algorithm turns out to work better than cross-validation (that used 1000 additional validation examples) and comparable to Rumelhart's weight-decay, although it did not reach the performance of Nowlan and Hinton's soft weight sharing.

Other than the just mentioned methods, our approach is not restricted to feed-forward-networks or differentiable activation functions, and our analysis even suggested ways to further enhance it's performance.

Tab. 1: Comparison of the original (left) and reduced (right) weights.

Original (left)	Reduced (left)	Original (right)	Reduced (right)
	-2.296660	-0.000761	
-1.269776		0.009543	0.0
-1.260177		0.021943	
-1.134541		0.027102	
-1.131305		0.040751	
-1.086930	-1.474317	0.051377	
-1.061369		0.060793	
-1.006712		0.068573	
-0.846008		0.072736	
-0.821840		0.096648	
-0.756132		0.098216	
-0.679395		0.107132	
-0.623208		0.119471	
-0.603662		0.135665	
-0.595839		0.143374	
-0.593972		0.154963	
-0.570125		0.155917	0.237863
-0.563382		0.180649	
-0.544735		0.183075	
-0.523402	-0.817952	0.230067	
-0.443304		0.261975	
-0.421148		0.265619	
-0.400527		0.273501	
-0.389916		0.306626	
-0.372866		0.320946	
-0.348698		0.321266	
-0.343247		0.350677	
-0.327538		0.357111	
-0.271977		0.390651	
-0.252070		0.391834	
-0.223026		0.418702	
-0.200253		0.443310	
-0.194693		0.450430	0.81792
-0.174757	-0.237863	0.460755	
-0.169060		0.506568	
-0.156351		0.521098	
-0.112623		0.537551	
-0.102760		0.545658	
-0.097726		0.555882	
-0.090511		0.622158	
-0.084352		0.651565	
-0.080913		0.689628	
-0.077237		0.693038	
-0.056424		0.732766	
-0.051268		0.783090	
-0.045109		0.846987	
-0.035603		0.880584	
-0.025031		0.908113	1.474317
-0.020784		1.010746	
-0.009105	0.0	1.495531	
-0.004331		1.695201	2.296660

6 Conclusion

This paper presented a novel approach for improving the generalization capabilities of neural networks: weight sharing on neural networks imposed by a distributed genetic algorithm.

In contrast to conventional distributed algorithms of this kind, here it has been suggested to exchange individuals between subpopulations after they reach some pre specified performance level instead of after some fixed number of generations. This should prevent far evolved individuals from being sent into a weak subpopulation and dominating that subpopulation immediately. Although leading to promising results, this novel migration strategy did not show significantly better performance than the conventional method. However, more experiments on other test problems should be performed before making a final statement on this strategy.

Furthermore, in connection with the performance driven migration strategy, a suitable load balancing strategy has been developed, where far evolved subpopulations can lend processors to slower subpopulations to speed up the evolutionary process.

The presented results show that the proposed algorithm is indeed appropriate to introduce weight sharing on neural networks and that this improves the network's generalization capabilities significantly. In addition, the algorithm turned out to be very robust to parameter changes. The analysis also suggests that even though the algorithm was successful, there is probably still room for improvement.

Future research in this area will include

- further experiments to better understand why and how this approach worked
- development of a new approach that does not limit the search space
- checking whether the algorithm can be helpful in understanding how a neural network actually represents the data and
- evaluating the new migration strategy separately on other problems.

References

[Abu-M89] Abu-Mostafa, Y. S.: *The Vapnik-Chervonenkis Dimension: Information versus Complexity in Learning*. Neural Computation 1 (1989), pp. 312-317

[Bäck94] Bäck, T.: *Selective Pressure in Evolutionary Algorithms: A Characterization of Selection Mechanisms*. Proceedings of the first IEEE conference on Evolutionary Computation, June 1994, Vol. 1, pp.57-62

[Br94] Branke, J.: *Weightsharing auf Neuronalen Netzen durch einen parallelen Genetischen Algorithmus*. Diplomarbeit, Institut fuer Angewandte Informatik und Formale Beschreibungsverfahren, Universität Karlsruhe, Germany, 1994

[CDS89] LeCun, Y., Denker, J. S. and Solla, S. A., *Optimal Brain Damage*. In: Advances in Neural Information Processing Systems 1, Denver 1989, D. S. Touretzky, ed., San Mateo, Morgan Kaufmann, pp. 598-605

[DMM91] Dodd, N., Macfalrlane, D. and Marland, C.: *Optimization of Artificial Neural Network Structure using Genetic Techniques on Multiple Transputers*. Transputing 91, P. Welch, D. Stiles, T. Kunii and A. Bakkers, eds., Conference-Proceedings of the World Transputer User Group (WOTUG), Amsterdam, The Netherlands: IOS Press, 1991, pp. 687-700

[GoDe90]   Golderg, D. E. and Deb, K.: *A Comparative Analysis of Selection Schemes used in Genetic Algorithms*. G. J. E. Rawlins, ed., Foundations of Genetic Algorithms, Morgan kaufman, san Mateo, CA, 1991, pp. 68-93

[Gol89]   Goldberg, D. E.: *Genetic Algorithms in Search, Optimization, and Machine Learning*. Addison-Wesley, 1989

[Han94]   Hancock, P. J. B.: *An Empirical Comparison of Selection Methods in Evolutionary Algorithms*. To appear in: proceedings of the AISB workshop on evolutionary computation, 1994

[LeCu89]   LeCun, Y., *Generalization and Network Design Strategies*. In: Connectionism in Perspective, Pfeifer, R., Schreter, Z., Fogelman, F. and Steels, L., eds., 1989, Zurich, Switzerland. Elsevier, pp. 143-155

[LWH90]   Lang, K. J., Waibel, A. H. and Hinton, G. E.: *A Time-Delay Neural Network Architecture for Isolated Word Recognition*. Neural Networks 3, 1990, pp. 22-43

[Mic94]   Michalewicz, Z.: *Genetic Algorithms + Data Structures = Evolution Programs*. second edition, Springer Verlag Berlin Heidelberg 1994

[NoHi92]   Nowlan, S. J. and Hinton, G. E., *Simplifying Neural Networks by Soft Weight-Sharing*. In: Neural Computation 4 (1992), pp. 473-493

[Ree93]   Reed, R.: *Pruning Algorithms - A Survey*. In: IEEE Transactions on Neural Networks, Vol.4, No.5 (September 1993), pp. 740-747

[Riss78]   Rissanen, J., *Modeling by shortest data description*. Automatica 14 (1978), pp. 465-471

[SWM90]   Starkweather, T., Whitley, D. and Mathias, K.: *Optimization using Distributed Genetic Algorithms*. In: H.-P. Schwefel, R. Männer (eds.), Parallel Problem-Soving from Nature, Springer, 1990

[VaCh71]   Vapnik, V. N. and Chervonenkis, A. Y.: *On the Uniform Convergence of Relative Frequencies of Events to Their Probabilities*. Theory of Probability and Its Applications 16 (1971), pp. 264-280

[WhSt90]   Whitley, D. and Starkweather, T.: *GENITOR II: a Distributed Genetic Algorithm*. Journal of Experimental and Theoretical Artificial Intelligence, V. 2(3), (1990), pp. 189-214

Learning Non-Monotonic Logic Programs: Learning Exceptions

Yannis Dimopoulos and Antonis Kakas
Department of Computer Science
University of Cyprus
CY-1678, Nicosia, Cyprus
{yannis, antonis}@turing.cs.ucy.ac.cy

Abstract. In this paper we present a framework for learning non-monotonic logic programs. The method is parametric on a classical learning algorithm whose generated rules are to be understood as default rules. This means that these rules must be tolerant to the negative information by allowing for the possibility of exceptions. The same classical algorithm is then used to learn recursively these exceptions.

We prove that the non-monotonic learning algorithm that realizes these ideas converges asymptotically to the concept to be learned. We also discuss various general issues concerning the problem of learning non-monotonic theories in the proposed framework.

1 Introduction

Over the last two decades research work in Artificial Intelligence has shown that many problems can not be captured fully within the realm of classical monotonic logic and that other logics which are non-monotonic are more suitable. In many cases these problems need a non-monotonic formalism if they are to be represented adequately. As a result if we want to develop methods for learning theories for these problems we need to develop learning formalisms that are based on non-monotonic representation (description) languages and concepts.

In this paper we will present a learning framework where the learned theories are non-monotonic. In particular, we will be interested in learning theories which are non-monotonic logic programs. We are thus interested in extending the language bias of the hypotheses from definite logic programs as in Inductive Logic Programming ([13]) to the language of non-monotonic logic programs. The development of this non-monotonic learning framework will be done primarily within the context of learning from a set of examples hierarchical concepts with their exceptions. The particular learning problem that we will study within this framework is the usual problem of learning a concept from a set of positive and negative examples with emphasis on problems that can not be captured by classical definite logic programs. To do this we will exploit a recently proposed formalism for non-monotonic logic programming which although like all other such formalisms is based on the principle of negation as failure it does not rely on a NAF construct within the language but instead uses a limited form of classical negation. We are thus interested in extending the language bias from definite logic programs to a more general class of logic programs that embodies both the non-monotonic principle of NAF as well as a form of explicit negation.

Within this formalism then the basic idea is to employ a classical learning algorithm to cover (as usual) the positive examples but with the difference that we are tolerant with respect to the negative information in the sense that we will allow a hypothesis generated by the classical algorithm even if this covers some of the negative examples. Hence a rule generated by the classical learning algorithm is now to be understood as a default rule in the sense that it holds in general but not always; it may have exceptions. In this way the logic program that we are building is not anymore a classical monotonic theory but now this constitutes a non-monotonic theory. If indeed it is the case that a generated rule also covers some of the negative examples the non-monotonic learning process can not stop but it will continue to address the problem of learning the concept that covers these negative examples i.e. the exceptions to the previously generated rule for the positive examples. This will be done by calling again the underlying classical algorithm that we are using in a dual form to learn the part of the negative concept that corresponds to these exception examples. As a result we will get a set of rules with the classical negation of the concept appearing in the head that imply the negation of the concept for these examples. These negative rules will then be added to the previously generated positive rules to form a new hypothesis.

Again we will allow anyone of these negative rules even if this covers some of the positive examples i.e. contains exceptions. The negative rules are also default rules and hence we need to be tolerant in the same way and allow for the possibility that they may cover some of the opposite (positive) examples. If this is so we will then iterate the above process by calling the classical algorithm to learn the "subpart" of the concept given by the subset of positive examples that form the exceptions to the negative rules generated in the previous step.

The problem of learning non-monotonic theories (logic programs) has already been address in the literature by several authors (e.g. [1], [11], [16]). In most of these works NAF is used in the object language of non-monotonic logic programs. This forces the need to invent new predicates (abnormality predicates) to handle exceptions. In [1, 11], exceptions are handled primarily at one level by some method of enumeration or with the use of inequality conditions. This makes it difficult to handle a hierarchy of exceptions (i.e. exceptions of exceptions etc).

Our approach is closely related to the algorithm presented in [16]. This is also capable of learning hierarchical concepts by using abnormality predicates and negation at the object level. In fact, this algorithm is, modulo the representation language, identical to the algorithm we present in this paper.[1] Our recursive treatment and the interpolation of the positive and negative information applies to that algorithm as well. Nevertheless, while in [16] the main task is to use the negative examples to learn the exceptions to the positive concept, we are also interested in learning (and using) the negative concept itself in a symmetric way to that of the positive concept. This task can be easily accommodated in the

---

[1] We thank the anonymous referees for pointing this connection out to us.

particular non-monotonic logic programming formalism that we are using.

The idea of learning the negative concept has already been studied in several earlier works. For example the work in CLINT ([5]) is concerned with learning the negative concept to be understood in a three valued logic. Our work has several points in common with this work but differs in the following ways. The main difference is the fact that here we are not only concerned with learning the negative concept per se but are also interested in a focused limited learning of parts of the negative concept as the need arises from the hierarchical nature of the positive concept. In this sense the two approaches are complementary in a way that our approach can adopt the other at the point where we need to learn the negative concept and conversely the extended CLINT system can adopt our method to learn hierarchical concepts. The two approaches also differ in the particular formalisms and description languages that they are using. Our approach with its tolerant rules seems to provide a simple framework in which non-monotonic learning algorithms can be developed.

Another method that is related to our work is that of [3]. This also uses a representation language which includes priorities but these are based on statistical information coming from the examples. Classical rules are generated for both the positive and negative concept and each one is attributed a statistical priority weight. However, like in [5], this method does not generate exceptions directly, as in our work and in [16], but exceptions come indirectly through the relative strength of the statistical weights of contradictory rules. Consequently, the theories generated in [3] will not have the multi-layered hierarchical structure that can be present in our theories. Again we believe that the two approaches can complement each other.

The rest of the paper is organised as follows. Section 2 gives some needed background information on the subject of non-monotonic logic programs. In section 3 we describe the non-monotonic learning algorithm and then show some of its main properties in section 4. Section 5 provides additional discussion on the non-monotonic learning algorithm and the issue of handling negative information.

2 Non-monotonic reasoning in Logic Programming

Non-monotonic reasoning in Logic Programming is done using the *negation as failure principle* (NAF) ([2]). This principle informally states that we can assume that some atom is false provided that it is not possible to derive the atom from our theory. Traditionally, in order to implement this principle a negation as failure operator is introduced in the language. Thus the language of Logic programming is extended from definite Horn clauses to general clauses of the form:

$$A \leftarrow L_1, \ldots L_n$$

where A is an atom and each L_i is either an atom A_i or a negation as failure literal *not* A_i. As usual each variable occurring in the clause is implicitly universally quantified. The semantics of this form of negation introduced in logic programs is given by some formalization of the NAF principle which can now be stated as:

not A holds iff A fails to hold

for any atomic goal A. Operationally, in order to satisfy a NAF goal, not p, an auxiliary computation is generated that checks that the goal, p, can not be derived. Consider for example the following program

$$fly(x) \leftarrow bird(x), not\ abnormal(x)$$
$$abnormal(x) \leftarrow penguin(x)$$
$$bird(x) \leftarrow penguin(x)$$
$$bird(Tweety)$$

From the first clause (rule) of the program we can prove that Tweety flies if we can prove that Tweety is a bird and that *not abnormal(Tweety)* holds. The first of these follows directly from the last clause (rule) of the program whilst to show that *not abnormal(Tweety)* holds we need (following the NAF principle) to check that *abnormal(Tweety)* can not be proved from the program. Indeed, there is no way to prove this form the above program. On the other hand, if we add to the program the new clause *penguin(Tweety)* then we will be able to prove *abnormal(Tweety)* and thus *not abnormal(Tweety)* and *flies(Tweety)* do not hold.

Notice here that the effect of the NAF condition in the first rule is to prevent the conclusion of the rule to hold in the cases where we know (the program knows) that the abnormality property holds. In other words, the first rule can be understood as *x flies if x is a bird unless x is abnormal*. Thus the NAF operator "not" can informally be given the meaning of "unless" and we can thus see that NAF can help to capture exceptions to rules.

Various semantics have been proposed for general logic programs with NAF in their language ([2], [6], [15], [18]). In this paper we will adopt a recent new proposal ([8]) for capturing the NAF principle in Logic Programming that does not employ a NAF operator in the language but instead uses a limited form of classical negation together with a priority relation amongst the sentences of the program. The semantics of this framework, called the admissibility (or more generally the acceptability) semantics, is defined within an argumentation-based formalism and has been shown to be powerful enough to encompass most of the earlier semantics for NAF in Logic Programming.

In this framework the above logic program will be written equivalently as the following theory

$$fly(x) \leftarrow bird(x)$$
$$\neg fly(x) \leftarrow penguin(x)$$
$$bird(x) \leftarrow penguin(x)$$
$$bird(Tweety)$$

with a (partial) ordering relation between the sentences that assigns the second rule higher than the first. (In the subsequent chapters this will be denoted by a directed arc between the rules.) Here "¬" denotes explicit negation and can be used to represent negative information about the world that the program is modelling. From this theory we can conclude that Tweety flies because we can derive this from the first rule and there is no way to derive $\neg fly(Tweety)$ from the program. If we add the sentence $penguin(Tweety)$ then we can derive both $fly(Tweety)$ and $\neg fly(Tweety)$ from the program understood as a classical theory. But in the non-monotonic admissibility semantics of the theory the second conclusion overrides the first since the part of the program that derives $\neg fly(Tweety)$ contains the second rule which is designated higher than the first rule which belongs to the part of the program that derives the first conclusion $fly(Tweety)$.

Note that the language bias given by this framework contains together with the NAF principle that it embodies a form of explicit (classical) negation.

In general, this argumentation-based framework for non-monotonic Logic Programs is defined as follows.

Definition 1. *(Background logic)*
Formulae in the language $\mathcal{L}$ of the framework are defined as $L \leftarrow L_1, \ldots, L_n$, where $L, L_1, \ldots, L_n$ are positive or explicit negative literals. The only inference rule is the classical modus ponens rule

$$\frac{L \leftarrow L_1, \ldots, L_n \qquad L_1, \ldots, L_n}{L} \qquad (n \geq 0) \qquad \square$$

We assume that, together with the set of sentences T, we are given a priority relation $<$ on these sentences (where $\phi < \psi$ means that ϕ has lower priority than ψ). The role of the priority relation is to encode locally the relative strength of rules in the theory, typically between contradictory rules. We will require that $<$ is irreflexive and antisymmetric.

Definition 2. *(Non-Monotonic Theory or Logic Program)*
A theory $(T, <)$ is a set of sentences T in $\mathcal{L}$ together with a priority relation $<$ on the sentences of T.

We now proceed to define a notion of attack on these theories based on the possible conflicts that we can have in a theory T between a literal L and its explicit negation $\neg L$ and on the priority relation $<$ on T.

Definition 3. *(Attacks)*
Let $(T, <)$ be a theory and $T, T' \subseteq T$. Then T' attacks T iff there exists L, $T_1 \subseteq T'$ and $T_2 \subseteq T$ such that

(i) $T_1 \vdash_{min} L$ and $T_2 \vdash_{min} \neg L$
(ii) $(\exists r' \in T_1, r \in T_2 \text{ s.t. } r' < r) \Rightarrow (\exists r' \in T_1, r \in T_2 \text{ s.t. } r < r')$. $\qquad \square$

$T \vdash_{min} L$ means that $T \vdash L$ under the background logic and that L can not be derived from any proper subset of T. Using this we then define the basic notion of an admissible subset of a given theory (program).

Definition 4. *(Admissibility)*
Let $(\mathcal{T}, <)$ be a theory and $T \subseteq \mathcal{T}$. Then T is *admissible* iff T is consistent and for any $T' \subseteq \mathcal{T}$ if T' attacks T then T attacks T'.

The (sceptical) semantics of a theory can then be defined in terms of its admissible subsets as follows.

Definition 5. Let $(\mathcal{T}, <)$ be a theory and L a ground literal. Then L is a *non-monotonic consequence* of the theory iff L holds in every maximal admissible subset of $\mathcal{T}$.

It can be shown that given a logic program P, with NAF in its object language we can define a corresponding equivalent theory $\mathcal{D}(P)$. This transformation is motivated from the interpretation of *not p* as *unless p*. For example, if we have a rule "$p \leftarrow q, not\ r$" then this transformed into two sentences "$p \leftarrow q$" and "$\neg p \leftarrow r$", and the second is assigned higher priority than the first.

Finally, we mention that for most of the work in this paper we will be concerned with a subclass of non-monotonic logic programs in this formalism. These will be theories where their set of contradictory rules (i.e. rules with opposite conclusions) can be separated into classes where the rules in each class are totally ordered by the priority relation of the theory. In such theories in order to decide if an atom, A, holds we need to show that A can be derived classically using some rule, r, for A and that $\neg A$ can not be derived (classically) using some rule r' which is designated higher than the rule r by the priority relation on the program.

3 Description of the Algorithm

The main learning problem we are interested in is the usual problem of learning a concept from a set of positive and negative examples. Hence given a background theory and a set of examples we want to generate a hypothesis within the language bias of non-monotonic logic programs described above that covers all the positive examples and does not cover any of the negative examples. In particular, we are interested in problems which can not be learned within the language bias of definite (classical) logic programs. For example these concepts may have an inherent hierarchical nature that cannot be captured by classical logic programs. In these cases in addition to the coverage of the examples by the generated hypothesis we also want to identify the hierarchical structure of concept. As a result of this the generated hypothesis (non-monotonic logic program) will also have as consequence the negation of the concept for some of the negative examples. In other words, part of the negative concept will also be learned.

The basic idea behind the algorithm that we are proposing is to use a classical learning algorithm in a tolerant way in the sense that the hypothesis computed to cover a set of positive examples may also cover some of the negative examples. We say that, given a background theory B, a hypothesis H covers an example *e* iff $B \cup H$ implies *l*, such that $|l| = e$, where $|l| = e'$ or $|l| = \neg e'$ where e' is an atom. If the example *e* is negative (resp. positive) and $B \cup H$ implies *e* (resp. $\neg e$) then this example is called an exception to *H*.

The set of negative examples that are covered by this generalization are considered to be an exception to this generalization, and the algorithm then attempts to learn this exception by using the classical algorithm on this set of examples. This procedure is applied iteratively on subsets of the original examples until a point is reached where, under the admissibility semantics, all the positive examples are covered and no negative example is covered. We illustrate the main features of the algorithm via the next example.

Example 1. Consider the background theory *B*
$bird(x) \leftarrow penguin(x)$
$superpenguin(x) \leftarrow penguin(x)$
$bird(a), bird(b), penguin(c), penguin(d), superpenguin(e), superpenguin(f)$
Consider also the set of examples $E = E^+ \cup E^-$ where $E^+ = \{flies(a), flies(b), flies(e), flies(f)\}$ and $E^- = \{flies(c), flies(d)\}$.
□

The algorithm in the first step will attempt to cover all the positive examples by calling a classical learning algorithm. This can be done by the rule $flies(x) \leftarrow bird(x)$. But this rule also covers the negative examples. These will then be considered to be exceptions to it, and a new phase will begin that will now attempt to learn the concept that these exceptions may form. The set of positive examples for the classical algorithm in this phase will be $E_1^+ = E^- = \{flies(c), flies(d)\}$. Since the concept of the exception should not cover any of the positive examples covered by the rule, the negative examples for this phase will be the set $E_1^- = E^+$. Suppose that the classical algorithm will now compute the rule $\neg flies(x) \leftarrow penguin(x)$. This new rule will be related to the one of the previous step via a link that gives priority to $\neg flies(x) \leftarrow penguin(x)$ over $flies(x) \leftarrow bird(x)$.

Note that we are learning the negative concept $\neg flies$ in exactly the same way as the positive concept *flies*. Again some of the examples in E_1^- are covered by the new rule. These are the "exceptions of the exceptions", and the algorithm again calls the classical learning algorithm to generate a rule with input examples $E_2^+ = \{flies(e), flies(f)\}$ and $E_2^- = E_1^+$. This rule is $flies(x) \leftarrow superpenguin(x)$ which is added to the theory together with a link from itself to the rule $\neg flies(x) \leftarrow penguin(x)$. This last rule does not cover any of examples in E_2^- and the procedure terminates. The result is the hypothesis *H*

flies(x) ← bird(x)

¬ flies(x) ← penguin(x)

flies(x) ← superpenguin(x)

The hypothesis H together with the background knowledge B cover, under the admissibility semantics, all the examples in E^+ and do not cover any of the examples in E^-.

The ideas presented so far can be captured formally in the following algorithm. Let P be the set of positive examples, N the set of negative examples, B the background knowledge, H the current hypothesis and R a rule initialized to be empty.

Algorithm NMLearn(P, N, B, R, H)
Begin
Classic-Learn(P, N, B, H')
if $E \subset E'$, where $E = \{e | e \in N$ and e covered by $H'\}$ and
$E' = \{e | e \in N$ and e covered by $R\}$
then

> begin
> $H = H \cup H'$; add priority links from each rule in H' to R;
> $M_i = \{e_i | e_i \in N$ and covered by rule $R'_i \in H'\}$.
> For each $M_i <> \emptyset$ do
> $NMLearn(M_i, P, B, R'_i, H'')$
> end

else enumerate the exceptions of R and terminate;
end

Some comments on the algorithm are in order. First note that is possible that at each step more than one rule may be needed to cover a set of the examples. Consider the following example.

Example 2. Let the background knowledge be $B' = B \cup \{plane(g), plane(h),$ $plane(k), plane(m), damaged(k), damaged(m)\}$, where B is the background knowledge of example 1. Moreover let the set of examples be the same with those of example 1 augmented with the positives $flies(g), flies(h)$ and the negatives $flies(k), flies(m)$. Then the algorithm will compute the hypothesis

Notice that the algorithm computes the hypothesis in a depth first manner. Sets of rules computed at each level are explicitly associated with a rule of the previous level and are considered to express the part of the negative concept that forms of the exception to the rule. Moreover, it is obvious from the recursive nature of the algorithm $NMLearn$ that the treatment of positive and negative examples is symmetric. At each odd level (starting from level one) a set of positive examples is generalized while at each even level set of negative ones.

Another important issue is the treatment of the negative examples by the $Classic\text{-}Learn$ algorithm. No special restriction is put on the rules that this algorithm returns. Nevertheless, it is clear that the procedure may also cover some of the negative examples. The non-monotonic algorithm can tolerate such a coverage, since in the subsequent steps these exceptions will be captured and introduced in the final hypothesis. We should though stress the fact that the amount of tolerance that the algorithm exhibits is an important issue to be discussed further in section 5.

4 Properties of the Algorithm

A learning problem is formally stated as a tuple $(\vdash, LB, LE, LH)$, where $\vdash$ is a correct provability relation, LB the language of the background knowledge, LE the language of examples and LH the hypothesis language. Then we are given a background knowledge $B \in LB$ and a set of positive and negative examples $E = E^+ \cup E^-$, $E \in LE$. The problem is to find a hypothesis $H \in LH$ such that $B, H \vdash E^+$ and $\forall e \in E^-$, $B, H \not\vdash e$. In this paper we are concerned with two particular learning problems. The first is defined by the tuple $(\vdash_C, LB, LE, LH)$ and the second by the tuple $(\vdash_N, LB, LE, NLH)$. The provability relation $\vdash_C$ refers to a correct provability relation for first order Horn clauses, while the relation $\vdash_N$ to a correct provability relation for non-monotonic logic programs under the admissibility semantics. Furthermore, LB and LH is the language of definite logic programs, while NLH denotes the language of non-monotonic logic programs. Finally, LE is a language of ground atoms.

In order to prove the formal results of this section we will assume that any input set of examples can be covered by the $Classic\text{-}Learn$ algorithm with a single clause and so $NMLearn$ uses only a single clause at each level. Hence, the NHL language is now restricted to non-monotonic theories of the form $H = (H_1, \ldots, H_n)$, where each H_i is a single rule and the links are of the form $H_{i+1} > H_i$ for $1 \leq i < n$. Furthermore, since in this section we are interested in learning hierarchies the language bias also imposes the restriction that $B \models \forall (\text{body}(H_{i+1}) \rightarrow \text{body}(H_i))$ for $1 \leq i < n$, where B is the given background knowledge. We call this language bias the *hierarchy language bias*. Combining this with the single clause bias we get the *single hierarchy language bias*.

Furthermore, assume that the algorithm $Classic\text{-}Learn$ always computes a clause $c(x) \leftarrow b_{min}(x)$ that covers all the examples for which the following minimality condition holds: For any other clause $c(x) \leftarrow b(x)$ that also covers the same set of examples, $B \models \forall x (b_{min}(x) \rightarrow b(x))$ holds.[2] We call such a clause a *minimal clause* or rule. A minimal clause together with the background

---

[2] Here we identify the variables of the two rules $c(x) \leftarrow b_{min}(x)$ and $c(x) \leftarrow b(x)$ by

knowledge entails a set of conclusions that is a subset of the consequences of any other clause that covers the positive examples at hand.

This minimality condition implies that the hypotheses computed by $NMLearn$ comply with the single hierarchy langauge we have assumed in this section. This is a straightforward consequence of the observation that for any H_{i+1} in the hypothesis $H = (H_1, \ldots H_m)$, H_{i+1} is a minimal rule that covers a set of examples E_{i+1}, which are the exceptions to the rule H_i and so H_i is a rule that also covers the examples E_{i+1}.

Next we prove that the procedure $NMLearn$ always terminates.

Proposition 6. *The algorithm $NMLearn$ terminates on any finite set of examples that is given as input.*

Proof. Let E be a finite set of examples given as input to the algorithm. We will show that at each iteration of the algorithm the classical algorithm is asked to cover less examples than at the previous step, and therefore, since E is finite, the algorithm terminates.

Let E_i^+ be the set of positive examples to be covered at step i (i odd) by a clause r_i. Suppose also that r_i covers a non-empty set of negative examples E_i^-. Otherwise, if $E_i^- = \emptyset$ then the algorithm terminates. This set E_i^- will be covered by a new (negative) rule r_{i+1}. At this step the algorithm either terminates by enumeration[3] when $E_{i+1}^+ \not\subset E_i^+$ or if $E_{i+1}^+ \subset E_i^+$ it continues to find a rule r_{i+2} to cover E_{i+1}^+. $\square$

Proposition 7. *The depth of the hypothesis computed by the algorithm $NMLearn$ on a set of examples $E = E^+ \cup E^-$ is minimum in the sense that there is no other hypothesis that identifies the concept and has smaller depth.*

Proof. Let M be an optimal hypothesis wrt the depth such that $M \vdash_N E^+$ and $M \not\vdash_N e$ for every $e \in E^-$. The algorithm in the first step has to cover the set E^+ with the minimal clause of E^+, say r_1. Due to the restricted single hierarchy language bias of NLH the same set of examples has also to be covered by of one of the rules of M, say r_1'. If r_1 does not cover any examples from E^- is optimal. If not, then since r_1 is minimal, and so $B \models \text{body}(r_1) \rightarrow \text{body}(r_1')$, every negative example that is covered by r_1 is also covered by r_1'. This means that if the depth is increased by the $NMLearn$ by one, then the depth in M is increased by one as well. Also if we denote by $E_1'^-$ the set of negative examples that have to be covered by the optimal hypothesis in the next level note that $E_1'^- \supseteq E_1^-$, where E_1^- is the set of negative examples that have to be covered by the algorithm $NMLearn$. Since $NMLearn$ computes the minimal clause of E_1^- we see that

---

identifying the corresponding variables in the heads of the rules. We assume that the heads do not contain any non-variable terms. If this is so, we first need to homogenise such rules by introducing explicit equality conditions in the body of the rule.

[3] Note that the additional condition of minimality on $Classic - Learn$ ensures that at each iteration $E_{i+1}^+ \subseteq E_i^+$, hence enumeration is only required if $E_{i+1}^+ = E_i^+$.

if during this step the algorithm covers some positive examples then the same positive examples will be covered by the optimal hypothesis and hence if the depth needs to be increased further by the algorithm this will also be true in M. Iterating these argument see that M has the same depth as the hypothesis computed by the algorithm. $\square$

We will now show that the algorithm $NMLearn$ identifies in the limit ([7], [9]) the learning problem $(\vdash_N, LB, LE, NLH)$, under some restrictions on the input examples.

Definition 8. Let LE be the language of examples, $E_\infty = \{e_1, e_2, \ldots\}$ denote an infinite stream of examples, such that $e_i \in LE \times \{+, -\}$ and E_∞ a complete enumeration of LE. Let also $E_\infty^+ = \{e| < e, + > \in E_\infty\}$ denote the positive examples and $E_\infty^- = \{e| < e, - > \in E_\infty\}$ the negative ones.
We say that the background knowledge B is **partially suitable** for E_∞ and LH if $\exists H \in LH$ such that $B, H \vdash E_\infty^+$. We also say that the background knowledge B is **suitable** for E_∞ and LH iff it is partially suitable and $\forall e \in E_\infty^-, B, H \not\vdash e$.
We say that a learning problem $(\vdash, LB, LE, LH)$ is **partially identified in the limit** by an algorithm $LEARN$ iff for every stream E_∞ and partially suitable background knowledge $B \in LB$, $LEARN$ accepts incrementally E_∞ and there exists a step i for which $\forall j \geq i : H_i = H_j$ and $B, H_i \vdash E_\infty^+$. $\square$

Definition 9. A learning problem $(\vdash, LB, LE, LH)$ is **identified in the limit** by an algorithm $LEARN$ iff for every stream $E_\infty = E_\infty^+ \cup E_\infty^-$ and suitable background knowledge $B \in LB$, $LEARN$ accepts incrementally E_∞ and there exists a step i for which $\forall j \geq i : H_i = H_j$ and $B, H_i \vdash E_\infty^+, \forall e \in E_\infty^-, B, H_i \not\vdash e$ holds. $\square$

The following definition is used in the next theorem.

Definition 10. A set of examples $E = E^+ \cup E^-$ is called **strictly consistent** wrt a background knowledge B, if there are no subsets, $E_i^+ \subseteq E^+$ and $E_j^- \subseteq E^-$ such that the minimal rules H_i of E_i^+ and H_j of E_j^- have equivalent bodies under B, i.e. $B \models \forall (\text{body}(H_i) \leftrightarrow \text{body}(H_j))$. $\square$

Theorem 11. *If the learning problem $(\vdash_C, LB, LE, LH)$ is partially identified in the limit by the algorithm Classic-Learn, then the learning problem $(\vdash_N, LB, LE, NLH)$ on any strictly consistent infinite set of examples E_∞ is identified in the limit by the algorithm $NMLearn$.*

Proof. Let $E_\infty = E_\infty^- \cup E_\infty^+$. Then since *Classic-Learn* partially identifies in the limit E_∞ then after some step it will stabilize and there will be a rule H_i such that $\forall j \geq i : H_i = H_j$ and $B, H_i \vdash E_\infty^+$. We call H_i H_S^1. If H_S^1 does not cover any negative example then the concept is identified. If not then at some point the negative examples will be encountered and the second level of the algorithm will be activated. So again because *Classic-Learn* partially identifies in the limit the classical learning problem, at some point after the stabilization of the first rule a second negative rule H_S^2 will be stabilized that will imply all the negative examples that H_S^1 covers. Note that this second rule will identify in the limit the infinite stream of examples $E_2 = E_2^+ \cup E_2^-$, where $E_2^+ = \{e|B \cup H_S^1 \vdash_C e, e \in E_1^-\}$ and $E_2^- = E_\infty - E_2^+$, where $E_1^- = E_\infty^-$. Iterating these arguments we can construct a sequence of rules $H_S^1, H_S^2, \ldots H_S^m$ each of which partially identifies a learning problem on an infinite stream of examples $E_i = E_i^+ \cup E_i^-$ where $E_i^+ = \{e|B \cup H_S^{i-1} \vdash_C e, e \in E_{i-1}^-\}$ and $E_i^- = E_\infty - E_i^+$. Such a finite sequence will not be computed by the algorithm only if the algorithm reaches a point where an enumeration is required or if an unbounded sequence of rules is needed in order to identify the set E_∞. The first case can not occur as E_∞ is strictly consistent. If the second case occurs then note that due to the optimality of the depth of the hypothesis constructed by the $NMLearn$ algorithm (proposition 7) no other finite set of rules can cover E_∞. So the background knowledge and the set E_∞ are not suitable and hence there is nothing to prove for algorithm.

Assume now that $NMLearn$ computes a finite set of rules $H = \{H_1, \ldots, H_m\}$ and terminates without enumeration. Let $E_j^{+/-}$ be the set of examples covered minimally by the rule H_j. We first prove that for every $e \in E_\infty^+$, $B, H \vdash_N e$ (the background knowledge B will be omitted from the premises for the rest of the proof). Let E_{2k+1}^+ be the last set on an odd level in which e occurs. If $2k + 1 = m$ we see that $H_m \vdash_C e$ and hence $H_N \vdash e$. Assume that $2k+1 \neq m$. If $H_{2k+2} \not\vdash_C e$ then for all $2n > 2k + 2$, $H_{2n} \not\vdash_C e$ and then $H \vdash_N e$. If $H_{2k+2} \vdash_C e$ then by construction of $NMLearn$, E_{2k+1}^+ can not be the last set in which e occurs. Hence $H \vdash_N e$, for every $e \in E_\infty^+$.

We next prove that if $e \in E_\infty^-$, then $H \not\vdash_N e$. Assume the contrary and let H_{2k+1} be the last rule on an odd level, such that $H_{2k+1} \vdash_C e$. If $2k + 1 = m$ then the $NMLearn$ will compute a new rule H_{m+1} such that $H_{m+1} \vdash_C e$. This gives a contradiction since H_m is the last such rule. Let $2k + 1 < m$. Then by construction $H_{2k+2} \vdash_C e$. Furthermore, $H_{2k+3} \not\vdash_C e$ since H_{2k+1} is the last rule on an odd level, such that $H_{2k+1} \vdash_C e$. Hence $H \not\vdash_N e$. $\square$

5 Further Discussion

The convergence result presented in the previous section is restricted to the case of strictly consistent sets of examples. Sets of examples that are not strictly consistent reveal important issues for practical systems that address the problem of learning exceptions, both on an algorithmic as well as a conceptual level. The following example is illustrative.

Example 3. Consider the background knowledge $B = \{bird(a), feathered(a),$ $bird(a'), feathered(a'), bird(b), light(b), bird(b'), light(b'), bird(c), feathered(c),$ $broken-wings(c), bird(c'), feathered(c'), broken-wings(c'), bird(d), light(d),$ $big(d), bird(d'), light(d'), big(d')\}$, and the examples $E = E^+ \cup E^-$ where $E^+ = \{flies(a), flies(b), flies(a'), flies(b')\}$ and $E^- = \{flies(c), flies(d), flies(c'),$ $flies(d')\}$. $\square$

In this example the minimal clause of both E^+ and E^- is $flies(x) \leftarrow bird(x)$. The algorithm $NMLearn$ of the previous section will terminate by enumerating the exceptions of the rule $flies(x) \leftarrow bird(x)$. Note however that the following hypothesis:

$$\text{flies(x)} \leftarrow \text{bird(x), feathered(x)}$$
$$\neg \text{flies(x)} \leftarrow \text{bird(x), feathered(x), broken-wings(x)}$$

$$\text{flies(x)} \leftarrow \text{bird(x), light(x)}$$
$$\neg \text{flies(x)} \leftarrow \text{bird(x), light(x), big(x)}$$

covers all the positive examples and none of the negative without the need for any enumeration. In this case (see also example 3.2) it is clear that the single hierarchy language bias is too restrictive as these examples are inherently multi-hierarchical and thus the algorithm is forced to enumerate. In general to avoid enumeration in the $NMLearn$ algorithm whenever it reaches a stage where $E = E'$ holds for R and H', the algorithm can backtrack to the point where R was computed to generate a set of new rules to replace R which are more specific than R in the sense that they have less consequences than those of R. One possible way to do this is to employ the standard "covering approach" where we split the set of examples that we want to cover into smaller subsets and try to cover each of these separately.

The negative input information present in the negative examples can be used in two different ways during the learning process of the algorithm $NMLearn$. On the one hand they can be used within the classical algorithm employed by $NMLearn$ to specialise the monotonic generalization rules that this generates. On the other hand, they can also be used as examples that define a part of the negative concept which forms an exception. We thus see that negative information can play a double role, either that of specialization or that of exception. Clearly each one of these roles on its own is not optimal. In the case where the only role is that of specialization we may have situations (e.g. hierarchical concepts) where it is not possible to find an appropriate theory. On the other hand, if we treat all negative information as exception then we run the risk of been overgeneral and thus overtolerant as the above example 3 shows. In general, a learning system must find a balance between the two different uses of the negative information. One possible strategy to achieve this balance in the algorithm $NMLearn$ is to allow the $Classic\text{-}Learn$ to use the negative examples to specialise as much as possible (without losing coverage of any of the positive examples) and then treat the remaining negative examples as exceptions.

Finally, note that it may happen that some of the negative examples are used neither in the specialization process by the $Classic\text{-}Learn$ algorithm nor as exceptions by $NMLearn$. Those examples remain essentially unused. Hence it is reasonable to require that the learning process should try to learn the part of the negative concept implied by these examples. In fact, this learning of the negated concept is necessary in some situations. Consider the following example.

Example 4. Let $B = \{Republican(a), Republican(b), Quacker(c), Quacker(d)$ and $E = E^+ \cup E^-$, where $E^+ = \{Pacifist(c), Pacifist(d)\}$ and $E^- = \{Pacifist(a), Pacifist(b)\}$. □

The obvious generalization is the clause $Pacifist(x) \leftarrow Quacker(x)$. However, note that from this theory we can entail $Pacifist(m)$ for any m such that $Republican(m)$ and $Quacker(m)$ holds although intuitively in view of the negative examples we do not expect this. If we require that we also learn the concept that generalizes the unused negative examples, the clause $\neg Pacifist(x) \leftarrow Republican(x)$ will be also computed. Then within this new theory under the admissibility semantics, the value of $Pacifist(m)$ is undefined.

This learning of the negative concept can easily be accommodated within our framework by requiring that after $NMLearn$ terminates on the original input of examples a second run is activated to learn input of examples a second run is activated to learn the negative examples unused in the first run. This will give a second (dual) hierarchy whose rules are not related to these of the first hierarchy and thus allow for the possibility of many admissible extensions. As a result of this, under the skeptical semantics, some literals may become undefined. Note that in this way we combine together the non-monotonic learning of a hierarchical concept, as in [16], with learning the negative concept as in [3] and [5].

6 Conclusions-Further work

We have proposed a framework for learning non-monotonic logic programs and have studied within this framework the problem of learning a hierarchical concept from a set of examples. The main features of our approach are (i) the exploitation of a classical learning algorithm that is tolerant to the negative information, (ii) the handling of exceptions through learning the relevant part of the negative concept and (iii) the ability to complete within the same framework the learning of the negative concept. These features have been naturally accommodated within the particular non-monotonic logic programming formalism that we have adopted that embodies together with the NAF principle a form of explicit negation.

Our approach is closely related to that of [16]. Nevertheless, we argue that a further step may be useful if the task is to learn the negative concept completely. This can be easily accommodated within the particular non-monotonic formalism used in this paper. The definition of the negative concept through explicit negation provides a more expressive representation language where undefinetness can be accommodated. The idea of learning the negative concept and thus allowing a three valued semantics, was also used in [5] and [3]. However, in these works the negative concept is not related so strongly to the positive one in the sense that they do not generate explicit hierarchical structures for the concept to be learned. Thus our work provides a framework that links together these works [3], [5], [16] where one can investigate how these different approaches can complement each other. We are planning to test empirically the theoretical work developed here, compare these results with those of [3], [5] and investigate how we can link our approach to these other methods in order to get better results. We also plan to investigate to what extend our techniques can be applied to problems of refining classifications learned by artificial neural network systems.

Other possible directions for further research are the following. One issue is the investigation of the dual nature of negative information for specialization and exceptions as pointed out in section 5.

Another issue is the extension of the non-monotonic learning algorithm along two main directions. The first is to modify the algorithm with incremental learning capabilities ([4]). Preliminary investigations indicate that this can be done in a way analogous to *NM Learn*. Also incremental specialization techniques (e.g. [11], [17]) may be useful in developing incremental variants of the algorithm. The second extension that needs further study is the problem of learning with a background knowledge which is itself non-monotonic. We are currently investigating how classical algorithms such as those based on inverse resolution ([12]) can be modified to work on non-monotonic background knowledge.

Acknowledgements We thank the anonymous referees for many valuable comments. This work was partly supported by the ESPRIT BRA project Compulog 2 no 6810.

References

1. M. Bain and S. Muggleton, Non-monotonic learning. In: J.E. Hayes-Michie and E. Tyugu, eds., *Machine Intelligence 12*. Oxford University Press, 1990
2. K.L. Clark. Negation as failure. In *Logic and databases*, Gallaire and Minker, eds., Plenum Press, 1978.
3. J. Cussens, A. Hunter and A. Srinivasan. Generating explicit ordering for non-monotonic logics. *Proc. of AAAI-93*.
4. L. De Raedt. *Interactive Theory Revision: an Inductive Logic Programming Approach*. Academic Press, 1992.
5. L. De Raedt and M. Bruynooghe. On negation and three-valued logic in interactive concept learning. *Proc. of the 9th European Conference on AI, ECAI-90*, 207-212, 1990.
6. M. Gelfond and V. Lifschitz. The stable model semantics for logic programs. *Proc. of the 5th International Conference and Symposium on Logic Programming*, 1070-1080, MIT Press, 1990.
7. E.M. Gold. Language identification in the limit. *Information and Control*, 10:447-474, 1967.
8. A. Kakas, P. Mancarela and P. M. Dung. The acceptability semantics for logic programs. *Proc. of 11th Inter. Conference on Logic Programming, ICLP-94*, 504-519, MIT Press, 1994.
9. J-U. Kietz and S. Dzeroski. Inductive logic programming and learnability. *SIGART Newsletters*, 5(1), 1994.
10. N. Lavrac and S. Dzeroski. *Inductive Logic Programming: Techniques and Applications*. Ellis Horwood, 1994.

11. C. Ling. Non-Monotonic specialization. *Proc. of the Inductive Logic Programming Workshop, ILP-91*, 1991.
12. S. Muggleton and W. Buntime. Machine invention of first order predicates by inverting resolution. *Proc. of the 5th Inter. Conference on Machine Learning*, 339-352, Kaufmann, 1988.
13. S. Muggleton. Inductive logic programming. *New Generation Computing, 8*, 295-318, 1991.
14. S. Muggleton and L. De Raedt. Inductive logic programming: Theory and methods. submitted.
15. T. Przymusinski, On the declarative and procedural semantics of logic programs. *Journal of Automated Reasoning*, 5, 167-205, 1989.
16. A. Srinivasan, S. Muggleton and M. Bain. Distinguishing exceptions from noise in non-monotonic learning. *Proc. of the International Workshop on Inductive Logic Programming*, S. Muggleton and K. Furukawa, Japan, 1992.
17. S. Wrobel. On the proper definition of minimality in specialization and theory revision. *Proc. of the European Conference on Machine Learning, ECML-93*, Vienna, 1993, LNAI 667, Springer Verlag.
18. A. Van Gelder, K. A. Ross and J. S. Schlipf. Unfounded sets and well-founded semantics for general logic programs. *Proc. of the 7th Symposium on Principles of Database Systems, PODS-88*, 221-230, ACM Press, 1988.

A Comparative Utility Analysis of Case-Based Reasoning and Control-Rule Learning Systems

Anthony G. Francis, Jr. and Ashwin Ram
College of Computing
Georgia Institute of Technology
Atlanta, Georgia 30332-0280
(404) 853-9381, (404) 853-9372
{centaur, ashwin}@cc.gatech.edu

Abstract

The utility problem in learning systems occurs when knowledge learned in an attempt to improve a system's performance degrades performance instead. We present a methodology for the analysis of utility problems which uses computational models of problem solving systems to isolate the root causes of a utility problem, to detect the threshold conditions under which the problem will arise, and to design strategies to eliminate it. We present models of case-based reasoning and control-rule learning systems and compare their performance with respect to the swamping utility problem. Our analysis suggests that case-based reasoning systems are more resistant to the utility problem than control-rule learning systems.[1]

1. Introduction

An interesting asymmetry exists in the patterns of retrieval in case-based reasoning (CBR) and control-rule learning (CRL) systems: to take advantage of past learning experiences, CRL systems need to retrieve rules from memory at each step, whereas CBR systems need retrieve a case only once. Under certain conditions, this asymmetry may provide CBR with an advantage in dealing with the *utility problem*, which arises when knowledge learned in an attempt to improve a system's performance degrades performance instead (HOLDER ET AL. 1990, MINTON 1990). In this paper, we analyze the differences between CBR and CRL systems in the context of a general methodology for the study of the utility problem. Our methodology couples a functional analysis of a problem solving system with a performance analysis of the system's algorithmic and implementational components. This computational model allows us to formally specify the root causes of the utility problem in terms of interactions within the system and to predict the threshold conditions under which the utility problem will arise. Using this methodology, we have found that, while both CBR and CRL systems can suffer from the utility problem, CBR systems have important advantages over CRL systems. In particular, because CBR systems amortize the cost of case retrieval over many adaptation steps, ideal case-based reasoners suffer less severely from the same overhead than CRL systems.

---

[1]This research was supported by the United States Air Force Laboratory Graduate Fellowship Program and the Georgia Institute of Technology.

2. Analyzing the Utility Problem

2.1. What is the Utility Problem?

The utility problem was first detected in PRODIGY/EBL (MINTON 1988). PRODIGY/EBL is a control-rule learning system,[2] a type of system that attempts to improve its problem-solving performance by learning search-control knowledge, called *control rules*, that reduce the amount of search it needs to perform by eliminating dead-end paths and selecting profitable ones. What Minton and others noticed about systems like PRODIGY/EBL was that the system could actually get slower after having learned control rules, rather than faster. At each step in the search space, a CRL system has to match all of its control rules against the current state to determine if they should fire. As that library of control rules grows in size, the cost of matching the control rules often increases to the point that they outweigh the savings in search the rules provide.

This side effect of learning was called the "utility problem": learning designed to improve the system's performance ended up degrading performance instead. Since Minton's discovery, researchers have identified many different types of utility problems, each manifesting itself in slightly different ways. Because some types of utility problems are affected by the hardware architecture of the system and others are largely independent of hardware concerns, we can group the different types of utility problems into two rough classes: architectural utility problems and search-space utility problems (FRANCIS & RAM 1993).

Architectural utility problems arise when learning has the side effect of causing an increase in the costs of basic operations the system performs; for example, in PRODIGY/EBL learning new control rules caused the cost of retrieval to rise. Two types of architectural utility problem have been identified: *swamping*, which arises in systems like PRODIGY/EBL when the cost of matching a large number of rules "swamps" the savings (MINTON 1990); and *expensive chunks*, which arises when a few individual rules are so expensive to match that they outweigh the benefits of the rest (e.g., TAMBE ET AL. 1990). *Search-space utility problems* arise because of the manner in which learning modifies the search performed by a problem solver, and not because of limitations in the system's underlying hardware architecture. Three have been identified in CRL systems: *branching*, which arises when a system learns macro-operators that increase the branching factor of the search space (ETZIONI 1992), *wandering*, which arises when a learner fails to achieve tractability (ETZIONI 1992), and *composability*, which arises when learned control rules interfere with each other (GRATCH & DEJONG 1991).

A full discussion of the different types of utility problems is beyond the scope of this paper; we will focus on swamping, which is the utility problem most commonly encountered in learning systems. In this paper, we will reserve the term "the utility

---

[2] Etzioni (1992) uses the term meta-level problem solvers for control-rule learning systems. We have avoided this term because of the possible confusion with metacognition, which includes systems that "know what they know" (metaknowledge) and systems that reason about their own reasoning processes (metareasoning, or introspection).

problem" for the general utility problem, and will refer to specific versions of the utility problem, such as swamping, by their names.

2.2. The Methodology

We propose the use of algorithmic complexity theory as a tool for the analysis of the utility problem. Our methodology involves analyzing different types of AI systems and decomposing their cognitive architectures into lower-level functional units, including problem-solving engines and memory systems, that can be represented by formal algorithmic models. Our algorithmic approach incorporates both functional-level aspects of the computation, such as the system's cognitive architecture and its knowledge base, and implementation-level aspects, such as the performance characteristics of the system's hardware architecture. This multi-level analysis is crucial for the study of the utility problem because many utility problems arise due to interactions between the functional level of the system and the way that functional computation is actually implemented.

For a comparative analysis to be successful, the AI systems being studied must be modeled with a uniform vocabulary of basic cognitive operations that is sufficient to describe the architectures of a wide range of systems. This uniform representational language will allow us to represent AI systems as *computational models* whose basic operations are identical and thus are suitable for comparative algorithmic complexity analysis. The performance of different systems can then be directly compared in terms of the costs of basic cognitive operations, such as memory retrieval or operator applications. These cognitive operations can in turn be modeled on different hardware architectures to determine their costs and the utility of learning in these systems. Our methodology can therefore be used to identify potential utility problems, as well as to design coping strategies to eliminate their effects.

3. A Quick Introduction to Utility Analysis

3.1. AI Systems and Learning

Formally, we can describe an AI system as a triple (**CA, KB, HA**) of cognitive architecture, knowledge base, and hardware architecture. The *cognitive architecture* **CA** specifies a system in terms of separate functional modules that carry out fixed subtasks in the system, while the *knowledge base* **KB** represents the internal "data" that the **CA** uses to perform its computations. The *hardware architecture* **HA** defines the types of operations that a system can perform at the implementation level, as well as the relative costs of such operations. The cost (and hence the utility) of an operation may be different on different **HA**'s: for example, retrieval might take longer on a serial machine than it would on a parallel machine.

Utility can only be defined in terms of "performance" measures that judge the efficiency of a reasoner, such as execution time, number of states searched, storage space used, or even quality of solution. These *evaluation metrics* measure the costs that a system incurs during its reasoning. Because many utility problems are dependent on the distribution of problems that a system encounters (e.g., TAMBE ET

AL. 1990), we must also represent the *problem set* **PS**, which is defined by a tuple (**S, D**) of a *problem space* **S**, the space of problems a system can encounter, and a *problem distribution* **D**, the probability that the system will encounter a particular problem.

3.2. Utility and the Utility Problem

Given a particular evaluation metric, the *utility* of a learned item can be defined as the change in expectation values of a problem solver's performance on the metric across a problem set (MARKOVITCH & SCOTT 1993). In other words, when we compute the utility of a change to the system's knowledge base with respect to some metric, we want to compute the costs that the system will incur for different problems weighted by the probability that the system will actually encounter those problems. Thus, utility is a function not only of the learned item but also of the learning system, the problem set, and the evaluation metric. The *utility problem* occurs when a learning system makes a change to its knowledge base **KB** with the goal of improving problem solving utility on some metric by a calculated improvement F_c, but which has the side effect of degrading problem solving utility for another (possibly identical) evaluation metric by some actual amount F_a that outweighs the savings (i.e., $F_c < F_a$).

3.3. Dissecting the Utility Problem

In general, utility problems are not global, emergent properties of computation but can instead be tied to specific interactions between the cognitive architecture, the knowledge base and the performance characteristics of the hardware architecture. In a CRL system, the interaction of interest is the relationship between match time and knowledge base size; in a CBR system, a similar interaction exists between case retrieval time and case library size.

We can formally define an *interaction* to be a combination of a set of parameters, a module, and a set of effects. The module represents the part of the **CA** that is responsible for the relationship between independent variables in the interaction (the parameters) and the dependent variables (the effects). *Parameters* represent characteristics of the system's knowledge base, while *effects* represent the performance measures that affected by the interaction. Thus, an interaction defines a function between learning (changes in the knowledge base) and performance (changes in the evaluation metric), mediated by the characteristics of the algorithmic component of the interaction (the module).

Utility problems arise when a learning module in the system causes parameter changes which interact with some cognitive architecture component to produce side effects that impact the performance measures a learning module is designed to improve. This kind of coupling between a learning module and an interaction is a potential *root cause* of a utility problem. For a particular root cause, the calculated improvement F_c is the savings that the learning module is designed to perform, while the actual cost F_a is the actual change in performance taking into account the side effects of the interaction.

By comparing the algorithmic behavior of the learning module, the root cause interaction it is paired with, and the cost and savings functions that they contribute, we can compute *threshold conditions* — limiting values for the parameter changes that the system can tolerate before the actual costs exceed the calculated improvement and the system encounters a utility problem. Eliminating the general utility problem involves identifying the root causes of particular utility problems that can arise in a system and designing *coping strategies* that prevent their threshold conditions from being satisfied.

4. Modeling CRL and CBR Systems

The baseline for comparison of the computational model approach is the *unguided problem solver*. Unguided problem solvers use knowledge-free weak methods, and are always guaranteed to find a solution if one exists; one such method is breadth-first search. Given a problem p whose solution is a path of length d—which we shall call the *depth* or *difficulty* of the problem—an unguided problem solver will expand on the average b^d nodes during its search, where b is the branching factor of the search space. The number of nodes that the system expands for a problem p is termed the *complexity* of a problem and is denoted C_p. Figure 1 depicts the search space of an unguided problem solver.

The only knowledge library that an unguided problem solver uses is its *operator library*; its algorithm consists of applying whatever operators are allowable in all of the possible sequences that begin with its starting point. The unguided problem solver serves as a "baseline" against which learning systems can be compared because it is the "worst" system, in terms of performance, that is capable of solving a particular problem in a given search space. An unguided problem solver solves problems in exponential time in the size of the problem; much of "intelligence" can be viewed as attempts to reduce this combinatorial explosion through the use of heuristics or other techniques (NEWELL & SIMON 1975; RAM & HUNTER 1992; SCHANK & ABELSON 1977; SIMON 1993).

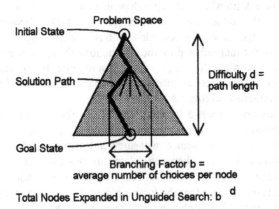

Figure 1. Unguided Search

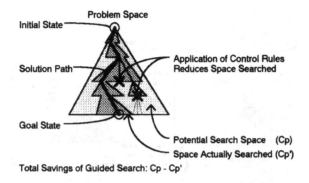

Figure 2. Search Guided by Control Rules

4.1. Control-Rule Learning Systems

Learning systems improve over the unguided problem solver model by finding ways to reduce or eliminate search. A control-rule learning system reduces search by retrieving and applying *control rules* at each state it visits during problem solving, giving it the ability to select or reject states. This control knowledge is a completely different kind of knowledge than operator knowledge and must be stored in a separate *control rule library*. If a system's control rule library is empty and control rules are not available, the problem solver resorts to blind search. Once a solution path has been found, the correct decisions can be cached in the library as control rules that will guide the problem solver in similar situations in the future. This model, while simplified, is a good approximation of many existing systems, including Soar and Prodigy. Figure 2 depicts the guided search of a CRL system.

4.2. Case-Based Reasoners

Case-based reasoning is primarily experience-based; when a case-based reasoner encounters a new problem, it checks its *case library* of past problem solving episodes, or *cases*, looking for a similar case that it can adapt to meet the needs of the new problem. Our model of CBR[3] has two primary knowledge libraries: the case library itself, indexed so that the most appropriate case can be retrieved in new problem-solving situations, and an *adaptation library* that stores *adaptation operators* that are used to transform the cases once they are retrieved. When a case-based reasoner is presented with a problem, it retrieves an appropriate past case based on the problem's features, its goals, and the indices it has in its case library. Once a case has been retrieved, the case is adapted by performing search in the space of problem paths: the

---

[3]This model leaves out some of the stages of a full-fledged case-based reasoner, such as situation assessment and credit/blame assignment (KOLODNER 1993), but contains the core "case-based" elements of the full case-based reasoning approach.

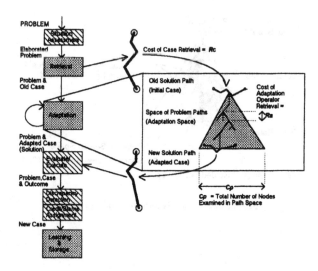

Figure 3. Search in the Space of Problem Paths

adaptation operators are used to transform entire paths into new paths until a satisfactory solution path is achieved. Figure 3 depicts this search in the space of problem paths. Once the new solution is found, it is stored in the case library, indexed by the goals of the current problem for future retrieval.

5. Analyzing Retrieval Costs

To illustrate how computational models can be used to analyze utility effects in different kinds of problem solving systems, consider retrieval costs in CRL and CBR systems—how many retrievals are made, and how much does each of those retrievals cost? Retrieval is often cited as the core source of power for CBR systems, yet the cost of retrieval is a critical factor in the swamping utility problem. An examination of retrieval costs, both before and after learning, in CRL and CBR systems reveals both the source of the swamping problem and potential mechanisms for its solution.

Because the focus of this comparison is on the differences in retrieval between CBR and CRL systems, we will make the simplifying assumption that "all other things are held equal." Specifically, we will assume that both the CRL and CBR systems operate on the same problem set, and moreover that the problem space they function in is defined by the same operator library.

We define a basic operation of retrieval, R, which extracts an item (such as a case or operator) from a knowledge library based on some matching function. In general, for a given hardware architecture **HA**, the cost of retrieval for a knowledge library i, denoted R_i, is a function of both the library i and the item to be retrieved, r: $R_i = f(r,i)$. Some of the features of a knowledge library that affect retrieval time are the number and organization of items in the system's knowledge library. However, for a serial hardware architecture, $\mathbf{HA_s}$, the most important variable in this cost function is the number of items in the knowledge library, K_i. We will approximate this serial cost function with $R_i = cK_i$, where c is a constant multiplier that approximates the (nearly) linear cost function for matching on serial systems like HA_s. For the purposes of this paper, we will ignore the possible variations in the match cost of each individual item, as well as other issues dependent on more specifics of the cognitive architecture of the memory system and the hardware architecture upon which it runs.

Because the learning operations in both case-based reasoners and control-rule learning systems have the effect of increasing the size of knowledge libraries in the system, the learning modules in both types of systems, combined with the retrieval time interactions in each, form potential root causes of the utility problem. The particular interaction we will examine, therefore is the retrieval time interaction: the relationship between the system parameters R_i (number of retrieval operations) and K_i (knowledge library size), and the effect t (running time). Given these definitions, let us examine the actual dynamics of learning and retrieval in CRL and CBR systems and attempt to establish the threshold conditions for the utility problem in each.

5.1. Retrieval in CRL systems

In its initial state, without control rules, a CRL system is equivalent to an unguided problem solver. It searches C_p states, retrieving a set of operators at each step with a cost of R_o. Thus, the total cost, in retrievals, of the initial system is C_pR_o. After the system has learned a set of control rules, it has the capacity to guide its search. The number of states searched is reduced to C_p', where $C_p' < C_p$. However, in addition to retrieving a set of operators, it also needs to retrieve control rules at each step; thus, the cost for solving a problem rises to $C_p'(R_o+R_c)$.

The expected savings that CRL brings are the costs of the states that the problem solver avoids, or just $(C_p - C_p')R_o$. The added costs are the costs of matching the control rules at each step, $C_p'R_c$. Obviously, the utility problem will arise when the added costs exceed the expected savings. Thus, the threshold condition is $(C_p - C_p')R_o < C_p'R_c$; in other words, when the cost of retrieval outweighs the benefits of individual rules. This is, in effect, the swamping utility problem. But will this threshold condition ever be met? To determine this, we must examine how large the expected savings in states can become, and how that compares to the added costs of retrieval.

In the limit, the maximum search reduction is to a single path ($C_p' = d$), and operator retrieval costs are constant ($R_o' = R_o$) since the library of operators the system uses does not change in size. The *maximum expected savings* possible for any problem are thus $(C_p - d)R_o$. In contrast, the cost of retrieving control rules (R_c) increases without bound as the control base K_c increases in size; in the limit, the added costs associated with a rulebase are $dR_c = dc(K_c)$ and thus can outweigh the maximum possible savings. Therefore, the threshold conditions *can* be met and the CRL system will encounter the utility problem.

These results indicate that swamping is a function of the potential speedup of learned items, the cost function of retrieval (which is itself dependent on retrieval strategies and machine architecture), and the number of items a system needs to learn. If the system converges on a bounded set of learned items and the hardware slowdown never approaches the utility of those items, the system will never be swamped.[4] If the learned items arc of low utility, or if the learner never converges on a bounded set, as might be the case for an open-world or multidomain system, then the swamping problem can eliminate the benefits of the learned rules.

5.2. Retrieval in Case-Based Reasoners

To analyze utility effects in case-based reasoning systems, we need to measure the performance of a CBR system as it learns. To provide a basis for this measurement, we assume that a CBR system that does not have an appropriate case in memory can resort to some method (e.g., adaptation of a "null case," or using first principles problem solving to produce a sketchy case which can then be adapted), and this method is no worse than an unguided problem solver. Most existing CBR systems have such a last-resort method; for example, the earliest case-based reasoner, MEDIATOR, had a rule-based problem solving method that it could fall back on if no case was available (KOLODNER & SIMPSON 1988).

A CBR system that resorts to null-case adaptation beginning with no experiences must still incur the cost of retrieving the null case (R_c) and then search the space of problem paths until the case has been adapted into a satisfactory solution. Under our earlier assumptions, the total number of paths the system examines is C_p, and one adaptation retrieval (R_a) occurs per step. Thus, the total cost of case adaptation before learning is $R_c + C_p R_a$. After the system has learned a library of cases, it will still need to retrieve a case from the library but each case will require much less adaptation, reducing the number of paths examined to C_p' where $C_p' << C_p$. Also, the cost of retrieving cases may increase to R_c' where $R_c' > R_c$. Thus, the total costs are $R_c' + C_p' R_a$.

To evaluate these results we must again examine the benefits and costs of case retrieval. The expected savings are the costs of the states that the problem solver avoids: $(C_p - C_p') R_a$, while the added costs are the increased costs of retrieval of cases $R_c' - R_c = \Delta R_c$. In the limit, the cost of retrieval increases without bound as the casebase increases in size: $R_c' = c(K_c)$. However, as we approach the limit the casebase contains many appropriate cases and little adaptation needs to be done— perhaps only one or two steps. In general, whenever the threshold condition $(C_p - C_p') R_a < \Delta R_c$ is met, the cost of retrieval outweighs the benefits of case adaptation; under these conditions, CBR systems will be swamped.

---

[4] For example, on a parallel machine with a logarithmic cost function $R_i = c(\log K_i)$, the threshold condition $(C_p - C_p') R_o < C_p' c(\log K_c)$ may never be met in a closed-world domain in which a small set of knowledge items learned by rote are adequate for performance. If the learning system successfully converges on a small enough set, the logarithmic slowdown will be negligible compared to the potential savings. (This condition can arise on serial architectures as well, but because the cost function is linear in the size of the knowledge base the constraints on the size of the learned set are much more severe.)

5.3. Advantages of Case-Based Reasoning

While this analysis reveals that both control-rule learners and CBR systems can suffer from the swamping utility problem, it also reveals that CBR systems have important advantages over CRL systems.

One advantage of CBR systems is that they have a greater potential improvement than CRL systems. Even if a CRL system learns enough rules to guide search completely, with no false paths, the control rules and operators must nevertheless be retrieved and applied at each step; this means the minimum cost of solution in a CRL system will be dR_oR_c. In contrast, if a case that completely solves the current problem is retrieved from the case library, no adaptation will need to be done and the minimum cost will be just R_c. In practice, it is just as unrealistic to assume that the case library will have an exact case as it is to assume that a CRL system will be able to completely guide search. Some adaptation will need to be done, for a total cost of $C_p'R_a + R_c$. The precise tradeoffs between case-based and CRL systems depend on the particular domain, but nevertheless the *potential* savings are greater for CBR systems.

Another advantage CBR systems have over CRL systems is that cases are retrieved only once during the lifetime of problem solving. For a CRL system to avoid swamping, the increase in cost of retrieval of a control rule must be less than the fraction of total states that the system avoids in guided problem solving times the cost of an operator: $\Delta R_c < R_o(C_p - C_p')/C_p'$. For a CBR system, on the other hand, the increase in cost of a case retrieval must be less than the cost of the number of adaptation steps avoided: $\Delta R_c < R_a(C_p - C_p')$. The missing C_p' term in the denominator of the CBR equation arises because the increased cost of retrieval of control rules are incurred at each step in the search space, whereas the increased cost

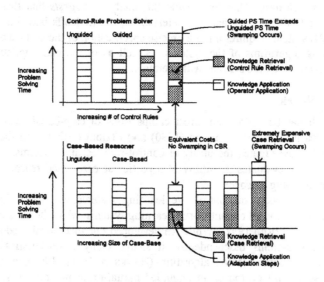

Figure 4. Comparing Control Rules and Cases

of case retrieval is incurred only once during problem solving for a case-based reasoner. In other words, CBR systems *amortize* the cost of case retrieval across all adaptations, making them much more resistant to increases in retrieval costs than CRL systems.

Figure 4 illustrates this phenomenon. Each bar graph represents the time a problem solver takes to solve a problem plotted against its knowledge base size; white blocks in the bar graph represent problem solving or adaptation steps, while grey blocks represent knowledge retrievals. Because a CRL system makes a retrieval from memory at each step, the costs of retrieval (illustrated by the size of the grey blocks) can outweigh the savings of reduced search more quickly than they can in a case-based reasoner, in which retrieval from a large knowledge library is (ideally) performed only once during problem solving.

This amortization also makes CBR more amenable to solutions to the swamping problem, such as deletion policies or indexing schemes. In order to be effective, any coping strategy needs to reduce retrieval time to the point that the threshold conditions are never satisfied. For a CRL system, this upper limit on retrieval time is $R_c < R_o(C_p-C_p')/C_p'$; for a CBR system, this upper limit is $R_c < R_a(C_p-C_p')$, a much higher (and hence much less stringent) limit on the maximum time retrieval can take for a system to be guaranteed to avoid swamping.

Whether the benefits suggested by this analysis will be realized in practice depends critically on other factors that may affect the cost-benefit relationships within the system. Specifically, this analysis claims that, for CBR and CRL systems operating over the same problem set and same operator library, an identical increase in retrieval costs is less harmful to the case-based system than it is to the CRL system. However, the actual retrieval costs of the two systems may be different over the same learning history; moreover, the two types of systems may differ in the amount of improvement they gain from learning. Therefore, while this analysis *suggests* that there may be advantages for CBR systems, actually determining the tradeoffs between particular CBR and CRL systems requires a more precise specification of the costs and specifics of the learning algorithms of the systems, as well as of the characteristics of the problem set over which the systems will operate.

6. Related Work

Little research has been done on direct comparisons of case-based reasoning and control-rule learning systems. Minton (1990) and Etzioni (1992) have theoretically and empirically investigated the utility of control-rule learning systems, and Koton (1989) empirically evaluates the utility of a particular case-based reasoning system against a non-learning reasoner.

Our theoretical model of control-rule learning systems was based in part on Etzioni's theoretical model of control-rule learning systems, which he calls meta-level problem solvers (ETZIONI 1992). While we developed our theoretical model of case-based reasoning systems independently, it shares many characteristics with the Systematic Plan Adaptor (SPA) algorithm (HANKS & WELD 1995), a case-based reasoning system built on top of an unguided partial-order planning system called SNLP (BARRETT & WELD 1994).

A closely related body of work concerns DerSNLP (IHRIG & KAMBHAMPATI 1994). DerSNLP is a derivational analogy system also layered on top of SNLP. Ihrig and Kambhampati use the DerSNLP framework to theoretically and empirically evaluate the efficiency of plan-space and state-space planning systems. While their work and ours both focus on comparative theoretical analysis of AI systems, their work compares two different planning algorithms in the context of the same learning algorithm and our work compares two different learning algorithms in the context of the same planning system.

7. The Bottom Line

The utility problem is caused by interactions between a system's learning modules and other portions of a system and can arise completely independently of hardware concerns. Analyzing the utility problem at an algorithmic level allows us to identify the root causes responsible for the problem and to identify the threshold conditions under which the problem will arise; solving the utility problem involves applying coping strategies which prevent these threshold conditions from occurring. Our uniform framework for utility analysis also facilitates the direct comparison of different systems on the utility issues. We are currently extending this framework to account for more factors that can affect the utility problem, such as domain boundedness, representation language and indexing vocabulary.

Several features of CBR make it resistant to the utility problem. First, cases have the potential to eliminate vast amounts of problem solving, providing improvements robust enough to survive large increases in retrieval time. Second, because the cost of case retrieval is amortized over many adaptation steps, ideal case-based reasoners suffer less severely from the same overhead than CRL systems. Finally, this amortization makes CBR systems more amenable to coping strategies than CRL systems.

References

Barret, A. & Weld, D. (1994). Partial order planning: evaluating possible efficiency gains. *Artificial Intelligence, 67* (1), 71-112.

Etzioni, O. (1992) An Asymptotic Analysis of Speedup Learning. In *Machine Learning: Proceedings of the 9th International Workshop*, 1992.

Francis, A. and Ram, A. (1993). Computational Models of the Utility Problem and their Application to a Utility Analysis of Case-Based Reasoning. In *Proceedings of the Third International Workshop on Knowledge Compilation and Speedup Learning*, pages 48-55, University of Massachusetts at Amherst, June 30, 1993.

Gratch, J.M. and Dejong, G.F. (1991) Trouble with gestalts: The composability problem in control learning. Technical Report, University of Illinois at Urbana-Champaign, April 1991.

Hanks, S. & Weld, D.S. (1995). A domain-independent algorithm for plan adaptation. *Journal of Artificial Intelligence Research* 2 (1995), 319-360.

Holder, L.B.; Porter, B.W.; Mooney, R.J. (1990). The general utility problem in machine learning. In *Machine Learning: Proceedings of the Seventh International Conference*, 1990.

Ihrig, L. & Kambhampati, S. (1994). On the Relative Utility of Plan-Space v. State-Space Planning in a Case-Based Framework, Technical Report 94-006, Department of Computer Science and Engineering, 1994. Arizona State University.

Kolodner, J.L. & Simpson, R.L. (1988). The Mediator: A case study of a case-based reasoner. Georgia Institute of Technology, School of Information and Computer Science, Technical Report no. GIT-ICS-88/11. Atlanta, Georgia.

Kolodner, J.L. (1993). *Case-based Reasoning*. Morgan Kaufmann, 1993.

Koton, P. A. (1989). A Method for Improving the Efficiency of Model-Based Reasoning Systems. Laboratory for Computer Science, MIT, Cambridge, MA. Hemisphere Publishing, 1989.

Markovitch, S. and Scott, P.D. (1993) Information Filtering: Selection Methods in Learning Systems. *Machine Learning*, 10: 113-151.

Minton, S. (1988). Quantitative results concerning the utility of explanation-based learning. In *Proceedings of the Seventh National Conference on Artificial Intelligence*, Morgan Kaufmann, 1988.

Minton, S. (1990). Quantitative results concerning the utility of explanation-based learning. *Artificial Intelligence*, 42(2-3), March 1990.

Newell, A. & Simon, H.A. (1975). Computer Science as Empirical Inquiry: Symbols and Search. Reprinted in Haugeland, J., (ed.). *Mind Design: Philosophy, Psychology, Artificial Intelligence*, chapter 1, pp 35-66. MIT Press, 1981.

Ram, A. & Hunter, L. (1992) The Use of Explicit Goals for Knowledge to Guide Inference and Learning. *Applied Intelligence*, 2(1):47-73.

Schank, R. & Abelson, R. (1977). *Scripts, Plans, Goals and Understanding*. Lawrence Erlbaum Associates, Hillsdale, NJ.

Simon, H.A. (1993). Artificial Intelligence as an Experimental Science. Invited Talk. Abstracted in *Proceedings of the Eleventh National Conference on Artificial Intelligence*, page 853, July 11-15, 1993.

Tambe, M.; Newell, A.; Rosenbloom, P. S. (1990). The Problem of Expensive Chunks and its Solution by Restricting Expressiveness. *Machine Learning*, 5:299-348, 1990.

A Minimization Approach to Propositional Inductive Learning

Dragan Gamberger

Ruđer Bošković Institute, 41000 Zagreb, Croatia

Abstract. An approach to the problem of propositional inductive learning of if-then-else rules, different from the commonly used ones, is presented in the paper. Main differences are: literal selection process that searches for the smallest set of literals so that the completely correct rule for all learning examples can be constructed and the nonnormal form of the generated rules built by the search for necessary and sufficient conditions of example classes. It is also presented how iterative application of the literal selection process can solve the problem of learning from noisy domains by appropriate exclusion of some learning examples. The results of application of the system that includes described algorithms on a few publicly available domains are discussed.

1 Introduction

The well known propositional inductive learning systems like ID3,AQ15,CN2, C4.5 have already been successfully applied on different learning domains [10, 8, 3, 12]. Although the research interests have moved towards learning first-order relations [11], some recent results have independently shown that the problem of propositional induction is neither completely solved yet. The main problem is, as shown in [2], that every of the known systems is well suited for some class of the problems while it can perform rather bad on the others. This is especially obvious for noisy domains when tree pruning or rule truncation must be used [1]. Also the results of application of m-estimates [4] as well as the application of CNF for generated rules [9] undoubtedly demonstrate that some modifications of the well known algorithms will be necessary in the future in order to make them more general. Besides, the development of LINUS shows that under some assumptions the propositional systems can be effectively used in building the first-order learning systems [7], what additionally stresses the importance of reliable and general propositional systems.

In this paper some novel ideas in building rule based propositional inductive learning systems, already applied on the ILLM (Inductive Learning by Logic Minimization) system will be presented [5]. Main differences to the known systems are as follows: literal selection process, the form of generated rules and noise handling procedure. These topics are described each in a separate section. At the end some comparative results are presented.

The term 'literal' is used in the paper in the sense as in [9]. It is equivalent to the term selector in AQ systems and logical test in ILLM. The form or complexity of literals is not restricted in any sense so that presented algorithms can be combined by some constructive induction methods or that new literals can be formed due to the background knowledge.

In the paper only the basic inductive learning problem with only two example classes, positive and negative, will be discussed. By known techniques the results can be applied on many-classes problems as well.

2 Literal Selection Process

All known propositional inductive learning systems select significant literals (attributes) and generate the rule (decision tree) at the same time. Some forms of information gain metric based on the total number of positive and negative examples before and after the selection is always used. Details can be found in [6, 3]. In ILLM system the procedures for literal selection and rule generation are separated. The aim of the first ILLM step is to select significant literals, and after it is completely done they are used in the rule generation process (second ILLM step described in the next section). Another difference is that the selection process does not use the information based metric. The significant literals are selected so that the smallest number of different literals should be used in the rule that will satisfy all learning examples.

This property has two main consequences. The first one is that in the basic form the suggested algorithm can work only on noise-free domains without contradictions. In Sec. 4 it will be shown how its iterative usage can enable its application on noisy domains as well. The second one is that total number of positive and negative examples that can be distinguished by some literal does not influence the selection process in the suggested algorithm. It means that, for example, presence or addition of example copies in the learning set can not change the subset of selected literals, what is not true for other systems. This characteristic enables elimination of example copies, and elimination of some other learning examples under conditions defined later in the section, before the actual beginning of the search process. This can simplify the learning task.

The two step inductive learning algorithm and so defined its first step introduces a completely new paradigm in inductive learning: the importance of the pairs of examples, each pair consisting of a positive and a negative learning example. Such pairs are called 1/0 pairs in the rest of the paper. Their importance stems from the fact that if we want to have a set of literals such that it is possible to form a rule that uses only literals from the set, then for any possible 1/0 pair a literal that covers it must be an element of the set [5]. A 1/0 pair is covered by a literal if it is true for the positive example and not true for the negative example in the pair. This directly implies the importance of 1/0 pairs built of the positive and negative learning examples that differ in a small number of attributes because such pairs are covered by a small number of literals and at least one of them must be an element of any minimal set of selected literals.

The main advantage of the algorithm is that it is concentrated on the search for the globally most relevant literals. The disadvantage is that it has space complexity $O(e \cdot l)$ and time complexity $O(e^2 \cdot l^K)$, where e is number of examples, l total number of possible literals and K number of selected literals. The algorithms time complexity can be reduced to $O(e^2 \cdot l \cdot K)$ if heuristic instead of exhaustive search is used. In this case space complexity is $O(e^2)$ and it can not be guaranteed that the real minimum is found. Practically, this algorithm characteristic limits its usage to the domains of up to 1000 learning examples. For greater domains a windowing procedure based on 1/0 pairs of small distance must be applied.

The search for the smallest subset of literals, either exhaustive or heuristic, can be realized in a few different ways. In the ILLM so called covering tables are introduced that, besides clear algorithm definition and fast manipulations, enable some reduction of the starting search space. These tables can be effectively used during the second algorithm step as well.

2.1 Definition and Reduction of Covering Tables

For learning domain two covering tables can be defined: one for positive and the other one for negative examples. The first one is called TO and it has as much rows as there are positive examples, while the other one is called TZ and it has as much rows as there are negative examples. Both tables have the same number of columns and it is equal to the number of possible literals that can be used. The elements of both tables are 1 and 0, including the cases when learning examples have some attributes of unknown value. An element of TO table has value 1 if the corresponding literal (by column) is true, or could be true by appropriate substitution of unknown values, for the corresponding example (by row). An element of TZ table has value 1 if the literal is *not true*, or could be *not true*, for the corresponding negative learning example. All other elements of TO and TZ tables have value 0. When a literal has value 1 for an example, either positive or negative, it is said that the example is covered by the literal.

After TO and TZ tables are formed for the domain, whole relevant information necessary for rule generation is contained in them. The algorithm does not need any further access to the learning examples.

The first ILLM step can be also defined as the minimal covering problem with object to find a minimal subset of literals that covers all *1/0 pairs*. The problem can be reduced if some columns and/or rows of TO and TZ tables are eliminated.

A column for a literal can be eliminated from both TO and TZ tables if there is another literal that covers the same, and potentially also some additional 1/0 pairs of examples. The condition is equivalent to the requirement that the column that can be eliminated has values 0 at least for all rows of both TO and TZ tables as some other column that will remain in the tables.

An example can be eliminated from either TO or TZ table if it is covered by same or potentially some additional literals as another example from the same class. The condition is equivalent to the requirement that the row that can be eliminated has values 1 in at least all columns as another row that would remain in the same table.

3 Form of Generated Rules

In most inductive learning systems that generate rules DNF is used. By experiments on 5 natural data sets, it has been recently shown that the application of CNF may lead in some cases to more concise rules [9]. In this section the concept of necessary and sufficient conditions which can result in the nonnormal form of rules that is generalization of both DNF and CNF will be presented. This algorithm is implemented in the second step of the ILLM system. It is supposed that the algorithm starts from the minimal set of literals generated by the first algorithm step although it can start from any set, including the set of all possible literals, that enables the rule that satisfies all learning examples to be constructed. The reason for the execution of the first step is, beside simplification of the rule generation process, selection of the globally significant literals.

A sufficient condition is a literal or conjunction of literals that covers some positive and all negative examples. A necessary condition is a literal or disjunction of literals that covers all positive and some negative examples. The rule generation process is iterative repetition of the following procedure:

For the given set of positive and negative learning examples (presented by TO and TZ tables respectively) find the minimal sufficient and the minimal necessary condition.

- If the minimal sufficient condition has less literals than the minimal necessary condition, or if the number of literals is equal but the sufficient condition covers greater number of examples than the necessary condition, then generate a part of the rule consisting of the minimal sufficient condition in the form of one literal or more literals connected by AND operation. Eliminate positive examples covered by the condition. If TO is empty stop rule generation process. Else add the sign of OR operation to the generated rule in order to connect the generated condition with the remaining part that will be generated in succeeding iterations.
- Else, if minimal necessary condition has less literals than minimal sufficient condition, or if the number of literals is equal but the necessary condition covers greater number of examples than the sufficient condition, then generate a part of the rule consisting of the minimal necessary condition. This condition has the form of one literal or more literals connected by OR operation and written in brackets. Eliminate negative examples covered by the necessary condition. If TZ table is empty stop the rule generation process. Else add the sign of AND operation to the generated rule in order to connect the generated condition with the remaining part that will be generated in succeeding iterations.

The main advantage of the approach is that it adapts the generated rule form to each domain. Beside DNF and CNF it can generate mixed forms that can be easily understood by users as well. The obtained rule form can be interpreted also as an extraction of common literals or groups of literals in order to simplify its presentation.

Example 1. A rule generated by literals lt1,lt2, .. , lt9 may look like:

$$\underbrace{lt1}_{\text{Suff.}} \lor \underbrace{lt2 \cdot lt3}_{\text{Suff.}} \lor \underbrace{[lt4 \lor lt5]}_{\text{Nec.}} \cdot [\underbrace{lt6}_{\text{Suff.}} \lor \underbrace{lt7}_{\text{Nec.}} \cdot \underbrace{lt8}_{\text{Nec.}} \cdot \underbrace{lt9}_{\text{Nec.}}]$$

4 Noise Handling Procedure

The algorithm described in Sec. 2 and 3 generates a rule that satisfies all learning examples. Because of its two step nature, truncation or similar procedures implemented on known inductive algorithms, can not be easily applied. However, this algorithm has rather precise measure of the complexity of the generated rules: the number of literals selected by its first step. This enables an iterative approach to the problem of noise in the learning domain.

The algorithm starts with the first step described in Sec.2. It selects the minimal set of literals that enables construction of the rule that satisfies all learning examples. Now, it is tested if by elimination of any of learning examples (or by elimination of a pair of learning examples in great domains) the minimal set of literals could be reduced. If yes, exclude the example (or the example pair) from the learning domain and repeat the procedure till the minimal set that can not be further easily reduced is obtained. That minimal set is input of the second step described in Sec.3. The formed rule will satisfy at least all nonexcluded examples.

The test that exclusion of an example (or an example pair) can reduce minimal literal set is a very complex task. But if the search space is reduced to the subsets of the already generated minimal set then it can be easily realized in the following way: for each literal from the minimal set find all 1/0 pairs of learning examples that are covered exclusively by the literal. If all this 1/0 pairs have an example (or an example pair) in common, by its elimination this literal will not be necessary any more.

The comparison of this noise handling procedure and the known truncation techniques is a problem of further research. It is obvious that the presented approach opens some novel possibilities like directed control of the class of excluded examples (positive or negative) what can be interesting for some, especially medical, domains.

5 Example

A small artificial learning domain is here included to show the presented concepts. In Table 1 the learning set is presented. There are 10 examples with 3 attributes of the quality type. Their names are c.bg (background color), c.frame (frame color), and c.object (object color). The classes are harmony 1 and 0. Attribute values are different colors.

For this learning set it is possible to generate 27 different literals of the form $(input = color)$, $(input \neq color)$, $(inputA = inputB)$, and $(inputA \neq inputB)$.

Table 1. Learning set used to learn the concept harmony

s	s	s	o
c.bg	c.frame	c.object	harmony
black	blue	yellow	1
red	yellow	yellow	1
blue	blue	white	1
red	white	white	1
yellow	blue	blue	1
white	yellow	yellow	0
black	red	red	0
red	white	blue	0
red	grey	white	0
white	grey	yellow	0

They are: $(c.bg = black)$, $(c.bg = red)$, $(c.bg = blue)$, $(c.bg = yellow)$, $(c.bg \neq white)$, $(c.bg \neq black)$, $(c.bg \neq red)$, $(c.frame = blue)$, $(c.frame = yellow)$, $(c.frame = white)$, $(c.frame \neq yellow)$, $(c.frame \neq red)$, $(c.frame \neq white)$, $(c.frame \neq grey)$, $(c.object = yellow)$, $(c.object = white)$, $(c.object = blue)$, $(c.object \neq yellow)$, $(c.object \neq red)$, $(c.object \neq blue)$, $(c.object \neq white)$, $(c.bg = c.frame)$, $(c.bg = c.object)$, $(c.frame = c.object)$, $(c.bg \neq c.frame)$, $(c.bg \neq c.object)$, $(c.frame \neq c.object)$. For these literals the generated TO and TZ tables are presented in Table 2.

Table 2. TO and TZ tables for 27 literals

TO

```
1 0 0 0 1 0 1 1 0 0 1 1 1 1 1 0 0 0 1 1 1 0 0 0 1 1 1
0 1 0 0 1 1 0 0 1 0 0 1 1 1 1 0 0 0 1 1 1 0 0 1 1 1 0
0 0 1 0 1 1 1 1 0 0 1 1 1 1 0 1 0 1 1 1 0 1 0 0 0 1 1
0 1 0 0 1 1 0 0 0 1 1 1 0 1 0 1 0 1 1 1 0 0 0 1 1 1 0
0 0 0 1 1 1 1 1 0 0 1 1 1 1 0 0 1 1 1 1 1 0 0 1 1 1 0
```

TZ

```
1 1 1 1 1 0 0 1 0 1 1 0 0 0 0 1 1 1 0 0 0 1 1 0 0 0 1
0 1 1 1 0 1 0 1 1 1 0 1 0 0 1 1 1 0 1 0 0 1 1 0 0 0 1
1 0 1 1 0 0 1 1 1 0 0 0 1 0 1 1 0 0 0 1 0 1 1 1 0 0 0
1 0 1 1 0 0 1 1 1 0 0 0 1 1 0 1 0 0 0 1 1 1 1 0 0 0
1 1 1 1 1 0 0 1 1 1 0 0 0 1 0 1 1 1 0 0 0 1 1 1 0 0 0
```

The columns in the tables correspond to the literals in the same order as they are cited. The rows of TO table correspond to ex1-ex5 and rows of TZ table to ex6-ex10. It can be noticed that in the tables there are some literals covered by other literals (e.g. column 1 is covered by column 8). After their elimination there remain only 11 literals that are interesting for rule generation. They are: $(c.bg = red)$, $(c.frame = blue)$, $(c.frame = white)$, $(c.object = yellow)$, $(c.object = white)$, $(c.bg \neq white)$, $(c.frame \neq red)$, $(c.frame \neq white)$, $(c.frame \neq grey)$, $(c.object \neq blue)$, $(c.frame = c.object)$. The reduced TO and TZ tables are presented in Table 3.

Table 3. TO and TZ tables after column reduction

TO

ex1	0 1 0 1 0 1 1 1 1 1 0
ex2	1 0 0 1 0 1 1 1 1 1 1
ex3	0 1 0 0 1 1 1 1 1 1 0
ex4	1 0 1 0 1 1 1 0 1 1 1
ex5	0 1 0 0 0 1 1 1 1 0 1

TZ

ex6	1 1 1 0 1 1 0 0 0 0 0
ex7	1 1 1 1 1 0 1 0 0 0 0
ex8	0 1 0 1 1 0 0 1 0 1 1
ex9	0 1 1 1 0 0 0 0 1 0 1
ex10	1 1 1 0 1 1 0 0 1 0 1

It can be noted that although none of the rows of the original tables is covered by any other row of the same table, after reduction of the number of the literals (Table 3) ex6 covers ex10. After elimination of the row for ex10, the result is presented by the tables in Table 4. Any further reduction of the number of their rows and columns is not possible.

Table 4. TO and TZ tables after row reduction

TO

ex1	0 1 0 1 0 1 1 1 1 1 0
ex2	1 0 0 1 0 1 1 1 1 1 1
ex3	0 1 0 0 1 1 1 1 1 1 0
ex4	1 0 1 0 1 1 1 0 1 1 1
ex5	0 1 0 0 0 1 1 1 1 0 1

TZ

ex6	1 1 1 0 1 1 0 0 0 0 0
ex7	1 1 1 1 1 0 1 0 0 0 0
ex8	0 1 0 1 1 0 0 1 0 1 1
ex9	0 1 1 1 0 0 0 0 1 0 1

From 4 it can be seen that there are 3 necessary conditions (columns 6,7,9) and 1 sufficient condition (column 2) consisting of only one literal. The sufficient condition is selected because it covers 3 positive examples while each of necessary conditions covers only one negative example. After this selection and elimination of the mentioned 3 positive examples, beside previous 3 necessary conditions two other necessary conditions (columns 1,11) that cover two negative examples each, can be detected in the reduced TO table. By selection of these conditions all negative examples are eliminated. The generated rule has the form:

harmony IF $(c.frame = blue) \lor (c.bg = red) \cdot (c.frame = c.object).$

6 Experimental Results

Apart from the results presented in [5] for the biodegradation domain, there are the concise results of application of the ILLM on three publicly available domains here.

For the 'Breast Cancer' database from the University of Wisconsin Hospitals obtained through UCI repository (699 learning examples), at first the ILLM excluded 24 examples and then selected following 5 literals:

A $(ClumpThickness > 5)$
B $(Uniformity of CellSize > 2)$
C $(Uniformity of CellShape > 2)$
D $(SingleEpithelialCellSize > 2)$
E $(BareNuclei > 3).$

The generated rule

$$\text{malignant IF } CD \lor AB \lor E[A \lor B[C \lor D]]$$

is not correct for 3 malignant and 18 benign learning cases. These results are very similar to those reported in [14] obtained by 3 other learning systems.

For the 'Mushrooms' database created at University of California at Irvine and obtained through the same repository (8124 learning examples), the ILLM used windowing based on 500 examples and after 4 iterations selected following 9 literals:

A $(cap - color = yellow)$
B $(bruises = yes)$
C $(bruises = no)$
D $(odor \neq none)$
E $(gill - spacing = close)$
F $(gill - size = narrow)$
G $(stalk - root = bulbous)$
H $(spore - print - color = green)$
I $(spore - print - color = white)$

The system does not suggest the exclusion of any example and generated the rule

poisenous IF H ∨ CD ∨ AC ∨ [F ∨ D][B ∨ E][I ∨ BE[F ∨ G]]

that is correct for all learning examples. According to the knowledge of the author of the domain, it is the first such result for the domain [13].

For the 'Australian Credit Approval' database obtained from LIACC, University of Porto (690 learning examples), ILLM suggested exclusion of 32 examples and selected 15 literals. Due to its complexity the rule is not presented here. To illustrate the time complexity of the algorithm, let us mention that for that domain with only 14 attributes (descriptors) the selected starting set contained 1010 literals. The reason for such rather great number is that 6 attributes are of continuous type with lot of possible separation values. Even the minimization of covering tables before the first algorithm step did not reduce this number significantly. The minimization algorithm started from 690 learning examples and 969 literals. The result is that for one iteration of the first algorithm step (nonexhaustive search) the execution time was about 2 hours on a HP-Apollo workstation. The total time for the complete rule generation was about 60 hours. Such long execution time in this case is due to attribute characteristics as much as the consequence of very noisy domain and relatively weak correlation between attribute values and example classes. The results obtained by ILLM and other systems prove this statements. Nevertheless, from the rules generated by ILLM for such domains, one can expect relatively good prediction accuracy as well. For 10-fold cross validation on the 'Australian Credit Approval' database the ILLM system had prediction error rate of 13% while the reported error rate for all 22 different systems tested under Statlog project was greater than 13% (according to the results at LIACC, University of Porto).

7   Conclusions

The work shows that although the theory of propositional inductive learning is already well defined there is a need and a possibility for other approaches as well. Specially the generation of rules in a nonnormal form, that is a generalization of both the DNF and CNF, could be interesting for all rule generation systems.

The presented results obtained by the ILLM system for a few publicly available domains show rather great correlation in accuracy of generated rules and in the level of detected noise when compared to the results of commonly used systems. Another encouraging fact shown by the results is that iterative exclusion of 'suspicious' examples from noisy domains is a real alternative to the known algorithm of rule truncation. However, the unsolved problem of both suggested processes for literal selection and noise handling is their time complexity.

Acknowledgements

The 'Wisconsin Breast Cancer' and 'Mushrooms' databases were copied by anonymous ftp from ics.uci.edu from directory pub/machine-learning-databases.

The 'Australian Credit Approval' database was copied by anonymous ftp from ftp.ncc.up.pt from directory pub/statlog/datasets.

References

1. I.Bratko, *Learning and Noise*. Proceedings of MLnet Summer School on Machine Learning and Knowledge Acquisition, Dourdan, France, 1994, pp.121-143.
2. P.Brazdil,J.Gama,B.Henery, *Characterizing the Applicability of Classification Algorithms Using Meta-level Learning*. Proceedings of MLnet Workshop on Industrial Applications of Machine Learning, Dourdan, France, 1994, pp.127-146.
3. P.Clark, T.Niblett, *The CN2 Induction Algorithm*. Machine Learning, Vol.3, 1989, pp.261-284.
4. S.Džeroski, B.Cestnik, I.Petrovski, *Using the m-estimate in Rule Induction*. Journal of Computing and Information Technology - CIT, Vol.1, 1993, pp.37-46.
5. D.Gamberger, S.Sekušak, A.Sabljić, *Modelling Biodegradation by an Example-Based Learning System*. Informatica, Vol.17, 1993, pp.157-166.
6. M.Holsheimer, A.Siebes,*Data Mining The Search for Knowledge in Databases*. Report CS-R9406, CWI, Amsterdam, 1994. (can be obtained by anonymous ftp from ftp.cwi.nl /pub/CWIreports/AA/CS-R9406.ps.Z)
7. N.Lavrač, S.Džeroski, *Weaking the Language Bias in LINUS*. J. Expt. Theor. Artif. Intell., Vol.6, 1994, pp.95-119.
8. R.S.Michalski, I.Mozetič, J.Hong, N.Lavrač, *The Multipurpose Incremental Learning System AQ15 and Its Testing Application to Three Medical Domains*. Proc. Fifth Nat'l Conf. Artificial Intelligence, Morgan Kaufmann, San Mateo, Calif., 1986, pp.1,041-1,045.
9. R.J.Mooney, *Encouraging Experimental Results on Learning CNF*. Technical report, University of Texas, October 1992.
10. J.R.Quinlan, *Induction of Decision Trees*. Machine Learning, Vol.1,1986, pp.81-106.
11. J.R.Quinlan, *Learning Logical Definitions from Relations*. Machine Learning, Vol.5, 1990, pp.239-266.
12. J.R.Quinlan, *C4.5:Programs for Machine Learning*, Morgan Kaufmann, 1992.
13. J.S.Schlimmer, *Concept Acquisition Through Representational Adjustment*, (Technical Report 87-19). Doctoral dissertation, Department of Information and Computer Science, University of California, Irvine, 1987.
14. W.H.Wolberg, O.L.Mangasarian, *Computer-Designed Expert Systems for Breast Cytology Diagnosis*. Analytical and Qauntitative Cytology and Histology, Vol.15, February 1993, pp.67-74.

On Concept Space and Hypothesis Space in Case-Based Learning Algorithms

A D Griffiths and D G Bridge

Department of Computer Science, University of York, YORK YO1 5DD, UK
Email: {tony|dgb}@minster.york.ac.uk

Abstract. In order to learn more about the behaviour of case-based reasoners as learning systems, we formalise a simple case-based learner as a PAC learning algorithm. We show that the case-based representation $\langle CB, \sigma \rangle$ is rich enough to express any boolean function. We define a family of simple case-based learning algorithms which use a single, fixed similarity measure and we give necessary and sufficient conditions for the consistency of these learning algorithms in terms of the chosen similarity measure. Finally, we consider the way in which these simple algorithms, when trained on target concepts from a restricted concept space, often output hypotheses which are outside the chosen concept space. A case study investigates this relationship between concept space and hypothesis space and concludes that the case-based algorithm studied is a less than optimal learning algorithm for the chosen, small, concept space.

1 Introduction

The performance of a case-based reasoning system [13] will change over time as new cases are added to the case base by the problem-solving process. A prudent knowledge engineer might wonder whether the performance will necessarily improve, how quickly the performance of the system might change, or how many exemplars would be required to reach some specific level of accuracy in problem solving.

A simple model of a case memory system is presented here as a basis for answering these questions analytically. The model used is a *functional* one in that the knowledge content of the case memory system is modelled as a mapping between input and output domains. The analysis applied to this model is a *probabilistic, worst case* analysis, in that we apply the PAC learning framework [3] [10] to case-based learning.

For the moment, a number of restrictions are made in order to gain leverage on the problems in hand. To focus on the learning behaviour of the systems, the model abstracts away from many aspects of case-based reasoning systems which are of interest in other contexts such as interactive properties, details of the reasoning process at conceptual and implementation levels and knowledge representation issues such as the choice of abstract indices. Additionally, this paper focuses only on case-based classifiers whose task is to decide whether or not the input description is an instance of some concept.

2 Definitions

Our model is of a case-based classifier operating over the space of N-bit binary vectors. Thus the *example space* in the current work will be referred to as $D_N \triangleq \{0,1\}^N$. $(d)_i$ will be used to stand for the i-th bit of a vector $d \in D_N$. The set of $\{0,1\}$-valued total functions defined over this domain will be denoted $B_N \triangleq (D_N \to \{0,1\})$.

By *hypothesis space* we refer to the set of possible hypotheses that might be output by the case-based learning algorithm over all possible training samples. The term *concept space* on the other hand will be used to refer to some specific subset of B_N from which target concepts for the learning algorithm might be drawn. In particular, section 5 considers the set of *monomial* functions as the concept space for a case-based learning algorithm. A monomial expression U is a combination of no more than N literals chosen without replacement from the set $\{u_1, \ldots, u_N\}$; additionally each chosen literal may be negated before being added to U. The classification function for the expression interprets U as a conjunction of the (possibly negated) literals:

$$h_U^N(d) = \begin{cases} 1 \; if \; \forall i \cdot (u_i \in U \to ((d)_i = 1)) \wedge (\overline{u_i} \in U \to ((d)_i = 0)) \\ 0 \; otherwise \end{cases} \quad (1)$$

The function $h_U^N(d)$ is therefore a $\{0,1\}$-valued function on D_N whose value is decided by a conjunction of the bits of d. The space of such functions will be referred to as M_N. Further, $M_{N,k}$ is defined as the set of monomials with exactly k literals ($\#U = k$).

3 Case-Based Learning Algorithms

Following the work of Jantke [11], a case memory system is modelled as the pair $\langle CB, \sigma \rangle$ where CB is the case-base, or set of stored exemplars, assumed here to be free from observational error, and σ is a similarity measure defined for the space D_N. Using the terminology of Dearden's model [7], the case-base is modelled as a set of pairs of 'descriptions' and 'reports'. As indicated above, a description is an N-bit vector from the space D_N. A report is a single bit denoting the classification of that exemplar, making CB an object of type:

$$CB : \mathcal{P}\,(D_N \times \{0,1\})$$

The similarity measure σ is a function over pairs of descriptions returning a normalised real value indicating the degree of similarity between the two instances:

$$\sigma : (D_N \times D_N) \to [0,1]$$

The pair $\langle CB, \sigma \rangle$ is treated as the representation of a function from B_N, according to the following interpretation related to the 'standard semantics' for a case-based classifier of Jantke and Lange [12]. The function represented by $\langle CB, \sigma \rangle$ is defined as:

$$h^N_{\langle CB, \sigma \rangle}(d) = \begin{cases} 1 \; if & \exists (d_{pos}, 1) \, \epsilon \, CB \cdot \forall (d_{neg}, 0) \, \epsilon \, CB \cdot \sigma(d, d_{pos}) > \sigma(d, d_{neg}) \\ 0 \; otherwise \end{cases}$$

(2)

Informally, a point d from D_N is positively classified by $h^N_{\langle CB, \sigma \rangle}$ if and only if there is a stored positive exemplar d_{pos} which is strictly more similar to d according to the chosen similarity measure σ than any of the stored negative exemplars d_{neg}. In relation to other semantics discussed by Jantke [11], this interpretation resolves 'ties' between equally similar near neighbours by imposing a preference ordering on the 'report' part of retrieved cases. Negative exemplars are preferred over positive ones in inferring the classification of a new problem instance, i.e. if the set of exemplars which are most similar to d contains both positive and negative exemplars, d will be classified negatively.

Since the interpretation of a case-based representation $\langle CB, \sigma \rangle$ depends on the interaction between the available cases and the similarity measure, a 'case-based' or 'instance-based' learning algorithm may alter its hypothesis by manipulating either of the two components [15, p.79]. The algorithms IB2 [1], VS-CBR [15] and PEBLS [5], for example, each show different ways of adjusting the represented hypothesis via changes to the case-base and/or the similarity measure. In the current paper, we restrict our study to the following family of very simple case-based learning algorithms.

Definition 1. $CB1(\sigma)$ **Learning Algorithm for Case-Based Classifiers**

```
set CB = ∅
for i = 1 to m do
    set CB = CB ∪ {(d_i, b_i)}
set CB1(σ)(s̄) = h_{⟨CB,σ⟩}
```

$CB1(\sigma)$ learns by adding each and every member of the training sample $\bar{s}$ (a series of m pre-classified examples (d_i, b_i)) to the case base, and constructs each hypothesis using a single, fixed similarity measure σ. Clearly the usefulness of $CB1(\sigma)$ will depend on the choice of σ; a similarity measure that assigns high similarity to *arbitrary* pairs of descriptions will not be of much use in defining a viable learning algorithm.

The best understood learning algorithms are those which consistent, i.e. those which are able to classify correctly at least the exemplars in their training sample. In the following section we demonstrate precisely which choices of similarity measure allow $CB1(\sigma)$ to behave consistently.

4   Consistency of $CB1(\sigma)$

Theorem 4 below gives necessary and sufficient conditions over σ to make $CB1(\sigma)$ a consistent consistent learning algorithm. Results elsewhere [12, Lemma 3] [14,

Lemma 7] formalise the intuition that a 'reasonable' similarity measure [14], which recognises that an object is more similar to itself than any other object, will be sufficient for consistency. This property is here called 'definiteness' after Day and Faith [6, p.183].

Definition 2. Definiteness of a Similarity Measure. A similarity measure σ is definite iff the comparison of two distinct objects yields a score strictly less than the score given to the comparison of an object to itself.

$$\forall d, d' : D_N \cdot d \neq d' \rightarrow \sigma(d, d') < \sigma(d, d) \tag{3}$$

This property ensures a consistent hypothesis since any exemplar in the case base will be judged strictly most similar to itself, and therefore those exemplars at least will be classified correctly by equation (2). Definiteness is not however a necessary condition for consistency. The exemplars in the case base will still be classified correctly as long as the most similar object to a positive exemplar is *any* positive exemplar and the most similar object to a negative exemplar is *any* negative one. In other words, two distinct objects may be assigned maximal similarity only if they are classified the same by all relevant classification functions f. This is recognised informally as a necessary condition by Wess and Globig [15, p.86]. We express it within our framework in our definition of predictivity and prove it a necessary and sufficient condition over σ to make $CB1(\sigma)$ a consistent learning algorithm.

Definition 3. Predictivity of a Similarity Measure with respect to a concept space C. A similarity measure is predictive of a concept space C iff, for any concept $c \in C$:

1. When d is a positive instance of c, the comparison of d and d' yields a score at least as large as the comparison of d to itself only if d' is also a positive instance.

$$\forall c \in C \cdot \forall d, d' \in D_N \cdot \sigma(d, d') \geq \sigma(d, d) \rightarrow c(d) = 1 \rightarrow c(d') = 1 \tag{4}$$

2. When d is a negative instance of c, the comparison of d and d' yields a score strictly greater than the comparison of d to itself only if d' is also a negative instance.

$$\forall c \in C \cdot \forall d, d' \in D_N \cdot \sigma(d, d') > \sigma(d, d) \rightarrow c(d) = 0 \rightarrow c(d') = 0 \tag{5}$$

Note how this relates to equation (2) in that the property of definiteness is relaxed precisely where no misclassification will occur under our chosen classification function (2). The asymmetry in equations (4) and (5) reflects the preference given to negative exemplars in the classification function. Hence we emphasise that choosing a different semantics in (2) would entail a slightly different form of the following theorem.

Theorem 4. Consistency of $CB1(\sigma)$. *For any concept space $C \subseteq B_N$, $CB1(\sigma)$ is a consistent learning algorithm for C if and only if the chosen similarity measure σ is predictive of C.*

Proof. Let $CB1(\sigma)$ infer a hypothesis from some training sample $\bar{s} = \langle(d_i, b_i)\rangle$ for a target concept c. According to the definition of $CB1(\sigma)$, the case-base will contain exactly those labelled examples presented in the training sample; in the absence of observational error we can assume $(d_i, n) \in CB \rightarrow c(d_i) = n$, for $n \in \{0, 1\}$. *a) Sufficiency:* Assume σ is predictive of the concept space C. Taking positive and negative exemplars in the case base separately, consider first d_i such that $b_i = 1$. For any negative exemplar $(d_{neg}, 0) \in CB$, we have $c(d_{neg}) = 0$ and hence by equation (4) $\forall d \in D_N \cdot \forall (d_{neg}, 0) \in CB \cdot \sigma(d, d_{neg}) < \sigma(d, d) \vee c(d) = 0$. Since $c(d_i) = 1$, we conclude $\forall (d_{neg}, 0) \in CB \cdot \sigma(d_i, d_{neg}) < \sigma(d_i, d_i)$, and thus $h_{\langle CB, \sigma \rangle}(d_i) = 1$ by equation (2). By a similar argument, for some d_i such that $b_i = 0$ we derive from equation (5), $\forall (d_{pos}, 1) \in CB \cdot \sigma(d_i, d_{pos}) \leq \sigma(d_i, d_i)$, and hence $h_{\langle CB, \sigma \rangle}(d_i) = 0$ by equation (2). Thus for any example d_i in an arbitrary training sample, $h_{\langle CB, \sigma \rangle}(d_i) = b_i$, making $CB1(\sigma)$ a consistent learning algorithm. *b) Necessity.* It will be shown that for any similarity measure σ' which violates either of equations (4) & (5), there is a target concept c' from the specified concept space for which a training sample can be constructed which will be mis-classified by $CB1(\sigma)$. The consistency of $CB1(\sigma)$ would therefore require a similarity measure satisfying both equations. If equation (4) does not hold, then there must be two descriptors d_1 and d_2 and a target concept c' such that:

$$\sigma'(d_1, d_2) \geq \sigma'(d_1, d_1) \wedge c'(d_1) = 1 \wedge c'(d_2) = 0 \qquad (6)$$

Thus $\langle(d_1, 1), (d_2, 0)\rangle$ will be a training sample for c'. Given the case base CB constructed by $CB1(\sigma')$ from this sample, note that $h_{CB, \sigma'}(d_1) = 0$ since equation (6) indicates that the negative exemplar d_2 will be at least as similar to d_1 as d_1 is to itself. Hence $h_{\langle CB, \sigma \rangle}$ disagrees with the training sample. In a similar way, if it assumed that equation (5) is relaxed, then there is a training sample $\langle(d_1, 0), (d_2, 1)\rangle$ resulting in a hypothesis such that $h_{\langle CB, \sigma' \rangle}(d_1) = 1$. Thus $CB1(\sigma)$ will be a consistent learning algorithm for a concept space C if and only if σ is predictive of C. $\square$

The close relationship between definition 2 (definiteness) and definition 3 (predictivity) means that the following additional result can be easily established:

Corollary 5. *$CB1(\sigma)$ is a consistent learning algorithm for the space B_N of all total functions on D_N if and only if σ is a definite similarity measure.*

As a further corollary, we can also state the following.

Corollary 6. *Given a similarity measure σ which is predictive of a concept space C, then for any target concept $c \in C$ there is a case-base CB s.t. $h_{\langle CB, \sigma \rangle} = c$.*

Proof. For some σ and C s.t. σ is predictive of C, take any $c \in C$ and any training sample $\bar{s}$ for c which contains an exemplar for every point in the example space D_N. Since Theorem 4 guarantees that the output of $CB1(\sigma)$ will be consistent with $\bar{s}$, clearly the function $h_{\langle CB, \sigma \rangle}$ output by $CB1(\sigma)$ on $\bar{s}$ will be exactly c. $\square$

Finally we observe that it is a basic result in the PAC framework that a learning algorithm which is consistent with respect to some concept space and which learns using a *finite* hypothesis space is a PAC-learning algorithm for that concept space [3, p.41]. Since the number of distinct boolean functions that can be defined on D_N is 2^{2^N} the hypothesis space of $CB1(\sigma)$ must be finite. Hence, trivially, a similarity measure predictive of any concept space $C \subseteq B_N$ is sufficient to make $CB1(\sigma)$ a PAC learning algorithm for C (c.f. PAC-Learnability results for case-based classifiers for concepts defined on real-valued attributes in [1] [2]). PAC learnability answers one of our original questions (§1): the performance of a consistent case-based reasoning system will eventually improve if enough exemplars are presented. What is more interesting however, is to ask *how many* examples must be processed to guarantee a good hypothesis.

5 Sample Complexity in Case-Based Learning

The sample complexity of a learning algorithm with respect to some concept space is defined within the PAC learning framework as the size of training sample which will ensure, to some level of confidence and accuracy, that the hypothesis chosen by the learning algorithm is a good approximation, for any target concept in the chosen concept space. Theorem 7 gives an upper bound on sample complexity in terms of the VC dimension of the hypothesis space used by an algorithm. The VC dimension of a space of $\{0, 1\}$-valued functions is a quantity related to the size of the function space, being defined as the size of the largest possible sample from the example space for which every possible dichotomy into positive and negative examples can be generated by some function in the set ('shattering') [4, p.934] [9, p.189]. Note the relationship of this theorem to the results of the previous section in that it refers specifically to consistent learning algorithms.

Theorem 7. *[4, Thm 2.1(ii)(a)] [9, Theorem 4.4] Suppose that an hypothesis space H has finite VC dimension $d_{VC}(H)$. Then any consistent learning algorithm L which uses hypothesis space H is PAC with sample complexity:*

$$m_L(H, \delta, \epsilon) \leq \left\lceil \frac{k_1.d_{VC}(H)}{\epsilon} \log_2 \left(\frac{k_2}{\epsilon} \right) + \frac{k_3}{\epsilon} \log_2 \left(\frac{k_4}{\delta} \right) \right\rceil$$

where δ & ϵ are the required levels of confidence and accuracy, and k_i constant.

In giving an upper bound on sample complexity, Theorem 7 shows that the size of training sample that can be processed before a consistent learning algorithm *necessarily* outputs a good hypothesis with high probability will increase with the VC dimension. In what follows, we assume that the converse also holds, and that as the VC dimension increases, the sample complexity of the learning algorithm also must increase. Although strictly this depends on the specific properties of the learning algorithm using the hypothesis space, we hold that, in general, the larger the hypothesis space, the more training examples the learner must see in order to discriminate between the available hypotheses, and choose a hypothesis that is accurate with high probability [10, p.1103].

Any such discussion, however, requires us to characterise the hypothesis space of our case-based learners. The hypothesis space of $CB1(\sigma)$ with respect to some concept space C will be referred to as $H_C^{CB1(\sigma)}$. The simplicity of $CB1(\sigma)$ means that, for a given target concept t, all possible case-bases $CB \subseteq t$ are reachable by the learning algorithm. This allows the following to be stated about the hypothesis space of $CB1(\sigma)$:

Proposition 8. *A function f is a member of the hypothesis space of $CB1(\sigma)$ with respect to the concept space $C \subseteq B_N$ if and only if there is some target concept $c \in C$ for which there is a case base $CB \subseteq c$ s.t. $h_{\langle CB,\sigma \rangle} = f$.*

$$\forall C \subseteq B_N \cdot \forall f \in B_N \cdot f \in H_C^{CB1(\sigma)} \leftrightarrow \exists c \in C \cdot \exists CB \subseteq c \cdot h_{\langle CB,\sigma \rangle} = f$$

As a corollary of proposition 8:

$$H_C^{CB1(\sigma)} = \bigcup_{t \in C} hyp_{t,\sigma} \tag{7}$$

where $hyp_{t,\sigma} = \{h_{\langle CB,\sigma \rangle} | CB \subseteq t\}$

These statements show how the hypothesis space of $CB1(\sigma)$ depends on the choice of both the similarity measure and the concept space. For smaller concept spaces, since we restrict the possible target concepts and hence the allowable training samples, only a restricted number of the possible functions in B_N may be output as hypotheses. On the other hand, it will not be uncommon that a case base CB which is extensible to some target concept $c \in C$ will be interpreted by equation (2) as a function from outside of the concept space C. In general then, the hypothesis space $H_C^{CB1(\sigma)}$ does not necessarily contain all functions $f \in B_N$, but may well contain functions from outside the chosen concept space.

Our contribution in the remainder of the paper is to establish a lower bound on the VC dimension of the hypothesis space of $CB1(\sigma)$ for particular instances of C and σ. Specifically, we will consider the (highly restricted) set of functions $M_{N,k}$ as concept space and the 'unweighted feature count' σ_F defined in equation (8) as similarity measure.

$$\sigma_F(d_1, d_2) = \frac{1}{N} \#\{i | 1 \leq i \leq N \wedge (d_1)_i = (d_2)_i\} \tag{8}$$

Proposition 15 below reports a surprising result which partly characterises the space of functions $H_{M_{N,k}}^{CB1(\sigma_F)}$. Corollary 16 re-expresses this result in terms of the VC dimension to give the promised lower bound. The following definitions and results, whose proofs are omitted for brevity, are given as necessary preliminaries to Proposition 15 and its corollary.

Definition 9. Extrapolations of monomial function. The extrapolations of a monomial function $h_U^N \in M_N$ are the functions $h_{U'}^{N+1} \in M_{N+1}$ such that $U' \in \{U, U \cup \{u_{N+1}\}, U \cup \{\overline{u_{N+1}}\}\}$.

$$h_{U'}^{N+1} \in \mathrm{extr}_N(h_U^N) \leftrightarrow (U' = U \vee U' = U \cup \{u_{N+1}\} \vee U' = U \cup \{\overline{u_{N+1}}\})$$

Proposition 10. *The union of the extrapolations of the functions $f \in M_N$ is equal to the class of functions M_{N+1}.*

$$\forall N \geq 0 \cdot \bigcup_{f \in M_N} \mathrm{extr}_N(f) = M_{N+1}$$

Definition 11. Projections of a description. The projections of a description are constructed by extending the description by a single new bit.

$$\forall d \in D_N, d' \in D_{N+1} \cdot d' \in \mathrm{proj}_N(d) \leftrightarrow \forall 1 \leq i \leq N \cdot (d)_i = (d')_i$$

Definition 12. Projections of a case-base. The projections of a case-base are constructed by adding a new bit, set to one specified value, to the description of each exemplar in the case-base.

$$P_i^N(CB) = \{(d', n) | (d, n) \in CB \wedge d' \in \mathrm{proj}_N(d) \wedge (d')_{N+1} = i\}$$

Proposition 13. *Given a function $f^{N+1} \in B_{N+1}$ defined on D_{N+1} and a second function $h_U^N \in M_N$ defined on D_N, it is concluded that $f^{N+1} = h_U^{N+1}$, i.e. f^{N+1} is the function on D_{N+1} represented by the same monomial expression U, if it can be shown that for any description $d \in D_N$, $h_U^N(d)$ will return the same value as $f^{N+1}(d')$, where d' is either of the projections of d in D_{N+1}.*

$$\forall N \geq 1 \cdot \forall f^{N+1} \in B_{N+1}, h_U^N \in M_N \cdot \forall d \in D_N, d' \in D_{N+1} \cdot$$
$$d' \in \mathrm{proj}_N(d) \rightarrow [(h_U^N(d) = 1 \leftrightarrow f^{N+1}(d') = 1)) \rightarrow f^{N+1} = h_U^{N+1}]$$

Proposition 14. *For a given case base CB containing exactly one positive exemplar, if there is a function $f \in M_{N,k}$ s.t. $CB \subseteq f$, then for any larger k' s.t. $k \leq k' \leq N$, there is some $f' \in M_{N,k'}$ so that also $CB \subseteq f'$.*

$$\forall N \geq 1 \cdot \forall 1 \leq k \leq N \cdot \forall CB \in \mathcal{P}\,(D_N \times \{0, 1\}) \cdot$$
$$(\#\{d_{pos} : D_N | (d_{pos}, 1) \in CB\} = 1 \rightarrow$$
$$\forall f \in M_{N,k} \cdot CB \subseteq f \rightarrow \forall k \leq k' \leq N \cdot \exists f' \in M_{N,k'} \cdot CB \subseteq f')$$

The following result can now be established:

Proposition 15. *The effective hypothesis space $H_{M_{N,k}}^{CB1(\sigma_F)}$ of the case-based learning algorithm $CB1(\sigma_F)$, defined with respect to the 'unweighted feature count' similarity measure σ_F and the set of k-literal monomial functions $M_{N,k}$, contains the set of all monomial functions M_N defined on D_N.*

$$\forall N \geq 1 \cdot \forall 1 \leq k \leq N \cdot M_N \subseteq H_{M_{N,k}}^{CB1(\sigma_F)}$$

Proof. By induction on N. Proposition 8 shows that the required result is equivalent to requiring that for each $f \in M_N$, there is a 'target concept' $t \in M_{N,k}$ for any value $1 \leq k \leq N$, and some case base $CB \subseteq t$, such that $h^N_{\langle CB, \sigma_F \rangle} = f$. Therefore, it will be sufficient to show $\forall N \geq 1 \cdot H(N)$, defining H as below. Introducing the extra restriction that case bases contain a single positive exemplar will allow reference to proposition 14 in subsequent argument:

$$H(N) \triangleq \forall f \in M_N \cdot \forall 1 \leq k \leq N \cdot \exists t \in M_{N,k} \cdot \exists CB \subseteq t \cdot p^+(CB) \wedge h^N_{\langle CB, \sigma_F \rangle} = f$$

where $p^+(CB) \triangleq \#\{d_{pos} : D_N | (d_{pos}, 1) \in CB\} = 1$.

Base Case $H(1)$. $M_1 = \{\{\}, \{u_1\}, \{\overline{u_1}\}\}$. $h_{\langle \{(1,1)\}, \sigma_F \rangle} = h_{\{\}}$, $h_{\langle \{(1,1),(0,0)\}, \sigma_F \rangle} = h_{\{u_1\}}$ and $h_{\langle \{(1,0),(0,1)\}, \sigma_F \rangle} = h_{\{\overline{u_1}\}}$. Hence $H(1)$.

Inductive Step $H(p) \to H(p+1)$. We make the inductive hypothesis $H(p)$:

$$\forall f \in M_p \cdot \forall 1 \leq k \leq p \cdot \exists t \in M_{p,k} \cdot \exists CB \subseteq t \cdot p^+(CB) \wedge h^p_{\langle CB, \sigma_F \rangle} = f \quad (9)$$

Proposition 10 indicates that it will be sufficient to infer from equation (9) that for any monomial function $f \in M_p$ each extrapolation of f is a member of the hypothesis space with respect to $M_{p+1,k}$ for values $1 \leq k \leq p+1$. Proposition 14 in turn shows that it will be sufficient to derive from the inductive hypothesis that for each $f' \in \text{extr}_p(f)$ there is a $t \in M_{p+1,1}$ and a case-base $CB \subseteq t$ containing just one positive exemplar which represents f', which will entail the results for all other values of k.

Hence it will be shown equation (9) entails that for each $h^p_U \in M_p$ there are functions t_1, t_2 and t_3 and case bases CB_1, CB_2 and CB_3 satisfying:

$$\forall h^p_U \in M_p \cdot \exists t_1 \in M_{p+1,1} \cdot \exists CB_1 \subseteq t_1 \cdot p^+(CB_1) \wedge h^{p+1}_{\langle CB_1, \sigma_F \rangle} = h^{p+1}_U \quad (10)$$

$$\forall h^p_U \in M_p \cdot \exists t_2 \in M_{p+1,1} \cdot \exists CB_2 \subseteq t_2 \cdot p^+(CB_2) \wedge h^{p+1}_{\langle CB_2, \sigma_F \rangle} = h^{p+1}_{U \cup \{u_{p+1}\}} \quad (11)$$

$$\forall h^p_U \in M_p \cdot \exists t_3 \in M_{p+1,1} \cdot \exists CB_3 \subseteq t_3 \cdot p^+(CB_3) \wedge h^{p+1}_{\langle CB_3, \sigma_F \rangle} = h^{p+1}_{U \cup \{\overline{u_{p+1}}\}} \quad (12)$$

For any function $h^p_U \in M_p$, equation (9) asserts there must be some case base CB s.t. there is some $h^p_T \in M_{p,1}$ where $CB \subseteq h^p_T$ and $h^p_{\langle CB, \sigma_F \rangle} = h^p_U$. It will be shown that there are case-bases defined in terms of CB and T which will satisfy each of equations (10) to (12):

a) Case-based representation of h^{p+1}_U.

It will be shown that either projection of CB (definition 12), $P^p_0(CB)$ and $P^p_1(CB)$ is a case-based representation of h^{p+1}_U; clearly either projection also has a single positive exemplar. It will first be shown that for any function $h^N_{\langle CB, \sigma_F \rangle}(d)$ defined on D_N the functions represented by the projections of CB will classify the projections of d positively iff $h^N_{\langle CB, \sigma_F \rangle}(d) = 1$:

$$\forall N \geq 1 \cdot \forall i \in \{0, 1\} \cdot \forall h^N_{\langle CB, \sigma_F \rangle} \in B_N \cdot$$

$$\forall d \in D_N, d' \in \text{proj}_N(d) \cdot (h^N_{\langle CB, \sigma_F \rangle}(d) = 1 \leftrightarrow h^{N+1}_{\langle P^N_i(CB), \sigma_F \rangle}(d') = 1) \quad (13)$$

Assume there is some $d \epsilon D_N$ such that $h_{\langle CB, \sigma_F \rangle}(d) = 1$, and let d' be a projection of d in D_{N+1}. There must be a positive exemplar in CB satisfying equation (2). For any $d_1, d_2, d_3 \epsilon D_N$ where $\sigma_F(d_1, d_2) > \sigma_F(d_1, d_3)$, consider the projections of d_1 in D_{N+1}, $d'_1 \epsilon \mathrm{proj}_N(d_1)$. Consider also projections of d_2 & d_3, $d'_2 \epsilon \mathrm{proj}_N(d_2)$, $d'_3 \epsilon \mathrm{proj}_N(d_3)$, such that $(d'_2)_{N+1} = (d'_3)_{N+1}$. Let $\gamma_{i,j}$ stand for the number of bits which d_i and d_j agree on; similarly, let $\gamma_{i',j'}$ stand for the number of bits agreed on by d'_i and d'_j. Since the extending bit $(d'_1)_{N+1}$ will either agree or disagree with the bit extending d_2 and d_3, we have $\gamma_{1',2'} - \gamma_{1,2} = \gamma_{1',3'} - \gamma_{1,3} = \delta$, where $\delta \epsilon \{0, 1\}$. Therefore we also have $\sigma_F(d'_1, d'_2) > \sigma_F(d'_1, d'_3)$, and, letting $d' = d'_1$, any d_{pos} from the projection of the case-base $= d'_2$ and any $d_{neg} = d'_3$:

$$\forall i \epsilon \{0, 1\} \cdot \exists (d_{pos}, 1) \epsilon P_i^N(CB) \cdot \forall (d_{neg}, 0) \epsilon P_i^N(CB) \cdot \sigma_F(d', d_{pos}) > \sigma_F(d', d_{neg}) \tag{14}$$

and $h_{\langle P_i^N(CB), \sigma_F \rangle}^{N+1}(d') = 1$, $i \epsilon \{0, 1\}$. Similarly $h_{\langle CB, \sigma_F \rangle}^N(d) = 0 \rightarrow h_{\langle P_i^N(CB), \sigma_F \rangle}^{N+1}(d') = 0$; hence (13).

We have shown that for any function $h_{\langle CB, \sigma_F \rangle}^N$, either projection of CB (definition 12) will represent a new function defined on D_{N+1} which classifies the projections of d positively iff $f^N(d) = 1$. Therefore by proposition 13:

$$h_{\langle P_0^p(CB), \sigma_F \rangle}^{p+1} = h_{\langle P_1^p(CB), \sigma_F \rangle}^{p+1} = h_U^{p+1} \tag{15}$$

It remains only to show $P_i^p(CB) \subseteq h_T^{p+1}$. For any $(d', n) \epsilon P_i^p(CB)$, there is a unique d such that $d' \epsilon \mathrm{proj}_p(d)$ and $(d, n) \epsilon CB$ (definition 12). Since $CB \subseteq h_T^p$, $(d, n) \epsilon CB \rightarrow h_T^p(d) = n$. Since d & d' agree on their first p bits and also $h_T^p \epsilon M_{p,k}$ so that T refers only to the first p bits of representation, $h_T^p(d) = 1 \leftrightarrow h_T^{p+1}(d') = 1$. Hence also $h_T^{p+1}(d') = n$ and therefore $(d', n) \epsilon P_i^p(CB) \rightarrow h_T^{p+1}(d') = n$. Hence the following result, concluding (10):

$$P_i^p(CB) \subseteq h_T^{p+1} \tag{16}$$

b) *Case-based representation of* $h_{U \cup \{u_{p+1}\}}^{p+1}$. It will be shown that the case base $P_1^p(CB) \cup \{(d_{new}, 0)\}$ is a case-based representation of $h_{U \cup \{u_{p+1}\}}^{p+1}$, where d_{new} is defined as follows:

$$
\begin{aligned}
(d_{new})_x &= |1 - (d_{pos})_x| \\
(d_{new})_i &= (d_{pos})_i \ where \ 1 \le i \le p \wedge i \ne x \\
(d_{new})_{p+1} &= 0
\end{aligned}
$$

d_{pos} is the description of the unique positive exemplar in $P_1^p(CB)$, inherited from CB, and x is the smallest value s.t. $u_x \epsilon T \vee \overline{u_x} \epsilon T$, T being the representation of the target function $h_T^p \epsilon M_{p,1}$.

By equation (2), we have $h_{\langle P_1^p(CB) \cup \{(d_{new}, 0)\}, \sigma_F \rangle}^{p+1} = f^{p+1}$, where:

$$f^{p+1}(d) = \begin{cases} 1 \ if \ h_{\langle P_1^p(CB), \sigma_F \rangle}^{p+1}(d) = 1 \wedge \sigma_F(d, d_{pos}) > \sigma_F(d, d_{new}) \\ 0 \ otherwise \end{cases} \tag{17}$$

From the definition of d_{new}, we have $\sigma_F(d, d_{pos}) > \sigma_F(d, d_{new})$ iff d agrees with d_{pos} on a strict majority of the bits $\{u_x, u_{p+1}\}$; note $(d_{pos})_{p+1} = 1$ since $(d_{pos}, 1) \in P_1^p(CB)$, while $(d_{new})_{p+1} = 0$ by definition. (All other bits are irrelevant to the comparison since they are common to both d_{pos} and d_{new}). Hence:

$$\sigma_F(d, d_{pos}) > \sigma_F(d, d_{new}) \leftrightarrow ((d)_x = (d_{pos})_x \wedge (d)_{p+1} = 1) \qquad (18)$$

Substituting (15) and (18) in (17):

$$h^{p+1}_{\langle P_1^p(CB) \cup \{(d_{new}, 0)\}, \sigma_F \rangle} = f^{p+1} = h^{p+1}_{U \cup \{u_{p+1}\}} \qquad (19)$$

since $h_U^{p+1}(d) = 1$ implies that $(d)_x$ must have the same value as $(d_{pos})_x$.

Clearly, the new case-base still contains a single positive exemplar; to satisfy equation (11), it must only be shown $P_i^p(CB) \cup \{(d_{new}, 0)\} \subseteq h_T^{p+1}$. From (16), we have $P_i^p(CB) \subseteq h_T^{p+1}$. Note also $h_T^{p+1}(d_{new}) = 0$ since by definition, d_{new} will fail to satisfy T. Hence $(d_{new}, 0) \in h_T^{p+1}$ and $P_1^p(CB) \cup \{(d_{new}, 0)\} \subseteq h_T^{p+1}$.

c) *Case-based representation of* $h^{p+1}_{U \cup \{\overline{u_{p+1}}\}}$. Equally, the case base $P_0^p(CB) \cup \{(d'_{new}, 0)\}$, where $d'_{new} = d_{new}$ as defined as above except $(d'_{new})_{p+1} = 1$, is an equivalent representation to $U \cup \{\overline{u_{p+1}}\}$. Hence (12). $\square$

Corollary 16. Lower bound on VC Dimension of $H_{M_{N.k}}^{CB1(\sigma_F)}$. *The VC Dimension of $H_{M_{N.k}}^{CB1(\sigma_F)}$, the effective hypothesis space of $CB1(\sigma_F)$ with respect to the concept space $M_{N,k}$, is at least $\mathcal{O}(N)$.*

Proof. $H_{M_{N,k}}^{CB1(\sigma_F)}$ contains M_N (proposition 15). Therefore any sample shattered by M_N will shattered by $H_{M_{N,k}}^{CB1(\sigma_F)}$, and the VC dimension of $H_{M_{N.k}}^{CB1(\sigma_F)}$ will be at least that of M_N, which is $\mathcal{O}(N)$ [3, p.76] [9, p.193]. $\square$

In contrast to corollary 16, note the following result:

Proposition 17. Upper bound on VC Dimension of $M_{N,k}$. *The VC Dimension of $M_{N,k}$ is no greater than $1 + \log_2 \binom{N}{k}$.*

Proof. Let $\overline{x}$ be a sample of size v, which orders the set of examples X and is shattered by $M_{N,k}$. Consider that there are 2^{v-1} subsets of X which contain a particular $x_i \in X$, and also that there are exactly $\binom{N}{k}$ functions $f \in M_{N,k}$ that classify x_i positively. Since each subset of X must be labelled by a distinct member of $M_{N,k}$, we have $2^{v-1} \leq \binom{N}{k}$, and hence $v \leq 1 + \log_2 \binom{N}{k}$ $\square$

Hence, while the VC dimension of the hypothesis space of $CB1(\sigma_F)$ with respect to the set of functions $M_{N,k}$ is at least $\mathcal{O}(N)$ (Corollary 16), the VC dimension of $M_{N,k}$ itself is $\mathcal{O}(\log N)$ (Proposition 17). Theorem 7 leads us to believe that this qualitative difference, reflecting the presence of a number of spurious functions in the hypothesis space of $CB1(\sigma)$ in this instance, indicates that $CB1(\sigma_F)$ is a less than optimal learning algorithm (with respect to sample complexity) for the space $M_{N,k}$. That is, as N increases, we would expect the number of examples $CB1(\sigma_F)$ needs to reach an accurate hypothesis will rapidly outgrow the number needed by a learning algorithm whose hypothesis space represents exactly the functions contained in $M_{N,k}$.

Finally, we note that Proposition 15 is very much a partial characterisation of the hypothesis space in this instance. In addition to that formal result, direct enumeration establishes the presence of functions such as $u_1 + u_2.u_3$ and $u_1.u_2 + u_1.u_3 + u_2.u_3$ in $H_{M_{3,1}}^{CB1(\sigma_F)}$, and in addition shows that only a fraction of B_N is output as hypotheses on training samples for functions in $M_{N,k}$ and that $|H_{M_{N,k}}^{CB1(\sigma_F)}|$ varies for different values of k.

6 Conclusions

$CB1(\sigma_F)$ is a general purpose learning algorithm with a rich hypothesis language. Specifically, for any fixed *predictive* similarity measure (Definition 2) such as σ_F, corollaries 6 and 5 indicate that there is a case-based representation $\langle CB, \sigma_F \rangle$ for any $\{0,1\}$-valued total function on D_N. In addition we have explored the nature of the hypothesis space of $CB1(\sigma_F)$. Considering the possible hypotheses that might be output on training samples for functions in specific concept spaces $M_{N,k}$, it has been shown here (Proposition 15) that the hypothesis space of $CB1(\sigma_F)$ with respect to the concept space $M_{N,k}$ includes not only $M_{N,k}$ but also *all* monomial functions M_N. Arguments related to Theorem 7 lead us to believe in addition that the presence of these spurious hypotheses will make $CB1(\sigma_F)$ a relatively inefficient learning algorithm for $M_{N,k}$ (with respect to sample complexity) compared to a consistent learning algorithm which can represent *only* the functions $M_{N,k}$. We suggest that this is a natural corollary of the generality of $CB1(\sigma_F)$.

In contrast, Wess and Globig have already pointed out and ably demonstrated that "the [similarity] measure (respectively the way to modify the measure) is the bias of case-based reasoning" [15, p.90]. That is, with some prior knowledge of the concept space to be learnt, the similarity measure can be manipulated so that the hypotheses output by the case-based learner are more likely to be close to the possible target concepts. Such strategies demonstrably improve efficiency with respect to sample size [8] [15], although performance will obviously be degraded outside the chosen concept space.

Where more sophisticated case-based learning algorithms outperform a simple but universal algorithm such as $CB1(\sigma_F)$, this must be seen as the result of some bias in the learning algorithm to the target concepts that the algorithms are being tested on. We believe that the formalisation presented here and its attention to the hypothesis space of the case-based learner provide a tool for the rigorous comparison of the many possible case-based learning algorithms and the different forms of bias they embody. Much work remains in carrying out these comparisons and in extending the model, for example to allow for the possibility of observational error in the cases of the case base.

Acknowledgements The first author is funded by an EPSRC grant and receives additional support under the CASE award scheme from Logica Cambridge Ltd. The authors would like to thank Robert Dormer for leading the way into Computational Learning Theory.

References

1. D W Aha, D Kibler, and M K Albert. Instance-based learning algorithms. *Machine Learning*, 6:37–66, 1991.
2. M K Albert and D W Aha. Analyses of instance-based learning algorithms. In *AAAI-91: Proceedings of the Ninth National Conference on Artificial Intelligence*, pages 553–558, 1991.
3. M Anthony and N Biggs. *Computational Learning Theory*. Cambridge University Press, 1992.
4. A Blumer, A Ehrenfeucht, D Haussler, and M K Warmuth. Learnability and the Vapnik-Chervonenkis dimension. *Journal of the ACM*, 36(4):929–965, Oct 1989.
5. S Cost and S Salzberg. A weighted nearest neighbour algorithm for learning with symbolic features. *Machine Learning*, 10(1):37–66, Mar 1993.
6. W H E Day and D P Faith. A model in partial orders for comparing objects by dualistic measures. *Mathemetical Biosciences*, 78(2):179–192, 1986.
7. A M Dearden and M D Harrison. The engineering of case memory systems. *submitted to the Journal of Intelligent Information Systems*.
8. C Globig and S Wess. Symbolic learning and nearest-neighbour classification. In *Proceedings of the 17th Annual Conference of the Gesellschaft fur Klassification e.V. University of Kaiserslautern, March 3-5, 1993*. Springer-Verlag, 1994.
9. D Haussler. Quantifying inductive bias: AI learning algorithms and Valiant's learning framework. *Artificial Intelligence*, 36:177–221, 1988.
10. D Haussler. Probably approximately correct learning. In *AAAI-90 Proceedings of the Eight National Conference on Artificial Intelligence, Boston, MA*, pages 1101–1108. American Association for Artificial Intelligence, 1990.
11. K P Jantke. Case-based learning and inductive inference. GOSLER report 08/92, FB Mathematik & Informatik, TH Leipzig, 1992.
12. K P Jantke and S Lange. Case-based representation and learning of pattern languages. In *EWCBR-93 Working Notes of the first European Workshop on Case-Based Reasoning*, volume 1, pages 139–144. University of Kaiserslautern, 1993.
13. E L Rissland, J Kolodner, and D Waltz. Case-based reasoning. In *Proceedings of DARPA Case-Based Reasoning Workshop May 1989*, pages 1–13. Morgan Kaufmann, 1989.
14. P Turney. Theoretical analyses of cross-validation error and voting in instance-based learning. Technical Report NRC-35073, Knowledge Systems Laboratory, Institute for Information Technology, National Research Council (Canada), 1993.
15. S Wess and C Globig. Case-based and symbolic classification algorithms - A case study using version space. In *Topics in CBR: Selected papers from EWCBR-93*, LNCS vol. 837, pages 77–91. Springer-Verlag, 1994.

The Power of Decision Tables

Ron Kohavi

Computer Science Department
Stanford University
Stanford, CA. 94305
ronnyk@CS.Stanford.EDU
http://robotics.stanford.edu/~ronnyk

Abstract. We evaluate the power of decision tables as a hypothesis
space for supervised learning algorithms. Decision tables are one of the
simplest hypothesis spaces possible, and usually they are easy to understand. Experimental results show that on artificial and real-world
domains containing only discrete features, IDTM, an algorithm inducing decision tables, can sometimes outperform state-of-the-art algorithms
such as C4.5. Surprisingly, performance is quite good on some datasets
with continuous features, indicating that many datasets used in machine
learning either do not require these features, or that these features have
few values. We also describe an incremental method for performing cross-
validation that is applicable to incremental learning algorithms including
IDTM. Using incremental cross-validation, it is possible to cross-validate
a given dataset and IDTM in time that is linear in the number of instances, the number of features, and the number of label values. The time
for incremental cross-validation is independent of the number of folds
chosen, hence leave-one-out cross-validation and ten-fold cross-validation
take the same time.

1 Introduction

Write the vision, and make it plain upon tables,
that he may run that readeth it.
—Habakkuk 2:2

Given a dataset of labelled instances, supervised machine learning algorithms
seek a hypothesis that will correctly predict the class of future unlabelled instances. In the machine learning literature, many representations for hypotheses
have been suggested, including decision trees, decision graphs, neural networks,
k-DNF formulae, automata, Lisp programs, and probability measures.

We investigate the power of one of the simplest representations possible—a
decision table with a default rule mapping to the majority class. This representation, called **DTM** (Decision Table Majority), has two components: a **schema**
which is a set of features that are included in the table, and a **body** consisting
of labelled instances from the space defined by the features in the schema. Given
an unlabelled instance, a decision table classifier searches for exact matches in
the decision table using only the features in the schema (note that there may

be many matching instances in the table). If no instances are found, the majority class of the DTM is returned; otherwise, the majority class of all matching instances is returned.

To build a DTM, the induction algorithm must decide which features to include in the schema and which instances to store in the body. In this paper, we restrict ourselves to the former problem, called feature subset selection.

Given a target function f and a hypothesis class $\mathcal{H}$, we define the **optimal features** to be the features used in a hypothesis h in $\mathcal{H}$ that has the highest future prediction accuracy with respect to f. Because the hypothesis space is limited in its expressive power, the optimal features may not include all relevant features.

To search for the optimal features, the wrapper model (John, Kohavi & Pfleger 1994) is used. In the wrapper model, the induction algorithm is used as a black box, and a search through the space of feature subsets is made by a "wrapper" algorithm. In this paper, we search using best-first search and estimate the future prediction accuracy (the heuristic required for the best first search) with **k-fold cross-validation**.

The goal of this paper is to evaluate the representation power of DTMs. In experiments with feature subset selection for decision tree algorithms, we have observed that in many cases the decision-trees were nearly complete, *i.e.*, the leaves represented almost all combinations of the chosen subset of the features. We then conjectured that a simple decision table on a subset of the features might be a good hypothesis space. While we use a specific technique for selecting the features—the wrapper model—our aim is not to show that the specific method for selecting features is good, but rather to show that at least one method for selecting the schema works well. It is conceivable that other methods, perhaps better and faster, exist.

The chances of getting a perfect match on the values of continuous features are slim: even a single truly continuous feature in the schema will make the table useless. Our initial experiments were therefore restricted to datasets containing only discrete features. To determine how weak the performance of IDTM is on datasets with continuous features, we also report on such experiments. Surprisingly, performance is not significantly worse than that of C4.5 (Quinlan 1993) in some cases. On those that performance is not significantly worse than C4.5, the algorithm ignores the continuous features or uses those features that have few values.

The paper is organized as follows. Section 2 formally defines DTMs and the problem of finding an optimal feature subset. Section 3 describes how we search for the optimal feature subsets using best-first search to guide the search and cross-validation to estimate the accuracy. Section 4 details the experimental methodology and the results. Section 5 describes related work on decision tables and feature subset selection. Section 6 concludes with a summary and directions for future work.

2   Decision Tables and Optimal Features Subsets

Given a training sample containing labelled instances, an induction algorithm builds a hypothesis in some representation. The representation we investigate here is a decision table with a default rule mapping to the majority class, which we abbreviate as **DTM**. A DTM has two components:

1. A **schema,** which is a set of features.
2. A **body,** which is a multiset of labelled instances. Each instance consists of a value for each of the features in the schema and a value for the label.

Given an unlabelled instance I, the label assigned to the instance by a DTM classifier is computed as follows. Let $\mathcal{I}$ be the set of labelled instances in the DTM exactly matching the given instance I, where only the features in the schema are required to match and all other features are ignored. If $\mathcal{I} = \emptyset$, return the majority class in the DTM; otherwise, return the majority class in $\mathcal{I}$. Unknown values are treated as distinct values in the matching process.

Let $\mathbf{err}(h, f)$ denote the error of a hypothesis h for a given target function f. Since f is never known for real-world problems, we estimate the error using an independent test set $\mathcal{T}$ as

$$\widehat{\mathrm{err}}(h, \mathcal{T}) = \frac{1}{|\mathcal{T}|} \sum_{(x_i, y_i) \in \mathcal{T}} L(h(x_i), y_i) \ ,$$

where L is a loss function. In the rest of the paper we assume a zero-one loss function, *i.e.*, zero if $h(x) = y$ and one otherwise. The **approximate accuracy** is defined as $1 - \widehat{\mathrm{err}}(h, \mathcal{T})$.

An **optimal feature subset**, $\mathcal{A}^*$, for a given hypothesis space $\mathcal{H}$ and a target function f is a subset of the features $\mathcal{A}^*$ such that there exists a hypothesis h in $\mathcal{H}$ using only features in $\mathcal{A}^*$ and having the lowest possible error with respect to the target function f. (Note that the subset need not be unique.) As the following example shows, relevant features are not necessarily included in the optimal subset.

Example 1.
Let the universe of possible instances be $\{0, 1\}^3$, that is, three Boolean features, say X_1, X_2, X_3. Let the distribution over the universe be uniform, and assume the target concept is $f(X_1, X_2, X_3) = (X_1 \wedge X_2) \vee X_3$. Under any reasonable definition of relevance, all variables are relevant to this target function.

If the hypothesis space is the space of monomials, *i.e.*, conjunctions of literals, the only optimal feature subset is $\{X_3\}$ The accuracy of the the monomial X_3 is 87.5%, the highest accuracy achievable within this hypothesis space. ∎

An induction algorithm using DTMs as the underlying hypothesis space must decide which instances to store in the table and which features to include in the schema. In this paper we assume the induction algorithm includes the projections of all instances defined by the schema in the DTM, but we do not restrict the subset of features to use in the schema in any way. Let $A = \{X_1, \ldots, X_n\}$ be a set of features and let S be a sample of m instances over the features in A. Given a subset of features $A' \subseteq A$, $DTM(A', S)$ is the DTM with schema A' and a body consisting of all instances in S projected on A'. The goal of the induction algorithm is to chose a schema A^* such that

$$A^* = \arg\min_{A' \subseteq A} \text{err}(DTM(A', S), f) \ . \tag{1}$$

The schema A^* consists of an optimal feature subset for a DTM under the assumption that all instances from the training set are stored in the body of the decision table.

3 Finding an Optimal Feature Subset

In this section, we describe **IDTM** (Inducer of DTMs), an induction algorithm that induces DTMs. The goal of IDTM is clear: find the feature subset A^* that is described in Equation 1. Since the target function f is unknown, no learning algorithm can compute the exact error: it can only be approximated. Furthermore, the number of feature subsets for n features is 2^n, a space too large to search exhaustively even for moderately sized n.

An interesting way to view the induction process is to think of the feature subset selection algorithm as wrapping around a trivial induction algorithm that simply creates a DTM from the full dataset it receives (see John et al. (1994) for details on the wrapper approach). The wrapper is the only part that makes the inductive leap of which features to use.[1]

We now give an overview of the feature subset selection mechanism, which transforms the problem into one of state space search with probabilistic estimates; further details can be found in Kohavi (1994c).

3.1 Searching the Space of Feature Subsets

In order to search the space of feature subsets effectively, we transform the problem into a state space search and use best-first search to heuristically search the space (Ginsberg 1993, Nilsson 1980).

The states in the space are feature subsets; operators can add or delete a feature; the initial node can be either the set of all features or the empty set; and the evaluation function is cross-validation (described below). Since we are aiming for the optimal feature subset, there is no goal node. The optimization problem requires a termination condition, and the algorithm we used stops after a fixed number of node expansions do not yield a node with a better estimated accuracy than the current best estimate.

---

[1] Holte (personal communication) remarked that this type of learning is basically a preprocessing step (feature selection), and an optional post-processing step to simplify the rules, with *nothing* in between.

To estimate future prediction accuracy, cross-validation, a standard accuracy estimation technique (Weiss & Kulikowski 1991, Breiman, Friedman, Olshen & Stone 1984, Stone 1974), is used. Given an induction algorithm and a dataset, k-fold cross-validation splits the data into k approximately equally sized partitions, or folds. The induction algorithm is executed k times; each time it is trained on $k-1$ folds and the generated hypothesis is tested on the unseen fold, which serves as a test set. The estimated accuracy is computed as the average accuracy over the k test sets.

The estimated accuracy for each cross-validation fold is a random variable that depends on the random partitioning of the data. We observed high variance in the accuracy estimates and ameliorate this disturbing phenomenon by repeating the cross-validation t times. Following John's suggestion (1994), we used a 10% trimmed mean of the kt folds.

3.2 Incremental Cross-Validation

Each feature subset, represented as a node in the state space, is evaluated by cross-validation. One of the main problems with regular k-fold cross-validation is that the algorithm is run k times, introducing a multiplicative factor of k in the running time. We now explain how to speed up cross-validation time for algorithms that support incremental addition and deletion of instances. We feel that this digression is important because the simple idea of incremental cross-validation is what makes the IDTM algorithm practical.

The idea in incremental cross-validation is that instead of training k times on $k-1$ folds each time, we train on the full dataset, then delete the instances in one fold, test on that fold, and insert the instances back. The delete-test-insert phase is repeated for each of the k folds. If the algorithm is guaranteed to produce the same results in incremental mode as in batch mode, this incremental version of cross-validation is guaranteed to produce the exact same result as batch cross-validation.

Proposition 1 Incremental Cross-Validation.
The running time of incremental cross-validation is

$$O(T + m(t_d + t_c + t_i)) \, ,$$

where T is the running time of the induction algorithm on the full dataset, m is the number of instances, and t_d, t_c, and t_i represent the time it takes to delete an instance, classify an instance, and insert an instance, respectively.

Proof: Incremental cross-validation starts out by running the original induction algorithm on the full dataset. Since each instance appears in exactly one fold, it is deleted once, classified once, and inserted once during the overall incremental cross-validation phase. ∎

Example 2.
Conducting k-fold cross-validating of a decision tree induction algorithm and a

dataset is deemed an expensive operation because one typically builds k decision trees from scratch, one for each fold. However, Utgoff (1994) shows how to incrementally add and delete instances in a way that is guaranteed to generate the same tree as a batch algorithm. Thus, one can incrementally cross-validate decision trees much faster.

Nearest neighbor algorithms support incremental addition and deletion of instances by simply adding and removing prototype points. Since these operations are fast, it can be shown that incremental cross-validation of a dataset with m instances and n features with a simple nearest neighbor induction algorithm takes $O(m(m \cdot n))$ time; incremental cross-validation of a weighted regression nearest neighbor takes $O(m(m \cdot n^2 + m^3))$ time as shown in Moore & Lee (1994), Maron & Moore (1994), and Moore, Hill & Johnson (1992).

We now describe the data structures that allow fast incremental operations on DTMs. The underlying data structure that we use is a universal hash table (Cormen, Leiserson & Rivest 1990). The time to compute the hash function is $O(n')$ where n' is the number of feature values in the DTM's schema, and the expected lookup time (given the hashed value of the instance) is $O(1)$ if all objects (unlabelled instances) stored are unique. To ensure that all stored objects are unique, we store with each unlabelled instance ℓ counter values, where ℓ is the number of label values. Each counter value c_i represents the number of instances in the training set having the same underlying unlabelled instance and label l_i.

To classify an instance, the unlabelled instance is found in the hash table and the label matching the highest counter value is returned.[2] The overall expected time to classify an instance is thus $O(n' + \ell)$.

To delete an instance, the underlying unlabelled instance is found and the appropriate label counter is decreased by one; if all counters are zero, the underlying unlabelled instance is deleted from the table. Inserting instances is done similarly. Class counts must be kept for the whole body of the DTM in order to change the majority class.

Corollary 2 Incremental Cross-Validation of IDTMs.
The overall time to cross-validate an IDTM with n' features in the schema and a dataset with m instances and ℓ label values is $O(m(n' + \ell))$.

Proof: All DTM operations have time complexity $t_d = t_c = t_i = O(n' + \ell)$. The overall time to build a DTM from scratch is the same as m insertions; thus by Proposition 2, the overall time for the cross-validation $O(m(n' + \ell))$. ∎

3.3 Choosing the Number of Folds

The time to incrementally cross-validate an IDTM and a dataset for any number of folds is the same. Leave-one-out is almost unbiased (Efron 1983) and was

---

[2] The running time could further decreased to $O(n')$ by computing the majority of every unlabelled instance in advance, but the counters are needed for the incremental operations.

commonly considered the preferred method for cross-validation. Recently Zhang (1992) and Shao (1993) proved that, for linear models, using leave-one-out cross-validation for model selection is asymptotically inconsistent in the sense that the probability of selecting the model with the best predictive power does not converge to 1 as the total number of observations approaches infinity. The theorems show that in order to select the correct model, as the number of instances in the dataset grows, the number of instances left out for testing should grow as well. Zhang showed that the models chosen by any k-fold cross-validation for any k will overfit in the sense that too many features will be selected. However, for moderately sized data sets, he claimed that 10 to 15 folds are reasonable choices.

Empirically, we have observed similar results, namely that using ten-fold cross-validation is slightly better than leave-one-out. Similar observations were made by Weiss (1991). While the differences are usually small, especially for feature subset selection where only the relative ranking of different subsets matters, there is one extreme case that deserves special mention: the Monk1 dataset.

Example 3 Leave-one-out on Monk1.
The Monk1 problem (Thrun etal. 1991) has a standard training and test set. There are no duplicate instances, nor is there noise in the training set. A DTM with a schema that has all the features and that is tested on a test set disjoint from the training set always predicts the majority class; hence it is equivalent to an induction algorithm that predicts a constant function—*True* or *False*—depending on the prevalent class in the training set.

The estimated accuracy using leave-one-out cross-validation on a DTM with all the features (or equivalently, a majority inducer) and the standard training set for the Monk1 problem is 0.0%! The example shows an inherent problem with cross-validation that applies to more than just a majority inducer. In a no-information dataset where the label values are completely random, the best an induction algorithm can do is predict majority. Leave-one-out on such a dataset with 50% of of the labels for each class and a majority inducer would still predict 0% accuracy. ∎

The reason for this phenomenon is that the standard training set for the Monk1 problem has 62 positive instances and 62 negative instances. Each time an instance is removed in leave-one-out, the other class is the more prevalent in the training set and the majority inducer predicts the wrong label for the test instance.

We have observed a similar phenomenon even with ten-fold CV. The iris dataset has 150 instances, 50 of each class. Predicting any class would yield 33.3% accuracy, but ten-fold CV using a majority induction algorithm yields 21.5% accuracy (averaged over 100 runs of ten-fold CV). The reason is that if there is a majority of one class in the training set, there is a minority of that class in the test set. (See Schaffer (1994) for a discussion along these lines.)

4   Experiments with IDTM

We now describe experiments conducted with IDTM, the induction algorithm for DTMs. The experiments were done on all the datasets at the UC Irvine repository (Murphy & Aha 1994) and StatLog repository (Taylor, Michie & Spiegalhalter 1994) that contain only discrete features. To test the performance on datasets with continuous features, we chose the rest of the StatLog datasets except shuttle, which was too big, and all the datasets used by Holte (1993).

4.1   Methodology

We now define the exact settings used in the algorithms. The estimated accuracy for each node was computed using ten-fold cross validation. Because of the high variability of the estimates, the cross-validation was repeated (shuffling the instances between runs) until the standard deviation of the mean went below one percent or until ten cross-validations runs have been executed.

The termination condition for the search was a consecutive sequence of five node expansions that did not generate a feature subset with an estimated accuracy of at least 0.1% better than the previous best subset.

For datasets with a specified training and test set, we executed the algorithm once. For the rest of the datasets, we performed ten-fold cross-validation around IDTM.[3] In the comparisons with C4.5, the same cross-validation folds were used for both algorithms.

As in Holte's work, we believe that the weakest part of the IDTM algorithm is the accuracy estimation. In order to derive an upper bound on the possible accuracy of DTMs, the test set was used to guide the search, and the termination condition for the best-first search was changed so that a maximum of 30 consecutive nodes need not show improvement before we stop (up from five).

Because the search is still a heuristic search, the best feature subset might not be found, and so this is not a true upper bound (it is a lower bound on the upper bound). As shown in the next section, the heuristic sometimes fails to find the best node. The upper bound usually leads to optimistic accuracy estimates, especially if the test set size is small and there are many features that allow perfectly fitting the test set (*e.g.*, the lung-cancer dataset). The upper bound does not show that the given accuracy is achievable, something we cannot expect, but rather that performance above this level is impossible without changing the hypothesis space or improving the search for the best feature subset.

4.2   Experimental Results

Table 1 shows the accuracy results for the following induction algorithms:

1. A majority induction algorithm, which simply predicts the majority class. The accuracy shown is sometimes referred to as baseline accuracy.

---

[3] Although IDTM performs cross-validations internally, the outer cross-validation is completely independent.

Dataset	Feat-ures	Train sizes	Test	Majority Accuracy	C4.5 Accuracy	IDTM Accuracy	IDTM* Accuracy
audiology	69	226	CV	25.2±2.8	**79.3±3.5**	71.3± 3.8	88.0±1.9
breast-cancer	9	286	CV	70.4±2.3	73.9±2.8	75.3± 2.4	83.7±1.9
chess	36	3196	CV	52.2±1.1	**99.5±0.1**	97.8± 0.2	98.4±0.2
corral	6	32	128	56.3±4.4	81.2±3.5	**100.0±0.0**	100.0±0.0
dna	180	2000	1186	50.8±1.5	92.3±0.8	**94.6±0.7**	94.9±0.6
lenses	4	24	CV	65.0±8.4	83.3±7.0	83.3± 7.0	91.7±5.7
lung-cancer	56	32	CV	41.7±9.0	49.2±7.5	53.3± 9.9	100.0±0.0
Monk1	6	124	432	50.0±2.4	75.7±2.1	**100.0±0.0**	100.0±0.0
Monk2	6	169	432	67.1±2.3	65.0±2.3	64.4± 2.3	81.9±1.9
Monk2-local	17	169	432	67.1±2.3	70.4±2.2	**100.0±0.0**	67.1±2.3
Monk3	6	122	432	47.2±2.4	97.2±0.8	97.2± 0.8	97.2±0.8
mushroom	22	8124	CV	51.8±0.5	100.0±0.0	99.9± 0.4	100.0±0.0
parity5+5	10	100	1024	50.0±1.6	50.0±1.6	**100.0±0.0**	50.0±1.6
tic-tac-toe	9	958	CV	65.4±1.7	**85.6±1.1**	78.2± 1.4	84.8±0.9
vote	16	435	CV	61.4±2.1	**95.6±0.5**	94.3± 0.4	99.1±0.4
vote1	15	435	CV	61.4±2.1	88.0±1.8	87.6±1.3	97.0±0.7

Table 1. Comparison of majority, C4.5, IDTM, and IDTM* on discrete domains. Bold indicates significantly better accuracies (either C4.5 or IDTM.)

2. The C4.5 decision-tree induction algorithm with the default parameter settings.
3. The IDTM induction algorithm described in this paper.
4. The IDTM* induction "algorithm," which gives an approximate upper bound on the performance of any induction algorithm using DTMs. We stress that this is not really a learning algorithm because it is given access to the test set.

The numbers after the "±" sign indicate the standard deviation of the reported accuracy. On cross-validated runs, the standard deviation of the fold accuracies is given; on runs that had a pre-specified test-set, the standard accuracy is the computed according to the Binomial model which assumes each test set instance is an independent Bernoulli experiment, and thus the standard deviation of the mean accuracy is $\sqrt{acc(1 - acc)/m}$ (see Breiman et al. (1984), Devijver & Kittler (1982)).

The results demonstrate that IDTM can achieve high accuracy in discrete domains using the simple hypothesis space of DTMs. In corral, dna, the Monk problems, and parity, IDTM significantly outperforms C4.5 (a difference of more than two standard deviations). In audiology, chess, tic-tac-toe, and vote, performance is significantly below that of C4.5. Performance is approximately the same for the rest.

The 94.6%±0.7% accuracy of IDTM on the DNA dataset, containing 180 binary features, 2,000 training instances, and 1,186, test instances, is higher than

Dataset	Feat-ures	Train sizes	Test	Majority Accuracy	C4.5 Accuracy	IDTM Accuracy	IDTM* Accuracy
australian	14	690	CV	55.5±2.3	85.4±1.1	84.9± 1.7	89.4±1.3
breast	10	699	CV	65.5±1.7	**95.4±0.7**	90.6± 0.9	96.1±0.6
cleve	13	303	CV	54.4±3.6	72.3±2.2	75.5± 3.2	90.8±2.2
crx	15	690	CV	55.5±2.0	85.9±1.4	86.7± 1.1	89.1±1.2
diabetes	8	768	CV	65.1±1.6	**71.8±1.0**	66.0± 1.1	71.0±1.2
german	24	1000	CV	70.0±1.3	69.8±1.1	69.4± 1.1	81.4±1.3
glass	9	214	CV	35.5±3.3	**65.5±3.2**	41.6± 3.0	55.6±1.8
glass2	9	163	CV	53.3±4.0	**70.6±2.0**	48.9± 4.0	69.2±2.8
hayes-roth	4	160	CV	31.8±2.6	**64.8±4.6**	57.5± 3.2	76.9±2.1
heart	13	270	CV	55.6±3.1	76.7±1.8	**80.4± 1.6**	91.5±1.5
hepatitis	19	155	CV	79.2±3.9	80.0±3.7	77.9± 2.8	96.0±2.0
horse-colic	22	368	CV	63.1±2.3	85.1±1.2	84.3± 0.7	92.1±0.9
hypothyroid	25	3163	CV	95.2±0.4	**99.1±0.2**	97.0± 0.4	97.9±0.3
iris	4	150	CV	23.3±2.5	95.3±1.4	94.7± 1.3	94.7±1.3
labor-neg	16	57	CV	65.3±7.7	**85.7±3.5**	75.3± 7.6	98.3±1.7
letter	16	15000	5000	3.7±0.3	**86.8±0.5**	69.2± 0.7	69.2±0.7
lymphography	18	148	CV	54.6±6.4	78.4±1.7	76.2± 3.6	93.9±1.61
satimage	36	4435	2000	23.1±0.9	**85.2±0.8**	78.9±0.9	78.9±0.9
segment	19	2310	CV	11.1±0.4	**96.4±0.3**	56.3±1.3	57.5±1.2
sick-euthyroid	25	3163	CV	90.7±0.6	**97.7±0.3**	94.9± 0.3	96.0±0.3
soybean-small	35	47	CV	36.0±6.7	100.0±0.0	97.5± 2.5	100.0±0
vehicle	18	846	CV	22.6±1.0	**69.8±1.8**	59.3± 1.5	63.4±1.4

Table 2. Comparison of majority, C4.5, IDTM, and IDTM* on non-discrete domains. Bold indicates significantly better accuracies (either C4.5 or IDTM.)

many other state-of-the-art induction algorithms reported for this dataset in (Taylor et al. 1994). For example, CART (Breiman et al. 1984) achieves 91.5% accuracy, Backprop (Rumelhart, Hinton & Williams 1986) achieves 91.2% accuracy, CN2 (Clark & Niblett 1989) achieves 90.5% accuracy, and k-nearest neighbor achieves 84.5% accuracy.

Table 2 shows some results for datasets containing continuous features. In these domains, we expected IDTM to fail miserably, given that the chances of matching continuous features in the table are slim without preprocessing the data. Although C4.5 clearly outperforms IDTM on most datasets, IDTM outperforms C4.5 on the heart dataset and achieves similar performance on nine out of the 22 datasets (australian, cleve, crx, german, hepatitis, horse-colic, iris, lymphography, and soybean).

Running times on a Sparc 10 varied from about one minute for the Monk datasets to 15 hours for the dna dataset. The long running time for the dna dataset was due to the branching factor of 180 in the feature-subset space.

4.3 Discussion

We believe that best-first search is doing a reasonable job at searching the space for good feature-subset candidates. The dna dataset is a clear example; out of $2^{180} = 1.5 \cdot 10^{54}$ possible subsets, only 21 nodes were expanded, resulting in a graph with 3,723 nodes, each representing a feature subset. Two interesting examples where best-first search fails to find a good subset are the Monk2-local and the parity5+5 problems. In these datasets, the IDTM* algorithm fails to find a feature subset at least as good as the subset chosen by IDTM. Monk2-local is a local encoding of the original Monk2 problem where out of eighteen features, only six are relevant. The baseline (majority) is 67.13% accuracy. All 268 nodes that were expanded did not result in any improvement, so the algorithm halted. IDTM, on the other hand, climbed a path of seemingly improving nodes, and found the correct subset. Parity5+5 is parity of five features with five random features; a similar event happened in this case.

The fact that IDTM's performance equals that of C4.5 in domains with continuous features indicates that many such features are not very useful, or that they contain few values, or that C4.5 is not using the information contained in them. The soybean dataset contains only one feature with more than four values, even though all are declared continuous. The german dataset contains 21 continuous features that have less than five values each (out of a total of 24 features); IDTM indeed chooses only the features with a few values. Iris contains over 20 to 43 values for each continuous feature, yet a table using a single feature—petal width—has 94.7% accuracy. The crx dataset contains six continuous features, five having more than 130 values each; in our experiments, IDTM usually used three non-continuous features that contained a total of 18 possible values (making the 18 line table extremeley easy to comprehend).

We conjecture that IDTM algorithm outperforms C4.5 in discrete domains when the features interact and not too many features are relevant. Decision trees are well suited for local relevances (*i.e.*, different features are relevant in different regions of the instance space), but the greedy top-down recursive partitioning algorithms tend to fail when features interact. DTMs are suited to concepts where some features are globally relevant; the feature subset selection algorithm used here is conducting a best-first search and is thus able to capture interactions. The tic-tac-toe dataset is an example where features are locally relevant; the Monk1, Monk2, and parity5+5 datasets have feature interactions.

5 Related Work

Because they permit one to display succinctly the conditions that must be satisfied before prescribed actions are to be performed, decision tables are becoming popular in computer programming and system design as devices for organizing logic.
—Reinwald & Soland (1966)

In the early sixties, algorithms were created to convert decision tables into optimal computer programs (decision trees) under different measure of optimality using branch and bound procedures (Reinwald & Soland 1966, Reinwald &

Soland 1967). In the early seventies, these procedures were improved using dynamic programming techniques (Garey 1972, Schumacher & Sevcik 1976). Hyafil & Rivest (1976) showed that building an optimal decision tree from instances (or from a table) is NP-complete. Hartmann, Varshney, Mehrotra & Gerberich (1982) show how to convert a decision table into a decision tree using mutual information. The algorithm is very similar to ID3 (Quinlan 1986). All these approaches, however, dealt with conversions that are information preserving, *i.e.*, all entries in the table are correctly classified and the structures are not used for making predictions.

The rough sets community has been using the hypothesis space of decision tables for a few years (Pawlak 1987, Pawlak 1991, Slowinski 1992). Researchers in the field of rough sets suggest using the degrees-of-dependency of a feature on the label (called γ) to determine which features should be included in a decision table (Ziarko 1991, Modrzejewski 1993). Another suggestion was to use normalized entropy (Pawlak, Wong & Ziarko 1988), which is similar to the information gain measure of ID3. These approaches ignore the utility of the specific features to the specific induction algorithm and to the hypothesis space used.

Much work in the rough sets community has focused on finding the **core** set of features, which are the indispensable features, and **reducts** which are sets of features that allow a Bayesian classifier to achieve the highest possible accuracy. The core is the set of **strongly relevant** features as described in John et al. (1994). While finding reducts is appealing in theory, they are not necessarily optimal subsets for a given induction algorithm. Much of the work presented here stemmed from a paper claiming that reducts are not necessarily useful (Kohavi & Frasca 1994).

Almuallim & Dietterich (1991) described the FOCUS algorithm which is equivalent to finding the DTM with the smallest number of features in the schema and with no conflicting instance projections. The main problem with FOCUS algorithm is that it has no way of dealing with noise and thus the table overfits the data. The algorithm is also unable to handle continuous features.

Almuallim & Dietterich (1992) discussed the "Multi-balls" algorithm that has high coverage—for a given sample size, the number of concepts it can PAC learn is close to the upper bound of any learning algorithm. DTMs can be viewed as a multi-balls hypothesis space because the centers are equidistant. However, the induction method is completely different and the maximal number of balls a DTMs creates is less than the upper bound given by the Gilbert-Varshamov bound.

A nearest-neighbor algorithm can be viewed as a generalization of a DTM with zero weights on the features not included in the schema. However, while nearest-neighbor algorithms use the nearest neighbor to classify instances, a DTM classifier defaults to the majority whenever the distance is greater than zero.

Feature subset selection has been long studied in the statistics community (Miller 1990, Boyce, Farhi & Weischedel 1974), in the pattern recognition community (Devijver & Kittler 1982), and lately in the machine learning community (John et al. 1994, Moore & Lee 1994, Caruana & Freitag 1994, Kohavi & Frasca 1994, Langley & Sage 1994, Aha & Bankert 1994).

Decision tables have a bias similar to that of oblivious read-once decision graphs (OODGs) (Kohavi 1994a, Kohavi 1994b): all of the features chosen for the schema are tested during classification. This implies that it is easy to convert a decision table into an OODG, perhaps making it more comprehensible.

6   Summary and Future Work

In this paper, we showed that a decision table with a default rule mapping to the majority class can be used to classify instances in discrete spaces with accuracy that is sometimes higher than state-of-the-art induction algorithms. Decision tables are easy for humans to understand, especially if not too big (e.g., the decision table for the crx dataset has 18 entries). For future classification, the resulting decision table provides a constant classification time on the average (using a hash table storing the majority) and is therefore well suited for applications in real-time environments.

We observed that on some datasets with continuous values, the prediction accuracy of IDTM is comparable to that of C4.5. This observation indicates that some real-world datasets from the StatLog and the UC Irvine repositories do not have much "information" in the real values or that C4.5 is unable to utilize this information.

Our goal in this paper has not been to claim that decision tables provide a very good hypothesis space for induction algorithms; rather, we have shown that such a simple hypothesis space can lead to high performance, a point previously made by Holte (1993), although he used a different algorithm. The IDTM algorithm described here performs better than Holte's algorithm and sometimes outperforms C4.5.

Generalization without a bias is impossible (Schaffer 1994, Wolpert 1994). IDTM is biased to select a feature subset maximizing cross-validation accuracy estimates. When the estimates are good, IDTM should choose a feature subset that leads to high prediction accuracy. Our empirical evidence indicates that the estimates are usually good, but have high variability.

We also formalized the idea of an **incremental cross-validation** algorithm, which is applicable whenever an induction algorithm supports incremental add and delete operations. We used this approach to show how cross-validation of an IDTM and a dataset can be performed in time that is linear in the number of instances, the number of features, and the number of label values. We suggested that incremental cross-validation can lead to fast accuracy estimates for decision-tree induction algorithm.

IDTM may be used to select a subset of features that yield good performance and which can provide a starting point for a feature subset selection search that uses a more complex algorithm. It is also possible to test constructive induction methods that construct new features (e.g., interval discretization) with this method.

Acknowledgments The work in this paper was done using the $\mathcal{MLC}$++ library, partly funded by ONR grant N00014-94-1-0448 and NSF grants IRI-9116399 and IRI-9411306. Special thanks to Brian Frasca and Yeogirl Yun who implemented some of the classes in $\mathcal{MLC}$++ that made this paper possible. Rob Holte provided excellent comments and useful pointers after seeing an earlier version of this paper. Scott Benson, Tom Dietterich, Jerry Friedman, George John, Pat Langley, Ofer Matan, Ross Quinlan, Rob Tibshirani, Paul Utgoff, and one anonymous referee provided useful comments. George Light and Pat Langley helped clear the presentation style.

References

Aha, D. W. & Bankert, R. L. (1994), A comparative evaluation of sequential feature selection algorithms, *in* "Proceedings of the Fifth International Workshop on Artificial Intelligence and Statistics", pp. 1–7.

Almuallim, H. & Dietterich, T. G. (1991), Learning with many irrelevant features, *in* "Ninth National Conference on Artificial Intelligence", MIT Press, pp. 547–552.

Almuallim, H. & Dietterich, T. G. (1992), On learning more concepts, *in* "Proceedings of the Ninth International Conference on Machine Learning", Morgan Kaufmann, pp. 11–19.

Boyce, D., Farhi, A. & Weischedel, R. (1974), *Optimal Subset Selection*, Springer-Verlag.

Breiman, L., Friedman, J. H., Olshen, R. A. & Stone, C. J. (1984), *Classification and Regression Trees*, Wadsworth International Group.

Caruana, R. & Freitag, D. (1994), Greedy attribute selection, *in* W. W. Cohen & H. Hirsh, eds, "Machine Learning: Proceedings of the Eleventh International Conference", Morgan Kaufmann.

Clark, P. & Niblett, T. (1989), "The CN2 induction algorithm", *MLJ* **3**(4), 261–283.

Cormen, T. H., Leiserson, C. E. & Rivest, R. L. (1990), *Introduction to algorithms*, McGraw-Hill.

Devijver, P. A. & Kittler, J. (1982), *Pattern Recognition: A Statistical Approach*, Prentice-Hall International.

Efron, B. (1983), "Estimating the error rate of a prediction rule: improvement on cross-validation", *Journal of the American Statistical Association* **78**(382), 316–330.

Garey, M. R. (1972), "Optimal binary identification procedures", *Siam Journal on Applied Mathematics* **23**, 173–186.

Ginsberg, M. L. (1993), *Essential of Artificial Intelligence*, Morgan Kaufmann.

Hartmann, C. R. P., Varshney, P. K., Mehrotra, K. G. & Gerberich, C. L. (1982), "Application of information theory to the construction of efficient decision trees", *IEEE Transactions on information theory* **IT-28**(4), 565–577.

Holte, R. C. (1993), "Very simple classification rules perform well on most commonly used datasets", *Machine Learning* **11**, 63–90.

Hyafil, L. & Rivest, R. L. (1976), "Constructing optimal binary decision trees is NP-complete", *Information Processing Letters* **5**(1), 15–17.

John, G. H. (1994), Cross-validated C4.5: Using error estimation for automatic parameter selection, Technical Report STAN-CS-TN-94-12, Computer Science Department, Stanford University.

John, G., Kohavi, R. & Pfleger, K. (1994), Irrelevant features and the subset selection problem, *in* "Machine Learning: Proceedings of the Eleventh International Conference", Morgan Kaufmann, pp. 121–129. Available by anonymous ftp from: starry.Stanford.EDU:pub/ronnyk/ml94.ps.

Kohavi, R. (1994a), Bottom-up induction of oblivious, read-once decision graphs, *in* "Proceedings of the European Conference on Machine Learning". Available by anonymous ftp from starry.Stanford.EDU:pub/ronnyk/euroML94.ps.

Kohavi, R. (1994b), Bottom-up induction of oblivious, read-once decision graphs : strengths and limitations, *in* "Twelfth National Conference on Artificial Intelligence", pp. 613–618. Available by anonymous ftp from Starry.Stanford.EDU:pub/ronnyk/aaai94.ps.

Kohavi, R. (1994c), Feature subset selection as search with probabilistic estimates, *in* "AAAI Fall Symposium on Relevance", pp. 122–126. Available by anonymous ftp from: starry.Stanford.EDU:pub/ronnyk/aaaiSymposium94.ps.

Kohavi, R. & Frasca, B. (1994), Useful feature subsets and rough set reducts, *in* "Third International Workshop on Rough Sets and Soft Computing", pp. 310–317. Available by anonymous ftp from: starry.Stanford.EDU:pub/ronnyk/rough.ps.

Langley, P. & Sage, S. (1994), Induction of selective bayesian classifiers, *in* "Proceedings of the Tenth Conference on Uncertainty in Artificial Intelligence", Morgan Kaufmann, Seattle, WA, pp. 399–406.

Maron, O. & Moore, A. W. (1994), Hoeffding races: Accelerating model selection search for classification and function approximation, *in* "Advances in Neural Information Processing Systems", Vol. 6, Morgan Kaufmann.

Miller, A. J. (1990), *Subset Selection in Regression*, Chapman and Hall.

Modrzejewski, M. (1993), Feature selection using rough sets theory, *in* P. B. Brazdil, ed., "Proceedings of the European Conference on Machine Learning", pp. 213–226.

Moore, A. W. & Lee, M. S. (1994), Efficient algorithms for minimizing cross validation error, *in* W. W. Cohen & H. Hirsh, eds, "Machine Learning: Proceedings of the Eleventh International Conference", Morgan Kaufmann.

Moore, A. W., Hill, D. J. & Johnson, M. P. (1992), An empirical investigation of brute force to choose features, smoothers and function approximators, *in* "Computational Learning Theory and Natural Learning Systems Conference".

Murphy, P. M. & Aha, D. W. (1994), UCI repository of machine learning databases, For information contact ml-repository@ics.uci.edu.

Nilsson, N. J. (1980), *Principles of Artificial Intelligence*, Morgan Kaufmann.

Pawlak, Z. (1987), "Decision tables — a rough sets approach", *Bull. of EATCS* **33**, 85–96.

Pawlak, Z. (1991), *Rough Sets*, Kluwer Academic Publishers.

Pawlak, Z., Wong, S. & Ziarko, W. (1988), "Rough sets: Probabilistic versus deterministic approach", *Internation Journal of Man Machine Studies* **29**, 81–95.

Quinlan, J. R. (1986), "Induction of decision trees", *Machine Learning* **1**, 81–106. Reprinted in Shavlik and Dietterich (eds.) Readings in Machine Learning.

Quinlan, J. R. (1993), *C4.5: Programs for Machine Learning*, Morgan Kaufmann, Los Altos, California.

Reinwald, L. T. & Soland, R. M. (1966), "Conversion of limited-entry decision tables to optimal computer programs i: Minimum average processing time", *Journal of the ACM* **13**(3), 339–358.

Reinwald, L. T. & Soland, R. M. (1967), "Conversion of limited-entry decision tables to optimal computer programs ii: Minimum storage requirement", *Journal of the ACM* **14**(4), 742–755.

Rumelhart, D. E., Hinton, G. E. & Williams, R. J. (1986), *Learning Internal Representations by Error Propagation*, MIT Press, chapter 8.

Schaffer, C. (1994), A conservation law for generalization performance, *in* "Machine Learning: Proceedings of the Eleventh International Conference", Morgan Kaufmann, pp. 259–265.

Schumacher, H. & Sevcik, K. C. (1976), "The synthetic approach to decision table conversion", *Communications of the ACM* **19**(6), 343–351.

Shao, J. (1993), "Linear model seletion via cross-validation", *Journal of the American Statistical Association* **88**(422), 486–494.

Slowinski, R. (1992), *Intelligent decision support : handbook of applications and advances of the rough sets theory*, Kluwer Academic Publishers.

Stone, M. (1974), "Cross-validatory choice and assessment of statistical predictions", *Journal of the Royal Statistical Society B* **36**, 111–147.

Taylor, C., Michie, D. & Spiegalhalter, D. (1994), *Machine Learning, Neural and Statistical Classification*, Paramount Publishing International.

Thrun etal. (1991), The monk's problems: A performance comparison of different learning algorithms, Technical Report CMU-CS-91-197, Carnegie Mellon University.

Utgoff, P. E. (1994), An improved algorithm for incremental induction of decision trees, *in* "Machine Learning: Proceedings of the Eleventh International Conference", Morgan Kaufmann, pp. 318–325.

Weiss, S. M. (1991), "Small sample error rate estimation for k-nearest neighbor classifiers", *IEEE Transactions on Pattern Analysis and Machine Intelligence* **13**(3), 285–289.

Weiss, S. M. & Kulikowski, C. A. (1991), *Computer Systems that Learn*, Morgan Kaufmann, San Mateo, CA.

Wolpert, D. H. (1994), The relationship between PAC, the statistical physics framework, the Bayesian framework, and the VC framework, Technical report, The Santa Fe Institute, Santa Fe, NM.

Zhang, P. (1992), "On the distributional properties of model selection criteria", *Journal of the American Statistical Association* **87**(419), 732–737.

Ziarko, W. (1991), The discovery, analysis, and representation of data dependencies in databases, *in* G. Piatetsky-Shapiro & W. Frawley, eds, "Knowledge Discovery in Databases", MIT Press.

Pruning Multivariate Decision Trees by Hyperplane Merging

Miroslav KUBAT[1], Doris FLOTZINGER[2]

1 Institute for Systems Sciences, Johannes Kepler University, Altenbergerstr. 69, A-4040 Linz, Austria, e-mail: mirek@cast.uni-linz.ac.at

2 Department of Medical Informatics, Institute of Biomedical Engineering, Graz University of Technology, Brockmanngasse 41, A-8010 Graz, Austria. e-mail: flotzi@dpmi.tu-graz.ac.at

Abstract

Several techniques for induction of multivariate decision trees have been published in the last couple of years. Internal nodes of such trees typically contain binary tests questioning to what side of a hyperplane the example lies. Most of these algorithms use *cut-off pruning* mechanisms similar to those of traditional decision trees. Nearly unexplored remains the large domain of *substitutional pruning* methods, where a new decision test (derived from previous decision tests) replaces a subtree. This paper presents an approach to multivariate-tree pruning based on merging the decision hyperplanes, and demonstrates its performance on artificial and benchmark data.

1 Introduction

Algorithms for decision-tree induction belong to the most successful machine-learning techniques. In most implementations, the decision tests in the internal nodes question the values of single attributes. For many realistic concepts such *univariate* trees tend to be large and inflexible and, therefore, some researchers investigate algorithms for the induction of *multivariate* trees where the decisions are based on n-ary predicates or functions.

One of the first representatives of this category was the system BTC (Chan, 1988) where the decision tests were boolean functions of symbolic attributes. More recent work concentrates on the relatively general class of decision tests based on hyperplanes—see Utgoff (1989), Utgoff and Brodley (1990), Park and Sklansky (1990), or Murthy et al. (1993)[1]. The hyperplane is defined as $c_j + \Sigma w_i x_i = 0$, where x_i is the value of the i-th attribute, w_i is its weight, and c_j is a constant. If the weighted sum of the numeric attributes is larger than c_j, the example is propagated down the left branch. Otherwise, it is propagated down the right branch. An analysis of various aspects of this approach, with an overview of previous work, can be found in Brodley and Utgoff (1994).

---

[1] Heng Guo and Gelfand (1992) go one step further and place, at the decision nodes, small neural networks capable of modeling nonlinear concept boundaries

Experiments with benchmark data indicate that multivariate decision trees often outperform univariate trees at the cost of decreased interpretability.

To prevent overfitting and to make decision trees more compact, *pruning* is used. Several pruning techniques are described in Breimann et al. (1984), Quinlan (1990, 1993), and Cestnik and Bratko (1991). Typically, some statistical criterion is used to decide whether to replace a subtree with a leaf or branch. In the sequel, we will call these techniques *cut-off* pruning because they simply dismiss decision tests without creating new ones. An alternative approach can be exemplified by the system Fringe (Pagallo, 1989), where a univariate tree is simplified by replacing some of its subtrees with new attributes constructed as Boolean combinations of existing attributes. This may be referred to as *substitutional* pruning.

The fact that multivariate-tree tests are based on n-ary functions implies a rich class of substitutional-pruning methods based on the idea of replacing the set of tests $t_1(x_1, \ldots, x_n), \ldots, t_m(x_1, \ldots, x_n)$ with a single test $t(x_1, \ldots, x_n)$, derived from them. For instance, a pair of hyperplanes can be replaced with a single hyperplane approximating them. The objective of this paper is to show that this *hyperplane merging* leads to smaller trees that can yield higher classification accuracies on unseen data than cut-off pruning.

2 The System Description

In the sequel, we will report an algorithm for multivariate-tree pruning with hyperplane merging (HPM). For simplicity, we will constrain ourselves to domains where the examples are classified into two classes. Moreover, we will ignore such important aspects of multivariate trees as the selection of features for a decision test—for a detailed treatment of this issue see Brodley and Utgoff (1994). We will suppose that any decision test at an internal node of the tree is a linear combination of *all* attributes. Boolean attributes are turned into numeric by putting -1 for *false* and 1 for *true*[2].

The coefficients of the decision tests for this class of problems can be found by pseudoinverse matrices (for more sophisticated approaches addressing more general tasks see the above mentioned papers). Below, we first describe this simple approach to the induction of multivariate decision trees. Then, the HPM-postpruning method is presented.

2.1 Multivariate Tree Induction

The decisions in multivariate trees usually test the sign of a weighted sum of attribute values, $c_j + \Sigma_i w_i x_i$. To determine the weights, we used *pseudoinverse* matrices described in Duda and Hart (1973, Section 5.8).

Denote by $\mathbf{Y}$ the matrix of training examples and assume that each row represents one example and each column represents one attribute. An additional

---

[2]Symbolic attributes can be turned into Boolean (and then into numeric) by considering the presence or absence of individual attribute-value pairs as *true* and *false*, respectively.

Table 1: Multivariate-Tree Induction

---

mti(S).

1. Determine, by Formula (6), the coefficients of the hyperplane that splits the space of examples with minimum mean square error;
2. Place the hyperplane at the root. The decisions made at this node will split S into S_L and S_R;
3. If S_L contains examples from more than one class, run *mti(S_L)*; otherwise substitute S_L by a leaf with the label of this class;
4. If S_R contains examples from more than one class, run *mti(S_R)*; otherwise substitute S_R by a leaf with the label of this class.

---

column in $\mathbf{Y}$, $C = [111\dots 1]^T$, is provided for the biases c_j. Denote by $\mathbf{b}$ the (column) vector of the classification values of the examples, where 1 denotes a positive example and -1 denotes a negative example. If $\mathbf{w}$ is the (column) weight vector, then the problem is formulated as follows:

$$\mathbf{Y} \cdot \mathbf{w} = \mathbf{b} \tag{1}$$

Generally speaking, Equation (1) cannot be solved by matrix inversion because the number of rows in $\mathbf{Y}$ is usually much larger than the number of columns. Hence, the alternative task is to find the vector $\mathbf{w}$ that minimizes the difference $\mathbf{e}$ between $\mathbf{Y} \cdot \mathbf{w}$ and $\mathbf{b}$:

$$\mathbf{e} = \mathbf{Y} \cdot \mathbf{w} - \mathbf{b} \tag{2}$$

This is equivalent to minimizing the mean square error

$$E = \Sigma_i (\mathbf{y_i} \cdot \mathbf{w} - b_i)^2 \tag{3}$$

where $\mathbf{y_i}$ is the i-th example multiplied by the weight vector $\mathbf{w}$, and b_i is the class of the i-th example.

To find an extreme of a function amounts to finding its gradient

$$\nabla E = \Sigma_i 2(\mathbf{y_i} \cdot \mathbf{w} - b_i)\mathbf{y_i} \tag{4}$$

and setting it equal to zero, which leads to the following matrix formula:

$$2\mathbf{Y}^T(\mathbf{Yw} - \mathbf{b}) = 0, \tag{5}$$

Equation (5) can be rewritten as $\mathbf{Y}^T\mathbf{Yw} = \mathbf{Y}^T\mathbf{b}$, and from here

$$\begin{aligned} \mathbf{w} &= (\mathbf{Y}^T\mathbf{Y})^{-1}\mathbf{Y}^T\mathbf{b} \\ &= \mathbf{Y}^P\mathbf{b}. \end{aligned} \tag{6}$$

$\mathbf{Y}^P = (\mathbf{Y}^T\mathbf{Y})^{-1}\mathbf{Y}^T$ is called the *pseudoinverse* matrix of $\mathbf{Y}$. Standard functions for its effective calculation are provided in most mathematical software packages.

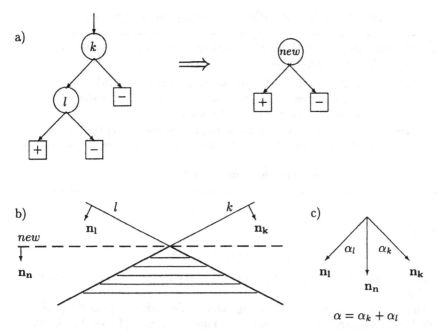

Fig.1. Hyperplane merging. The hyperplanes l and k are substituted by the hyperplane *new*. The shaded area is the original positive subspace. The positive subspace after HPM is below the dashed line. $\mathbf{n_l}, \mathbf{n_k}$ and $\mathbf{n_n}$ are the normal vectors of the respective hyperplanes.

To summarize, knowing the matrix $\mathbf{Y}$ of training examples and knowing the vector $\mathbf{b}$ of their classifications, one can use Formula (6) to determine the weight vector $\mathbf{w}$ minimizing the mean squared error. The only requirement is that $\mathbf{Y^T Y}$ must not be singular, which is satisfied in most cases.

Formula (6) is used within the recursive algorithm for the decision-tree induction, as indicated in Table 1.

2.2 Hyperplane Merging

Figure 1 shows a 2-dimensional illustration of HPM. Two consecutive nodes in the multivariate-tree branch in Figure 1a are represented by two hyperplanes that, if conjuncted, form a subspace boundary (Figure 1b). Cut-off pruning would solely eliminate hyperplane l and the resulting subspace would be bordered by k. HPM, however, replaces the two hyperplanes with a new hyperplane approximating them. Subtree *new* will in many cases better generalize to unseen examples than subtree k.

Let us now specify the HPM procedure (see Figure 1c). The new hyperplane is characterized by its normal vector, $\mathbf{n_n}$, and an arbitrary intersection point of l and k. The normal vector $\mathbf{n_n}$ is a linear combination of the normal vectors of

Table 2: Combined HPM and cut-off pruning algorithm

---

1. Generate a multivariate decision tree with the algorithm from Table 1;
2. Starting from the bottom level:
   a) For each decision node, attempt its replacement with a leaf;
   b) For each pair of consecutive decision tests, attempt their replacement with a single test using Formula (10), as indicated in Figure 1;
3. Among the replacements attempted in the previous step, select the one with the smallest 'pessimistic error estimate' (Quinlan, 1990). If no error decrease can be achieved, *stop*.
4. Carry out the selected replacement and go to 2.

---

hyperplanes l and k:

$$\mathbf{n}_{n0} = a_l \cdot \mathbf{n}_{l0} + a_k \cdot \mathbf{n}_{k0} \tag{7}$$

where $\mathbf{n}_{n0}, \mathbf{n}_{k0}$, and $\mathbf{n}_{l0}$ are normalizations of the respective normal vectors to unit length.

The angles between $\mathbf{n}_n$ and $\mathbf{n}_l$ ($\mathbf{n}_k$) can be defined as a percentage of the angle between $\mathbf{n}_l$ and $\mathbf{n}_k$ weighted by the number of examples used to create l (k):

$$\begin{aligned} \mathbf{n}_{l0} \cdot \mathbf{n}_{n0} &= \cos(\alpha_l) \\ \mathbf{n}_{k0} \cdot \mathbf{n}_{n0} &= \cos(\alpha_k) \end{aligned} \tag{8}$$

$$\alpha_l = \frac{\#ex_k \cdot \alpha}{\#ex_l + \#ex_k} \qquad \alpha_k = \frac{\#ex_l \cdot \alpha}{\#ex_l + \#ex_k} \tag{9}$$

where $\#ex_l$ ($\#ex_k$) is the number of examples below hyperplane l (k) and α is the angle between $\mathbf{n}_l$ and $\mathbf{n}_k$.

Substituting (7) into (8), we obtain

$$\begin{bmatrix} \mathbf{n}_{l0}^T \mathbf{n}_{l0} & \mathbf{n}_{l0}^T \mathbf{n}_{k0} \\ \mathbf{n}_{k0}^T \mathbf{n}_{l0} & \mathbf{n}_{k0}^T \mathbf{n}_{k0} \end{bmatrix} \cdot \begin{bmatrix} a_l \\ a_k \end{bmatrix} = \begin{bmatrix} \cos(\alpha_l) \\ \cos(\alpha_k) \end{bmatrix} \tag{10}$$

and, from here, the values of coefficients a_l and a_k can easily be found, considering Equations (9).

Note that cut-off pruning can be understood as a special case of HPM, where $\alpha_l = 0$ and $\alpha_k = \alpha$.

The overall pruning algorithm using HPM is described in Table 2. Note that the program has to decide, at each step, whether to use traditional cut-off pruning or hyperplane merging.

3 Experiments

To test the utility of the approach, we experimented with artificial as well as public-domain benchmark data files. Throughout the experiments, we observed whether HPM leads to smaller decision trees with comparable, or even increased, classification accuracy on unseen data. We wanted to know how learning curves are affected and what the behavior in the presence of noise is.

3.1 Experimental Data

Three artificial and four benchmark data were used. Below we provide their brief description and motivation.

Artificial data

To observe the performance on learning concepts with axis-parallel, oblique, and non-linear concept boundaries, we generated the following artificial data sets,

Axis-Parallel Concept (APC). A decision tree involving five numeric attributes from the interval [0,1] was manually drawn. Then 800 examples were constructed so that 50% of them were positive, according to this tree, and 50% were negative. 320 examples were used as a testing set. Note that this concept is not very suited for a learner searching for oblique hyperplanes.

Oblique Concept (OC). The concept was defined as the space between two hyperplanes in a 3-dimensional cube $[0, 1] \times [0, 1] \times [0, 1]$. 3000 examples were generated, 50% of them positive and 50% negative. 1200 examples were used as a testing set.

Nonlinear Concept (NC). The concept was defined as the space inside a sphere positioned in the center of the 3-dimensional cube $[0, 1] \times [0, 1] \times [0, 1]$. 2000 examples were generated, 50% of them positive, 50% negative. 640 examples were used as a testing set.

Public domain benchmark data

We have tested HPM also on some well-known benchmark data. An important methodological note is necessary.

The fact that the number of examples in these data files was relatively small (considering the number of attributes) weakens the validity of error estimates. To insure the statistical reliability of the results, we used the *random subsampling* strategy, as suggested, for instance, by Weiss and Kapouleas (1989): each file is split into two non-overlapping subsets, one for learning and one for testing; the experiments are repeated for several (10 in our case) random splits, and the results are averaged. This methodology is known to provide very good error estimates. In our experiments, the training set contained 60% of the examples, the rest was used as a testing set.

The following public-domain benchmark data files were used:

Table 3: Artificial data: axis-parallel concept (APC), oblique concept (OC), and non-linear concept (NC). Classification accuracy on unseen examples and tree sizes are shown for cut-off pruning and for HPM

	Classif.accuracy		Tree size	
	cut-off	HPM	cut-off	HPM
APC	71.3	72.7	101.0	87.4
OC	97.8	97.7	54.6	48.8
NC	82.8	83.4	281.6	233.6

Congressional Vote. 435 examples described by 16 Boolean attributes. Values *false* are treated as -1 and values *true* are treated as 1. No missing values. The noise was generated in such a way that in $n\%$ of the cases (where n is the noise level) the attribute value was flip-flopped to its opposite.

Hepatitis. 155 examples described by 19 mixed Boolean/numeric attributes. Missing values are replaced with medium values (0 in the case of a Boolean variable).

Liver disorders (BUPA). 345 examples described by 7 numeric attributes. No missing values.

Chess domain. 3197 examples described by 36 symbolic attributes. No missing values.

3.2   Results

Table 3 summarizes the classification accuracy and size of the trees induced from the artificial data. Two kinds of decision trees are compared: multivariate trees with the traditional cut-off pruning, and multivariate trees with HPM. As the examples are noise-free, an increase in classification accuracy was not the primary objective. Rather, we wanted to see, for different shapes of concept boundaries, whether the tree size is reduced by HPM without detriment to performance. This is indeed the case in all of the three domains. The trees are more compact and the classification accuracy after HPM is comparable to that achieved with cut-off pruning.

Table 4 summarizes results achieved on benchmark data. In the hepatitis domain, HPM clearly outperformed cut-off pruning in terms of accuracy, while in the other domains the accuracy remained virtually unchanged. However, in three domains the tree size is dramatically reduced. For instance, in the chess domain, the program was able to find (in all 10 runs) a single decision test providing about the same classification accuracy as cut-off pruning and only about 2 percent deterioration of the accuracy as compared to the original tree that contained, on average, 56 nodes (the chess domain is noise-free). Interestingly, such decision test was not found with the pseudoinverse matrix minimizing the mean square error.

Table 4: Learning from benchmark data under various approaches to pruning: no pruning, cut-off pruning, and hyperplane merging

	Classif.accuracy			Tree size		
	no prng	cut-off	HPM	no prng	cut-off	HPM
Congr.vote	92.4	96.1	96.1	11.6	1	1
Hepatitis	73.1	72.1	77.4	8.6	4.8	2.6
Bupa	60.4	60.0	60.7	61.8	54.8	51.4
Chess	95.8	94.2	94.0	56.0	5.0	1.0

Table 5: Congressional vote in the presence of noise: no pruning, cut-off pruning, and hyperplane merging

noise	Classification accuracy			Tree size		
	no prng	cut-off	HPM	no prng	cut-off	HPM
0%	92.4	96.1	96.1	11.6	1	1
5%	90.4	93.7	93.3	14.2	1	1
10%	86.4	90.2	89.1	17.4	5.8	4.2
15%	85.9	87.9	89.5	18.8	9.6	4.6
20%	83.1	85.1	87.6	20.4	12.8	5.2
25%	77.7	78.7	79.5	23.2	17.0	15.0

Table 5 contains similar results for the congressional-vote data corrupted with noise. HPM performance is more evident for noise levels exceding 10%.

A series of supplementary experiments have revealed that the method of pruning did not affect the learning curves of the systems. In all domains, hyperplane merging provided somewhat better accuracy by arbitrary number of learning examples.

It should be noted that the results provided by the program are not always superior to those that can be achieved by other machine learning systems. Here we concentrate exclusively on the effect of pruning techniques in multivariate trees, ignoring the question whether multivariate trees represent the ideal solution for the given data.

4 Conclusion

A technique for *substitutional pruning* of multivariate decision trees has been presented. The approach is based on replacing a pair of decision hyperplanes with a single hyperplane (hyperplane merging, HPM). To verify the feasibility of the basic idea, we implemented a simple system for the induction of multivariate decision trees with subsequent HPM-pruning.

Experiments indicate that this simplification mechanism leads to substantially smaller decision trees than traditional cut-off pruning techniques. In many cases, the simplified trees yielded even better classification accuracies on unseen examples with smaller standard deviations. HPM seems to perform well especially in the presence of noise.

Improvements to the current version are, of course, possible. For instance, the *new* hyperplane in Figure 1 is always positioned at the intersection of the original two hyperplanes, k and l. It is likely that further tuning is possible by moving the substituted hyperplane along its norm vector. Moreover, we believe that alternative algorithms for more general substitutional pruning (not necessarily limited to hyperplanes) can be found and supplemented to existing multivariate-tree generating programs such as OC1, described in Murthy et al. (1993).

Even though the decision hyperplanes of the trees considered in this study always involved *all* features (which is not an ideal solution, as pointed out by Brodley and Utgoff, 1994), the approach can be easily generalized to decision hyperplanes created from subsets of features when the coefficients of the non-involved features are put equal to 0. Also the application of the technique in multiclass domains should not pose serious problems.

Acknowledgement

The first author was supported by the grant S7002-MAT from the Austrian Science Foundation (FWF).

References

L. Breiman, J. Friedman, R. Olshen, and C.J. Stone (1984). *Classification and Regression Trees*. Wadsworth International Group, Belmont, CA

C.E. Brodley and P.E. Utgoff (1994). Multivariate Decision Trees. *Machine Learning* (in press)

B. Cestnik and I. Bratko (1991). On Estimating Probabilities in Tree Pruning. *Proceedings of the European Working Session on Mashine Learning*, Porto, Portugal, March 6–8, 138–150

P.K. Chan (1988). Inductive Learning with BCT. *Proceedings of the 5th International Conference on Machine Learning*, Morgan Kaufmann

R.O. Duda and P.E. Hart (1973). *Pattern Classification and Scene Analysis*. John Wiley & Sons, New York

Heng Guo and S.B. Gelfand (1992). Classification Trees with Neural Network Feature Extraction. *IEEE Transactions on Neural Networks*, 3:923–933

S. Murthy, S. Kasif, S. Salzberg, and R. Beigel (1993). OC1: Randomized Induction of Oblique Decision Trees. *Proceedings of the 11th National Conference on Artificial Intelligence*, Washington, DC

G. Pagallo (1989). Learning DNF by Decision Trees. *Proceedings of the 11th International Joint Conference on Artificial Intelligence, IJCAI'89*

Y. Park and J. Sklansky (1990). Automated Design of Linear Tree Classifiers. *Pattern Recognition* 23:1393–1412

J.R. Quinlan (1990). Probabilistic Decision Trees. In Kodratoff,Y.–Michalski,R.S. (eds.) *Machine Learning: An Artificial Intelligence Approach*, Volume III, Morgan Kaufmann, 140–152

J.R. Quinlan (1993). *C4.5: Programs for Machine Learning*. Morgan Kaufmann, San Mateo

P.E. Utgoff (1989). Perceptron Trees: A Case Study in Hybrid Concept Representations. *Connection Science* 1:377–391

P.E. Utgoff and C.E. Brodley (1990): An Incremental Method for Finding Multivariate Splits for Decision Trees. *Proceedings of the 7th International Conference on Machine Learning*, Morgan Kaufmann

S.M. Weiss and I. Kapouleas (1989). An Empirical Comparison of Pattern Recognition, Neural Nets, and Machine Learning Classification Methods. *Proceedings of the 11th International Joint Conference on Artificial Intelligence, IJCAI'89*, Detroit, MI, 781–787

Multiple-Knowledge Representations in Concept Learning

Thierry Van de Merckt & Christine Decaestecker

IRIDIA, Université Libre de Bruxelles
Av. Franklin Roosevelt 50, 1050 Brussels, Belgium.
Phone: +32.2 - 650 31 69 Fax: +32.2 - 650 27 15
{THVDM, CDECAES@ULB.AC.BE}

Abstract. This paper investigates a general framework for learning concepts that allows to generate accurate and comprehensible concept representations. It is known that biases used in learning algorithms directly affect their performance as well as their comprehensibility. A critical problem is that, most of the time, the most "comprehensible" representations are not the best performer in terms of classification! In this paper, we argue that concept learning systems should employ Multiple-Knowledge Representation: a *deep* knowledge level optimised from recognition (classification task) and a *shallow* one optimised for comprehensibility (description task). Such a model of concept learning assumes that the system can use an interpretation function of the deep knowledge level to build an *approximately* correct *comprehensible* description of it. This approach is illustrated through our GEM system which learns concepts in a numerical attribute space using a Neural Network representation as the deep knowledge level and symbolic rules as the shallow level.

1. Introduction

Concept Learning has much evolve during the last decade. Referring to the goal stated by Michalski in 1983 [Michalski 83] Conceptual Inductive Learning "designates a type of Inductive Learning whose final products are *symbolic descriptions* expressed in high level, *human oriented* terms and forms." Besides the implicit goal of inductive learning, i.e., to produce a theory that is able to explain observed facts and to make correct predictions about unseen cases, Concept Learning also relies on a strong cognitive motivation: the system should be able to express the underlying theory (the concept) under a human-understandable language, which is by essence symbolic. Therefore, concept descriptions have been biased in a way that is close to human way of *understanding and explicating concepts*, that is, by using symbolic descriptions under the form of logical-based languages for Nominal attributes or under the form of intervals (producing orthogonal hyper-rectangles) for continuous ones. Some well-known examples are AQ [Michalski 83], Decision Trees [Quinlan 86a] and Decision Lists [Clark & Niblett 89]. This goal on the representation of induced theories was a characteristic that drew a clear frontier between AI Concept Learning and any "classifier" algorithm issued from Statistical Inference or Pattern Recognition techniques.

Nowadays many subsymbolic algorithms like Neural Networks [Hertz & al. 91], Exemplar-based [Aha & al. 91] and Prototype-based [Kohonen 90; Decaestecker 93] are actively investigated by the machine learning community. Concurrently, symbolic algorithms make an increasing use of techniques issued from Statistical Inference or

Pattern Recognition to improve some aspects of concept recognition: Bayesian Trees [Buntine 89] and Flexible Concept Matching [Esposito & al. 91; Bergadano & al. 92; Van de Merckt 92] are some examples of this trend. A major problem of these algorithms is that it is no longer easy to get the semantic of the knowledge used to encode the concept membership function: they use *interpretation* functions of the encoded knowledge under the form of complex matching mechanisms where the semantic of the concept is (partially) encoded in real valued parameters. In this case, *semantic* means to have a comprehension on how instances are allocated or not to a particular concept. Hence, most of them do not produce a concept *description* in "human-oriented terms and forms" any more. It is clear then that the actual trend of many works done in Machine Learning does not reflect the original definition of Concept Learning. However, these algorithms were developed to answer some important weaknesses of early concept learning systems with respect to classification accuracy. From one side, most early symbolic systems produced *crisp* concept descriptions, i.e., descriptions under the form of explicit concept boundaries that discriminate classes in the description space (see AQ [Michalski 83], ID3 [Quinlan 86a] or CN2 [Clark & Niblett 89]). Whilst more difficult learning tasks have been attacked, it became clear that these algorithms entailed strong limitations, especially regarding graded concepts [Aha & al. 91], noisy and incomplete data [Aha & al. 91; Esposito & al. 91; Van de Merckt 92], and complex concepts [Bergadano & al. 91; Michalski 90]. From another side, it became clear that the relation between biases implemented in the algorithms and their efficiency to infer correct hypothesis is crucial [Utgoff 86; Benjamin 90]. Hence, Brodley speaks about "selective superiority" among different algorithms and concept domains [Brodley 93].

A critical problem of concept learning lies in satisfying two conflicting goals. From one side, one wants the algorithms to produce simple and human-understandable descriptions, which imposes strong (cognitive) constraints. From the other side, one wants them to reach high levels of classification accuracy, which requires one to use complex (as far as human comprehensibility is concerned) knowledge representations. How these two goals can be reconciled? Simply by assuming that an agent might possess multiple-knowledge representations on the same problem. In this paper we present a new approach to Concept Learning, called the Two-functional Model, which is based on this idea. In this framework, we present a system called GEM, which uses a Neural Network to optimise a concept representation using a prototype-based representation and which produces symbolic descriptions reflecting "its knowledge" of the target concept. Section 3 presents our neural-symbolic system. Section 4 presents some experimental results using GEM. Section 5 makes a quick review of closer related works. Section 6 identifies limitations and future works.

2 . Concept Learning Revisited: the Two-Functional Model

The basic idea of the TF model is that symbolic descriptions, as far as concepts are concerned, is a characteristic of human beings and hence, results from our high linguistic skill to communicate *what we have in mind*. It does not mean however, that what we communicate is equivalent to the complex knowledge encoded in our brain. Therefore communicating complex concepts, such as *friendship*, entails some kind of reduction in both complexity and efficiency by introducing a human understandable language and cognitive description biases, as simplicity, that constitute a common

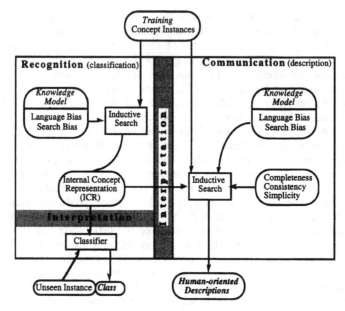

Fig. 1: A flow-chart of the Two-Functional Model of Concept Learning

semantic ground shared by all people. Therefore we argue that there is no need to merge both functions (recognition and description) into one single concept representation as it is done by most symbolic approaches. On the contrary, an *internal concept representation* (ICR), based on any knowledge model[1], should be optimised regarding recognition efficiency without conflict of its further description which is performed by a distinct system that produces a (good) approximation of it. In the Two-Functional model (TF) a "Concept Learner" entails two distinct parts (see Fig. 1):

(i)   **Recognition** - It is the "deep knowledge" level which results from an inductive learning process whose bias focus on accuracy of the concept representation. This bias may include any kind of Background Knowledge that helps the system to choose a specific knowledge model regarding the domain (as done by [Brodley 93]) or that encodes *a priori* domain theory that generates constraints on the possible concept representations. The resulting representation, called the *Internal Concept Representation* (ICR), is further used by a classifying function which aims to recognise instances from non-instances of the concept;

(ii) **Communication** - It is the "shallow knowledge" level using human-oriented descriptions that reflect the concept encoded by the ICR. It results from an exploration of the ICR guided by biases focusing on cognitive aspects of the descriptions, such as background knowledge that provides preferences and constraints on the descriptions or that help the system to choose among possible search techniques regarding the type of knowledge model encoded by the ICR. As it is the case for human beings, preferences may entail parameters like

---

1   By Knowledge Model we mean the way the knowledge is encoded (prototype, examplar, DNF, NN, etc.) and its interpretation function (matching used for classification).

completeness ("tell me more about it"), consistency ("be more precise") and simplicity ("I don't care about the exceptional cases"). Because its bias may be very different from those of the ICR, many different descriptions consistent with the ICR and the background knowledge might exist and hence, the communication function performs an inductive search in a space of possible descriptions.

In early symbolic systems, both parts were merged into one single algorithm where the ICR also stood for the human-oriented description. It should be noted that the TF model does not provide a framework for generating symbolic descriptions *independently* of the recognition function. On the contrary, the link between the ICR and the inductive description engine in Fig. 1 entails an interpretation of the semantic content of the ICR (it will be explained in details later) and this interpretation defines the class of classifying functions that could be easily implemented within a particular implementation of the TF model.

Although this model is inspired from Cognitive Science, it offers two major advantages resulting from the clear separation between recognition and communication. The first one is that the classification function may be optimised regarding accuracy by using many kinds of powerful techniques that throw off the yoke of cognitive biases linked to human-oriented descriptions (in our case we use a Neural Network (NN) for that purpose). This allows to get rid of the compromises between accuracy and understandability of complex concepts that are always to be chosen in single concept representation algorithms [Stepp & Michalski 83; Iba & al. 88]. The second advantage is that starting from an optimised ICR and explicitly introducing cognitive biases to generate concept descriptions allow to evaluate the cost of introducing these biases. Indeed, by looking at the loss of accuracy due to their introduction one may *know the cost of being explicit and human understandable* and hence, to evaluate the adequacy of the description bias regarding the target concept. This is not the case of most Symbolic and several Neural Net algorithms [Tshichold & al. 92; Goodman & al. 92] which directly produce biased class descriptions also used for classification.

3. The Hybrid Neural-Symbolic GEM System

GEM has been designed to work in continuous attribute spaces in which cognitive biases encoded in symbolic algorithms are especially constraining. Indeed, many algorithms (ID3-like, AQ's or CN2) produce descriptions under the form of orthogonal hyper-rectangles (whose edges are perpendicular to the description axis). It is well known that this representation may be inadequate for many domains, leading to poor descriptions from a cognitive as well as from a recognition point of view. Many recent algorithms using other kinds of knowledge models like Instance-Based Learning [Aha & al. 91], Prototypes [Decaestecker 93], Neural Trees [Samkar & Mammone 91; Utgoff 88] or Neural Networks [Hertz & al. 91] achieve better results in these domains. Therefore, the whole potential of the TF approach may be particularly highlighted for such numerical-featured concepts. To illustrate the behaviour of GEM, we will use a two-class problem defined in a two-dimension space as shown in Fig. 2, named the Diamond problem. The instances are uniformly distributed in a square of side 30 and allocated to the classes following the decision surface drawn in the figure. A training set of 400 instances has been used.

3.1 The Recognition Function

In GEM, the recognition function uses a Prototype-based *Knowledge Model* implemented through a neural network (a detailed presentation may be found in [Decaestecker 93]).

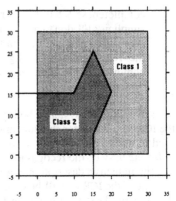

Fig. 2: The Diamond Problem

The Knowledge Model - NNP uses a three-layer, fully connected, feedforward net (Fig. 3). The hidden layer stands for a set of Prototypes whose locations are to be optimised. The weights of the input-to-hidden units are the prototype vector descriptions (location in the pattern space). The hidden-to-output weights are binary and *fixed*: they indicate the class of each prototype. Only the weights of the hidden units are trained. NNP globally optimises the location of prototypes in order to minimise the classification error rate. Hence, the vector descriptions of prototypes are adapted through a gradient procedure which minimises an original error function. A deterministic annealing procedure is introduced to avoid local minima and to distribute the prototypes in each class. The whole optimisation process is biased in order to minimise the resubstitution error rate with a *minimum number of prototypes* (simplicity

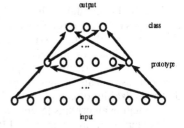

Fig. 3: Network architecture

bias). Hence, redundant prototypes (a prototype is redundant if all its covered instances may be correctly classified by other prototypes of the same class) are eliminated. Hence, the remaining ones are "forced" to cover the largest area of the instance space. At the end of the optimisation, the ICR is constituted by the list of prototypes and its interpretation function for doing classification becomes a simple nearest neighbour rule applied on their locations. Thus the ICR produces Piecewise-linear decision boundaries.

Bias - A major bias of NNP results from the fact that it belongs to Piecewise Linear Classifiers. Indeed, each prototype defines implicitly a convex decision surface by the means of the nearest neighbour competition (see Fig. 4). The set of all individual prototype's decision surface realises a partition of the input space (Voronoï Diagram) and hence, the ICR is always complete but may be partially inconsistent. Besides this language bias, the inductive search algorithm applies a *global optimisation* process focusing on the minimisation of the resubstitution error rate by modifying the prototypes' location. An important bias of NNP is its hill-climbing search for generating *simple* ICR (redundant prototypes elimination): this process imposes a *greatest generalisation* strategy by forcing each prototype to cover the largest area in the instance space, allowing the algorithm to better handle noisy data.

Empirical evaluations of NNP show that it generates highly performing ICR in terms of: (i) classification accuracy and simplicity (small number of prototypes); (ii) regularity (small standard deviations when tested on many different random training sets) and (iii) robustness against noise and domain dependency (even for highly nonlinear concepts). For detailed results see [Decaestecker 93] and [Van de Merckt & Decaestecker 94].

On the Diamond problem, NNP produces an ICR which consists of 6 prototypes. In Fig. 4, the classification boundaries resulting from the prototype's location and from the nearest neighbour competitive process is compared to the underlying target concept boundary. The difference between the real frontier and the decision surface produced by NNP results from the lack of training instances in some places of the instance space.

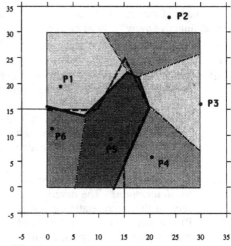

Fig. 4: NNP ICR on the Diamond problem

ICR Interpretation - It is essential, in the framework of the TF model, to have a clear interpretation of the semantic content of the ICR. Indeed, this knowledge must be available to the communication function to generate descriptions that correctly reflect the knowledge encoded in the ICR. The semantic interpretation of the ICR relies upon the identification that each prototype implicitly draws (or covers) a *convex* decision surface in the instance space, called the *Prototypical Region* (PR). Because of NNP's bias for simplicity, we assume that each PR is necessary to approximate the concept's class membership function and hence that, regarding their instance space convexity, each PR stands for a disjunction of the target concept. Therefore, to produce a symbolic description of the concept underlined by the ICR, a description of each individual PR will be searched, each of them being the description of a *disjunct* of the concept.

3.2 The Communication Function

The problem of "understanding" a piece of knowledge representation (as a list of prototypes' location, symbolic descriptions or a matrix of weighted connections of a NN) is related to its *interpretation*, i.e. the function that *gives a protocol on how to use the knowledge*. For NNP, the interpretation is a nearest neighbour rule that entails a competitive process between all prototypes and hence, getting a clear view of the encoded concept's *shape* is a complex calculation problem, as far as human being is concerned.

The Form of Human-oriented Descriptions - The communication function identifies the *classification boundaries* encoded by the ICR and produces a *crisp* description of them. Crisp descriptions have been chosen because they have a "self-contained" meaning: they take the form of DNF implication rules where the precondition part entails disjunctive sets of conjunctive predicates and where the conclusion part specifies the resulting class.

Bias - Each PR of the ICR is approximated by a set of closed geometrical figures. There are three basic biases used by GEM in its search for symbolic descriptions: (i) the shape of the crisp geometrical figures used to approximate each PR; (ii) the use of a "disjunctive view" instead of a "class view" when searching for descriptions; (iii) the assumption that noise has been correctly treated by the recognition function when producing the ICR.

(i)   *Symbolic language* - To approximate a PR drawn by the ICR, GEM uses orthogonal hyper-rectangles under the form of intervals defined over the instance space. This approach is widely used by Symbolic Learning systems (see for example ID3 [Quinlan 86a], AQ [Michalski 83] or Nearest Hyperrectangles [Salzberg 91]) because of their natural understanding: an orthogonal box can be easily represented by a conjunctive rule where each term tests a cut-point value of an attribute.

(ii)   *A Disjunctive view when searching for descriptions* - The descriptions rely on the interpretation given to PRs which assumes that each of them represents a typical disjunct of the target concept. It is a considerable advantage of the prototypical approach to produce an ICR allowing such a nice interpretation of the distinct areas of its decision surface, as shown in Fig. 4. The target concept is described by approximating each PR individually. As a result, the inductive search focuses on disjunctive terms (the PRs), each one being considered as a distinct new class (called the ICR_class in the algorithms), instead of focusing

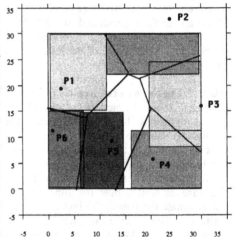

Fig. 5: The ICR and the resulting discriminant descriptions

on real classes given by the training set (called the Training_class). As a consequence, each Training_class represented by *n* prototypes will be described by at least *n* disjunctive terms, one for each PR (see in Fig. 5). The whole concept description is then simply the union of all disjunctive rules. However this bias is *relaxed when looking at near boundary regions of two adjacent PRs of the same class*. Indeed, prototypes also implicitly draw boundaries separating two adjacent PRs of the same class (called adjacent disjunctive PRs) whose locations are arbitrary. Therefore, describing the PRs individually accommodates a relaxing facility near adjacent disjunctive PR boundaries.

(iii)   *Noise treatment* - A basic assumption of the TF model is that the ICR is better optimised regarding classification accuracy than the symbolic descriptions that are produced using cognitive biases (as orthogonal concept boundaries) and hence, that the optimised ICR avoids noise overfitting. In GEM, noise overfitting avoidance is implemented by the simplicity bias described above. Therefore, training instances that are covered by a PR of a distinct class (inconsistent) are considered to be noisy and are hidden to the description inductive search. As a consequence, the symbolic algorithm relies on the recognition function for the treatment of noise and hence, will not incorporate procedures for taking noise into account.

Preference Criteria - Given these considerations, the inputs of the symbolic description engine are the ICR and the training set. In order to produce symbolic descriptions, a number of other preferences must be decided on: (i) the *simplicity* of the concept description or, in other words, the level of approximation of the ICR's decision surface; (ii) the *consistency* and the *completeness* of the descriptions.

(i)   *Simplicity* - Because the language bias differs among the ICR and the description (Piecewise linear versus orthogonal boundaries), more than one hyper-rectangles might be used to correctly approximate the decision surface drawn by one single Prototype. The number of hyper-rectangles needed to correctly approximate one single PR depends on the adequacy of the description's language bias (orthogonality) regarding the target concept. Thus, the number of disjunctive *rules* describing a single PR depends on a preference criterion for simplicity that fixes the maximum number of hyper-rectangles that will be used to approximate one single PR. Using this criterion, one may favour the simplicity of a concept description (sacrificing its consistency or its completeness) or one may ask for complete and consistent descriptions. Once a simplicity level has been chosen, consistency or completeness has to be fixed. In the current state of GEM implementation, there are two simplicity levels available: one box (hyper-rectangle) per prototype and a free number of boxes, which results in producing "perfect" approximations of the target concept.

(ii)   *Consistency and Completeness* - Given a level of simplicity, consistency and completeness are related: once a level of consistency for the descriptions has been chosen, the level of completeness is given as a result of the inductive search and inversely. Descriptions may therefore be oriented towards characteristic (100% complete) or discriminant (100% consistent). Any level between 0 and 100% may be asked to the system for consistency or completeness.

Bias Evaluation - Given a level of simplicity and a 100% consistent preference, the level of completeness gives information on the adequacy of the symbolic language towards the domain. Indeed, a PR is a *convex* region in the instance space and hence, if the concept boundaries are orthogonal, one single hyper-rectangle should adequately approximate a PR. If it is not the case, by increasing the complexity of the concept description, one may be able to obtain consistent descriptions that are more complete. In fact, increasing complexity is a mean to produce "closer" complete and consistent descriptions and hence, simplicity is no more a bias to avoid overfitting, as usually in symbolic learning, but *it stands for adjusting biased descriptions (hyper-rectangles) to the underlying shape of the target concept.*

3.3   The Description Algorithm

Two different algorithms have been implemented, one that produces a description with a simplicity level of one box per prototype, and another one, based on ID3 [Quinlan 86a], to produce descriptions of unconstrained complexity (called the free-complexity algorithm). Two important processes are common to the two algorithms: the *Filtering* process that implements the bias related to the treatment of noise and the *Re-Labelling* process that implements the Disjunctive view bias.

The Filtering Procedure - Given the training set, the ICR and its interpretation function, this function eliminates from the training all wrongly covered instances with respect to the ICR. It then returns a list of PR-instances organised into clusters, one per prototype. These filtered ICR_clusters will be further used to build the symbolic description of the target concept.

The Re-Labelling Procedure - This process creates a new attribute for each filtered instance, called the ICR_class, that indicates to which PR they belong. ICR_clusters and ICR_class are used by the algorithm to implement the Disjunctive view bias.

The One-complexity Algorithm - This algorithm follows a bottom-up approach with a *least generalisation strategy*. A PR may be described by two extreme boxes: a *complete Hyper-Box* (complete-HB) and a *discriminant Hyper-Box* (discriminant-HB). The complete-HB is the *smallest* hyper-rectangle covering all PR-instances (least generalisation strategy) and the discriminant-HB is the *largest* consistent hyper-rectangle included in the complete-HB, i.e., which covers the largest part of training examples belonging to the PR-class while covering no training examples of another class (greatest generalisation strategy within complete-HBs). Once the ICR_clusters have been built, producing a complete-HB for one PR is straightforward. It consists in the list of intervals defined by the minimum and maximum values observed among PR-instances for each attribute. In case of scarce training sets, the least generalisation strategy may produce uncovered instance space regions of known class regarding the ICR: the in-between regions of two adjacent disjunctive PRs (of same class). Therefore, complete-HBs are slightly extended, in each direction, towards the closest instance belonging to an adjacent disjunctive PR if it exists (no new negative instances should be included in the box extension). It should be noted that complete-HBs may share large overlapping areas and hence that they may include instances from another class or from an adjacent disjunctive PR, as Fig. 6 shows. The complete-HB is the starting point of the algorithm. To generate an HB of consistency χ, a deflation of the current complete-HB is done by the *Deflate-HB* procedure. Several HBs included into a Complete-HB can be χ-consistent while differing by their cover. Hence, the algorithm performs a hill climbing search biased to *maximise the cover* in terms of completeness and volume (to keep a maximum of positive examples as well as a maximum of the initial complete-HB volume). Starting from the complete-HB and the filtered ICR_clusters, it iteratively searches to shrink the complete-HB along one single direction (an attribute generates 2 directions) to obtain the consistency or completeness level asked for. The iterative procedure excludes *one single* negative example per step. To choose among all possible directions, two

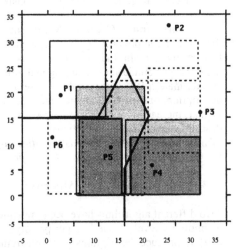

Fig. 6: Effect of the deflation process on the Diamond problem. Dashed-line boxes are complete-HBs where the deflation process didn't shrink the box. For P5 and P4, the darker boxes (discriminant) compared to the lighter ones (complete) show the effect of the deflation process.

heuristics are used: the direction that minimises the number of positive instances excluded is chosen and in case of equality, the one that minimises the reduction in volume is chosen. A *positive* example, regarding an HB, is an instance which shares the same class value (Training-class) than the box (which inherits its class value from its associated PR). Therefore, instances belonging to adjacent disjunctive PRs are considered as positive by the deflation heuristic, relaxing the Disjunctive view bias at near frontier regions. Fig. 6 shows the results of the one-complexity algorithm on the Diamond problem: the complete-HBs and 100%-consistent (discriminant-HBs) are presented. It shows that the deflation is high in the areas *where the orthogonal bias is inadequate to approximate the concept boundary*: P4 and P5 regions are good examples of this. In other regions, like in P2 and P3 where there is (nearly) no contact with the Diamond boundary, or like in P6, where the contact involves an orthogonal boundary, the bias is adequate and hence, the deflation process had nothing to do, leaving discriminant- and complete-HBs being identical. It can be seen from this example that discriminant descriptions may leave large uncovered instance space areas in the neighbourhood of those inadequate regions (see Fig. 5). In the following description of class 2, issued by GEM on this problem, the discriminant description is only about 60% complete, 40% are lost in the area inside the diamond:

```
Characteristic description (simplicity 1):
    2 Prototypes
    P5  (x ⊂ [5.5 19.0] ∧ y ⊂ [0.0 21.5])    (cover 79%; consist 87%)
    P6  (x ⊂ [0.0  7.0] ∧ y ⊂ [0.0 15.0])    (cover 21%; consist 100%)
    ≡ Class2
Discriminant description (simplicity 1):
    2 Prototypes
    P5  (x ⊂ [5.5 14.7] ∧ y ⊂ [0.0 15.0])    (cover 40%; consist 100%)
    P6  (x ⊂ [0.0  7.0] ∧ y ⊂ [0.0 15.0])    (cover 21%; consist 100%)
    ≡ Class2
```

The Free-complexity Algorithm - This algorithm can produce complete and consistent descriptions of the concept encoded in the ICR (with respect to the training of course). It uses a Decision Tree technique similar to ID3 [Quinlan 86a] but in this case the training set has been first Filtered and Re-Labelled. Unlike the one-complexity algorithm, this one follows a top-down approach and uses a *greatest generalisation strategy*. A decision tree is grown on the filtered instances *using the ICR_class*, that is, a partition of the PRs is produced. After this first stage, the relaxation of the Disjunctive bias is done by a simple pruning mechanism: a subtree is pruned if all its children nodes are leaves of the same Training_class. Indeed, due to its top-down search strategy, two leaves of the same Training_class represent a specialisation in a near border region of two adjacent disjunctive PRs. As result,

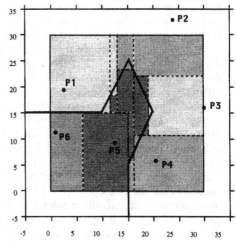

Fig. 7: A description of the Diamond problem with a free complexity

this pruning mechanism merges small hyper-boxes of the same real class value that have been separated due to the Disjunctive view bias. Each leaf is viewed as a disjunctive rule describing a PR. A rule is the conjunction of the predicates tested at each node on the path from the root to the leaf. Fig. 7 shows the result obtained on the Diamond problem. It can be seen that most of the consistent boxes found by the one-complexity algorithm are also produced by the free-complexity one (P1, P4, P5 and P6), despite the drastic change in the search method used. This is a result of the Disjunctive view bias used in both methods and the small number of dimension of the instance space. As a consequence, the main tendency provided by each prototype is preserved and represented by the largest box associated with it, while smaller ones are specialisations in complex shape regions: it can be seen that P1, P4 and P5 recover the "lost" regions due to the deflation process used to generate the discriminant-HBs (compare Fig. 6 and Fig. 7). An advantage, illustrated by this example, of the Disjunctive view bias in GEM is that we know that each main disjunction (resulting from a prototype) is a convex region and therefore that *each internal disjunctive rule (in a PR) is not a real disjunctive decision region in the instance space but rather is an artificial disjunctive term resulting from the inadequacy of the description language towards the domain.*

4. Empirical Evaluation

Experiments did not focus on the efficiency of the recognition function (ICR generated by NNP) of GEM. This aspect only concerns the classification part of the system that has been largely tested against other algorithms and has proven its high performance [Decaestecker 93; Van de Merckt & Decaestecker 94]. Instead, the experiences have been done in order to evaluate the claims concerning the advantages of GEM in the framework of the TF model.

The first aspect concerns the treatment of noise through the Filtering process, the question being: is the ICR Filtering reliable regarding noise? To evaluate this point, we have checked that (i) the ICR does not make noise overfitting and (ii) that the Filtering process is more active when noise is present than when it is absent. This may be evaluated by looking at the number of prototypes generated in the absence versus the presence of noise and the corresponding number of instances filtered out of the ICR_clusters. The second aspect concerns the capacity to evaluate the adequacy of the description bias regarding the target concept. The key point is the observation of the consistency of complete-HBs or its dual aspect, the completeness of discriminant-HBs produced by the one-complexity algorithm. A rating that entails this aspect has been designed: the *Bias Cost* is the difference of the resubstitution omission rate (computed *on the training set*) between discriminant-HB and complete-HB. If, at a given level of simplicity, this measure is too high, the system could propose to increase the complexity level in order to obtain a better approximation of the target concept encoded in the ICR. Our tests aim to evaluate the validity of such an analysis. The last aspect concerns the evaluation of the quality of the descriptions as a mean to communicate the concept encoded in the ICR. To evaluate this point, we used the descriptions as classification rules and compared their results to the classification performed by the ICR on the same data sets. These tests aim to appreciate how the descriptions may represent the central tendencies of the concept and localise "safe" classification areas in the instance space. These aspects have been evaluated along three dimensions: (i) domain dependence: seven different data sets are used presenting different concept shapes, sometimes adapted (Square data) and sometimes not adapted (Geometrical, Wave and Diamond) to the orthogonal bias of symbolic descriptions; (ii) noise dependence: each data set has been tested before and after noise addition; (iii) scarcity of training sets dependence: tests have been done on small and large training sets. The experiments only widely tested the one-complexity algorithm. However, the effects of using the free-complexity algorithm will be commented when appropriate.

4.1   Experimental Set-up

There are two real world data sets and five artificial ones that have been chosen in order to evaluate the TF model against various concept shapes:

- *Iris*: it contains 3 classes of 50 instances each, where a class refers to a type of Iris plant.

- *Diabetes*: it contains 145 records of 3 different diagnostics for Diabetes (the class repartition is C1=26 , C2= 35, C3=84 instances) based on 5 numerical attributes representing clinical tests.

- *Diamond Data*: it is the two-class problem presented at Fig. 2.

- *Wave Forms* [Breiman 84]: it is composed of 3 classes, each of them being a linear combination of three distinct wave forms. Each instance is composed by a vector of 21 continuous values.

- *Geometrical Data*: it is a two-class problem defined in a two-dimension space. The classes are delimited by two circles (centre: (0,0); diameter 20 and 40) entailed in a square (side 60) (see Fig. 8). Class 1 is represented by grey areas and class 2 by the white ring. Instances are uniformly distributed over the whole surface of the square.

Fig. 8: Geometrical

- *Gauss-Square Data*: it is a three-class problem shown in Fig. 9. Instances in each class are artificially generated by Gaussian distributions (several by class). The centre of each Gaussian is shown by a black triangle in the figure; the standard deviations are relatively small. The instances are attributed to the class corresponding to the nearest centre which have been chosen in order to generate orthogonal implicit decision boundaries (black lines in Fig. 9). The centre of the Gaussian can be considered as optimal prototype's location.

Fig. 9: Square data

- *Uniform-Square Data*: it is the same as the previous problem where the instances are uniformly distributed in the square and allocated to the class following the decision surfaces showed in Fig. 9.

Noise Addition - Each data set was tested before and after noise addition. For Diabetes and Iris, a Gaussian noise $N(0,\sigma)$ on each attribute (with σ equals to 1/2 the standard deviation of the whole population for this attribute) has been artificially added. For Geometrical data, noise was introduced by an overlapping between the clusters. For Wave Forms, a Gaussian noise $N(0,1)$ on each attribute has been added like in [Breiman & al. 84]. The same process has been made on Diamond and Uniform-square.

For Gauss-square, each instance has been reallocated following the location of the centre of the Gaussian that generated it: this process introduces overlapping between the classes.

Training & Test Sets - For each data set, 10 runs were done with two training sets of distinct sizes (small and large). Large sets were built using the small ones by *adding* a number of randomly chosen *new* instances. Table 1 indicates the number of elements in each set. Except for Iris and Diabetes, the test set was generated independently.

Table 1: Sizes of training and test sets.

| Data Set | Training sets | | Test set |
	small	large	
Iris	20% per class	50% per class	the rest
Diabetes	20% per class	50% per class	the rest
Geometrical	115	575	1000
Wave	10 per class	100 per class	5000
Diamond	100	400	1000
Gauss-square	130	390	1000
Uniform-square	130	390	1000

4.2   Noise Treatment

On average, the results obtained from NNP (see [Decaestecker 93]) are: (i) ICR complexity (the number of prototypes) increases very little when moving from small to large sets and (ii) complexity on noisy versions of the data sets are slightly less than on noise-free ones. These results (and others largely analysed in [Van de Merckt & Decaestecker 94]) show that the ICR produced by NNP does not cause overfitting. Concurrently to this general tendency to produce less complex ICR when noise is present, it can be seen in Fig. 10 that the effect of the Filtering procedure works as expected: the percentage of training instances provided to the description algorithm decreases proportionally to the presence of noise and to the size of the training set.

4.3   Evaluation of the Description Bias

The average Bias Cost over all data *for large sets* is presented in Fig. 11. In this chart, the two first bars present the average Bias Cost on noise-free *training* and *test* sets respectively and the two last ones present the same figures after noise addition. This chart shows that the difference in omission between discriminant versus complete descriptions is nearly the same on training and test sets and that this property is observed independently of the presence of noise in data. This result has a strong practical implication: it means that the adequacy of the description bias and hence, the complexity that should be used to correctly approximate the target concept, may be validly evaluated *on the training set*, even in case of noisy data. However, this result should not be misinterpreted: it doesn't mean that the observed level of omission on the training gives a reliable approximation of its level on the test set. On the Geometrical problem, for example, the Bias Cost is about 6% on large noise-free sets, meaning that if the system produces a description under the form of discriminant-HBs, it "looses" a cover of about 6% on the concept instances, but the level of omission of a discriminant description on the test set is about 12% (while complete-HBs omission is 6%). The estimation of the real omission rate depends on the statistical representativeness of the training and hence, the adequacy of description bias should be carefully evaluated regarding the size of the training compared to the dimension of the instance space: the fewer instances we have, the smaller space covered and hence, simple descriptions may appear to correctly approximate the target concept although they don't. When using the free-complexity algorithm, the adequacy of the description bias may be evaluated by looking at the number of disjunctive rules (leaves) necessary to approximate a single PR.

4.4 Evaluation of the Fidelity of the Descriptions

In GEM, a symbolic description should "reflect" the concept encoded in the ICR. This means that, given a level of detail asked by the user through the simplicity parameter, a description *should allow to easily identify the major classification areas entailed in the recognition function.* Therefore, the quality of descriptions may be evaluated by comparing classification results of the descriptions with the ICR's ones *on the test sets.* Fig. 12 presents two bar charts for each type of training, averaged over all data sets. The first bar presents, from bottom to top, the percentage of correct classifications, the omission rate (no decisions) and the error rate (% of incorrect classification) of *discriminant* descriptions produced by the *one-complexity* algorithm. Three main observations may be done from this chart: (i) on average (except on small noisy ones) *simple* descriptions correctly cover a large part (at least 70%) of the concept; (ii) the error

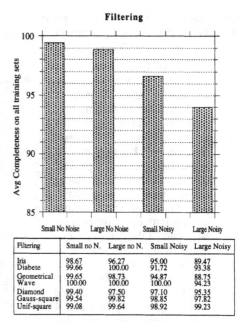

Filtering	Small no N.	Large no N.	Small Noisy	Large Noisy
Iris	98.67	96.27	95.00	89.47
Diabete	99.66	100.00	91.72	93.38
Geometrical	99.65	98.73	94.87	88.75
Wave	100.00	100.00	100.00	94.23
Diamond	99.40	97.50	97.10	95.35
Gauss-square	99.54	99.82	98.85	97.82
Unif-square	99.08	99.64	98.92	99.23

Fig. 10: Effect of the *Filtering* procedure

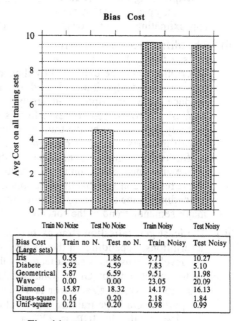

Bias Cost (Large sets)	Train no N.	Test no N.	Train Noisy	Test Noisy
Iris	0.55	1.86	9.71	10.27
Diabete	5.92	4.59	7.83	5.10
Geometrical	5.87	6.59	9.51	11.98
Wave	0.00	0.00	23.05	20.09
Diamond	15.87	18.32	14.17	16.13
Gauss-square	0.16	0.20	2.18	1.84
Unif-square	0.21	0.20	0.98	0.99

Fig. 11: Effect of deflation on omissions

rate of the descriptions is always less than the ICR, particularly on small training sets (however, at the cost of high omission rate); (iii) the omission rate depends on the size of the training and on the level of noise.

(i) By "simple" concept description, we mean a description that contains a small number of disjunctions covering a large number of concept instances. In this case, since one box has been used to approximate each single PR, the description is to most simple one GEM can produce. The fact that such simple descriptions correctly cover a large part of the concept is due to the Disjunctive view bias of GEM. On the Diamond problem for example, class 1 could not be correctly described with a higher simplicity than 4 convex regions and hence, the description algorithm produces 4 hyper-rectangles approximating these regions.

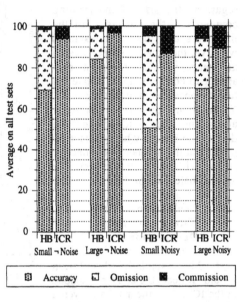

Fig. 12: Average results of 100%-consistent HBs

(ii) The difference among error rates of the ICR and the descriptions may be explained by their opposite generalisation strategies. The one-complexity algorithm is biased by a least generalisation strategy in order to produce "safe" descriptions adversely to the recognition function which uses a greatest generalisation strategy. In this latter case, when the concept is only partially represented by the training (due to scarce or noisy data) the inductive algorithm does not have enough data in some instance space regions and performs "best guess" generalisation that mainly relies on its *a priori* bias (Piecewise linear and simplicity), resulting in higher chances to perform errors. These results confirm that the descriptions, while being more or less incomplete, depending on the size of the training and the level of noise, correctly capture the major semantic trend of the concepts.

(iii) The least generalisation strategy has the "drawback" of producing incomplete descriptions, depending on the training size and the level of noise in the data. The level of omission is also affected by the adequacy of the description language for the target concept. On the Diabetes data, for example, the omission on small sets (not noisy) is 49% (error is 1%) while the ICR makes 98% of correct recognition. On large training, the level of omission decreases to 29% (error is still 1%) while the ICR is 99% accurate. It is clear in this case that the description bias is inadequate to approximate the concept boundary with an equivalent simplicity as the ICR. Clearly, the Diabetes concept is a good candidate for the free-complexity algorithm.

In conclusion, the symbolic descriptions correctly reflect the semantic content of the concept encoded by the ICR and the level of "correctness" reflects the statistical representativeness of the training set and the adequacy of the description language.

5. Related Works

The idea of coping with accuracy and comprehensibility in the same time is not new. Knight & Gil [91] proposed an architecture for problem-solving composed of an efficient "reasoner" (the problem-solver), such as a NN, and a "rationalizer" which aims to explain the output of the reasoner. However, both modules are completely separated and the rationalizer is a tool for *convincing* a user to accept the solution rather than for *explaining* how its has been reached. The closer work is certainly the one of Towell & Shavlik [93]. They use a special NN architecture (Knowledge-Based NN) in order to improve knowledge given under the form of a set of rules. After optimisation, a new and more accurate set of rules is extracted from the network. Their method differs from GEM in many respects: (i) they use KNN which encode horn clauses describing the domain whilst we use a prototype-based representation; (ii) their algorithm is restricted to discrete (nominal) features whilst GEM is restricted to numerical features; (iii) they don't use the training set to guide the interpretation of the knowledge encoded in the network whilst GEM makes an intensive use of it to constraint its interpretation. However, their algorithm fits the TF model where the recognition function uses a KNN whose accuracy has been empirically demonstrated and the communication function uses m-of-n type of rules.

6. Conclusions

We have presented a hybrid Neural-Symbolic Learning algorithm which implements the Two-Functional model of Concept Learning. This algorithm uses two different inductive engines that use two different knowledge representations: one for building an Internal Concept Representation optimised regarding accuracy, and the other for producing symbolic concept descriptions optimised for comprehensibility. This Multiple-Knowledge Representation schema has shown several advantages over Single-Knowledge Representation concept learning algorithms. Firstly, no compromise should be made concerning accuracy and/or comprehensibility. From the classification point of view, the inductive learning may be optimised without the interference of "human-oriented" biases. From the concept description point of view, stronger cognitive biases may be used (as accepting omission due to a least generalisation strategy). Secondly, the adequacy of biases used to produce concept descriptions may be evaluated regarding the target concept. This allows one to know the cost of being explicit and human understandable. Thirdly, regarding concept descriptions, completeness, consistency and simplicity become "real" preference parameters, since they should not be "optimised" to avoid noise overfitting.

We hope that the TF model approach will provide a framework for integrating many different classifier algorithms as well as to help developing new approaches for generating comprehensible concept descriptions. Indeed, in GEM we have used simple DNF-like rules for describing a concept. However, many different types of descriptions could be produced like m-of-n decision rules (like in [Towell & Shavlik 93]) or a mix among decision rules and typical examples that could be more understandable to an expert than a set of rules. The advantage of the TF model is that the type of descriptions that might be generated could depends on contextual factors such as the level of expertise of the user or explicit preferences for one kind of description among several available ones. From the recognition side and from a theoretical point of view, GEM's TF model implementation could be applied to a whole set of classification functions defined by their ability to account for the two essential biases of the system: (1) Noise Treatment by a Filtering process and (2) Disjunctive view by a Re-Labelling process. However, in practise, GEM benefits from the prototypical knowledge model used by the ICR which performs *generalisation over the instance space*. Using lazy learning algorithms like exemplar-based algorithms would cause problems to apply the Disjunctive view bias. Other kinds of neural networks, such as those using back-propagation, would also cause a problem since these NN creates a single non-linear decision surface for each class (although Towell and Shavlik have open promising ways for KNN). Therefore, GEM's implementation of the TF model may not be applied to any classifier algorithm without extensive work. However, we believe that the idea of the TF model, i.e., the separation between the knowledge used for prediction and explanation and the "interpretation bridge" between them, could be further explored in order to integrate powerful subsymbolic learning algorithms in the framework of "comprehensible" concept learning.

Our close future work will extend the description algorithm to any complexity level and will better evaluate the performance of GEM with respect to its capacity to communicate the semantic content of the ICR by a closer analysis of the effect of gradual increase of noise as well as gradual increase of the complexity of the tested domains (by increasing the number of dimensions). In a second stage we will also investigate how to extend our approach to mix nominal-numeric attribute spaces as well as how to introduce a feature selection process in NNP and/or in the one-complexity description algorithm.

References

Aha W. David, Kibler D., Albert K. M. (1991) Instance-Based Learning Algorithms, *Machine Learning vol.6, n° 1, January 1991*, Kluwer Academic Publishers.

Bergadano F., Esposito F., Rouveirol C. and Wrobel S. (1991) Evaluating and Changing Representation in Concept Acquisition, *Proceedings of the European Working Session on Learning*, Springer Verlag

Bergadano F., Matwin S., Michalski R.S., Zhang J. (1992) Learning Two-Tiered Descriptions of Flexible Concepts: The POSEIDON System, *Machine Learning vol.8, n° 1*, Kluwer Academic Publishers.

Benjamin Paul D. (Ed) (1990) *Change of Representation and Inductive Bias*, Kluwer Academic Publishers.

Brodley Carla E. (1993) Addressing the Selective Superiority Problem: Automatic Algorithm/ Model Class Selection, *Proceedings of the Tenth International Conference on Machine Learning ML'93*, Morgan Kaufmann.

Buntine Wray (1989) Learning Classification Rules using Bayes, *Proceedings of the Sixth International Workshop on Machine Learning ML'89*. Morgan Kaufmann.

Clark P. and Niblett T. (1989) The CN2 Induction Algorithm, *Machine Learning Vol.3 n°4, March 1989*, Kluwer Academic Publishers.

Decaestecker C. (1993) NNP: a neural net classifier using prototypes, *Proceedings of the IEEE International Conference on Neural Networks*, San Fransisco.

Esposito Floriana, Malerba Donato and Semeraro Giovanni (1991) Flexible Matching for Noisy Structural Descriptions, *Proceedings of the Thirteenth International Joint Conference on Artificial Intelligence IJCAI'91*, Morgan Kaufmann.

Goodman R.M., Higgins C.M. & Miller J.W. (1992) Rule-based neural networks for classification and probability estimation, *Neural Computation Vol.4 n° 6.*

Hertz J., Krogh A. & Palmer R.G. (1991) *Introduction to the theory of neural computation,* Addison-Wesley.

Knight K. and Gil Y. (1991), Automated Rationalization, *Proceedings of the First International Worshop on Multistrategy Learning,* Ed. by R.S. Michalski and G. Tecuci, Center of Artificial Intelligence, George Mason University.

Kohonen T. (1990) The Self-Organizing Map, *Proceedings of the IEEE, vol. 78, N° 9.*

Iba W., Wogulis J., Langley P. (1988) Trading Off Simplicity and Coverage in Incremental Concept Learning, *Proceedings of the Fith International Conference on Machine Learning ML'88,* Morgan Kaufman.

Michalski Ryszard S. (1983) A Theory and Methodology of Inductive Learning. *Machine Learning, An Artificial Intelligence Approach.* Ed. by Ryszard S. Michalski, Jaime G. Carbonell and Tom M. Mitchell, Tioga Publishing.

Michalski Ryszard S. (1990) Learning Flexible Concepts: Fundamental Ideas and Method Based on Two-Tiered Representation, *Machine Learning: An Artificial Intelligence Approach Vol. III.* Edited by Y. Kodratoff and Ryszard S. Michalski , Morgan Kaufmann.

Quinlan J.Ross (1986a) Induction of Decision Trees. *Machine Learning Vol 1, n°1,* Kluwer Academic Publishers.

Salzberg Steven (1991) A Nearest Hyperrectangle Learning Method. *Machine Learning vol. 6, n° 3, May 1991,* Kluwer Academic Publishers.

Samkar A. & Mammone R.J. (1991) *Neural Tree Networks. Neural Networks, Therory and Applications.* R.J. Mammone & Y. Zeevi Eds, Academic Press.

Stepp Robert E. and Michalski Ryszard S. (1983) Conceptual Clustering: Inventing Goal-oriented Classification of Structured Objects, *Machine Learning, An Artificial Intelligence Approach volII.* Ed. by Ryszard S. Michalski, Jaime G. Carbonell and Tom M. Mitchell, Morgan Kaufmann.

Towell G. G. and Shavlik J. (1993) Extracting Refined Rules from Knowledge-Based Neural Networks, *Machine Learning, vol. 13, n° 1,* Kluwer Academic Publishers.

Tschichold N., Ghazvini M. and Diez D. (1992), M-RCE: a self configuring ANN with rule extraction capabilities, Proceedings of the International Conference on Artificial Neural Networks ICANN'92, Brighton.

Utgoff Paul E. (1986) *Machine Learning of Inductive Bias.* Kluwer Academic Publishers.

Utgoff P.E. (1988) Perceptron Trees: A case Study in Hybrid Concepts Representations, *Proceedings of AAAI-88.*

Van de Merckt T. (1992) NFDT: A Sytem that Learns Flexible Concepts based on Decision Trees for Numerical Attributes. *Proceedings of the Ninth International Conference on Machine Learning ML'92,* Morgan Kaufmann.

Van de Merckt T. and Decaestecker C. (1994), An unifying framework for analysing bias in Similarity Based Learning, *Proceedings of the MlNet Workshop on Declarative Bias,* European Conference on Machine Learning, Catania.

The Effect of Numeric Features on the Scalability of Inductive Learning Programs

Georgios Paliouras* and David S. Brée

Department of Computer Science, University of Manchester, Oxford Road,
Manchester M13 9PL, UK
email: paliourg@cs.man.ac.uk, dbree@cs.man.ac.uk

Abstract. The behaviour of a learning program as the quantity of data increases affects to a large extent its applicability on real-world problems. This paper presents the results of a theoretical and experimental investigation of the scalability of four well-known empirical concept learning programs. In particular it examines the effect of using numeric features in the training set. The theoretical part of the work involved a detailed worst-case computational complexity analysis of the algorithms. The results of the analysis deviate substantially from previously reported estimates, which have mainly examined discrete and finite feature spaces. In order to test these results, a set of experiments was carried out, involving one artificial and two real data sets. The artificial data set introduces a near-worst-case situation for the examined algorithms, while the real data sets provide an indication of their average-case behaviour.

Keywords: empirical concept learning, scalability, decision trees, numeric features

1 Introduction

During the last two decades, a large number of empirical concept learning algorithms have been developed. Out of those, the ones we will examine here cover three major categories. The first (C4.5 [18]) induces decision trees and is the most recent version of the well-known ID3 algorithm [17]. The next two (AQ15 [10] and CN2 [2]) generate lists of decision rules and are based on the AQ algorithm [9]. The last (PLS1 [19]) is a conceptual clustering program which is based on the same principle as ID3.

The selected programs have several features which are important to the scalability analysis presented in the paper:

1. Despite differences in the representation of the learned concepts, all four algorithms perform *orthogonal clustering* of the feature space. In other words, the resulting concept can be graphically represented by a set of rectangles,

* The author was partially funded for this work by a research studentship from the Engineering and Physical Sciences Research Council.

aligned in parallel to the axes of the hyper-space, defined by the feature set[2]. This imposes a restriction to the concepts that can be efficiently learned by the algorithms.

2. The algorithms belong to two types, which have been shown (e.g. [21]) to have different computational requirements. The first type consists of algorithms like ID3 and PLS1, which are called *specialisation* algorithms, because they start from the most general concept description and specialise this until it discriminates perfectly between positive and negative examples of the concept. The second type corresponds to *generalisation* algorithms (e.g. AQ15 and CN2), which start from individual positive examples and generate all possible rules that discriminate between them and all negative ones.

3. All four programs can handle numeric features. With the exception of AQ15, the programs deal with numeric features in the following way: at each stage of the learning process they select a threshold value for the feature, which dichotomises the examined set of examples. AQ15 can only deal with integer features, with an upper bound on their value set (*bounded integer* features). It treats those like ordered discrete features, looking for characteristic value ranges.

There have been numerous analyses and comparisons of learning algorithms in the past (e.g. [15], [8], [2], [21], [22], [6], [12], [23], [11], etc.), most of which have concentrated on the classification accuracy of the algorithms. In general, the issue of scalability has been neglected, as only a few of these analyses have dealt with the computational performance of the examined algorithms. The ones which bear some relevance to the work presented here are those carried out by O'Rorke [15], Rendell et al. [21] and Clark and Niblett [2].

The common conclusion of the work on the computational performance of concept-learning algorithms is that *specialisation* algorithms are faster than *generalisation* ones, because they employ less expensive search methods. Additionally, the worst-case complexity of the algorithms has been estimated to be near-linear, in the size of the training set. For example, Rendell et al. [21] estimate the complexity of specialisation algorithms to be of order $O(kae)$, where e is the number of examples, a the number of features and k the number of nodes in the final decision tree or the number of hyper-rectangles generated by the clusterer. k is assumed to be independent of a and e, being determined by the complexity of the problem. Clark and Niblett [2] examine also the use of numeric features, deriving the worst-case estimates $O(ae \log e)$ and $O(as(e + \log(as)))$ (where s is the maximum star size parameter) for the core components of ASSISTANT (a variant of ID3) and the AQ-based algorithms respectively. These estimates do not deal with the size of the final concept, implicitly making the same assumption as in Rendell et al. [21].

The work presented in the following sections includes a theoretical analysis and an experimental comparison of the examined algorithms. Section 2 describes worst-case scenarios for the two types of algorithms and estimates their computational complexity. Worst-case estimates of the size of the learned concept are

---

[2] A more extensive account of the orthogonality problem appears in [18], chapter 10.

included in the scenarios. Section 3 presents the results of three experiments, comparing the near-worst-case and average performance of the programs. Finally, Sect. 4 and 5 summarise and compare the results of the theoretical and the experimental analyses.

2 Theoretical Analysis

2.1 The focus points

For the purpose of calculating the computational complexity of the algorithms, the scale of a learning problem can be defined in terms of two parameters: the *size of the training set* and the *size of the search space*. The former is determined by the number of instances in the training set, while the latter depends on the number of features and their value-sets, which define the set of all possible target concepts that can be learned. This paper concentrates on the size of the training set, examining its effect on the computational requirements of the algorithms. However, the type and value-sets of the features are also used in the definition of the worst-case scenarios.

In most of the previous studies, dealing with the complexity of ML algorithms, the assumption is made that only finite value-sets are used for the features. This assumption was valid for early versions of the algorithms, which could only deal with nominal features. More recent versions, however, can deal with numeric features, whose value-sets need not be finite. The effect of allowing infinite value-sets is that the search space becomes infinite and needs to be limited, typically using the feature values encountered in the training set. As a result, the order of complexity of the algorithms, with respect to the size of the training set, increases.

Most of the above-mentioned studies have also assumed that the size of the final concept description is determined only by the nature of the problem, not the feature-types nor the number of examples. In a worst-case situation, however, it will be shown that the size of the concept description depends on the size of the training set. There are some empirical results [1] which suggest that this is also true in some real-world learning problems.

2.2 Specialisation Algorithms

The two specialisation algorithms examined here, i.e., C4.5 and PLS1, behave in a very similar way to the basic ID3 algorithm, which is described in Fig. 1. Thus, ID3 can be used to derive an estimate of the complexity of the algorithms.

The main computational cost of ID3 arises at the stage where all the features are evaluated, in order for the best discriminant to be selected. At this stage, C4.5 discretises numeric features by evaluating all binary splits, based on the feature-values that are observed in the examined subset of the training set. This involves a sorting of the values and the calculation of the entropy for each binary split. In the worst case, each example will assign a different value to the numeric

---

Input: A set of examples E, a set of features A, a set of class values C.
Output: A decision tree T.

Initially $S = E$ and $N = T =$ root node.

Dichotomise(S, N):

1. **If** all the members of S belong to the same class make N a *leaf node* and stop dichotomisation.
   Else select feature a_i that best discriminates between positive and negative examples in S.
2. **For each** value of a_i: v_{ij} **do:**
   Create new node N_j under N.
   Dichotomise(S_{ij}, N_j), where S_{ij} is the subset of examples corresponding to v_{ij}.
3. **Return** T.

Fig. 1. The basic ID3 algorithm

feature, resulting in $e' - 1$ possible splits, where e' is the size of the examined subset of examples. Combining this with the linear complexity of the entropy calculation, would result in a quadratic estimate for this stage alone. However, as the feature-values are sorted, the entropy calculations can be optimised, by maintaining frequency counts (see [18]). As a result, the most expensive process is the sorting, which is of order $O(e' \log e')$. This process has to be repeated for all features, resulting in a total cost of $O(ae' \log e')$ for the calculations per node, where a is the number of features.

In the above worst-case situation, it is possible that one node is generated for each value of the numeric feature in the training set. This would happen in the case where perfect discrimination was sought and no better features were provided. Thus, the maximum size of the generated decision tree, measured by the number of non-leaf nodes, is $e - 1$, where e is the size of the training set. An additional worst-case assumption is that the resulting tree be highly skewed, which is the case if a single example is discriminated at each node. In that situation the average size of the subset of the training set examined at each node would be $e' = e/2$. Based on those results, the total cost of the algorithm is $O(ae^2 \log e)$.

Therefore, by estimating the size of the learned concept description, in the worst case, it is shown that the complexity of the ID3 algorithm is over-quadratic in the size of the training set. The assumptions, underlying this result are:

1. Numeric features are used.
2. Each example in the training set assigns a different value to the numeric features.
3. A complete and highly skewed tree results. This means that there are no informative features to support generalisation and no pre-pruning takes place.

These assumptions are strong and are not expected to hold in a typical learning problem. They illustrate, however, how the use of numeric features can affect the computational requirements of the algorithm. Section 3.2 presents a simple artificial problem, which satisfies most of the above assumptions.

2.3 Generalisation Algorithms

Out of the two generalisation algorithms examined here, i.e., AQ15 and CN2, only the latter can handle unbounded numeric features, i.e., real numbers and integers of an unlimited range. AQ15 can only deal with integer features, the range of which has to be specified. Therefore the behaviour of CN2, will be examined here. Figure 2 reproduces the description of the algorithm, presented in [2].

As with ID3, the most expensive process, during the search for the best decision rule (*complex*) in CN2, is the evaluation of all possible complexes. The evaluation in this case is done using the likelihood ratio statistic and the complexity of this calculation for each complex is $O(ce)$, where c is the number of classes and e the number of examples in the training set. This process has to be repeated for all the generated complexes, the number of which is determined by the size of the *SELECTORS* set. The maximum size of this set, in the worst-case scenario described above for ID3, is $ae/2$, where a is the number of features, which is the upper limit for the length of the complex. This process is repeated a maximum of a times, since each complex gets specialised by the addition of a selector (conjunctively added condition), which uses a feature that has not been used in the complex so far. Thus the complexity of the search process is $O(a^2e^2)$. Again this estimate can be improved, by optimising the calculation of the likelihood ratio. As in ID3, this involves sorting the numeric feature values and updating the frequency counts, instead of recalculating them. The revised worst-case estimate is $O(a^2 e \log e)$.

The number of times this search has to be repeated is k, the size of the final concept description (set of decision rules). In the worst case, a complex is generated for each example in the training set and $k = e$. The computational complexity of the process is then $O(a^2 c e^2 \log e)$. One interesting observation is that the *maximum star size* parameter does not affect the worst-case complexity of the algorithm. The reason for this is that the maximum number of distinct complexes in the worst case is bounded by the size of the *SELECTOR* set, $O(ae/2)$.

Due to the fact that AQ15 can only handle bounded numeric features, the worst-case scenario for the algorithm differs slightly from CN2. In brief, this scenario involves:

1. The generation of as many complexes, as the size of the training set.
2. The examination of all negative examples, each time a new complex is produced, i.e., each complex is maximally specific.
3. The use of an evaluation function that needs to examine the whole training set each time.

Let E be a set of classified examples.
Let *SELECTORS* be the set of all possible selectors.

Procedure *CN2(E)*
    Let *RULE-LIST* be the empty list.
    Repeat until *BEST-CPX* is nil or E is empty:
        Let *BEST-CPX* be *Find-Best-Complex(E)*.
        If *BEST-CPX* is not nil,
        Then let E' be the examples covered by *BEST-CPX*.
            Remove E' from E.
            Let C be the most common class of examples in E'.
            Add the rule 'If *BEST-CPX* then the class is C'
                to the end of the *RULE-LIST*.
    Return *RULE-LIST*.

Procedure *Find-Best-Complex(E)*
    Let *STAR* be the set containing the empty complex.
    Let *BEST-CPX* be nil.
    While *STAR* is not empty,
        Specialise all complexes in *STAR* as follows:
        Let *NEWSTAR* be the set:
            $\{x \wedge y | x \in STAR, y \in SELECTORS\}$.
        Remove all complexes in *NEWSTAR* that are either in *STAR*
            (i.e., the unspecialised ones) or null.
        For every complex C_i in *NEWSTAR*:
            If C_i is statistically significant and better than
            BEST-CPX by user-defined criteria when tested on E,
            Then replace the current value of *BEST-CPX* by C_i.
        Repeat until size of *NEWSTAR* $\leq$ user-defined maximum:
            Remove the worst complex from *NEWSTAR*.
        Let *STAR* be *NEWSTAR*.
    Return *BEST-CPX*.

Fig. 2. The CN2 algorithm

The second element of this list is the main difference between the two algorithms and increases the complexity of the algorithm, with respect to the size of the training set, by an order of magnitude[3]. The complexity estimate for AQ15 is $O(sa^2ve^3)$, where v is the largest set of feature-values.

---

[3] The details of the calculation of the complexity estimate for AQ15 are not of particular interest to the paper, and can be found in [16].

2.4 Summary of Results

Table 1 presents the results of the computational complexity analysis for each of the four algorithms and for each type of feature they can handle[4].

Table 1. Summary of complexity estimates.

Algorithms	Attribute Types			
	nominal/ bounded integer	value-sets[a]	numeric	
			unbounded integer	continuous
C4.5	$O(ca^2ve)$	$O(c^2av^4e^2)$	$O(ae^2\log e)$	$O(ae^2\log e)$
PLS1	—	—	$O(cae^2\log e)$	—
CN2	$O(ca^3v^{a+1}e)$	—	$O(ca^2e^2\log e)$	$O(ca^2e^2\log e)$
AQ15	$O(sa^2ve^3)$	—	—	—

[a] Value-sets for nominal features.

Notes:
a = *number of features*, c = *number of classes*, e = *the size of the training set*, s = *maximum star size*, v = *maximum number of values per feature*.

The following conclusions can be drawn from the presented results:

1. Most of the algorithms can handle nominal features quite efficiently, with respect to the size of the training set. This is because the search space is bounded by the domain-definition of the features.
2. AQ15 is more expensive than the other algorithms.
3. The value-grouping facility provided by C4.5, is expensive in terms of computations.
4. The complexity of the algorithms which can handle integer and real features is the same for both these types. Moreover, this complexity is higher than quadratic for all algorithms.

Nevertheless, one has to be very careful with the interpretation of the results of a worst-case analysis. The situations which were assumed in order to obtain those results are extreme and very atypical of the problems that concept-learning systems are usually required to solve.

3 Experimental Investigation

3.1 The Set-up

The analysis presented in this section examines the scaling behaviour of the four algorithms, using one artificial and two large real data sets. The desired

---

[4] These are the results of an extensive analysis, presented in [16].

outcome of the scalability analysis is a relationship between the performance of each algorithm and the size of the training set, which can be compared to the corresponding computational complexity estimate. This relationship can be derived, by measuring the rate at which the CPU-time consumption[5] changes, as the size of the training set increases. For that purpose, the CPU-time consumption of the learning process is measured at different *size-steps*, i.e., training sets of different sizes. The size-steps are determined on a logarithmic scale, starting from a small power of 2, usually $2^6 = 64$ and multiplying by 2 each time. For the real data sets three randomly sampled training sets are used at each size-step and the results of the three individual tests are averaged. The results of the analysis are plotted on a logarithmic scale for both axes and the slope at each point is examined.

In order to reduce the possibility of implementation inefficiencies, the examined algorithms are written in similar, procedural programming languages (C and Pascal) and are all original versions, provided by their developers. Especially CN2 was provided only in the form of executables. Finally, all the experiments were carried out on a 'Sun-SPARCsystem-400' machine (a server similar to a SPARC2), which contains 32 MBytes of fixed memory and 100 MBytes of swap memory. The system runs the 'SUNOS 4.1.2' operating system.

3.2 Learning Even Numbers

This is a simple artificial problem, whose purpose is to verify the results of the theoretical analysis. The task is the discrimination between even and odd natural numbers, provided no more information but the numbers themselves. Training sets range from 64 examples to the maximum number that each algorithm can handle and each set contains the first n numbers, where n is the size of the set. With the exception of AQ15, the examined algorithms can deal with this problem, because they can handle unbounded numeric features. However, AQ15 can also be included in the experiment, by varying its upper limit for numeric feature-values, according to the size of the training set. In this way, $v = e$ (Table 1), raising the worst-case complexity estimate to quartic: $O(sa^2e^4)$.

The problem examined here has a number of properties which generate a near-worst-case situation for most of the algorithms:

1. The key element is that there are no similarities between the instances on which induction can be based. In a typical learning problem informative features would be defined, usually by a domain expert, and the data would be represented using these features[6]. For example, in this problem the feature **divisible-by-2**, which would examine the divisibility of each number by 2 is very informative. Since, however, the raw data are used, such additional information is not available.

---

[5] The built-in C and Pascal functions **getrusage** and **clock** are used for the measurement of time consumption.

[6] Rendell [20] estimates that in the fifteen puzzle problem the feature extraction process provides about 80% of the acquired knowledge.

2. The pattern followed by the data is one that cannot be detected by orthogonal clustering algorithms. As mentioned above, the examined algorithms look for ranges of numeric feature-values that correspond to objects of the same class. In this problem, the largest range of that kind contains a single example.

3. The outcome of the learning process is complete and highly skewed decision trees and complete decision-rule lists. In other words, no generalisation is achieved.

4. The problem is easy to reproduce and uses a single discrete numeric feature and a binary class, minimising the effect of parameters other than the size of the training set.

The only algorithm for which this problem does not approximate the worst-case scenario is AQ15. The reason for this is that the concept-description generated by AQ15 consists of single-selector complexes, decreasing the complexity of the process by two orders of magnitude:

1. Not all negative examples need to be examined during the search for each complex.

2. The evaluation of each complex does not depend on the size of the value-set of the feature, which in this case is equal to the size of the training set.

The results of this experiment are shown in Fig. 3 and 4. Figure 3 presents, on a logarithmic scale, the CPU-time in seconds over the number of examples, so straight lines indicate a polynomial relationship, with the slope indicating the power. In Fig. 4 the slope of the curves at each point is plotted.

The main conclusion to be drawn from these results is that, although polynomial, the performance of the algorithms is mostly worse than quadratic, as predicted by the theoretical analysis. However, the algorithms perform significantly different from each other. More specifically, the generalisation algorithms (AQ15 and CN2) have a consistent, near-quadratic behaviour throughout the experiment. As expected, the performance of AQ15 is better than its worst-case estimate. PLS1 is somewhat worse, starting with an over-quadratic time consumption, which quickly approaches the cubic threshold. The results are less clear for C4.5, which starts below quadratic, but deteriorates to reach the cubic threshold for large sets, which is worse than predicted. A possible explanation for this is that the optimisation assumed in the analysis of the ID3 algorithm (Sect. 2.2) is not implemented.

3.3 Letter Recognition

While worst-case analysis serves as a warning, most applications will not encounter such extreme conditions. For this reason, we have carried out experiments using two real data sets, in order to get an indication of the average-case performance. The first set deals with the problem of classifying typed upper case letters of the Latin alphabet, based on a number of statistical properties of their pixel images. The data set was acquired from the UCI Repository [13] and its

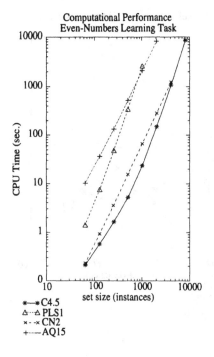
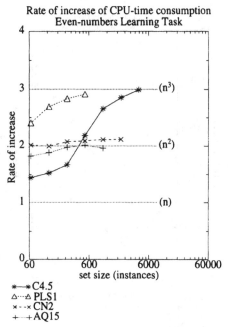

Fig. 3. Scalability Results, using the *Even-Numbers* learning task.

Fig. 4. *Even-Numbers Learning Task:* The rate of increase of the CPU-time consumed at each size-step.

original donor was D.J. Slate. Its author has used it as an application domain for Holland-style genetic classifier systems [7]. More recently the data set has also been used in the StatLog project [11]. The data set contains 20,000 instances, of which roughly 16,000 have been used for learning in this experiment. Each instance corresponds to an upper case letter, described in terms of 16 integer features, which take values in the range of 0–15. All of the algorithms examined here can handle bounded integer features and can thus participate in this experiment.

Figures 5 and 6 present the results of the experiment, in the same manner as previously. In addition, the deviations between the three measurements at each size-step are indicated. These are sufficiently small not to affect the results of the comparison.

The performance of the algorithms, in this problem, is polynomial and near-linear. However, despite their similar performance, the actual CPU-time consumption of the algorithms varies substantially. In general, the two generalisation algorithms (CN2 and AQ15) seem to have a higher computational *unit cost* than the specialisation ones (C4.5 and PLS1). This agrees with previously re-

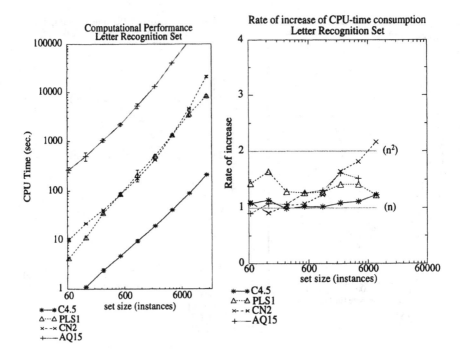

Fig. 5. Scalability Results, using the *Letter Recognition* data set.

Fig. 6. *Letter Recognition Set:* The rate of increase of the CPU-time consumed at each size-step.

ported comparisons (Sect. 1). Another interesting observation, drawn from Fig. 6 is that most of the algorithms start with a very close to linear performance, which worsens as the size of the training set increases. This may be explained by the effect of fixed start-up costs.

3.4 Chromosome Classification

The second real data set describes a chromosome analysis task. It is the Copenhagen data set, also used in [4], where an artificial Neural Network system was used for the classification of chromosomes. The data set was provided by the Department of Medical Biophysics, University of Manchester and contains 8,106 examples, of which roughly 6,000 were used for learning in this experiment. Each example corresponds to an instance of a set of 24 chromosomes and is described in terms of 15 real-valued features, which correspond to the grey-level profile of the chromosome. Due to the use of continuous numeric features, only two of the algorithms could be used in this experiment, i.e., C4.5 and CN2.

Figures 7 and 8 present the results, which are similar to the letter recognition experiment, with the exception of an overall increase in the actual CPU-time consumption values, as a result of the increased difficulty of the problem. The performance of the algorithms remains close to linear.

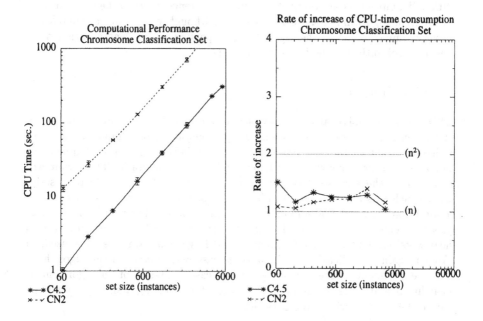

Fig. 7. Scalability Results, using the *Chromosome Classification* data set.

Fig. 8. *Chromosome Classification Set:* The rate of increase of the CPU-time consumed at each size-step.

4   Discussion of Results

The results of the experiment on the artificial data illustrate how the use of numeric features can increase the computational requirements of the examined algorithms. This is in accordance to the theoretical over-quadratic complexity estimates, presented in Sect. 2, which give an explanation of why this happens. Despite the extreme assumptions of the worst-case scenarios, this analysis supports attempts to reconsider the methods of handling numeric features in concept-learning problems (e.g. [3], [5], [14]).

Another observation, drawn from the results of the first experiment, is that although the generalisation algorithms are in general more expensive, their behaviour is very stable and their CPU-time consumption is comparable to that of the specialisation ones for large data sets. This points to a potential advantage of the AQ-based programs, which however is not observed in the two experiments that use real data.

The average-case performance of the algorithms is significantly better than the worst-case. Their behaviour in both the experiments using real-world data sets was near-linear, despite the fact that non-nominal features were used. Additionally, during these experiments a large difference between the real unit cost of different algorithms has been observed. Although their order of complexity is very similar, some of the algorithms, in particular the generalisation ones, became prohibitively slow for large data sets.

5 Conclusion

This paper has looked at the behaviour of four empirical concept learning algorithms on data sets of variable size. Using a computational complexity analysis, it has been shown that, in the worst case, the behaviour of the algorithms is not linear, as previously reported, but higher than quadratic. This result was achieved by the analysis of a parameter, i.e., the size of the concept description, which was assumed to be independent of the size of the training set, an assumption that does not hold in a worst-case situation. The results of this analysis were empirically confirmed, using an artificial problem, which generates a near-worst-case situation. Additionally, two large real data sets were used, in order to gain an indication of the average-case performance of the algorithms. These experiments suggest that the average-case behaviour of the algorithms is near-linear and some of the algorithms (i.e., those having a smaller unit cost) can deal efficiently with large data sets.

Acknowledgements
We are grateful to the following people for supplying programs, documentation, data sets and other valuable information:

G. Blix, E. Bloedorn, R. Boswell, P. Errington, J. Graham, R. Michalski, R. Nakhaeizadeh, T. Niblett, P. O'Rorke, R. Quinlan, L. Rendell, M. Rissakis, D. Slate, D. Sleeman

This work was greatly facilitated by the exchange of materials available within the *Concerted Action of Automated Cytogenics Groups*, supported by the European Community, Project No. II.1.1/13, and the use of material from the *UCI Repository of machine learning databases* in Irvine, CA: University of California, Department of Information and Computer Science.

References

1. J. Catlett. Megainduction: a test flight. In *Proceedings of the Eighth International Workshop in Machine Learning*, pages 596–599, 1991.
2. P. Clark and T. Niblett. The CN2 Algorithm. *Machine Learning*, 3(4):261–283, 1989.
3. T. V. de Merckt. Decision Trees in Numerical Attribute Spaces. In *Proceedings of the Int. Joint Conf. on Artificial Intelligence*, pages 1016–1021, 1993.

4. P. Errington and J. Graham. Application of Artificial Neural Networks to Chromosome Classification. *Cytometry*, 14:627–639, 1993.

5. U. Fayyad and K. Irani. Mutli-Interval Discretization of Continuous-Valued Attributes for Classification Learning. In *Proceedings of the Int. Joint Conf. on Artificial Intelligence*, pages 1022–1027, 1993.

6. D. Fisher and K. McKusick. An Empirical Comparison of ID3 and Backpropagation. In *Proceedings of the Int. Joint Conf. on Artificial Intelligence*, pages 788–793, 1991.

7. P. Frey and D. Slate. Letter Recognition Using Holland-Style Adaptive Classifiers. *Machine Learning*, 6:161–182, 1991.

8. M. Gams and N. Lavrač. Review of Five Empirical Learning Systems Within a Proposed Schemata. In *Proceedings of 2nd European Workshop on Machine Learning*, pages 46–66, 1987.

9. R. Michalski. A Theory and Methodology of Inductive Learning. In R. Michalski, J. Carbonell, and T. Mitchell, editors, *Machine Learning: An Artificial Intelligence Approach*, pages 83–138. Kaufmann, 1983.

10. R. Michalski, I. Mozetic, J. Hong, and N. Lavrač. The Multi-purpose incremental learning system AQ15 and its testing application to three medical domains. In *AAAI Proceedings*, pages 1041–1045, 1986.

11. D. Michie, D. Spiegelhalter, and C. Taylor. *Machine Learning, Neural and Statistical Classification*. Ellis Harwood, 1994.

12. R. Mooney, J. Shavlik, G. Towell, and A. Gove. An Experimental Comparison of Symbolic and Connectionist Learning Algorithms. In *Proceedings of the Int. Joint Conf. on Artificial Intelligence*, pages 775–780, 1991.

13. P. Murphy and D. Aha. UCI Repository of machine learning databases. Machine Readable data repository, 1994.

14. S. Murthy, S. Kasif, S. Salzberg, and R. Beigel. OC1: Randomised Induction of Oblique Decision Trees. In *AAAI Proceedings*, pages 322–327, 1993.

15. P. O'Rorke. A Comparative Study of Inductive Learning Systems AQ11P and ID3 Using a Chess-End Game Problem. Technical Report ISG 82-2, Computer Science Department, University of Illinois at Urbana-Champaign, 1982.

16. G. Paliouras. The Scalability of Machine Learning Algorithms. Master's thesis, Department of Computer Science, University of Manchester, 1993.

17. J. Quinlan. Learning Efficient Classification Procedures and Their Application to Chess End Games. In R. Michalski, J. Carbonell, and T. Mitchell, editors, *Machine Learning: An Artificial Intelligence Approach*, pages 463–482. Kaufmann, 1983.

18. J. Quinlan. *C4.5: Programs for Machine Learning*. Morgan Kaufmann Publishers, Inc., San Mateo, CA, 1993.

19. L. Rendell. A New Basis for State-Space Learning Systems and a Successful Implementation. *Artificial Intelligence*, 20(4):369–392, 1983.

20. L. Rendell. Conceptual Knowledge Acquisition in Search. In L. Bolc, editor, *Computational Models of Learning*, pages 89–159. Springer Verlag, 1987.

21. L. Rendell, H. Cho, and R. Seshu. Improving the Design of Similarity-Based Rule-Learning Systems. *International Journal of Expert Systems*, 2:97–133, 1989.

22. P. Utgoff. Incremental Induction of Decision Trees. *Machine Learning*, 4(2):161–186, 1989.

23. S. Weiss and I. Kapouleas. An Empirical Comparison of Pattern Recognition, Neural Nets, and Machine Learning Classification Methods. In *Proceedings of the Int. Joint Conf. on Artificial Intelligence*, pages 781–787, 1991.

Analogical Logic Program Synthesis from Examples

Ken Sadohara and Makoto Haraguchi

Department of Systems Science Tokyo Institute of Technology
4259 Nagatsuta, Midori-ku, Yokohama 227, Japan
E-mail:sadohara@sys.titech.ac.jp and makoto@sys.titech.ac.jp

Abstract. The purpose of this paper is to present a theory and an algorithm for analogical logic program synthesis from examples. Given a source program and examples, the task of our algorithm is to find a program which explains the examples correctly and is similar to the source program. Although we can define a notion of similarity in various ways, we consider a class of similarities from the viewpoint of how examples are explained by a program. In a word, two programs are said to be similar if they share a common explanation structure at an abstract level. Using this notion of similarity, we formalize an analogical logic program synthesis and show that our algorithm based on a framework of model inference can identify a desired program.

1 Introduction

This paper is concerned with Logic Program Synthesis from examples (LPS). LPS is generally regarded as one of the frameworks of learning from examples, and has been widely studied by many authors [5, 11, 9]. Any LPS system receives an example set from a target program, and tries to find the target program in a huge search space. Some researchers [13, 10] have pointed out that the use of analogy might be helpful in LPS. Such Analogical Logic Program Synthesis (ALPS) systems try to find a correct program[1] which is similar to a source program. They have considered that analogy is useful for reducing the search space to a space of "similar programs". However, no studies have established or proved that the use of analogy really makes such a contribution. Furthermore, there exists a criticism that analogy makes LPS more difficult. Because the ALPS system must find not only a correct program but also a similarity; that is, the system must find which program is appropriate as a source program and how the correct program is similar to the source program. Even if we admit such a disadvantage, we think that ALPS is worth investigating because of another role of analogy which is pointed out in [2]. It is the role as a device to shift a bias. The bias is a tendency to select a class of programs from the correct programs. Therefore, an ALPS system inheriting the role of analogy enables us to lead the system to identify a desired program , depending on which program we give the system as a source program. For example, let us consider programs for sorting lists. An

---

[1] A correct program means a program which can explain given examples correctly.

ALPS system might be able to identify *insert-sort* program rather than *naive-sort* program, provided we give the system a source program to which *insert-sort* is similar, such as *natural-number*[2]. To borrow from Michalski's word [4], we can change a *preference criterion* of programs dynamically. This aspect of ALPS seems to be important from a viewpoint of the change of representation (the program transformation). In the last section, we briefly discuss this viewpoint. These reasons mentioned above motivate us to investigate ALPS.

In ALPS, a notion of similarities between logic programs plays a crucial role. In the literatures [7, 10], the authors have precisely defined that notion from which only small classes of similarities are derived. On the other hand, in the literature [13], the authors have considered a wider class of similarities that has no firm theoretical basis. Because of the lack of an appropriate theoretical basis on similarities between programs, we have not been able to evaluate ALPS's usefulness. A purpose of this paper is to present a class of non-trivial similarities between programs with a firm theoretical basis.

There may exist various kinds of similarities between logic programs. According to [7] and [10], a source program is regarded as a second-order schema. A program is considered to be similar to the source program, provided it is an instance of the schema. For example, a program

$$Q = \left\{ \begin{array}{l} \texttt{ancestor(X,Y)} \leftarrow \texttt{parent(X,Y)} \\ \texttt{ancestor(X,Y)} \leftarrow \texttt{ancestor(X,Z),parent(Z,Y)} \end{array} \right\}$$

is similar to a source program

$$P = \left\{ \begin{array}{l} \texttt{connected(X,Y)} \leftarrow \texttt{link(X,Y)} \\ \texttt{connected(X,Y)} \leftarrow \texttt{connected(X,Z),link(Z,Y)} \end{array} \right\}$$

because Q is an instance of P, where connected and link are instantiated to ancestor and parent, respectively. This kind of similarity can be thus defined as a symbol-to-symbol mapping, and is therefore too much dependent on their surface syntax. On the other hand, we can observe a more internal similarity between the above programs. In fact, they share a common explanation structure. If any ground atom ancestor(x,y) corresponds to the ground atom connected(x,y) and any ground atom parent(x,y) corresponds to the ground atom link(x,y), then any proof of any ground atom ancestor(x,y) is similar to a proof of the ground atom connected(x,y). Considering in this way, we justify our intuition that a logic program

$$reverse = \left\{ \begin{array}{l} \texttt{rev([],[])} \leftarrow \\ \texttt{rev([A|X],Y)} \leftarrow \texttt{rev(X,Z),append(Z,[A],Y)} \end{array} \right\}$$

is similar to a logic program

$$natural\text{-}number = \left\{ \begin{array}{l} \texttt{nn(0)} \leftarrow \\ \texttt{nn(s(X))} \leftarrow \texttt{nn(X)} \end{array} \right\}$$

---

[2] These programs are similar because they have a similar recursive structure. The programs mentioned here are in [12].

although *reverse* is not an instance of *natural-number*. Because examples of *reverse* are explained in the similar way (not in the same way) as examples of *natural-number* under the following correspondence between rev and nn. Any ground atom $\mathtt{rev}(x,y)$ corresponds to the ground atom $\mathtt{nn}(\mathtt{s}^n(\mathtt{0}))$, where x is a list whose length is $n \geq 0$ and $\mathtt{s}^n(\mathtt{0})$ is an abbreviation of $\underbrace{\mathtt{s}(\mathtt{s}(\cdots \mathtt{s}(\mathtt{0})\cdots))}_{n}$.

In this paper, we formalize such a non-trivial similarity from the viewpoint of how the examples are explained. Although the paper [13] has considered this kind of similarity, it has not formalized the similarity completely.

The ALPS problem which we consider here is stated informally as follows.

Given
- a source program P and
- a set of positive examples E^+ and a set of negative examples E^-, where the examples are ground atoms,

Find a target program Q such that $Q \vdash E^+$, $Q \nvdash E^-$ and Q is similar to P.

Firstly we present a formal theory on ALPS, especially a theory on similarities between logic programs. Secondly we show an algorithm for ALPS which is obtained by extending Shapiro's incremental model inference algorithm [11], and prove that the algorithm identifies a solution in the limit.

2 Preliminaries

In this paper, concepts for logic programs are based on [3], unless stated otherwise. For any clause C and D, we define pre-order $C \geq D$, which is called θ-subsumption, iff there exists a substitution θ such that $C\theta \subseteq D$. In addition, for any set of clauses S and T, we define $S \geq T$ iff for any clause C in T, there exists a clause D in S such that $D \geq C$. For any definite clause $C = A \leftarrow B_1,\ldots,B_n$, $\mathrm{He}(C)$ denotes the positive literal A and $\mathrm{Bo}(C)$ denotes the set of atoms $\{B_1,\ldots,B_n\}$. A ground goal is a clause of the form $\leftarrow B_1,\ldots,B_n$, where each $B_i(1 \leq i \leq n)$ is a ground atom. The symbol $\bot$ denotes the empty clause. In the remainder of this paper, we consider a logic program as a finite set of definite clauses whose lengths are finite.

For any function symbol or any predicate symbol s, $\sharp s$ denotes the arity of s. For any set of function symbols Σ and any set of predicate symbols Π, we call the pair $\langle \Sigma, \Pi \rangle$ a vocabulary. For any logic program P, $\mathrm{V}(P)$ denotes a vocabulary $\langle \Sigma, \Pi \rangle$, where Σ is a set of function symbols including function symbols occurring in P and Π a set of predicate symbols including predicate symbols occurring in P. Moreover we assume that Σ and Π are finite sets. When we consider several logic programs, we assume that their vocabularies are disjoint.

Throughout this paper, we assume a set of variables $\mathcal{V}$, and a set of special constants $\mathcal{C}$ whose elements never appear in any program. We also assume that $\mathcal{V}$ and $\mathcal{C}$ contain enough elements.

For any set of function symbols Σ and any set of predicate symbols Π, $\mathrm{Trm}(\Sigma)$ denotes the set of terms constructed from Σ, $\mathcal{V}$ and $\mathcal{C}$. Likewise, $\mathrm{Sub}(\Sigma)$, $\mathrm{Atm}(\Sigma, \Pi)$ and $\mathrm{Cls}(\Sigma, \Pi)$ denote the set of substitutions constructed from $\mathrm{Trm}(\Sigma)$, the set of atoms constructed from $\mathrm{Trm}(\Sigma)$ and Π, and the set of clauses constructed from $\mathrm{Atm}(\Sigma, \Pi)$ respectively. $\mathrm{Exp}(\Sigma, \Pi)$ denotes $\mathrm{Trm}(\Sigma) \cup \mathrm{Sub}(\Sigma) \cup \mathrm{Atm}(\Sigma, \Pi) \cup \mathrm{Cls}(\Sigma, \Pi)$ and we call each elements of this set an expression. In addition, $\mathrm{Trm}(P)$, $\mathrm{Sub}(P)$, $\mathrm{Atm}(P)$ and $\mathrm{Cls}(P)$ denote $\mathrm{Trm}(\Sigma)$, $\mathrm{Sub}(\Sigma)$, $\mathrm{Atm}(\Sigma, \Pi)$ and $\mathrm{Cls}(\Sigma, \Pi)$ respectively for any logic program P, where $V(P) = \langle \Sigma, \Pi \rangle$.

For any logic program P, $B(P)$ denotes the Herbrand base which is the set of ground atoms constructed from $V(P)$ and $\mathcal{C}$. A mapping $T_P : 2^{B(P)} \to 2^{B(P)}$ is defined as follows. For any $I \subseteq B(P)$,

$$T_P(I) = \left\{ A \in B(P) \,\middle|\, \begin{array}{l} \text{There exists a ground instance } A \leftarrow B_1, \ldots, B_n \\ \text{of a clause in } P \text{ such that } \{B_1, \ldots, B_n\} \subseteq I \end{array} \right\}$$

Then,

$$T_P \uparrow 0 = \emptyset$$
$$T_P \uparrow n = T_P(T_P \uparrow (n-1)) \text{ for any positive integer } n$$
$$T_P \uparrow \omega = \bigcup_{n < \omega} T_P \uparrow n \text{ for the first transfinite ordinal } \omega$$

$M(P)$ denotes the least Herbrand model of P. It is known that $M(P) = T_P \uparrow \omega$.

For any mapping ϕ, $\mathcal{D}(\phi)$ denotes the domain of ϕ and $\phi \mid_S$ denotes the restriction of ϕ whose domain is $S \cap \mathcal{D}(\phi)$.

For any substitution $\{X_1/t_1, \ldots, X_n/t_n\}$, if each $t_i (1 \leq i \leq n)$ is a special constant then we call it a special substitution. In addition, a ground substitution θ is grounding substitution of a clause C if $C\theta$ is a ground clause.

3 Similarities between Logic Programs

There may exist various kinds of similarities between logic programs. In this section, we consider a class of similarities from the viewpoint of how examples are explained. This is because we think that programming can be viewed as fixing the way of explanation of examples. Formally, it can be viewed as giving a *Primitive Explanation Structure* defined as follows.

Definition 1. Let P be a logic program. The following relation $R \subseteq B(P) \times 2^{B(P)}$ is called *Primitive Explanation Structure (PES)* of P.

$$R = \left\{ (A, S) \,\middle|\, \begin{array}{l} A \leftarrow B_1, \ldots, B_n \text{ is a ground instance of a clause in } P, \\ \{B_1, \ldots, B_n\} \subseteq S \subseteq B(P) \end{array} \right\}$$

Because generalizing this possibly infinite PES, we get a finite expression of the structure and this is a program. Therefore, we consider similarities between programs based on this PES as follows: a target logic program Q is similar to a source logic program P if we can abstract the PES of Q into that of P. So, we first define a notion of abstraction relation between the PESs (the programs).

A partial mapping defined as follows enables to abstract the PES of the target program.

Definition 2. Let P and Q be logic programs. A partial mapping $\phi : B(Q) \to B(P)$ is called an *abstraction mapping from Q to P*. For $J \subseteq B(Q)$, $\phi(J) = \{\phi(B) \mid B \in J \cap \mathcal{D}(\phi)\}$.

The following proposition shows properties of abstraction mappings.

Proposition 3. *Let P and Q be logic programs. Let ϕ be an abstraction mapping from Q to P. For any $I, J \subseteq B(Q)$,*

$$I \subseteq J \Rightarrow \phi(I) \subseteq \phi(J) \qquad \phi(I \cup J) = \phi(I) \cup \phi(J)$$

Now, using the abstraction mappings, we define a class of abstraction relations between programs. The following definition says that for any logic programs P and Q, if we can abstract the PES of Q into that of P then P is more abstract than Q. That is, P is more abstract than Q when there exists an abstraction mapping ϕ from Q to P such that for any $\langle A, S \rangle$ in PES of Q, $\langle \phi(A), \phi(S) \rangle$ is in PES of P.

Definition 4. Let P and Q be logic programs. Let ϕ be an abstraction mapping from Q to P. P is *more abstract than Q w.r.t.* ϕ iff

$$T_P(\phi(I)) \supseteq \phi(T_Q(I))$$

for any $I \subseteq B(Q)$.

From the definition, we have the following theorem.

Theorem 5. *Let P and Q be logic programs. Let ϕ be an abstraction mapping from Q to P. If P is more abstract than Q w.r.t. ϕ then $M(P) \supseteq \phi(M(Q))$.*

The following proposition shows an equivalence condition of the abstraction relation. This is useful for decision whether there exists an abstraction relation w.r.t a given abstraction mapping.

Proposition 6. *Let P and Q be logic programs. P is more abstract than Q w.r.t. an abstraction mapping ϕ iff for any ground instance C of any clause in Q such that $He(C) \in \mathcal{D}(\phi)$, there exists a ground instance D of a clause in P such that $He(D) = \phi(He(C))$ and $Bo(D) \subseteq \phi(Bo(C))$.*

Example 1. Using Proposition 6, we can confirm the following abstraction relations.

For programs

$$append = \left\{ \begin{array}{l} \texttt{append([],X,X)} \leftarrow \\ \texttt{append([A|X],Y,[A|Z])} \leftarrow \texttt{append(X,Y,Z)} \end{array} \right\}$$

and

$$plus = \left\{ \begin{array}{l} \texttt{plus(0,X,X)} \leftarrow \\ \texttt{plus(s(X),Y,s(Z))} \leftarrow \texttt{plus(X,Y,Z)} \end{array} \right\}$$

Let ϕ_1 be an abstraction mapping such that

$$\phi_1(\texttt{append}(x,y,z)) = \texttt{plus}(\texttt{s}^n(\texttt{0}),\texttt{s}^m(\texttt{0}),\texttt{s}^{n+m}(\texttt{0}))$$

where x, y and z are lists whose lengths are $n \geq 0$, $m \geq 0$ and $n+m$ respectively. Then, *plus* is more abstract than *append* w.r.t. ϕ_1.

For *natural-number* and *reverse* in the introduction, Let ϕ_2 be an abstraction mapping such that

$$\phi_2(\texttt{rev}(x,y)) = \texttt{nn}(\texttt{s}^n(\texttt{0}))$$

where x is a list whose length is $n \geq 0$. Then, *natural-number* is more abstract than *reverse* w.r.t. ϕ_2.

For *natural-number* and

$$parity = \left\{ \begin{array}{l} \texttt{even(0)} \leftarrow \\ \texttt{odd(s(X))} \leftarrow \texttt{even(X)} \\ \texttt{even(s(X))} \leftarrow \texttt{odd(X)} \end{array} \right\}$$

if we define an abstraction mapping ϕ_3 as

$$\phi_3(\texttt{even}(x)) = \texttt{nn}(x), \phi_3(\texttt{odd}(x)) = \texttt{nn}(x)$$

then *natural-number* is more abstract than *parity* w.r.t. ϕ_3.

Now, let us consider how the abstractions defined above affect a proof tree. The consideration amplifies abstraction of the explanation structure mentioned in introduction.

Definition 7. Let P be a logic program. *Ground refutation node in P* is a pair $\langle G, C \rangle$, where $G \subseteq \text{B}(P)$ and C is a ground instance of a clause in P such that $\text{He}(C) \in G$.

Definition 8. Let P be a logic program and G a ground goal. *Ground refutation of G in P* is a finite sequence $\langle G_1, C_1 \rangle \cdots \langle G_n, C_n \rangle$ of ground refutation nodes in P, where

1. $G_1 = \text{Bo}(G)$.
2. For all i $(1 \leq i \leq n - 1)$, $G_{i+1} = G_i \setminus \{\text{He}(C_i)\} \cup \text{Bo}(C_i)$.
3. $G_n = \{A\}$ and $C_n = A \leftarrow$, where $A \in \text{B}(P)$.

The following theorem describes how the abstractions affect ground refutations in a target program. For any given ground refutation in a target program, the procedure in the theorem abstracts it into a ground refutation in a source program.

Theorem 9. *Let P and Q be logic programs. Assume P is more abstract than Q w.r.t. an abstraction mapping ϕ. For any ground goal G and any ground refutation GR of G in Q, any sequence GR' obtained by the following procedure is a ground refutation of $\phi(G)$ in P, where $\phi(G)$ denotes $\leftarrow B_1, \ldots, B_n$ $(\{B_1, \ldots, B_n\} = \phi(\text{Bo}(G)))$ and $\phi(G) \neq \bot$.*

1. *Assume* $GR = \langle G_1, C_1 \rangle \cdots \langle G_n, C_n \rangle$. *Let* GR' *be the empty sequence* ε *and* G_1' *be* G_1.
2. *For all* $1 \leq i \leq n$, *if* $\mathrm{He}(C_i) \in \mathcal{D}(\phi) \cap G_i'$ *then*
   (a) *non-deterministically choose a ground instance* D *of a clause in* P *such that* $\mathrm{He}(D) = \phi(\mathrm{He}(C_i))$ *and* $\mathrm{Bo}(D) \subseteq \phi(\mathrm{Bo}(C_i))$, *where there always exists such a clause because of Proposition 6,*
   (b) $G_{i+1}' \leftarrow G_i' \setminus \phi^{-1}(\{\mathrm{He}(D)\}) \cup \{A \in \mathrm{Bo}(C_i) \mid \phi(A) \in \mathrm{Bo}(D)\}$, *and*
   (c) *let* GR' *be the concatenation of* GR' *and* $\langle \phi(G_i'), D \rangle$.
   else let G_{i+1}' *be* G_i'.

In the procedure, ϕ^{-1} is defined as $\phi^{-1}(A) = \{B \mid \phi(B) = A\}$ and for any ground clause C such that $\mathrm{He}(C) \in \mathcal{D}(\phi)$, $\phi(C)$ denotes $\phi(\mathrm{He}(C)) \leftarrow B_1, \ldots, B_n$ $(\{B_1, \ldots, B_n\} = \phi(\mathrm{Bo}(C)))$.

There exist three types of abstraction of resolution by the above procedure. The following example shows them.

Example 2. Let a target program Q and a source program P as follows.

$$
Q = \left\{
\begin{array}{l}
s_1 \leftarrow \\
s_2 \leftarrow \\
t \leftarrow \\
r \leftarrow \\
p \leftarrow q, r \\
q \leftarrow s_1, s_2, t
\end{array}
\right\}
\qquad
P = \left\{
\begin{array}{l}
s' \leftarrow \\
t' \leftarrow \\
p' \leftarrow q' \\
q' \leftarrow s'
\end{array}
\right\}
$$

Let an abstraction mapping ϕ be $\phi(s_1) = \phi(s_2) = s'$, $\phi(t) = t'$, $\phi(p) = p'$ and $\phi(q) = q'$. Then P is more abstract than Q w.r.t. ϕ.

In the Fig. 1, GR is a ground refutation of a goal $\leftarrow p$ in Q and GR' is a ground refutation of a goal $\leftarrow p'$ in P obtained by the procedure stated above, where GR and GR' are represented by ordered binary tree. There exist three types of abstraction of resolution. The first one stems from the partiality of the abstraction mapping ϕ: the resolution (a) is abstracted because $r \notin \mathcal{D}(\phi)$. The second one stems from that ϕ is not injective: the resolution (b_1) and (b_2) are simplified into (b') because $\phi(s_1) = \phi(s_2) = s'$. The last one stems from that the image of a ground clause of Q is weaker than the corresponding clause of P: the resolution (c) is abstracted because $\phi(q \leftarrow s_1, s_2, t) = q' \leftarrow s', t'$ is weaker than $q' \leftarrow s'$.

The notion of abstraction defined in this paper differs from the notions of abstraction in [6, 14, 1] at least in abstraction mapping's partiality. As far as we concern ground atoms, our notion of abstraction is a partial *TI-abstraction* as Theorem 5 shows. The difference comes from a difference of motivation: while their notions of abstraction are motivated by theorem-proving with abstraction, our notion of abstraction is motivated by extracting similarity with abstraction.

Using the class of abstraction relations between logic programs we have seen, we define a class of similarities between programs.

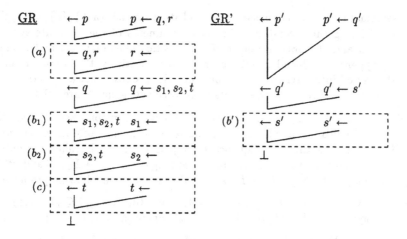

Fig. 1.

Definition 10. Let P and Q be logic programs. Let ϕ be an abstraction mapping from Q to P. Q is *similar to* P *w.r.t* ϕ iff P is more abstract than Q w.r.t. ϕ.

Q is *similar to* P iff there exists an abstraction mapping ϕ and Q is similar to P w.r.t. ϕ.

4 Restricted Similarities for Decidability

If the Herbrand base of a target program is finite then the PES is also finite and the decision whether the target program is similar to a source program w.r.t. an abstraction mapping is clearly decidable. Then, when the Herbrand base is infinite, is the decision decidable? This question is open. In this section, we restrict the class of the similarities defined in the previous section so that the decision is decidable even if the Herbrand base is infinite. By restricting the class of abstraction mappings in the preceding section, we restrict the class of the similarities. The restricted class of abstraction mappings can deal with the following abstractions, which are introduced in [6].

1. Renaming symbols abstraction. For a ground atom A, the predicate symbol and function symbols appearing in A are renamed in some systematic way. The renaming is not necessarily one-to-one. For example, ground atoms cup(a) and bottle(a) are renamed into container(a).
2. Permuting arguments abstraction. For a ground atom A, the order of the arguments of the predicate symbol or function symbols appearing in A changes in some systematic way. For example, a ground atom child(a,father(a)) is changed into parent(father(a),a). In this example, renaming symbols abstraction is applied at the same time.
3. Deleting arguments abstraction. For a ground atom A, certain arguments of the predicate symbol or function symbols appearing in A are deleted in some

systematic way. Let us consider a ground atom append([a,b],[c],[a,b,c]). By deleting the second and the third arguments of the predicate symbol append and the first argument of the function symbol [_|_], and renaming append, [_|_] and [] into nn, s and 0 respectively, the ground atom is abstracted into nn(s(s(0))). Note that the propositional abstraction is a special case of this (all arguments of all predicate symbols are deleted).

Definition 11. Let Σ_1 and Σ_2 be sets of function symbols. Let Π_1 and Π_2 be sets of predicate symbols. Let S is the set of sequences of different natural numbers including the null sequence ε. A pair $\langle \phi^\Sigma, \phi^\Pi \rangle$ is called a *symbol-abstraction mapping*, where ϕ^Σ is a total mapping $\phi^\Sigma : \Sigma_1 \to \Sigma_2 \times S$ and ϕ^Π is a partial mapping $\phi^\Pi : \Pi_1 \to \Pi_2 \times S$, and they have the following properties.

- For any $f \in \Sigma_1$, $\phi^\Sigma(f) = \langle g, a_1 \cdots a_{\sharp g} \rangle$, where $\{a_1, \ldots, a_{\sharp g}\} \subseteq \{1, \ldots, \sharp f\}$.
- For any $p \in \mathcal{D}(\phi^\Pi)$, $\phi^\Pi(p) = \langle q, a_1 \cdots a_{\sharp q} \rangle$, where $\{a_1, \ldots, a_{\sharp q}\} \subseteq \{1, \ldots, \sharp p\}$.

$\Phi^s(\langle \Sigma_1, \Pi_1 \rangle, \langle \Sigma_2, \Pi_2 \rangle)$ denotes the class of symbol-abstraction mappings

In the above definition, $\phi^\Sigma(f) = \langle g, a_1 \cdots a_m \rangle$ means that any term s whose function symbol is f is mapped to a term t whose function symbol is g and the a_i-th argument of s is mapped to the i-th argument of t for all $1 \leq i \leq m$.

Definition 12. For any symbol-abstraction mapping $\langle \phi^\Sigma, \phi^\Pi \rangle \in \Phi^s(\langle \Sigma_1, \Pi_1 \rangle, \langle \Sigma_2, \Pi_2 \rangle)$, a partial mapping $\phi : \mathrm{Exp}(\Sigma_1, \Pi_1) \to \mathrm{Exp}(\Sigma_2, \Pi_2)$ is defined as follows.

1. For any variable $X \in \mathcal{V}$, $\phi(X) = X$.
2. For any special constant $c \in \mathcal{C}$, $\phi(c) = c$.
3. For any constant $c \in \Sigma_1$, $\phi(c) = c'$, where $\phi^\Sigma(c) = \langle c', \varepsilon \rangle$.
4. For any term $f(t_1, \ldots, t_n) \in \mathrm{Trm}(\Sigma_1)$, $\phi(f(t_1, \ldots, t_n)) = g(\phi(t_{a_1}), \ldots, \phi(t_{a_m}))$, where $\phi^\Sigma(f) = \langle g, a_1 \cdots a_m \rangle$.
5. For any atom $p(t_1, \ldots, t_n) \in \mathrm{Atm}(\Sigma_1, \Pi_1)$ such that $p \in \mathcal{D}(\phi^\Pi)$, $\phi(p(t_1, \ldots, t_n)) = q(\phi(t_{a_1}), \ldots, \phi(t_{a_m}))$, where $\phi^\Pi(p) = \langle q, a_1 \cdots a_m \rangle$.
6. For any clause $C \in \mathrm{Cls}(\Sigma_1, \Pi_1)$ such that $\mathrm{He}(C) \in \mathcal{D}(\phi)$, $\phi(C) = \phi(\mathrm{He}(C)) \leftarrow \phi(B_1), \ldots, \phi(B_n)$, where $\{B_1, \ldots, B_n\} = \mathrm{Bo}(C) \cap \mathcal{D}(\phi)$.
7. For any substitution $\theta = \{X_1/s_1, \ldots, X_n/s_n\} \in \mathrm{Sub}(\Sigma_1)$, $\phi(\theta) = \{X_1/\phi(s_1), \ldots, X_n/\phi(s_n)\}$.

Moreover, for any set of clauses $S \subseteq \mathrm{Cls}(\Sigma_1, \Pi_1)$, $\phi(S) = \{\phi(C) \mid C \in S \cap \mathcal{D}(\phi)\}$. $\Phi(\langle \Sigma_1, \Pi_1 \rangle, \langle \Sigma_2, \Pi_2 \rangle)$ denotes the class of the mappings defined as above.

Let P and Q be logic programs. For any $\phi \in \Phi(\mathrm{V}(Q), \mathrm{V}(P))$, note that $\phi \mid_{\mathrm{B}(Q)}$ is an abstraction mapping from Q to P. So, we also call ϕ an abstraction mapping.

Example 3. Abstraction mappings ϕ_1, ϕ_2 and ϕ_3 introduced in Example 1 are obtained as follows.

$$
\begin{array}{lll}
\phi_1^\Sigma([]) = \langle 0, \varepsilon \rangle & \phi_2^\Sigma([]) = \langle 0, \varepsilon \rangle & \phi_3^\Sigma(0) = \langle 0, \varepsilon \rangle \\
\phi_1^\Sigma([\_|\_]) = \langle s, 2 \rangle & \phi_2^\Sigma([\_|\_]) = \langle s, 2 \rangle & \phi_3^\Sigma(s) = \langle s, 1 \rangle \\
\phi_1^\Pi(\mathrm{append}) = \langle \mathrm{plus}, 1 \cdot 2 \cdot 3 \rangle & \phi_2^\Pi(\mathrm{rev}) = \langle \mathrm{nn}, 1 \rangle & \phi_3^\Pi(\mathrm{even}) = \langle \mathrm{nn}, 1 \rangle \\
& & \phi_3^\Pi(\mathrm{odd}) = \langle \mathrm{nn}, 1 \rangle
\end{array}
$$

Lemma 13. *Let Σ_1 and Σ_2 be sets of function symbols. Let Π_1 and Π_2 be sets of predicate symbols. Let ϕ be in $\Phi(\langle \Sigma_1, \Pi_1 \rangle, \langle \Sigma_2, \Pi_2 \rangle)$. For any $t \in \mathrm{Trm}(\Sigma_1)$, any $A \in \mathrm{Atm}(\Sigma_1, \Pi_1)$, any $S \subseteq \mathrm{Atm}(\Sigma_1, \Pi_1)$, and any $\theta \in \mathrm{Sub}(\Sigma_1)$,*

$$\phi(t \cdot \theta) = \phi(t) \cdot \phi(\theta) \quad \phi(A \cdot \theta) = \phi(A) \cdot \phi(\theta) \quad \phi(S \cdot \theta) = \phi(S) \cdot \phi(\theta)$$

Theorem 14. *Let P and Q be logic programs. Q is similar to P w.r.t. $\phi \in \Phi(\mathrm{V}(Q), \mathrm{V}(P))$ iff $P \geq \phi(Q)$.*

Since whether $P \geq \phi(Q)$ or not is decidable, the decision whether Q is similar to P w.r.t. ϕ is also decidable.

Example 4. For the abstraction mapping ϕ_2 in Example 3, *natural-number* $= \phi_2(reverse)$. Therefore, *reverse* is similar to *natural-number* w.r.t. ϕ_2. Likewise, we can confirm similarities w.r.t. ϕ_1 and ϕ_3.

5 ALPS Algorithm

In this section, using the restricted class of the similarities introduced in the preceding section, we consider an algorithm for ALPS. By virtue of a decidability of the similarities, we get such an algorithm easily. Here, we show an algorithm using Shapiro's [11, page 33] incremental model inference algorithm. Concepts and notations for the model inference are based on [11], unless stated otherwise.

Using the terminology of the model inference, we restate the problem in the introduction as follows.

Assume
- vocabulary $\langle \Sigma, \Pi \rangle$,
- observational language L_o which is the set of ground atoms in $\mathrm{Atm}(\Sigma, \Pi)$
- hypothesis language $L_h \subseteq \mathrm{Cls}(\Sigma, \Pi)$,

Given
- a source program P and
- an oracle for unknown model M over $\langle \Sigma, \Pi \rangle$,

Find a finite L_o-complete axiomatization of M which is similar to P.

L_o-complete axiomatization of M ([11, page 8]) means a subset of L_h which is true in M and deduces all positive examples in L_o.

We get the following result of this problem.

Theorem 15. *If M is a h-easy model and there exists a solution in L_h then the Algorithm 1 identifies a solution in the limit.*

The algorithm is illustrated as follows: while switching abstraction mappings, the algorithm searches the hypothesis space constrained by the similarity w.r.t the abstraction mapping with the top-down (i.e. from general to specific) strategy.

The algorithm assumes the followings in the same way as [11].

1. The refinement operator ρ is complete for L_h and conservative for the resolution "$\vdash$".
2. $\alpha_1, \alpha_2, \alpha_3, \ldots$ is a enumeration of all elements of L_o and $\langle \alpha_1, V_1 \rangle, \langle \alpha_2, V_2 \rangle, \ldots$ is a enumeration of facts of M, where a fact $\langle \alpha, V \rangle$ means that $\alpha \in L_o$ has a validity V in M which is taught by the oracle for M.
3. h is a total recursive function.

Moreover, the algorithm assumes the followings.

1. $\phi_1, \ldots, \phi_{len}$ is a enumeration of all elements of $\Phi(\langle \Sigma, \Pi \rangle, V(P))$ except for elements ϕ such that $\mathcal{D}(\phi^\Pi) = \emptyset$, where $len = |\Phi(\langle \Sigma, \Pi \rangle, V(P))|$.
2. A set of clauses $L_\rho^m(\phi_i)$ denotes $\{C \in L_\rho^m \mid C \notin \mathcal{D}(\phi_i) \text{ or } P \geq \{\phi_i(C)\}\}$, where L_ρ^m denotes the source set of the marking m ([11, page 32]), i.e. the set of clauses which are not marked 'false' and all antecedent clauses by ρ are marked 'false' in m. A set of clauses $L_\rho^m(\phi_i) \mid_k$ denotes $\{C \in L_\rho^m(\phi_i) \mid size(C) \leq k\}$, where $size(C)$ denotes the size of the clause C ([11, page 23]). Note that $L_\rho^m(\phi_i) \mid_{k(i)}$ is computable.

The differences between the algorithm and Shapiro's algorithm are as follows. Firstly, our algorithm must find not only an axiomatization but also an abstraction mapping. So, the algorithm has two-dimensional search space: refinements and abstraction mappings. The algorithm can search this search space exhaustively. Secondly, our algorithm use $L_\rho^m(\phi_i)$ instead of L_ρ^m because a solution must be similar to the source program. By the constraint of the similarity, the hypothesis space L_h is reduced to $\bigcup_\phi L_h^\phi$, where $L_h^\phi = \{C \in L_h \mid C \notin \mathcal{D}(\phi) \text{ or } P \geq \{\phi(C)\}\}$. Of course, this does not mean that our algorithm converges on a solution faster than Shapiro's.

Algorithm 1

For all i $(1 \leq i \leq len)$, $S_F(i) \leftarrow \emptyset$, $S_T(i) \leftarrow \emptyset$, $n(i) \leftarrow 0$, and $k(i) \leftarrow 0$
$i \leftarrow 1$ and mark $\perp$ 'false'.
repeat
  if there exists an $\alpha \in S_F(i)$ such that $L_\rho^m(\phi_i) \mid_{k(i)} \vdash_{n(i)} \alpha$ **then**
    apply the contradiction backtracing algorithm
      and mark the refuted hypothesis 'false'.
    $i \leftarrow i + 1$
  else if there exists an $\alpha_j \in S_T(i)$ such that $L_\rho^m(\phi_i) \mid_{k(i)} \nvdash_{h(j)} \alpha_j$ **then**
    $k(i) \leftarrow k(i) + 1$, $i \leftarrow i + 1$
  else
    output $L_\rho^m(\phi_i) \mid_{k(i)}$
    $n(i) \leftarrow n(i) + 1$ and read a fact $\langle \alpha_{n(i)}, V_{n(i)} \rangle$
    if $V_{n(i)} = true$ **then** $S_T(i) \leftarrow S_T(i) \cup \{\alpha_{n(i)}\}$
    else $S_F(i) \leftarrow S_F(i) \cup \{\alpha_{n(i)}\}$
  endif
  if $i > len$ **then** $i = 1$
forever

6 Concluding Remarks

In this paper, we firstly have proposed a class of similarities between programs and a theory of ALPS using the similarities. We believe that further research based on the theory reveals that ALPS is effective for improvement of LPS system's performance and useful as a device to shift a bias. Secondly, we have showed that an algorithm for ALPS which is obtained by extending Shapiro's incremental model inference algorithm, and the algorithm identifies a solution in the limit.

However, the algorithm is impractical. This mainly stems from the enumeration of abstraction mappings. To overcome the difficulty, we are now developing an algorithm which constructs an abstraction mapping step by step. In addition, this algorithm incorporates the idea from theorem-proving with abstraction.

Furthermore, we are now investigating to utilize the aspect of ALPS as a device to shift a bias for the change of representation (the program transformation). For instance, given *natural-number* as a source program, an ALPS system transforms *naive-sort* into *insert-sort* which is similar to *natural-number*. That is, from the examples provided by *naive-sort*, the ALPS system synthesizes *insert-sort*. We expect that this method enable us to refine our initial program into more efficient or more comprehensible one depending on a source program.

A Appendix

Proof sketch of Theorem 5. We can show $T_P \uparrow n \supseteq \phi(T_Q \uparrow n)$ by induction on n ($0 \le n < \omega$). Since $\bigcup_{n<\omega} T_P \uparrow n \supseteq \bigcup_{n<\omega} \phi(T_Q \uparrow n) = \phi(\bigcup_{n<\omega} T_Q \uparrow n)$, $M(P) \supseteq \phi(M(Q))$ is proved. $\square$

Proof sketch of Theorem 9. We can verify the conditions in Definition 8. For instance, the condition 2 is verified as follows. Let $N_k = \langle \phi(G_i'), D_k \rangle$ and $N_{k+1} = \langle \phi(G_j'), D_{k+1} \rangle$ be ground refutation nodes in GR', where $1 \le i < j \le n$. Then, $G_j' = G_i' \setminus \phi^{-1}(\{He(D_k)\}) \cup \{A \in Bo(C_i) \mid \phi(A) \in Bo(D_k)\}$.

$$\phi(G_j') = \phi(G_i' \setminus \phi^{-1}(\{He(D_k)\})) \cup \phi(\{A \in Bo(C_i) \mid \phi(A) \in Bo(D_k)\})$$
(By Proposition 3.)
$$= \phi(G_i' \setminus \phi^{-1}(\{He(D_k)\})) \cup Bo(D_k) = \phi(G_i') \setminus \{He(D_k)\} \cup Bo(D_k)$$
(By $Bo(D_k) \subseteq \phi(Bo(C_i))$.)

$\square$

Proof sketch of Theorem 14. (if part) For any $I \subseteq B(Q)$ and any $A \in \phi(T_Q(I))$, there exists a clause $C \in Q$ and a grounding substitution $\theta \in Sub(Q)$ of C such that $\phi(He(C)\theta) = A$ and $Bo(C)\theta \subseteq I$. By the assumption, there exists a clause $D \in P$ and a substitution $\sigma \in Sub(P)$ such that $D\sigma \subseteq \phi(C)$. Thus, by Proposition 3 and Lemma 13, $He(D)\sigma\phi(\theta) = \phi(He(C)\theta) = A$ and $Bo(D)\sigma\phi(\theta) \subseteq \phi(Bo(C)\theta) \subseteq \phi(I)$. This means $A \in T_P(\phi(I))$.

(only-if part) We prove it by the contraposition. Assume there exists a clause $C \in Q$ such that $D \not\succeq \phi(C)$ for any clause $D \in P$. Then, there exists a special and grounding substitution $\theta \in \mathrm{Sub}(P)$ of $\phi(C)$ such that for any clause D in P and any grounding substitution $\sigma \in \mathrm{Sub}(P)$ of D, $D\sigma \not\subseteq \phi(C)\theta$. Therefore, $\phi(\mathrm{He}(C))\theta \not\in \mathrm{T}_P(\phi(\mathrm{Bo}(C))\theta$. On the other hand, there exists a ground substitution $\mu \in \mathrm{Sub}(Q)$ such that $\theta\mu$ is a grounding substitution of C. If we assume $I = \mathrm{Bo}(C)\theta\mu$ then $\phi(\mathrm{He}(C)\theta\mu) = \phi(\mathrm{He}(C))\theta \in \phi(\mathrm{T}_Q(I))$. This means $\mathrm{T}_P(\phi(I)) \not\supseteq \phi(\mathrm{T}_Q(I))$ because $\phi(I) = \phi(\mathrm{Bo}(C))\theta$. $\qquad\square$

Proof sketch of Theorem 15. We can show that if $L_\rho^m(\phi_i) \mid_{k(i)}$ is not a solution then the algorithm transfers the index i to next value. Let us fix ϕ_i, Since $\langle L_o, L_h^{\phi_i} \rangle$ is admissible pair and ρ is complete for $L_h^{\phi_i}$, we can show that the algorithm identifies a solution if the solution is in $L_h^{\phi_i}$ by Theorem 6.3 in [11]. $\quad\square$

References

1. Fausto Giunchiglia and Toby Walsh. A theory of abstraction. *Artificial Intelligence*, 57:323–389, 1992.
2. Bipin Indurkhya. On the role of interpretive analogy in learning. In *Proceeding of ALT'90*, pages 174–189, 1990.
3. J.W. Lloyd. *Foundations of Logic Programming*. Springer Verlag, second edition, 1987.
4. Ryszard S. Michalski. A theory and methodology of inductive learning. *Artificial Intelligence*, 20:111–161, 1983.
5. Stephen Muggleton. Inductive logic programming. In *Inductive Logic Programming*. ACADEMIC PRESS, 1992.
6. David A. Plaisted. Theorem proving with abstraction. *Artificial Intelligence*, 16:47–108, 1981.
7. Luc De Raedt and Maurice Bruynooghe. Constructive induction by analogy. In *Proceeding of ML'89*, pages 476–477, 1989.
8. Luc De Raedt and Maurice Bruynooghe. Interactive concept-learning and constructive induction by analogy. *Machine Learning*, 8:107–150, 1992.
9. Céline Rouveirol. Extension of inversion of resolution applied to theory completion. In *Inductive Logic Programming*. ACADEMIC PRESS, 1992.
10. Seiichiro Sakurai and Makoto Haraguchi. Towards learning by abstraction. In *Proceeding of ALT'91*, pages 288–298, 1991.
11. Ehud Y. Shapiro. Inductive inference of theories from facts. Technical Report 192, Yale University Computer Science Dept., 1981.
12. Leon Sterling and Ehud Shapiro. *The Art of Prolog*. The MIT Press, 1986.
13. Birgit Tausend and Siegfied Bell. Analogical reasoning for logic programming. In *Inductive Logic Programming*. ACADEMIC PRESS, 1992.
14. Josh D. Tenenberg. Abstracting first-order theories. In *Change of Representation and Inductive Bias*, pages 67–79. Kluwer Academic Publishers, 1990.

A Guided Tour Through Hypothesis Spaces in ILP

Birgit Tausend

Fakultät Informatik, Universität Stuttgart, Breitwiesenstr. 20-22, D-70565 Stuttgart

Abstract. In spite of the desirable properties of using Horn logic as hypothesis language, the expressivness leads to huge hypothesis spaces containing up to millions of hypotheses for even simple learning problems. Controlling hypothesis spaces by biases requires knowledge on the effects and applicability of biases in different domains. This knowledge can be gained experimentally by comparing the size of hypothesis spaces with respect to the language bias and the application domain. This approach contrasts theoretical comparisons of the complexity where the results are very general and small bias variations mostly cannot be considered. In order to yield more detailed information on small bias variations and to compare the results independently of systems, their implementations and additional more or less hidden biases, we use MILES-CTL for the experiments. As application domains, we selected a function-free domain including family relations and a non-function-free domain including list-processing programs.

1 Introduction

Obviously, expressive hypothesis languages as Horn logic in Inductive Logic Programming (ILP) offer a wide range of desirable properties, e.g., the representation of relational knowledge, or a better understandability of hypotheses. However, a closer look to the size of hypothesis spaces raises the question how a learning system is able to find an acceptable hypothesis among several thousands of alternative hypotheses. Exploiting the background knowledge, another goal of to ILP systems, seems to worsen the problem of very large hypothesis spaces, and one may ask if a step back to attribute-value representations as in LINUS [LD92] is the only reasonable solution.

The feeling of helplessness facing the mere size of hypothesis spaces of even very simple learning problems contrasts the success of ILP systems learning in different more or less real application domains, e.g. GOLEM [MKS92], Progol [SMKS94] or MOBAL [MWKE94, SMAU93]. In spite of the temptation to believe so, this success cannot be ascribed to some kind of magic but is the result of choosing appropriate language, search, or validation biases. Using strong language biases, e.g. predicate types, leads to considerably smaller hypothesis spaces. Another solution of the size problem is to apply heuristic search instead of complete search, e.g., beam or best search, guided by powerful heuristics.

To avoid exploding hypothesis spaces the designer of an ILP system needs to know a lot about biases, e.g.,

- which parameters of inductive learning systems can be affected by biases,
- which effects particular biases have,
- which combinations of biases are useful,
- which biases are appropriate to solve a particular learning problem.

Concerning a particular parameter of the learning system to design, he has to decide either to use more general and widely applicable biases, e.g. the information gain heuristic, or more specific and domain-dependent biases, e.g. predicate types. Another decision concerns the adaption of the learning system that can be supported by parameterizable biases, e.g., the parameters i and j in the ij-determinacy.

The knowledge about biases can be gained either by theoretical considerations or by experiments. Theoretically, the complexity of a learning algorithms with particular biases can be computed [Coh93, KL94, MP94]. Another theoretical approach is to approximate the size of the hypothesis space with respect to the language bias [PK92, Tau94b]. In contrast, experimental comparisons study for example the effects of some language biases on the size of the starting clauses in bottom-up ILP approaches [ADRB94] or on the size of the hypothesis space [PK92].

In this paper, we focus on the experimental setting comparing the effects of a particular class of biases, the language biases in ILP systems measuring the size of the hypothesis space by the number of clauses to be constructed with respect to the bias and the application domain. In the experiments, we use two domains, the domain of family relations and the domain of list-processing programs. The biases are represented in MILES-CTL [Tau94d, Tau94a], a declarative, scheme-based representation for language biases in ILP since using MILES-CTL offers several advantages. First, in contrast to the experiments in [ADRB94], language biases can be compared independently of particular systems and their implementations, i.e., independently of other more or less obvious biases in the systems compared. Second, a wider range of language biases as well as new combinations can be investigated because most of them can be represented. Third, in comparison to theoretical results, experiments using MILES-CTL give more detailed information on the effects of language biases since the represention enables small bias variations.

This paper is organized as follows. The following section describes the problem setting of ILP and classifies the language biases used in ILP systems. Section 3 gives a short introduction to MILES-CTL. In section 4, different language biases are experimentally evaluated with respect to the size of the hypothesis space using the function-free domain of family relations. Section 5 describes similar experiments in the domain of list-processing programs that is not function-free. The last section discusses the results and concludes.

2 ILP and Language Biases

Using the general model in [Tau94c] shown in figure 1, the problem setting of Inductive Logic Programming can be defined as follows. Given positive and negative examples E and a logic program B as background knowledge, the task is to learn a logic program H that fulfills A. Thus, L_H is restricted to subclasses of Horn logic. All other parameters may vary with respect to particular algorithms and systems, e.g. accptance criteria A mostly include the necessity, the completeness and the consistency.

Given

- the examples E in L_E,
- the background knowledge B in L_B,
- and the setting of the induction parameters including
    - the representation language of the examples L_E, i.e., classified fact or clauses with their classification,
    - the representation language of the background knowledge L_B, i.e., facts and/or clauses,
    - the representation language of the hypothesis L_H,
    - the parameters S^* of the search procedure S,
    - the operators O to proceed in the hypothesis space,
    - the initial hypotheses H',
    - the criterion $\leq_H$ to order the hypotheses,
    - the acceptance criterion A.

Find

- a hypothesis H in L_H that fulfills A.

Table 1. A general model for inductive learning systems

The hypothesis language is defined by the so-called language bias. Since a particular set of Horn clauses can be defined by a signature and rules to construct terms and clauses, the languages biases can be classified with respect to which of them they affect. In addition, several model-dependent biases are used in ILP, e.g. functionality, that depend on the Herbrand universe derived from the background knowledge B and the examples E. This leads to the following classification of biases described in more detail in [Tau94a]

- **Signature**: function-free clauses, constant-free clauses, predicate types, argument types, sort hierarchies, mode declarations, ... ;
- **Rules of Term Construction**: no term construction, term construction limited to head terms/subterms, limited depth of term construction, ... ;
- **Rules of Clause Construction**: generative/ range restricted clauses, constrained clauses, limited number of new variables, restrictions of variable sharing, limited clause length, limited arity of literals, ... ;
- **Model-dependend Restrictions**: functionality, determinacy, ...

Although these biases are very different, MILES-CTL [Tau94b] offers a unifying approach to represent most of them declaratively.

3 Representing the Language Bias in CTL

The basic idea of the representation MILES-CTL [Tau94d] is to describe sets of hypotheses by schemes. A scheme for a hypothesis clause called clause template includes schemes for each literal in the clause. Similar to a record data type, a literal template consists of several identifiers followed by a scheme variable or a constant. The domain of a scheme variable in a literal template can be further restricted by conditions. Since the items in a literal template describe the set of covered literals, they have to include at least an item for the predicate name and the arguments. Other items, for example, describe the arity, the number of new variables, argument or predicate types, or the depth of the covered literals.

Additionally, the vocabulary Σ including predicates, functors, and types, and an instantiation function I have to be specified in order to give a complete declaration of a hypothesis language $L_H = (T, \Sigma, I)$ in MILES-CTL. Given T and Σ, I constructs hypotheses by instantiating the scheme variables in a clause template.

For example, the clause template $T1$ with

$$T1: \begin{bmatrix} predicate : P21, \\ arguments : A21 \end{bmatrix} \leftarrow \begin{bmatrix} predicate : P22, \\ arguments : A22, \\ predicate\_type : comp \end{bmatrix}, \begin{bmatrix} predicate : P23, \\ arguments : A23, \\ arity : Ar23 || (Ar23 \geq 3) \end{bmatrix}.$$

covers clauses with two body literals where the predicate type of the first is *comp* and the arity of the second is greater or equal than 3. Let the language L_H be defined by $T = \{T1\}$, Σ containing the predicates *member/2,leq/2* and *geq/2* of type *comp* and the predicates *append/3, reverse/2* and *intersection/3* of type *listp*, and an instantiation function I. Given a clause head *intersection([A|B], C, [A|E])* induced from the examples, the following clauses can be constructed, for example:

$intersection([A|B], C, [A|E]) \leftarrow member(A, C), intersection(B, C, E).$
$intersection([A|B], C, [A|E]) \leftarrow member(A, C), intersection([A|B], C, E).$
$intersection([A|B], C, [A|E]) \leftarrow member(A, C), intersection(B, C, [A|E]).$
$intersection([A|B], C, [A|E]) \leftarrow member(B, C), intersection(B, C, D).$
$intersection([A|B], C, [A|E]) \leftarrow member([A|B], C), append(B, C, D).$
$intersection([A|B], C, [A|E]) \leftarrow geq(A, C), intersection(B, C, E).$
$intersection([A|B], C, [A|E]) \leftarrow geq(B, C), intersection(B, C, E).$
$intersection([A|B], C, [A|E]) \leftarrow leq(A, C), intersection([A|B], C, E).$

. . .

However, the clauses

$intersection([A|B], C, [D|E]) \leftarrow reverse(B, E), intersection(B, C, E).$
$intersection([A|B], C, [A|E]) \leftarrow member(A, C), leq(A, A).$
$intersection([A|B], C, [A|E]) \leftarrow member(A, C), reverse(B, E).$

cannot be constructed because of the first, respectively the second, body literal description in $T1$.

4 Effects of Language Biases in a Function-Free Domain

In the first five experiments, we restrict the hypothesis language to function-free Horn clauses because this restriction applies for a wide range of ILP systems, e.g., CLINT[DR91], ITOU[Rou92], FOIL [Qui90]. A function-free domain often used for comparisons is the domain of family relations. In the following experiments, the concept *father* is learned from a set of positive and negative examples given by

positive	negative
$father(theo, marc)$.	$father(penelope, arthur)$.
$father(theo, anna)$.	$father(penelope, victoria)$.
$father(peter, lisa)$.	$father(anne, lisa)$.
$father(peter, jennifer)$.	$father(anne, jennifer)$.
$father(peter, ina)$.	$father(anne, ina)$.
$father(klaus, jan)$.	$father(maria, jan)$.
$father(rainer, robin)$.	$father(helga, robin)$.
$father(andreas, susanne)$.	$father(doris, susanne)$.

The hypothesis languages in the experiments are represented by clause templates in T_1 and the signature Σ_1 given by

$$\Sigma_1 = [\ s\_data : \{person, numeric\},$$
$$s\_pred : \{relative, relation, sex, date, comp\},$$
$$s\_relation : \{\ \}$$
$$func : \{\ \},$$
$$const : \{\ \}$$
$$pred : Predicates,$$
$$modes : \{\ \}\ ]$$

The sets s_data and s_pred contain the argument and predicate types, $func$ and $const$ the functors and constants to be used in hypotheses, $pred$ contains the predicates and $modes$ the mode declarations in this domain. $Predicates$ is varied to study the effect of increasing background knowledge B, and it includes subsets of

$$\{\ father(X : person, Y : person)/relative$$
$$male(X : person)/sex,$$
$$female(X : person)/sex,$$
$$parent(X : person, Y : person)/relative,$$
$$greater(X : person, Y : numeric)/comp$$
$$married(X : person, Y : person)/relation$$
$$age(X : person, Y : numeric)/date\ \}.$$

Given Σ_1, the most general hypothesis language covering clauses with arbitrary literals is defined by clause templates $T_{unrestricted}$ with

$$T_{unrestricted} : \begin{bmatrix} predicate : P1, \\ arguments : A1 \end{bmatrix} \leftarrow \begin{bmatrix} predicate : P2, \\ arguments : A2 \end{bmatrix}, \ldots, \begin{bmatrix} predicate : Pn, \\ arguments : An \end{bmatrix}.$$

The first experiment FD_1 compares the size of the hypothesis space with respect to biases affecting the signature of the clauses. Among these biases, argument types can be exploited either by defining partially fixed argument types for the arguments of each literal or by checking the argument type of a term distributed to a particular argument position with the definition of the predicate in the signature. Predicate types can be fixed or specified as one of several alternatives. Thus, we vary Σ_1 and T_1 including one of the clause templates for

- checking argument types

$$T_1 : \begin{bmatrix} predicate : P1, \\ arguments : A1 \\ argument\_types :T1 \end{bmatrix} \leftarrow \begin{bmatrix} predicate : P2, \\ arguments : A2, \\ argument\_types :T2 \end{bmatrix} , \begin{bmatrix} predicate : P3, \\ arguments : A3, \\ argument\_types :T3 \end{bmatrix} .$$

- partially fixed argument types

$$T_2 : \begin{bmatrix} predicate : P1, \\ arguments : A1 \\ argument\_types :T1 \end{bmatrix} \leftarrow \begin{bmatrix} predicate : P2, \\ arguments : A2, \\ argument\_types :T2 :(\{person :\langle 1\rangle\} \subseteq T2) \end{bmatrix} ,$$

$$\begin{bmatrix} predicate : P3, \\ arguments : A3, \\ argument\_types :T3 :(\{person :\langle 1\rangle, \\ \qquad\qquad person :\langle 2\rangle\} \subseteq T3) \end{bmatrix} .$$

- fixed predicate types

$$T_3 : \begin{bmatrix} predicate : P1, \\ arguments : A1 \end{bmatrix} \leftarrow \begin{bmatrix} predicate : P2, \\ arguments : A2, \\ predicate\_type : sex \end{bmatrix} , \begin{bmatrix} predicate : P3, \\ arguments : A3, \\ predicate\_type : relative \end{bmatrix} .$$

- alternative predicate types

$$T_4 : \begin{bmatrix} predicate : P1, \\ arguments : A1 \end{bmatrix} \leftarrow \begin{bmatrix} predicate : P2, \\ arguments : A2, \\ predicate\_type : Y2 : (Y2 \in \{sex, date\}) \end{bmatrix} ,$$

$$\begin{bmatrix} predicate : P3, \\ arguments : A3, \\ predicate\_type : Y3 : (Y3 \in \{relative, relation\}) \end{bmatrix} .$$

The size of the hypothesis space is measured by the number of hypotheses constructed from T_1 and Σ_1 in FD_1 with respect to an increasing set of predicates in *Predicates*. The results are shown in the following table.

Clause Template	Predicates in Σ_1 in experiment FD_1					
	father female	father female male	father female male parent	father female male parent greater	father female male parent greater married	father female male parent greater married age
$T_{unrestricted}$	302	418	1238	2494	4168	6232
T_1 : check arg. types	302	418	1238	1374	2678	3035
T_2 : part. arg. types	51	122	210	210	298	298
T_3 : fix pred. types	44	88	176	176	176	176
T_4 : altern. pred. types	44	88	176	176	274	918

This experiment shows that predicate types strongly restrict the hypothesis space. The reason is that all variabilizations of a predicate are excluded if its type does not agree with the type specified for the literal. Fixed argument types as well result in strong reductions of the number of hypotheses because they implicitely fix the minimum arity of the predicate to be used. Thus, all variabilizations of literals with smaller arity are excluded. Compared to the other biases, checking argument types in this domain imposes minor restrictions on the search space. But satisfying reductions of more than 50% compared with the number of hypotheses constructed from an unrestricted clause template are gained if the types information can be exploited as in the last columns of the table.

In the next experiment FD_2, we study the effect of biases restricting the rules of clause construction. In particular, we compare several widely used biases, the restrictions to constrained and generative clauses, to clauses without recursive literals and to clauses with unique variables. Additionally, a new bias is compared, namely the restriction to clauses without single variable, that is similar to the search bias in SIERES [WO91] and INDICO [STW93]. This bias is defined by

$$A \text{ clause } C : l_1 \leftarrow l_1 \ldots l_n \text{ does not include single variables if}$$
$$\forall l_i \in C : vars(l_i) \subseteq vars(\{l_0, l_1, \ldots l_n\} - \{l_i\})$$

For example, the clause $father(A, B) : -male(A), parent(A, C)$ includes the single variable C.

These biases in experiment FD_2 are represented by the clause templates for

- constrained clauses

$$T_1 : \begin{bmatrix} predicate : P1, \\ arguments : A1 \end{bmatrix} \leftarrow \begin{bmatrix} predicate : P2, \\ arguments : A2, \\ new\_variables : \emptyset \end{bmatrix}, \begin{bmatrix} predicate : P3, \\ arguments : A3, \\ new\_variables : \emptyset \end{bmatrix}.$$

- range restricted/generative clauses

$$T_2 : \begin{bmatrix} predicate : P1, \\ arguments : A1, \\ generative : yes \end{bmatrix} \leftarrow \begin{bmatrix} predicate : P2, \\ arguments : A2 \end{bmatrix}, \begin{bmatrix} predicate : P3, \\ arguments : A3 \end{bmatrix}.$$

- clauses without recursive literals

$$T_3 : \begin{bmatrix} predicate : P1, \\ arguments : A1 \end{bmatrix} \leftarrow \begin{bmatrix} predicate : P2 || (P2 \neq P1), \\ arguments : A2 \end{bmatrix}, \begin{bmatrix} predicate : P3 || (P3 \neq P1), \\ arguments : A3 \end{bmatrix}.$$

- clauses with unique variables

$$T_4 : \begin{bmatrix} predicate : P1, \\ arguments : A1 \end{bmatrix} \leftarrow \begin{bmatrix} predicate : P2, \\ arguments : A2, \\ unique\_variables : yes \end{bmatrix}, \begin{bmatrix} predicate : P3, \\ arguments : A3, \\ unique\_variables : yes \end{bmatrix}.$$

- clauses without single variables

$$T_5 : \begin{bmatrix} predicate : P1, \\ arguments : A1, \\ no\_singles : yes \end{bmatrix} \leftarrow \begin{bmatrix} predicate : P2, \\ arguments : A2 \end{bmatrix}, \begin{bmatrix} predicate : P3, \\ arguments : A3 \end{bmatrix}.$$

A growing number of predicates in *Predicates* yields the numbers of hypotheses in the hypothesis space shown in the following table.

Clause Templates	Predicates in Σ_1 in experiment FD_2				
	father female	father female male	father female parent	father female male parent	father female male parent married
$T_{unresrricted}$	302	418	1033	1238	2498
T_1 : constrained	30	56	90	132	240
T_2 : range resticted	116	150	406	468	962
T_3 : no recursive literals	7	34	302	418	1238
T_4 : unique variables	206	302	683	848	1672
T_5 : no single variables	71	111	246	314	623

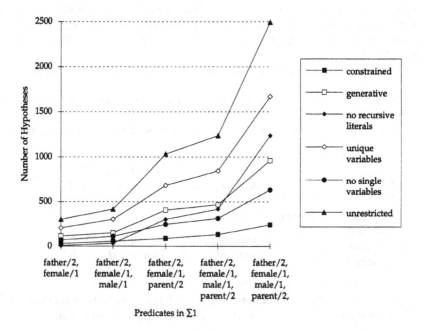

Fig. 1. The size of the hypothesis space in experiment FD_2

In this experiment, the restriction to constrained clauses is the strongest among the biases as shown in the table and in figure 1. Although *father* can be learned, many other concepts are excluded because the body literals of hypothesis clauses must not include new variables. The new restriction to clauses without single variable also imposes considerable restrictions to the hypothesis space. In contrast to the first restriction, this bias is useful from a computational point of view since it excludes unbound variables in the body of hypothesis clauses. Excluding recursive literals helps only when the number of predicates in the background knowledge is small. If it increases, the reductions decrease if compared to the number of hypotheses covered by the unrestricted clause template. The weakest bias in this experiment is the restriction to clauses with unique variables because it does not exclude many variabilizations.

The next experiment FD_3 investigates the effect of controlling the number of new variables since the bias of several ILP systems mainly relies on this restriction, e.g., CLINT [DR91]. We vary the maximum number of new variables by the scheme conditions i_1 and i_2 in the following clause template T in T_1.

$$T : \begin{bmatrix} predicate : P1, \\ arguments : A1 \end{bmatrix} \leftarrow \begin{bmatrix} predicate : P2, \\ arguments : A2, \\ new\_variables : i_1 \end{bmatrix} , \begin{bmatrix} predicate : P3, \\ arguments : A3, \\ new\_variables : i_2 \end{bmatrix} .$$

Experiment FD_3 results in the following sizes of hypothesis spaces.

	i_1, i_2	Predicates in Σ_1 in experiment FD_3				
		father female	father female male	father female parent	father female male parent	father female male parent married
1	$i_1 : \emptyset$ $i_2 : \emptyset$	30	56	90	132	240
2	$i_1 : \emptyset$ $i_2 : N3\| (|N3| \leq 1)$	78	128	240	324	608
3	$i_1 : N2\| (|N2| \leq 1)$ $i_2 : \emptyset$	118	182	390	500	976
4	$i_1 : N2\| (|N2| \leq 1)$ $i_2 : N3\| (|N3| \leq 1)$	254	362	855	1044	2080
5	$i_1 : \emptyset$ $i_2 : N3\| (|N3| \leq 2)$	84	136	260	348	656
6	$i_1 : N2\| (|N2| \leq 2)$ $i_2 : \emptyset$	187	205	460	578	1141
7	$i_1 : N2\| (|N2| \leq 1)$ $i_2 : N3\| (|N3| \leq 2)$	268	379	905	1100	2197
8	$i_1 : N2\| (|N2| \leq 2)$ $i_2 : N3\| (|N3| \leq 1)$	287	400	979	1178	2368
9	$i_1 : N2\| (|N2| \leq 2)$ $i_2 : N3\| (|N3| \leq 2)$	302	418	1033	1238	2498
10	$i_1 : N2\| (|N2| \leq 3)$ $i_2 : N3\| (|N3| \leq 3)$	302	418	1033	1238	2498

In this table, row 10 equals row 9 as the maximum arity of the predicates in this domain is 2. Thus, limiting the number of new variables to a bound greater than the maximum arity in the domain does not restrict the hypothesis space. Increasing the background knowledge shows that the growth of the hypothesis space depends on the arity of the predicate. For example, adding unary predicates like $female/1$ does not increase the number of hypothesis as much as $parent/2$.

This table shows that restricting the number of new variables is not very effective in this domain. For example, there is only a small difference between the rows 8 and 7, and row 9. Only excluding all new variables in one or more body literals as in the rows 1 to 3 or 5 considerably restricts the hypothesis space. The reason is that the maximum arity of the predicates in this domain is 2. Thus, at most two new variables can be distributed to the argument positions and restricting their number to one does not reduce very much the number of variables to be distributed.

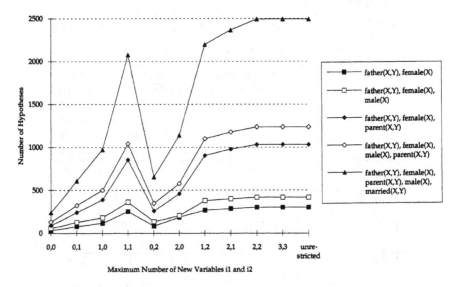

Fig. 2. The size of the hypothesis space in experiment FD_3

Another effect to be seen from the results is that restricting the number of new variables in the first literals of a clause imposes stronger restrictions than restricting the latter literals. For example, the clause templates in row 5 and 6 only differ in the order of the restrictions of new variables. But the order in row 5 results in stronger restrictions since there are less variables available to be distributed to the argument positions of the second literal as in case of row 6.

In experiment FD_4, the growth of the hypothesis space with respect to the limit of the clause length is investigated. T_1 includes one of the three clause templates $T1$, $T2$, and $T3$ that differ in the number of literal descriptions but are not restricted by further biases.

$$T_1 : \begin{bmatrix} predicate : P1, \\ arguments : A1 \end{bmatrix} \leftarrow \begin{bmatrix} predicate : P2, \\ arguments : A2 \end{bmatrix} .$$

$$T_2 : \begin{bmatrix} predicate : P1, \\ arguments : A1 \end{bmatrix} \leftarrow \begin{bmatrix} predicate : P2, \\ arguments : A2 \end{bmatrix} , \begin{bmatrix} predicate : P3, \\ arguments : A3 \end{bmatrix} .$$

$$T_3 : \begin{bmatrix} predicate : P1, \\ arguments : A1 \end{bmatrix} \leftarrow \begin{bmatrix} predicate : P2, \\ arguments :A2 \end{bmatrix}, \begin{bmatrix} predicate : P3, \\ arguments :A3 \end{bmatrix}, \begin{bmatrix} predicate : P4, \\ arguments :A4 \end{bmatrix}.$$

Using these clause templates and varying the predicates in Σ_1 results in the numbers of hypotheses shown in the following table.

Clause Template	Predicates in Σ_1 in experiment FD_4				
	father married age	father married age female	father married age female male	father married age female male parent	father married age female male parent greater
T_1 : 1 *body literals*	18	21	24	30	36
T_2 : 2 *body literals*	534	679	844	1358	1994
T_3 : 3 *body literals*	23304	31432	41456	86908	160620

These results show that the clause length is an important factor for the size of the hypothesis space, in particular when the background knowledge includes many predicates.

In experiment FD_5, both restrictions affecting the signature and the rules for clause construction are combined, namely the restrictions to constrained and generative clauses, to clauses without recursive literals, to clauses unique variables, and to using predicate types. *Predicates* includes the predicates *father*, *female*, *male*, *parent*, and *married* as given in experiment FD_1.

Bias 2	Bias 1 in experiment FD_5				
	constrained	predicate types	generative	no recur. literals	unique variables
unique variables	90	136	704	848	1672
no recursive literals	132	88	468	1238	
generative	200	56	962		
predicate types	32	176			
constrained	240				

This table shows that weak biases like the restriction to clauses with unqiue variables can be considerably improved by further biases since combinations lead to reductions between 5.3% and 50% of the original size of the hypothesis space. A similar effect occurs in case of clauses without recursive literals, another weak bias, where the hypothesis space can be reduced up to 7.1% of its original size.

In general, combining biases of different classes strongly decreases the size of the hypothesis space, e.g. combining predicate types with the restrictions affecting clause construction. In particular, combinations with the restrictions to generative constrained clauses yield strong reductions. Obviously, a second reason is that in both cases strong restrictions have been combined whereas combinations with weaker restrictions like clauses without recursive literals result in smaller reductions.

Another useful combination is given by the restriction to clauses with unique variables and constrained clauses since the clause must not include new variables and the distribution of the old variables is restricted.

5 Effects of Language Biases in a Non-Function-Free Domain

In contrast to the family domain, the second domain LPD containing list-processing clauses allows for using functors in the literals. In the following experiments the concept *merge* is to be learned given the positive and negative examples

positive	negative
$merge([1], [2], [1, 2])$.	$merge([1], [2], [2, 1])$.
$merge([2, 3, 4, 5], [4, 7], [2, 3, 4, 4, 5, 7])$.	$merge([55, 66], [22, 33, 55], [55, 66, 22])$.
$merge([55, 66], [22, 33, 55], [22, 33, 55, 55, 66])$.	$merge([2], [54, 66, 77, 88, 97], [])$.
$merge([5], [54, 66, 77], [54, 66, 5, 77])$.	$merge([22, 23, 24, 25], [], [23, 24, 25])$.
$merge([1], [5, 10], [1, 5, 10])$.	$merge([4], [3], [4])$.
$merge([22, 23, 24], [25], [22, 23, 24, 25])$.	$merge([22, 23, 24], [25], [25])$.
$merge([22, 23, 24, 27], [12], [12, 22, 23, 24, 27])$.	$merge([22, 23, 24], [12], [22, 12, 23, 24])$.
$merge([24, 33], [25], [24, 25, 33])$.	$merge([22, 23, 24, 25], [], [24, 25])$.

and the signature Σ_2 given by

$$\Sigma_2 = [\ s\_data : \{list, number, atomic\},$$
$$s\_pred : \{comp, listbasic, listcomb, listset\},$$
$$s\_relation : \{number : atomic\}$$
$$func : \{\ . : (X : atomic, Y : list)/list\},$$
$$const : \{\ \}$$
$$pred : Predicates,$$
$$modes : \{\ \}\ ],$$

and the head literal $merge([A|B], [C|D], [A|E])$. The set $Predicates$ in Σ_2 including clauses from the set

$$\{merge(X : list, Y : list, Z : list)/listcomb,$$
$$leq(X : number, Y : number)/comp,$$
$$geq(X : number, Y : number)/comp,$$
$$reverse(X : list, Y : list)/listcomb,$$
$$append(X : list, Y : list, Z : list)/listbasic,$$
$$intersect(X : list, Y : list, Z : list)/listset,$$
$$union(X : list, Y : list, Z : list)/listset,$$
$$subset(X : list, Y : list, Z : list)/listset\ \}$$

is varied as in the experiments in the familiy domain in order to study the biases with resepct to increasing background knowledge.

In experiment LPD_1, we study the effect of increasing the number of literals in $Predicates$ for unrestricted clauses of length 3, i.e., clause template $T2$ from experiment FD_4 is used. This experiment yields the results shown in figure 3.

Compared to the results of experiment FD_4 in the family domain, the hypothesis space grows much faster. The reason is that not only variables can be

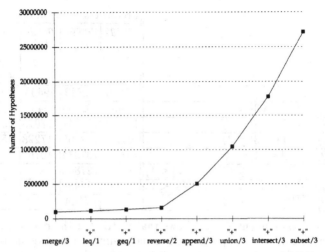

Fig. 3. The size of the hypothesis space in experiment LPD_1

distributed to argument positions of the body literals, but all subterms of the head literal. Thus, further language biases or powerful search biases have to be used in order to learn effectively in this domain.

In the next experiment LPD_2, several of the language biases studied in experiment FD_1 and FD_2 are compared in the non-function-free domain of list-processing programs. To learn the concept *merge*, the respective clauses from the family domain defined in the previous section are used. So, experiment LPD_2 results in the numbers of hypotheses shown in the next table.

Clause Template	Predicates in Σ_2 in experiment LPD_2			
	merge	merge leq	merge leq geq	merge leq geq append
T_2 : *constrained*	46010	47742	49506	192282
T_2 : *predicate types*	0	3087	6174	12348
T_3 : *no recursive literals*	0	116	482	151778
T_4 : *unique variables*	3478	4124	4892	16502

In contrast to the family domain, the restriction to constrained clauses results in minor reductions whereas the restriction to unique variables gives better results because it excludes all terms not resulting in unique variables in the literals. As in the family domain, predicate types turn out to be a powerful restriction. Again, the effect of the restriction to clauses without recursive literals is strong as long as the total number of predicates is small.

As in experiment FD_3 in the family domain, we investigate the effects of limiting the maximum number of new variables. For this experiment LPD_3, clause template T from experiment FD_3 is used and the scheme conditions i_1 and $i2$ are varied as shown in the following table. This experiments yields the results shown in the following table.

i_1, i_2	Predicates in Σ_2 in exp. LPD_3			
	$merge$	$merge$ lcq	$merge$ leq geq	$merge$ leq geq $append$
$i_1 : \emptyset, i_2 : \emptyset$	46010	47742	49506	192282
$i_1 : \emptyset, i_2 : N3\ \|\ (|N3| \leq 1)$	98496	102054	98496	410026
$i_1 : \emptyset, i_2 : N3\ \|\ (|N3| \leq 2)$	107715	112347	117075	451292
$i_1 : \emptyset, i_2 : N3\ \|\ (|N3| \leq 3)$	107930	112566	117298	452170
$i_1 : N2\ \|\ (|N2| \leq 1), i_2 : \emptyset$	103370	107034	110762	407114
$i_1 : N2\ \|\ (|N2| \leq 1), i_2 : N3\ \|\ (|N3| \leq 1)$		127848		
$i_1 : N2\ \|\ (|N2| \leq 1), i_2 : N3\ \|\ (|N3| \leq 2)$		134480		
$i_1 : N2\ \|\ (|N2| \leq 2), i_2 : \emptyset$		95944		

In general, experiment LPD_3 shows that restricting the maximum number of new variables does not apply as well as the family domain. Again, the reason is that reducing the set of terms to be distributed to the argument positions by the new variables does not have strong effects because the total number is large.

6 Conclusions

For comparing language biases, the representation MILES-CTL turned out to be very useful because it enables fine-grained variations of the language bias and investigating language biases in isolation of other biases in the learning system. In addition, new biases, e.g. the restriction to clauses without single variables, can be tested easily.

The results of the experiments in this paper give detailed knowledge of the effects of language biases in the two domains that have been investigated. As the experiments show, some of the biases, e.g. predicate types, perform well in both domains. Other biases, e.g. the restriction to clauses with unqiue variables, apply well in one domain but not in the other. Another result is that biases often used in ILP, e.g. restrictions of the new variables, result in minor restrictions compared to other language biases. A general observation is that biases from different classes in section 2 can be combined successfully, e.g., using predicate types together with the restriction to generative clauses.

Because of the size of the hypothesis spaces, especially in the domain of list-processing programs, efficient learning procedures require carefully selected language biases and additional powerful search biases. Most of the biases studied in this paper are syntactic biases applying to many domains. However, for better restrictions, the designer of new ILP systems should try to find and use more specific and domain-dependent restrictions like predicate types because this knowledge is not well exploited by the biases currently used in ILP.

References

[ADRB94] H. Adé, L. De Raedt, and M. Bruynooghe. Declarative bias for specific-to-general ILP systems. Deliverable D.KUL.4, ESPRIT Proj. 6020 ILP, 1994.

[Coh93]   W.W. Cohen. Rapid prototyping of ILP systems using explicit bias. In *Proc. of IJCAI-93 Workshop on Inductive Logic Programming*. Morgan Kaufmann, 1993.

[DR91]   L. De Raedt. *Interactive Concept-Learning*. PhD thesis, Katholieke Universiteit Leuven, 1991.

[KL94]   J.-U. Kietz and M. Lübbe. An efficient subsumption algorithm for inductive logic programming. In S. Wrobel, editor, *Proc. of 4th Workshop on Inductive Logic Programming ILP-94*, GMD-Studien Nr. 237, 1994.

[LD92]   N. Lavrac and S. Dzeroski. Inductive learning of relational descriptions from noisy examples. In S. Muggleton, editor, *Inductive Logic Programming*. Academic P., 1992.

[MKS92]   S.H. Muggleton, R.D. King, and M.J.E. Sternberg. Protein secondary structure prediction using logic-based machine learning. In *Protein Engineering*, 5(7), 1992.

[MP94]   S.H. Muggleton and C.D. Page. A learning model for universal representations. In S. Wrobel, editor, *Proc. of 4th Workshop on Inductive Logic Programming ILP-94*, GMD-Studien Nr. 237, 1994.

[MWKE94] K. Morik, S. Wrobel, J. Kietz, and W. Emde. *Knowledge Acquisition and Machine Learning: Theory Methods and Applications*. Academic P., 1994.

[PK92]   M. Pazzani and D. Kibler. The utility of knowledge in inductive learning. *Machine Learning*, 9(1), 1992.

[Qui90]   J. R. Quinlan. Learning logical definitions from relations. *Machine Learning*, 5:239–266, 1990.

[Rou92]   C. Rouveirol. Extensions of inversion of resolution applied to theory completion. In S. Muggleton, editor, *Inductive Logic Programming*. Academic Press, 1992.

[SMAU93]   E. Sommer, K. Morik, J.M. Andre, and M. Uszynski. What on-line machine learning can do for knowledge acquisition - a case study. GMD-Studien Nr. 757, GMD, St. Augustin, 1993.

[SMKS94]   A. Srinivasan, S.H. Muggleton, R.D. King, and M.J.E. Sternberg. Mutagenesis: ILP experiments in a non-determinate biological domain. In S. Wrobel, editor, *Proc. of 4th Workshop on Inductive Logic Programming ILP-94*, GMD-Studien Nr. 237, 1994.

[STW93]   I. Stahl, B. Tausend, and R. Wirth. Two methods for improving inductive logic programming systems. In *Machine Learning: ECML-93, European Conference on Machine Learning, Wien, Austria*. Springer, 1993.

[Tau94a]   B. Tausend. *Beschränkungen der Hypothesensprache und ihre Repräsentation in der Induktiven Logischen Programmierung*. Dissertation, Fakultät Informatik, Universität Stuttgart, 1994. (in German).

[Tau94b]   B. Tausend. Biases and their effects in inductive logic programming. In *Machine Learning: ECML-94, European Conference on Machine Learning, Catania, Italy*. Springer, 1994.

[Tau94c]   B. Tausend. Modelling inductive learning for knowledge acquisition tasks. In *ECAI 94 Workshop Integration of Knowledge Acquisition and Machine Learning. Amsterdam, NL*, 1994.

[Tau94d]   B. Tausend. Representing biases for inductive logic programming. In *Machine Learning: ECML-94, European Conference on Machine Learning, Catania, Italy*. Springer, 1994.

[WO91]   R. Wirth and P. O'Rorke. Constraints on predicate invention. In *Eighth International Conference on Machine Learning*. Morgan Kaufmann, 1991.

Part III:

Extended Abstracts

JIGSAW: puzzling together RUTH and SPECTRE (Extended Abstract)

Hilde Adé[1] and Henrik Boström[2]

[1] Department of Computer Science, Katholieke Universiteit Leuven
Celestijnenlaan 200A, B-3001 Heverlee, Belgium
[2] Department of Computer and Systems Sciences, Stockholm University
Electrum 230, S-164 40 Kista, Sweden

1 Introduction

In this work we present JIGSAW, which is a theory revision system within the Inductive Logic Programming (ILP) framework. In essence it is an enhanced version of the system RUTH [2], which is a non-interactive theory revisor built on the ideas presented by De Raedt and Bruynooghe [6]. The main contribution of this work is that we incorporated unfolding as a theory specialization operator into RUTH. This was done by integrating RUTH with SPECTRE [5] which is a theory specialization system based on unfolding and clause removal. The theory revision problem addressed by our system can be formalized as follows:

- **Given:**
  - an integrity constraint theory I
  - a new integrity constraint IC
  - a database D, satisfying I, but possibly not satisfying IC
- **Find:** a transaction $Trans$ such that database $Trans$(D) satisfies I $\cup$ {IC}

In our framework an *integrity constraint theory* is a set of integrity constraints. An *integrity constraint* is a clause of the form $p_1 \wedge ... \wedge p_k \rightarrow q_1 \vee ... \vee q_m$, ($k \geq 0$, $m \geq 0$), which can be read as: if p_1 and ... and p_k are true, then at least one of the q_j should be true. A *database* is a set of definite clauses. Finally, a *transaction* is a list of actions, where an action in our framework is of the form *add(fact)*, *add(clause)*, *delete(fact)*, *delete(clause)* or *replace(clause,set_of_clauses)*.

2 JIGSAW

The system JIGSAW is based on the overall structure of the RUTH system, and integrates the theory specialization technique of SPECTRE. In this section, we first briefly describe RUTH and SPECTRE, and then present JIGSAW.

RUTH. The system RUTH is a theory revision system built on ideas presented in [6]. However, it works non-interactively, replacing queries to an oracle by an intelligent search strategy based on an iterative deepening schema [7]. A full description of the system can be found in [2] and [3], and theoretical properties are described in [1].

```
procedure RUTH( I , D )
begin
        Trans ← ∅
        Hypo ← ∅
        while I is still violated by Trans(D) do
                select a violated constraint Ic from I
                hypothesize an example Ex
                Hypo ← Hypo ∪ Ex
                while Hypo ≠ ∅ do
                        choose an example Ex from Hypo
                        if Ex is an uncovered positive example
                        then handle_positive(Trans,I,Hypo,Ex)
                        else { Ex is a covered negative example }
                                handle_negative(Trans,I,Hypo,Ex)
        Output : Trans(D)
end procedure RUTH
```

The top level algorithm of RUTH

The central idea in the algorithm is the following. Upon violation of an integrity constraint $p_1 \wedge ... \wedge p_k \rightarrow q_1 \vee ... \vee q_m$ with answer substitution θ, the system hypothesizes that at least one of the $p_i\theta$ should be false, or at least one of the $q_j\theta$ should be true in the transformed database. As in concept learning $p_i\theta$, resp. $q_j\theta$, is called a covered negative example, resp. an uncovered positive example. Transforming the database is done by adding or deleting clauses or facts.

The operators of RUTH are contained in the procedures *handle_positive* and *handle_negative*. For handling a covered negative example RUTH uses an MIS-like specialization operator. It constructs an SLD-tree for the example, hypothesizes that one of the clauses used in the proof is incorrect, and removes this clause from the database. To handle an uncovered positive example the system has three operators: (1) add the example as a ground fact to the database, (2) construct a maximally general clause that covers the positive example, and that is consistent with the integrity theory and (3) abduce new facts $l_i\theta$ using a clause $h \leftarrow l_1 \wedge ... \wedge l_n$ of the database such that $h\theta$=Ex and for which not all literals $l_i\theta$ are true.

SPECTRE. Boström and Idestam-Almquist [5] have argued that the specialization of logic programs can be viewed as the pruning of SLD-trees. In their system SPECTRE, the actual pruning is done by applying the transformation rule *unfolding* [8] together with clause removal. The specialization of a logic program with respect to positive and negative examples is realized in the following way. As long as there is a clause in the program that covers a negative example, it is checked whether it covers any positive examples or not. If it covers no positive examples, then it is removed, otherwise it is unfolded. The choice of which literal to unfold upon is made using a computation rule, which is given as input to the algorithm. In [5] the optimal choice of literal to unfold upon is approximated by selecting the literal that results in the minimal residual impurity of the resolvents when having applied unfolding.

JIGSAW. For the new system JIGSAW we keep the top level algorithm of RUTH as well as the iterative deepening schema. Changes are only introduced at the operator level : the procedure *handle_negative* is enhanced with an unfolding and clause removal operator. Thus the set of possible actions of RUTH (*add(clause)*, *delete(clause)*, *add(fact)*, *delete(fact)*) is extended with the action *replace(clause, set_of_clauses)*.

For the evaluation of JIGSAW the "Student Loan" domain from the UCI repository of Machine Learning Databases was used. We randomly generated 40 corrupted domain theories and sets of 20 randomly selected examples. We also tested JIGSAW on the smaller CUP domain as described in [4]. Because of space constraints we cannot fully report on the results. We limit ourselves to the discussion the advantages and also a caveat

There are several advantages in using an unfolding technique for theory specialization. First, plain clause removal might affect the proofs of positive examples, whereas the unfolding technique first specializes the selected clause, and only removes clauses that do not cover any positive examples. Second, an unfolding operator can speed up the theory revision process. One can easily imagine situations where one unfolding step has the same effect as the removal of a clause, followed by the construction of a new - more specific - clause. The following small experiment taken from the CUP domain illustrates both these aspects.

Rules in the Database
cup(X) ← liftable(X), stable(X), open_vessel(X)
liftable(X) ← weighs(X,Y), light(Y)
stable(X) ← part_of(X,Y), bottom(Y), small(Y)
stable(X) ← part_of(X,Y), bottom(Y), large(Y)
stable(X) ← part_of(X,Y), body(Y), part_of(X,Z), support(Z), above(Y,Z)
open_vessel(X) ← part_of(X,Y), concavity(Y), upward_pointing(Y)

Solutions
RUTH: *delete* cup(X) ← liftable(X), stable(X), open_vessel(X)
add cup(X) ← liftable(X), open_vessel(X),
part_of(X,Y), bottom(Y), small(Y)
Time: 2.48 secs
JIGSAW: *replace* cup(X) ← liftable(X), stable(X), open_vessel(X)
by cup(X) ← liftable(X), open_vessel(X),
part_of(X,Y), bottom(Y), small(Y)
and cup(X) ← liftable(X), open_vessel(X), part_of(X,Y)
body(Y), part_of(X,Z), support(Z), above(Y,Z)
Time: 0.06 secs

Third, one can regard unfolding as a specialization technique that makes explicit use of the available background knowledge. Finally, one unfolding step can introduce more than one literal in the body of a clause. Hence one application of unfolding may correspond to several specialization steps. However, this can also be seen as a disadvantage, since there is a danger of overspecialization. This was illustrated by a small number of experiments where RUTH found a solution but JIGSAW did not.

3 Conclusion

The system JIGSAW that we have presented in this work is an example of integrating independently developed techniques. Benefiting from the common logical framework of the ILP research field, we were able to extend the theory revision system RUTH. More specifically, we integrated SPECTRE's specialization operator together with the impurity measure used for formulating a preference criterion. Experimental results using the Student Loan domain and the CUP domain show that the integration effort is beneficial, and they point out the advantages (and also some caveats) concerning the use of an unfolding technique.

Acknowledgements. Research for this paper is funded by the ESPRIT BRA project Nr.6020 (Inductive Logic Programming). Part of the work reported was done during a visit of Hilde Adé to the University of Stockholm, made possible by a grant of the Belgian Fund for Scientific Research.

We wish to thank Gunther Sablon, Maurice Bruynooghe and Luc De Raedt for their comments on earlier versions of this paper.

References

1. H. Adé, L. De Raedt, and M. Bruynooghe. Theory Revision. In *Proceedings of the 3rd International Workshop on Inductive Logic Programming*, pages 179–192, 1993.
2. H. Adé, B. Malfait, and L. De Raedt. RUTH : an ILP Theory Revision System. In *Proceedings of the 8th International Symposium on Methodologies for Intelligent Systems (ISMIS94)*, 1994.
3. H. Adé, B. Malfait, and L. De Raedt. RUTH : an ILP Theory Revision System. Technical Report CW-194, Department of Computer Science, Katholieke Universiteit Leuven, 1994.
4. F. Bergadano and A. Giordana. A knowledge intensive approach to concept induction. In *Proceedings of the 5th International Workshop on Machine Learning*. Morgan Kaufmann, 1988.
5. H. Boström and P. Idestam-Almquist. Specialization of Logic Programs by Pruning SLD-Trees. In S. Wrobel, editor, *Proceedings of the 4th International Workshop on Inductive Logic Programming*, volume 237 of *GMD-Studien*, pages 31–48. Gesellschaft für Mathematik und Datenverarbeitung MBH, 1994.
6. L. De Raedt and M. Bruynooghe. Belief updating from integrity constraints and queries. *Artificial Intelligence*, 53:291–307, 1992.
7. R. Korf. Depth-first iterative deepening : an optimal admissible search. *Artificial Intelligence*, pages 97–109, 1985.
8. H. Tamaki and T. Sato. Unfold/fold Transformations of Logic Programs. In *Proceedings of the Second International Logic Programming Conference*, pages 127–138, 1984. Uppsala University, Uppsala, Sweden.

Discovery of Constraints and Data Dependencies in Relational Databases (Extended Abstract)*

Siegfried Bell & Peter Brockhausen
Informatik VIII University Dortmund
44221 Dortmund Germany
email: {*bell, brockh*}@ls8.informatik.uni-dortmund.de

1 Introduction

Data dependencies are the most common type of semantic constraints in relational databases which determine the database design. Despite the advent of highly automated tools, database design still consists basically of two types of activities: first, reasoning about data types and data dependencies and, second, normalizing the relations. Automatic database design may serve as a process to support database designers with a dependencies proposing system, which may help to design optimal relation schemes for those cases where data dependencies are not obvious. The so called dependency inference problem is described in [Mannila and Räihä, 1991] as: Given a relation r, find a set of data dependencies which logically determines all the data dependencies which are valid in r.

Unfortunately, it is impractical to enumerate all data dependencies and to try to verify each of them. Alternatively, a second approach to discovery is to avoid unnecessary queries by inferring as much as possible from already verified data dependencies. A third approach is to draw inferences not only from verified data dependencies but also from invalid data dependencies, the so called independencies. In this paper we will follow this approach. A second problem is that real world databases are known to be very large. Therefore they only can be accessed via a database management system.

We present a rough sketch of our main algorithms and in the last section a comparision with some similiar approaches.

Our system can be seen at the first glance as an optimized version of CLAUDIEN regarding functional dependencies, [Dehaspe et al., 1994]. But there are differences: first, in CLAUDIEN the relationship between the dependencies is based on θ-subsumption and the verification of the hypotheses on theorem proving. In our approach, the relationship of the dependencies is based on an axiomatization of FDs and UINDs. The verification is done by the database management system which groups the rows. This offers several advantages: First, theorem proving is for this purpose too powerful and we can infer dependencies by transitivity which is really simple. Second, we can find dependencies in relational databases, which can not be stored in the main memory as PROLOG assertions.

---

* The full paper is available from the authors.

2   Discovering Data Dependencies

2.1   Value Restrictions

Value restrictions are the upper and lower bounds of attribute domains. We select the minima and maxima for all attributes in all relations with the corresponding SQL statements. The SQL statement uses the normal order on numbers for numerical attributes and the lexicographic order on the character set for attributes of a symbolic type. Since it is possible to compute the two values in one query, the overall costs are $\mathcal{O}(n*m)$. Throughout this section n denotes the number of attributes in all tables and m the maximal number of tuples in the table which possesses the most.

2.2   Unary Inclusion Dependencies

A naive algorithm for computing inclusion dependencies has a time complexity of $\Theta(n^2*m^2)$. It generates exactly $\frac{n*(n-1)}{2}$ database queries, if the corresponding UINDs are valid or not. In contrast our algorithm has a overall time complexity of $\mathcal{O}(n^4 + n^2 * m^2)$.

At a first glance, this result looks strange because of the $\mathcal{O}$–notation. But our algorithm has one very important property. Given a fixed sequence of attributes for hypotheses testing, our algorithm always poses a minimal number of database queries for the discovery of UINDs, by exploiting discovered UINDs and the transitivity of UINDs, and hence it saves all superfluous queries to the database, cf. [Brockhausen, 1994]. The correctness of the algorithm is considerably based on the axiomatization of UINDs and UINIs, cf. [Bell, 1995].

2.3   Functional Dependencies

To determine functional dependencies we have integrated two main ideas, namely to exploit the transitivity of FDs and to concentrate on the computation of most–general FDs. For a discussion in full detail on the algorithm and the design choices being made see [Brockhausen, 1994]. Our algorithm uses a top–down and breadth–first search strategy. We should mention that we also use information of the database system on primary keys, indexes and null values and the discovered inclusion dependencies to reduce the search space in our algorithm.

Figure 1 lists the statement and the condition which must hold. The clue is the GROUP BY instruction. The computational costs of this operation are dependent on the database system, but it can be done in time $\mathcal{O}(m*log\,m)$. However, the worst case time complexity of every such an algorithm is exponential, due to the results of [Mannila and Räihä, 1991].

3   Evaluation and Conclusions

We compared our algorithm with two approaches presented at the AAAI workshop on knowledge discovery in databases in 1993. Savnik and Flach call their method "bottom–up induction of functional dependencies from relations", see

1.   SELECT SUM (COUNT (DISTINCT A_1)),
           SUM (COUNT (DISTINCT B))
     FROM R
     GROUP BY $A_1, \ldots, A_n$ $=: a_1, b$
2. $a_1 = b \Rightarrow A_1 \ldots A_n \rightarrow B$

Fig. 1. A SQL–statement for the Computation of Functional Dependencies

[Savnik and Flach, 1993]. Briefly, they start with a bottom–up analysis of the tuples and construct a negative cover, which is a set of FIs. Therefore they have to analyze all combinations between any two tuples.

In the next step they use a top–down search approach similar to ours in order to discover the functional dependencies. They check the validity of a dependency by searching for FIs in the negative cover. Schlimmer also uses a top–down approach, but in conjunction with a hash–function in order to avoid redundant computations [Schlimmer, 1993].

Algorithm by	Database	$|r|$	$\|R\|$	$\|X\|$	Time
Savnik and Flach	Lymphography	150	19	7	9 min.
Schlimmer	Breast Cancer	699	11	4	1 h 14 min.
Bell and Brockh.	Lymphography	150	19	7	> 33 h
Bell and Brockh.	Breast Cancer	699	11	11	8 Min. 53 sec.
Bell and Brockh.	Breast Cancer	699	11	4	4 Min. 19 sec.

Table 1. Comparison of the Experimental Results from [Savnik and Flach, 1993] and [Schlimmer, 1993] with the algorithm FUNCTIONAL DEPENDENCIES.

But in contrast to our algorithm, in both articles mentioned, the authors do not use a relational database like OracleV7 or any other commercial DBMS. They even do not use a database at all. And this has some important effects on the results, which will be discussed in the next paragraph. Table 1 shows a summary of their results, where $|r|$ denotes the number of tuples, $|R|$ the number of attributes, $|X|$ the maximal number of attributes on the left–hand side of a FD and time is the time needed for the discovery of a most–general–cover. For comparison reasons we introduced such a bound on the number of attributes in our algorithm.

First, our algorithm cannot detect the FDs in the lymphography domain in reasonable time, because we do not hold the data in main memory like Savnik and Flach. And since most of the FDs are really long, for some attributes the shortest most–general FDs have already seven attributes on the left side, the search space and the overhead for the communication with the database is to big. But it cannot be said that our approach is inferior to the one of Savnik and Flach, because the circumstances are to different, namely the presence or absence of a database for the storage of the tuples.

Second, in the breast cancer domain our algorithm is really fast, more than seventeen times faster than Schlimmer's algorithm. Even without any bound on the length of the FDs it is still eight times faster and it uses a database.

Database	$|r|$	$||R||$	$|X|$	Time	N
Books	9931	9	9	4 h 44 min.	25
Books	9931	9	6	4 h 40 min.	25
Books	9931	9	3	2 h 10 min.	20

Table 2. Summary of the results of the algorithm FUNCTIONAL DEPENDENCIES.

But of course the two domains above are not typical database applications. Table 2 shows the results of our algorithm with respect to a real database, the library database of the computer science department. Here it becomes obvious that our pruning criterions are efficient, because with a bound of six attributes and without any bound the time needed is nearly the same. The differences are neglectable because there are many more users working on the network and the results are only reproducible within some bounds. But apart from the known primary key of the database the discovered FDs are semantically meaningless.

In summary, one can say that the algorithm which we present in our work has one important advantage over the two approaches mentioned above. The algorithm is capable of dealing with great amounts of data, because we use a real database for the storage. And as a side effect, because we use standard SQL–statements for the discovery of FDs, our approach is portable and we can use any database which "understands" SQL as a query language.

Acknowledgment: This work is partly supported by the European Community (ESPRIT Basic Research Action 6020, project Inductive Logic Programming) and the Daimler–Benz AG, Contract No.: 094 965 129 7/0191.

References

[Bell, 1995] Bell, S. (1995). Inferring data independencies. Technical Report 15, University Dortmund, Informatik VIII.

[Brockhausen, 1994] Brockhausen, P. (1994). Discovery of functional and unary inclusion dependencies in relational databases. Master's thesis, University Dortmund, Informatik VIII. in german.

[Dehaspe et al., 1994] Dehaspe, L., Laer, W. V., and Raedt, L. D. (1994). Applications of a logical discovery engine. In Wrobel, S., editor, *Proc. of the Fourth International Workshop on Inductive Logic Programming*, GMD-Studien Nr. 237, pages 291–304, St. Augustin, Germany. GMD.

[Mannila and Räihä, 1991] Mannila, H. and Räihä, K.-J. (1991). *The design of relational databases*. Addison-Wesley.

[Savnik and Flach, 1993] Savnik, I. and Flach, P. (1993). Bottum-up indution of functional dependencies from relations. In Piatetsky-Shapiro, G., editor, *KDD-93: Workshop on Knowledge Discovery in Databases*. AAAI.

[Schlimmer, 1993] Schlimmer, J. (1993). Using learned dependencies to automatically construct sufficient and sensible editing views. In Piatetsky-Shapiro, G., editor, *KDD-93: Workshop on Knowledge Discovery in Databases*. AAAI.

Learning Disjunctive Normal Forms in a Dual Classifier System (Extended Abstract)

Cathy Escazut   Philippe Collard

University of Nice-Sophia Antipolis-CNRS, Laboratory I3S, Bât. 4
250 Av. Albert Einstein, Sophia Antipolis, 06560 Valbonne — FRANCE
{escazut,pc}@unice.fr

Abstract. Genetics-Based Machine Learning systems suffer from many problems as representational weaknesses. We propose to introduce more general structures we used to learn disjunctive normal forms. Results show how our model can be used to discover and maintain complete classifier solutions.

1 Genetics-Based Machine Learning

Genetics-Based Machine Learning systems use *Genetic Algorithms* (GAs) as discovery heuristic. Such algorithms modify a population of potential solutions, using operators stemmed on natural genetics: reproduction, crossover, mutation. *Learning Classifier System* (LCS) implementations have shown the potential of this paradigm for machine learning, and also some limitations. LCSs automatically discover rules to perform tasks [2]. Each classifier is an "if-then" rule, with a condition part and an action part. New classifiers are generated by genetic operators applied to existing rules. Each condition part of a classifier, also called *schema* or *hyperplane*, is a string of length λ over the alphabet $\{0,1,\#\}$, where # is a wildcard character. Classifier representations appear to be a simple, effective method for implementing computational systems. However, many subtleties arise within the representation [5]. Indeed, disjunctions are hardly represented with a single rule. Consequently, the solution set and the search effort are increased.

2 Relational Schemata

In order to allow a more natural expression of solutions we propose to consider not only the value on each locus but also the relations (equality and inequality) between the values on different locus. We thus define *relational schemata*, called *R–schema*, as a string built over the alphabet $\{X,X',\#\}$[1]. As standard schema only express values on the different locus, we call them *P–schemata* or *positional* schemata. We are now going to study R–schemata in relation to properties Radcliffe [4] thinks requisite for a useful representation. Our aim is not to show R–schemata are better than P–schemata but to show they are complementary.

---

[1] The two symbols X and X' represent two complementary variables.

The closure: *The intersection of any pair of compatible[2] schemata should itself be a schema.* This property allows search to be gradually refined. Obviously, P–schemata and corroborating[3] R–schemata possess the closure property. Whereas the intersection of two non-corroborating R–schema is not a R–schema. In this sense, we say that R–schemata are semi-closed for intersection.

The respect: *Crossing two members of any schema should produce another member of that schema.* This property is necessary to keep good schemata. Crossover operators respect P–schemata but not R–schemata.

The proper assortment: *Given instances of two compatible schemata, it should be possible to cross them to produce a child which is an instance of both schemata.* This property allows the recombination of usefull schemata. Only uniform crossovers properly assort P–schemata, but not R–schemata.

Using R–schemata, we are able to represent more hyperplanes. For instance, the R–schema XX represents the subset {00,11}. But all the hyperplanes, for instance {011,000}, are not representable. We are thus going to extend the expressiveness of a schema defining a RP–schema as a string built over the alphabet {0,1,X,X',#}. So, a RP–schema can be obtained by the intersection of a R–schema and a P–schema. For instance, the intersection of 0## and #XX is the RP–schema 0XX. R–schemata don't possess the requisite properties and the use of variables increases the size of the space. That is why R–schemata are not explicitly used in LCS. Thus, a solution is to implement the notion of R–schema in an implicit way.

3 Implementation of Relational Schemata

The aim of a implicit implementation of R–schemata is to keep the alphabet {0,1,#} unchanged and to have the properties possessed. A string, in our system, will consist of two parts: the first one, a single bit called *head-bit*, contains the information needed for understanding the rest of the string. More formally, let the search space be $\Omega=\{0,1\}^\lambda$, and the *dual space* be $<\Omega>=\{0,1\}\times\Omega$. We define a *transcription* function, τ, from the dual space $<\Omega>$ to the basic space Ω by $\forall\omega \in \Omega$ $\tau(0\omega) = \omega$ and $\tau(1\omega) = \omega'$ where ω and ω' are complementary strings. It is worth noticing that different strings may be interpreted in the same way. For instance the two conditions $\underline{0}\,0101$ and $\underline{1}\,1010$ are both decoded as 0101. We call them *dual* strings. Moreover, when the head-bit is undetermined the use of a variable is requisite. For instance, the P–schema $\underline{\#}\,01\#0$ becomes the R–schema XX'#X. Does implicit R–schemata possess all the properties stated previously?

The respect: A GA applied on $<\Omega>$, through a choice between dual strings, allows R–schemata of Ω to be respected. For example, the set of the members of R–schema X#X' is not closed, but a corresponding one in $<\Omega>$, for instance $\{\underline{0}\,001,\underline{0}\,011,\underline{1}\,011,\underline{1}\,001\}$, is the P–schema $\underline{\#}\,0\#1$ possessing the respect property.

---

[2] Two schemata are *compatible* if there exists a string being a member of both.

[3] Two compatible R–schemata are *corroborating* if they share at least one locus with variable.

The proper assortment: A GA applied on $<\Omega>$ through a choice between dual strings, allows a uniform crossovers to properly assort R–schemata. For example, let us consider the compatible R–schemata X#X' and #XX and be 001 and 000 two members. If we represent them in $<\Omega>$ by respectively $\underline{0}\,001$ and $\underline{1}\,111$, a uniform crossover breeds $\underline{0}\,011$ in the intersection XX'X'.

The ergodicity: *It should be possible through a finite sequence of application of genetic operators, to access any point in the search space.* This property is the "raison d'être" of the mutation. For two λ-strings of Ω, at least λ mutations are needed to reach a point, while in $<\Omega>$, this number is smaller than $int(\frac{\lambda}{2}) + 1$.

A RP–schema is the intersection of a P–schema and a R–schema. So it can be represented by a conjunction $[a, b]$ where a is a P–schema of $\Omega(\lambda)$ and b a P–schema of $\Omega(\lambda+1)$[4]. The condition is satisfied when the two fields are satisfied [3]. Another way to implement RP–schemata, is to use a *mask*: the condition is composed with a mask (λ bits), and with a P–schema of $\Omega(\lambda+1)$. Only the loci of the P–schema corresponding to a 1 in the mask will be influenced by the head bit. For instance the RP–schema 0XX can be implemented by $[011, \underline{\#}\,000]$.

4 Learning disjunctive normal forms

To validate our proposition, we applied the algorithm on a similarity-based learning problem: the LCS has to learn a concise disjunctive normal form [6]. Each rule represents a conjunction of attributes. A set of classifiers represents a disjunction of such conjunctions. We test our system on two well-known problems: the XOR problem and the multiplexer function. The LCS used, is an adaptation of the one described by D.E. Goldberg [2]. The results obtained do not represent our "best efforts"; rather, they are intended as comparative results.

The XOR Problem

Schemata in the XOR problem are highly epistatic. LCSs have difficulties in learning such problems. In both cases (dual and basic approach), the initial population is randomly created with 22 classifiers. Results show that our system behaves in a better way than a standard LCS: approximately beyond cycle 2000, the solution set is found out: the final population contains 2 dominating classifiers ($\underline{\#}\,00{:}0$ and $\underline{\#}\,01{:}1$). The undetermined head-bit leads to the use of variables (XX:0 and XX':1) and so the use of less specialized classifiers. While the standard LCSs needs 5000 cycles to discover the four totally specialized classifiers: 00:0, 01:1, 10:1 and 11:0[5]. The dual learning is realized at an upper level of abstraction.

The Multiplexer Function

Two multiplexer functions, like the one described in [2], have been tested with different goals. The first one was to make good RP-schemata to appear in the population and the second one as to improve the success rate. In both trials, two fields compose the condition of the classifiers: the rightmost bits are for the

---

[4] Nervertheless, the head-bit of b must be undetermined and the schema a must be undetermined on the specified locus of b.

[5] The system has no other possibility than learning the solution by heart.

address lines, and the remaining ones are for the data. A head-bit is added in the dual approach. The action part represents the system's answer.

In the 6-line multiplexer, 2 bits are for the address and 4 for the data. The R.P–schemata are expressed using a mask. For instance, the rule X###11:X will be represented by the string: [111100, #0###11]:0. Moreover, in this case, the head-bit has to influence the action in order to make variables emerged. The initial population is randomly created with 100 classifiers. The GA is invoked every 2500 iterations, and 20% of the current population undergoes genetic operators. After 50,000 iterations the minimal solution set[6] dominates into the dual population, while in the standard one 8 rules are needed. Once more, the use of R–schemata allowed to learn at an upper level of abstraction.

We also test our system on an 11-line multiplexer (3 lines for the address and 8 for the data), in order to improve the success rate of the LCS. The initial population is randomly created with 300 classifiers. The GA is invoked every 5000 iterations, and 20% of the current population undergoes genetic operators. The performance average of the two systems increases from the beginning, but the one of our LCS evolves faster. Indeed, since the cycle 35,000 the average is above 80%, against 71% for standard LCS. At the end, it reaches 83% with our system, while it is only near 72% with standard LCS.

5 Conclusion

This paper has presented a new LCS based on general structures called *relational schemata*. To each string is associated its bitwise complement. So we introduce in the population dual strings having the same meaning. We have shown how minimal classifier sets can be found using implicit relationl schemata. Further work is aimed at applying the dual LCS to more difficult tasks.

References

1. P. Collard, J.P. Aurand. DGA: An efficient genetic algorithm. In *ECAI'94: European Conference on Artificial Intelligence*, 1994.
2. D. E. Goldberg. *Genetic algorithms in search, optimization, and machine learning.* Reading, MA : Addison-Wesley, 1989.
3. J. H. Holland. Escaping brittleness : The possibilities of general purpose learning algorithms applied to parallel rule-based systems. In *Machine Learning II*. Morgan Kaufmann, 1986.
4. N. J. Radcliffe. Forma analysis and random respectful recombination. In *Proceedings of the Fourth International Conference on Genetic Algorithms*, San Mateo, CA, 1991. Morgan Kaufmann.
5. D. Schuurmans, J. Schaeffer. Representational difficulties with classifier systems. In *Proceedings of the Third International Conference on Genetic Algorithms*, 1989.
6. S. W. Wilson. Classifier systems and the animat problem. *Machine Learning*, 2(3),1987.

---

[6] {X###11:X, #X##10:X, ##X#01:X, ###X00:X}.

The Effects of Noise on Efficient Incremental Induction (Extended Abstract)

Gerard V. Conroy (gvc@sna.co.umist.ac.uk)
David M. Dutton (ddutton@sna.co.umist.ac.uk)

Department of Computation,
UMIST,
PO BOX 88,
Manchester,
M60 1QD, UK.

Abstract

This paper presents an algorithm JITTER, that aims to eliminate any unnecessary work done whilst incrementally building decision trees. In particular, we illustrate how high levels of noise can greatly affect the efficiency of induction and how a straightforward approach can ameliorate these effects.

1 Introduction

Incremental learning has the potential to offer many advantages over one-step learning. New information can be added to a concept representation piecemeal, one can start with a small sample and refine the concept over time etc.. ID5 [2] achieves incrementality by maintaining statistics at each decision tree node that summarise class distributions, in terms of attribute values. ID5 can then judge whether a sub-tree has become sub-optimal with respect to entropy and will restructure a sub-tree in order to keep the most informative attributes near the top of the tree.

There are a number of aspects of incremental tree formation that can be reduced to increase the efficiency with which an algorithm works. These include entropy calculations, tree restructures, aborted restructures[1], the cost of individual restructures, and tree size/complexity. To reduce these quantities we propose the use of a more knowledge-based approach, one that utilises information easily available during induction. ID5 often does more tree restructuring than is necessary in order to maintain tree quality, e.g. accuracy (see [1]). Best

---

[1] Attempted restructures where entropy does not divulge a better test attribute thus leaving the tree unchanged.

'splits' are always tentative [3], especially during the early stages of a tree's development, as there is less information on which to base one's decisions. Entropy can cause a tree node to be swapped for another when in fact it does not increase the tree's accuracy or decrease its complexity.

2   JITTER

Our algorithm JITTER is based on ID5 and so we will concentrate on the extensions we have made. At each node in a tree is a list of the potential test attributes and their respective values, as for ID5. Each decision node has an associated weight that is used to indicate the efficacy (with respect to the partitioning of the example set) of the current test attribute. As an example is propagated down the tree, all that changes are the various counts at each node. The automatic entropy recalculations as seen in ID5 are omitted for the time being. When an example reaches a leaf, a correction factor (cf) is generated that is based on the class distribution of the examples at the leaf. The accuracy of a leaf should give a good indication of the effectiveness of the tests on the path to the leaf. A relatively pure leaf should thus give rise to increased confidence in it's contributory attributes while less pure leaves should result in a weakening. We use the ratio of majority class to the total of all classes at a leaf: *majority class count / total examples at leaf* and prepend this real with a '+' or '-' according to whether the last example to arrive is correctly or incorrectly classified, respectively. Once this cf is generated, it is weighted by the proportion of examples at that leaf to the total number in the tree. The factor is then propagated back up the tree from the leaf to the root and at each node along the path, we update the attached weight. Weights are updated using a formula that takes account of previous successes and failures and the current cf, similar to some neural net algorithms :- $w_i(t + 1) = w_i(t) + cf$, where $w_i(t + 1)$ is weight w_i at time $t + 1$, similarly for $w_i(t)$ and cf is the correction factor. The weights along this 'active' path are now checked against zero, starting with the leaf and moving up to the root. If a weight is found to be less than or equal to zero then restructuring as per ID5.

In [1] we test JITTER with a number of training sets. In one set in particular, it was noted that as the percentage of noise was increased, the level of tree manipulation activity increased also. Specifically, the number of actual and aborted restructures increases significantly. In order to make use of this salient information, we add another weighting factor to the cf as it is generated at the leaf. This factor involves the number of global actual and aborted tree restructures and is calculated as: $w = $ *no. aborted restructures / no.restructures*. It is used thus :-

IF no. aborted restructures $>=$ no. restructures THEN $cf = cf + w$

Therefore as the number of aborted restructures increases in proportion to the number of actual restructures, we conclude that noise is playing a significant part in the tree manipulation history and the node weights should be increased sufficiently to preclude further unnecessary change.

3 Evaluation

Each data set is randomly divided into a training set (two thirds) and a testing set (one third) and is repeated ten times. We use $I\hat{D}5$, instead of ID5, as it is more efficient with respect to entropy calculations and restructuring. The column headings signify time (seconds) to build the tree, the number of nodes and leaves (Nodes), the number of entropy calculations (Ecalcs), the number of restructures (Restrs), the number of *aborted* restructures (Aborts), the number of nodes restructured in total (Nodes Restr) and the accuracy of the tree (Acc) in percent. First we look at the seven-segment L.E.D. display. This concept has

Alg	Time	Nodes	Ecalcs	Restr	Aborts	Nodes Restr	Acc
ID3	8.6	158.0	236.0	0.0	0.0	0.0	72.7
$I\hat{D}5$	82.9	152.8	5411.2	127.8	890.9	1841.6	72.5
JITTER	14.5	161.4	462.1	7.4	11.1	46.1	72.5

Table 1: Results for 7-bit LED Set - 10% noise

1000 examples, ten classes, seven boolean attributes and is shown here with 10% noise. In this instance, accuracy and tree size are very similar but run-time, the number of entropy calculations and restructure costs are all significantly reduced for JITTER as compared to $I\hat{D}5$ (e.g. by some 82% for run-time). Indeed, JITTER's results are more comparable with the *non-incremental* ID3. Next we look at the L.E.D. set with 50% noise (table 2). The output, especially accuracy, deteriorates dramatically for all algorithms and illustrates that the ID3 family has a lot to improve upon. Nonetheless, JITTER again vastly improves in performance over $I\hat{D}5$. Our next set is the even parity concept with added noise

Alg	Time	Nodes	Ecalcs	Restr	Aborts	Nodes Restr	Acc
ID3	9.4	253.0	367.9	0.0	0.0	0.0	8.9
$I\hat{D}5$	1615.3	253.6	12974.8	506.5	1955.9	19261.0	8.8
JITTER	14.1	253.4	596.7	16.0	18.2	122.7	8.8

Table 2: Results for 7-bit LED Set - 50% noise

(10%). In this case we have 11 bits, 5 of which are relevant to classification (see table 3). In this instance JITTER has managed to improve over even ID3, with respect to node count and accuracy, albeit very slightly. The various costs of induction (entropy, restructures etc.) all show considerable differences between

Alg	Time	Nodes	Ecalcs	Restr	Aborts	Nodes Restr	Acc
ID3	37.9	1262.4	1987.3	0.0	0.0	0.0	62.4
$I\hat{D}5$	5967.8	1324.3	23090.2	594.5	1567.3	75986.7	64.8
JITTER	100.8	1255.4	6853.3	384.6	306.7	2615.6	64.8

Table 3: Results for Parity Error - 10% noise

$I\hat{D}5$ and JITTER. Finally, note with the 11-bit multiplexor with added noise (10%) JITTER again significantly decreases the time and effort taken to produce the trees over $I\hat{D}5$ and simultaneously improves node count and accuracy.

4   Conclusion

In [1] we show how ID4/5 can do unnecessary recalculations and restructures whilst building decision trees. Here, we show how simple extensions of these algorithms can use information available during the induction process to render them more knowledge-based. We use this information to implement an accuracy heuristic that reduces the automatically repetitive nature of the ancestor algorithms and significantly improves their inductive efficiency. This has been achieved with no significant decrease in accuracy. In addition, we have augmented our algorithm with a simple and effective measure for detecting and controlling the effects of noise during concept induction.

5   Acknowledgements

D. M. Dutton's work is funded by the E.P.S.R.C. (U.K.).

References

[1]   Conroy, G. and Dutton, D. (1994), JITTER: A Lazy Machine's Guide to Induction, *Technical Report, UMIST-COM-AI-94-4* , Dept. of Computation, UMIST, PO BOX 88, Manchester, M60 1QD, UK.

[2]   Utgoff, P. E., (1989), Incremental Induction of Decision Trees, *Machine Learning 4* , pp161-86, Kluwer Academic Publishers.

[3]   Van de Velde, W., (1990), Incremental Induction of Topologically Minimal Trees, *Proceedings, 7th International Conference on Machine Learning* , pp 66-74, Morgan Kaufmann.

Analysis of Rachmaninoff's Piano Performances Using Inductive Logic Programming (Extended Abstract)

Matthew J. Dovey,
Programming Research Group,
Oxford University Computing Laboratory,
Oxford, OX1 3QD, Great Britain.

Introduction

The project outlined here is an attempt to use inductive logic programming ([6]) to determine various interpretative rules which the pianist, Sergei Rachmaninoff, may have used during his pianoforte performances. During the 1920's Rachmaninoff recorded a number of recitals on the Ampico Recording Piano ([4]). This method of capturing the performance not only recorded the notes, duration and tempo, but also the dynamics of the key pressure and pedalling, in a digital (in actual fact, binary) format, which easily lends itself to conversion into a computer readable representation. To complement this performance information, it was also necessary to represent the musical structure of the piece being performed, so that a general analysis could be achieved, rather than one specific to that particular piece. For simplicity, only the melodies of the pieces involved were subjected to analysis, although better results may be obtained from a full analysis of the accompanying harmonic and contrapuntal structures. The two sets of information, structural analysis and performance analysis were encoded into PROGOL scripts ([5]), which were used to attempt to determine general rules (in the form of universal predicates) underlying the data set. Two pieces were analysed in this manner: Rachmaninoff's Prelude in C Sharp Minor, Opus 3 Number 2 (Ampico Roll Number 57504) and Mendelssohn's Song Without Words Opus 67 Number 4 (Ampico Roll Number 59661).

Performance Data

The Ampico Recording and Reproducing Piano, devised by Charles Stoddart in the early 1900's, provides a digital and fairly accurate representation of the performance of many pianists of the time by recording and reproducing the dynamics of the piano keys in terms of their speed and pressure ([2]). However, there are a few caveats of which to be aware. Rather than recording the dynamics of each key individually, only two sets of dynamics were recorded: one set for the bass notes and one set for the treble notes. As the analysis for this project was only performed on the melody line of the pieces concerned, this was not a major consideration. The dynamics were recorded using a mixture of analogue and discrete techniques. Punches on the piano roll could be used to set the air-pressure in the pneumatic mechanism to one of seven different levels, giving seven different levels of volume. In addition, the roll could also control slow and fast *crescendos* (gradual increases in volume) and *decrescendos* (gradual decreases in volume), which enabled smooth articulation of the dynamics between the seven steps. There was also a control for the *una chorda* (left) pedal, but since the mechanism used on Ampico grand pianos was that normally found on uprights, namely that of moving the hammers nearer the strings, thereby reducing the tone, this was used by the Ampico roll editors as a method to further modify the dynamics. Despite the fact that the rolls were edited, both to reduce any wrong notes and to capture the subtleties of the use of the damper pedal by extending the lengths of certain notes, the reproductions are fairly accurate to the original performances. Indeed an article by O'Connell contains a quantitative proof that Rachmaninoff's Ampico recording of the C Sharp Minor Prelude is very close to the 78 rpm disc recording ([7]). Using this data, therefore, it was possible not only to extract the timing and durations of the notes, but also their volume, which were quantised on a scale of 1 (quietest) to 14 (loudest).

Structural Data

As regards the encoding of the musical score, a number of different encoding techniques were used. On the surface level the encoding consisted of the note duration, dynamic as indicated in the score (on the same scale of 1 to 14 as for the performance dynamic), position in bar, pitch, touch (varying from *staccato*, i.e. detached, to *portamento*, i.e. smoothly linking between notes), accent (from *leggiero*, i.e. lightly to *sforzando*, i.e. heavily accented) and whether the note occurred at the beginning of, end of, or within a phrase. A more general encoding method consisted of merely noting whether the pitch of the melody was moving up, down or remaining on the same note. Such a method has been used to index musical themes with some success. A small modification was to encode high and low neighbourhoods, where a note is surrounded by two lower or higher notes, both of which have the same pitch. A more complicated attempt to encode the general structure of the music was to apply a method of classification devised by Cope for analysing compositional style ([1]). While Cope's classification can also be applied to harmony and rhythm in a hierarchical manner, here it was merely applied in a non-hierarchical way to individual notes, classifying their context within the musical phrase. In this scheme there are five classes or contexts: *Statements, Preparations, Extensions, Antecedents* and *Consequences* (the initials spelling SPEAC). These should not be confused with their use and meaning in logic programming. *Statements* can exist alone, and not as a result of other activity, with nothing expected except iteration. They can be prefaced by *Preparations* or lengthened by *Extensions*. *Antecedents* cause a significant musical implication in the structure and require musical resolution. They typically demand a *Consequence*. *Consequences* are often harmonically similar to *Statements* but have different musical implications in respect to their function and positioning within the musical phrase.

PROGOL Encoding

The PROGOL predicates devised take constants of the type "note" as their parameters, and defined various characteristics of each note in the piece. The predicates used can be divided into fourteen groups, the first six of which describe the performance of the note, while the remaining eight describe various properties of the note as indicated in the score. The six performance-related groups are: *rubato_hold* - describing whether the note is played longer or shorter than indicated in the score;

rubato_detach - describing whether the time interval between the note and the preceding note is longer or shorter than indicated; *rubato_overlap* - describing whether the overlap (if any) of the note with the preceding note is longer or shorter than indicated; *rubato_timing* - indicating whether the note occurs earlier or later in the bar than indicated; *dynamic_force* - describing whether the note is played louder or softer than indicated; and *dynamic_actual*, describing crescendos or decrescendos between the note and the preceding one. The nine musical score related groups are: *accent, touch, phrasing* - which were encoded directly from the relevant information mentioned in the section on "Structural Data" above; *structure* - illustrating the note's context using the SPEAC system; *pitch* - which describes whether the note is higher or lower than the preceding note and if it is a low or high neighbourhood note (as described above); *dynamic_expected* - describing whether the note as written is louder or softer than the preceding note; *syncopation* - describing whether the note occurs on a beat, or barline; *rhythm* - describing the value of the note (e.g. crotchet, which equals one beat, or minim, which equals two beats, or quaver, which equals half a beat, etc.). Two other predicates used are: *note,* to define the type ("note") of the constants used (which were of the form *note_1, note_2,* etc.), and finally *pre,* which is used to indicate the ordering of the notes in the score. Certain simplifications were introduced at this point. No predicates took integers as parameters, so comparisons are qualitative only, e.g. the *rubato_hold* predicates merely indicate that a note is shorter, longer, or over twice as long or short than indicated in the score, but does not give a more precise value as to how much longer or shorter. Also the PROGOL searches involved in the analysis only processed chains of up to four consecutive notes.

Since the first six groups of predicates (the performance-related ones) could appear in both the head and the body of the rules generated, six PROGOL scripts were generated for each piece, so that each of these six groups took it in turns to be goals, (i.e. they were declared with *modeh* declarations while the others were declared with *modeb* declarations). In each case, the negative data consisted of the set of negative predicates from the *modeh* declared group which were not properties of each note in turn. In all six scripts, the positive data from all fourteen groups were included. In this manner, the positive and negative examples come from the *modeh* declared group while the other groups form the background knowledge.

Results and Conclusions

A number of expected result came out of the analysis as well as some more interesting results, including a number of common or similar rules between the pieces, hinting at a performance style rather than predicates merely generated by style of the music being performed. Amongst the expected results is a one indicating that a note marked staccato resulted in a severe shortening of the note, followed by a corresponding lengthening of the gap before the next note. A more satisfying predicate is one characterising Rachmaninoff's technique of accentuation described by Martyn as his "rhythmic snap" ([4]), namely that he slightly anticipates notes occurring at the beginning of a bar. Other rules found include a tendency to exaggerate the detachment between two notes if he were to linger on the second note and to stick closely to the written dynamic of a note when playing it slightly quicker than indicated.

Future Research Directions

There are a number of areas in which further research could be done, and there is a wealth of data in the form of Piano rolls (from other manufacturers as well as Ampico) and that supplied from modern performances through MIDI. A more comprehensive structural analysis than the SPEAC system outlined here could be applied, making use of other forms of musical analysis such as Schenkerian analysis ([3]); the structural analysis could incorporate the entire score rather than just the melody, possibly with some form of automation using optical character recognition to scan the score and an expert system to perform the musical analysis; the use of more powerful inductive logic tools, allowing longer chains in the search space and the identification of numeric ranges rather than the qualitative analysis performed in this project. However, even with the shortcomings of the method described here, I believe a number of interesting results were obtained, indicating that this may be a rich avenue for further investigation.

Acknowledgements

I acknowledge support given by the ESPRIT Basic Research Action 6020 on Inductive Logic Programming. I would also like to thank Stephen Muggleton for his assistance and guidance as regards inductive logic programming, and Rex Lawson and Dennis Hall for their help and advice as regards the Ampico Reproducing Piano. Finally, I would like to thank Sergei Rachmaninoff for his piano recordings.

Bibliography

[1] David Cope, *Computers and Musical Style*, Oxford University Press 1991.
[2] John Farmer, "The Reproducing Piano" in *Journal of the Pianola Institute*, No. 6 1993.
[3] Allen Forte and Steven Gilbert, *Introduction to Schenkerian Analysis*, W. W. Norton 1982.
[4] Barrie Martyn, *Rachmaninoff - Composer, Pianist, Conductor*, Scolar Press 1990.
[5] Stephen Muggleton, *Inductive Logic Programming*, SIGART Bulletin, Vol. 5 Num. 1, 1994.
[6] Stephen Muggleton (editor), *Inductive Logic Programming*, Academic Press 1992.
[7] Sid O'Connell, "Rachmaninoff Performance Analysis" in *Rachmaninoff Society Journal*, No. 20 September 1994.

Handling real numbers in ILP: a step towards better behavioural clones (Extended abstract)

Sašo Džeroski, Ljupčo Todorovski, Tanja Urbančič

Institut Jožef Stefan, Jamova 39, 61111 Ljubljana, Slovenia

1 Introduction

The automated acquisition of knowledge for dynamic systems control is receiving increasing attention among machine learning researchers [9, 1]. Controllers can be designed by machine learning using different kinds of information in the learning process. Recent approaches make use of the existing skill of a human operator at performing a particular control task. In this case, traces of human performance serve as sources of learning examples. This approach is named behavioural cloning [7].

The task of learning a control rule for a dynamic system from examples can be formulated as follows: given examples of the form (*Time, Action, State*), find a functional relation between the *State* and *Action*, i.e., *Action(Time)* = $f(State(Time - Delay))$ [9]. For simplicity, we will assume no delay, i.e., *Action* = $f(State)$. The examples are derived from a successful performance trace, where the controlled system is brought from an initial to a goal state by applying a sequence of appropriate control actions.

Current experiments in behavioural cloning assume mostly the above formulation, where the goal is implicit in the performance trace. The learned controllers can thus be applied only to the very same control task that was used to generate the examples. Obviously, it is desirable to obtain controllers that are applicable to a wider range of similar tasks. A formulation of the behavioural cloning task that assumes *Action* = $f(State, Goal)$ instead of *Action* = $f(State)$ would facilitate the induction of controllers that would be more flexible in this sense.

Another important issue is the form of the function f. Present approaches to behavioural cloning use propositional learning and represent f as a set of classification rules, a classification tree or a regression tree. Using inductive logic programming (ILP) instead of propositional learning would facilitate the use of background knowledge and would allow for a more expressive formalism for representing f. Given background knowledge B, an appropriate formulation of the behavioural cloning problem would be *Action* = $f_B(State, Goal)$.

The capability of handling real numbers is essential for applying ILP systems to the problem of behavioral cloning. To achieve this capability, we transform ILP problems to propositional form, using the DINUS [3] algorithm. This allows us to use propositional learning approaches that have elaborate number-handling capabilities, including systems for learning classification rules/trees and regression rules/trees. The former predict a discrete-valued class and are suitable for learning bang-bang control, while the latter predict a real-valued class and are suitable for learning continuous control. We will refer to the task of predicting a real-valued class in the presence of background knowledge as the task of relational regression. We will use DINUS with CN2 [2] to induce bang-bang control rules for an ice cube, and DINUS with RETIS [4] to solve the relational regression problem of inducing continuous control rules for the inverted pendulum.

2 Learning bang-bang control

This section is concerned with the task of learning control rules for a simple dynamic system: an ice cube. The cube with mass 1kg slides without friction along one dimension. The goal is to bring the cube to a pre-specified position and keep it there. The control actions, applied at regular time intervals are: push the cube right or left with force 10N (bang-bang control). The particular control rule that we will try to reconstruct is shown in Figure 1. As the magnitude of the force is fixed (10N), the rule only determines the direction ($+$ right, $-$ left).

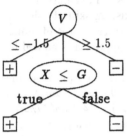

Fig. 1. A bang-bang controller for the ice cube.

If we use the formulation $Action = f(State)$, the task is to learn the relation $cube(Action, X, V)$, where X [m] denotes the current position and V [m/s] the current velocity of the cube. To generate training examples, we used two different traces where the cube was moved from the initial states $X = -2$ and $X = 5$ to the target position $G = 3$. Control decisions were made every 0.02 seconds. DINUS with CN2 (as no background knowledge is present, this is equivalent to using CN2) generated the four rules below.

The rules successfully bring the cube to the particular target position from an arbitrary initial state. However, they don't work if we change the target position.

$cube(left, X, V)\leftarrow$
    $X > 3.00, V > -1.45.$
$cube(left, X, V)\leftarrow V > 1.45.$
$cube(right, X, V)\leftarrow$
    $X < 3.01, V < 1.45.$
$cube(right, X, V)\leftarrow V < -1.45.$

$cube(left, X, V, G)\leftarrow$
    $X > -5.01, V > -1.45, G < -1.00.$
$cube(left, X, V, G)\leftarrow$
    $X > 3.00, V > -1.45.$
$cube(left, X, V, G)\leftarrow V > 1.45.$
$cube(right, X, V, G)\leftarrow$
    $X < 3.01, V < 1.45, G > -1.00.$
$cube(right, X, V, G)\leftarrow$
    $X < -5.00, V < 1.45, G < -1.00.$
$cube(right, X, V, G)\leftarrow V < -1.45.$

For the setting $Action = f(State, Goal)$, we used four behaviour traces to generate training examples: the positions ($G = -5$ and $G = 3$) were reached from the states ($X = -2$ and $X = 5$). The six rules below were induced. They are successful for $G = 3$ and $G = -5$, but fail for other goals.

Finally, the background knowledge predicate $leq(X, Y)$ (meaning $X \leq Y$) was used in the learning process, with the same training examples as above. DINUS transformed the ILP problem to a propositional learning problem where the class is the appropriate control action and the attributes are as follows: $X, V, G, leq(X, G)$ and $leq(G, X)$. The four rules below were induced.

$cube(left, X, V, G)\leftarrow$
    $V > -1.45, not\ leq(X, G).$
$cube(left, X, V, G)\leftarrow V > 1.45.$
$cube(right, X, V, G)\leftarrow$
    $V < 1.45, leq(X, G).$
$cube(right, X, V, G)\leftarrow V < -1.45.$

These rules successfully bring the cube from any initial state to any target position. Having the prerequisite number handling capabilities and the appropriate background knowledge, DINUS was able to construct a successful control rule.

285

3 Learning continuous control

In this section, we describe how DINUS was used to induce a continuous control rule for the inverted pendulum, a standard benchmark problem for control synthesis [9]. The inverted pendulum consists of a cart that can move along a horizontal track, and a pole hinged on top of the cart, so that it can rotate in the vertical plane defined by the track and its fixed point.

The state of the cart is described with the variables $X, \dot{X}, \varphi$ and $\dot{\varphi}$. X denotes the position of the cart, i.e., its distance from the origin point on the track, while φ denotes the inclination angle of the pole relative to the vertical line through its fixed point. $\dot{X}$ and $\dot{\varphi}$ denote the time derivatives of X and φ, i.e., the velocity of the cart and the angular velocity of the pole. A force F parallel to the track can be applied to the cart. A standard control task is to bring the cart from an initial state to a particular goal position G on the track, while balancing the pole at the same time.

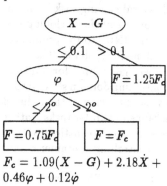

$F_c = 1.09(X - G) + 2.18\dot{X} + 0.46\varphi + 0.12\dot{\varphi}$

Fig. 2. A piece-wise linear controller.

The problem addressed by DINUS was to reconstruct the piece-wise linear controller shown in Figure 2. The predicate $diff(X, Y, Z)$, where $Z = X - Y$, was given as background knowledge. In ILP terminology, the task was to find a definition of the target predicate $pole(F, X, \dot{X}, \varphi, \dot{\varphi}, G)$. Given $X, \dot{X}, \varphi, \dot{\varphi}$, and G, the definition has to determine F. This is a relational regression problem and thus RETIS [4] was used within DINUS. RETIS induces regression trees and employs linear regression in the leaves. Using a simulator of the inverted pendulum, four behaviour traces were generated: the controller brought the cart from $X = 0.5$ and

$X = -0.7$ to each of $G = -0.5$ and $G = 0.3$. The control force was determined by the rule in Figure 2, and was applied every 0.02 seconds. Each trace lasted five seconds, giving 250 examples per behaviour trace.

Given the target predicate and the background knowledge above, the propositional task for RETIS was to predict F. The attributes were $X, \dot{X}, \varphi, \dot{\varphi}, G$, and $D = X - G$. The last variable was introduced by the determinate literal $diff(X, G, D)$. From the training examples generated in this manner, RETIS built a regression tree of 11 leaves, using linear regression in the leaves, without pre-pruning. Post-pruning with $m = 8$ yielded the following tree:

$pole(F, X, \dot{X}, \varphi, \dot{\varphi}, G) \leftarrow diff(X, G, D), D > 0.1$,
    F is $1.4D + 2.7\dot{X} + 0.58\varphi + 0.15\dot{\varphi}$.
$pole(F, X, \dot{X}, \varphi, \dot{\varphi}, G) \leftarrow diff(X, G, D), D \leq 0.1, \varphi > 2.04$,
    F is $-0.23 + 0.83D + 2.7\dot{X} + 0.47\varphi + 0.13\dot{\varphi} - 0.54G$.
$pole(F, X, \dot{X}, \varphi, \dot{\varphi}, G) \leftarrow diff(X, G, D), D \leq 0.1, \varphi \leq 2.04$,
    F is $0.82D + 1.6\dot{X} + 0.35\varphi + 0.09\dot{\varphi}$.

The tree has the same structure as the original controller and (almost) the same numerical parameters. In addition to performing each of the four training example tasks successfully, the tree also works for other initial and goal positions.

Further experiments have shown that learning with background knowledge produces more general, more concise and more reliable rules.

4 Discussion

The transformation approach, implemented in DINUS, allows for handling real numbers in ILP. In this respect, DINUS compares favorably to existing ILP systems. As compared to LINUS [6], it can use determinate new variables. Most other ILP systems do not deal with real numbers at all. Exceptions are FOIL [8] and INDLOG [1], which can use inequalities in the induced clauses. However, DINUS is the first to address the problem of relational regression and at the same time include noise handling. Both ingredients are necessary for practical applications, such as behavioural cloning. Karalič [5] is currently developing a relational regression system that builds first-order clauses to predict the value of a continuous-valued class. The system has some noise-handling capabilities and can, in principle, use linear regression.

We first generalized the formulation of the behavioral cloning task by introducing the goal state and background knowledge. Thus, behavioral cloning was formulated as an ILP task. We applied the ILP system DINUS to the problem of learning bang-bang and continuous control for two dynamic systems. The more general formulation and the use of background knowledge allowed for inducing general control rules. Extensive testing in the pole balancing domain showed that background knowledge also improves the reliability and precision of the induced rules. The induced controllers are applicable to a range of similar tasks, rather than a single specific task. Further work will address the more realistic problems of cloning human operators' skill in the domains of controlling container cranes [9] and flight simulators [1].

Acknowledgements This research is supported by the ESPRIT Project 6020 Inductive Logic Programming and the Slovenian Ministry of Science and Technology.

References

1. Camacho, R. (1994). Learning stage transition rules with Indlog. In *Proc. Fourth International Workshop on Inductive Logic Programming*.
2. Clark, P. and Boswell, R. (1991). Rule induction with CN2: Some recent improvements. In *Proc. Fifth European Working Session on Learning*.
3. Džeroski, S., Muggleton, S., and Russell, S. (1992). PAC-learnability of determinate logic programs. In *Proc. Fifth ACM Workshop on Computational Learning Theory*.
4. Karalič, A. (1992). Employing linear regression in regression tree leaves. In *Proc. Tenth European Conference on Artificial Intelligence*.
5. Karalič, A. (1994). Relational regression: first steps. Technical report IJS-DP-7001, Jožef Stefan Institute, Ljubljana.
6. Lavrač, N., Džeroski, S., and Grobelnik, M. (1991). Learning nonrecursive definitions of relations with LINUS. In *Proc. Fifth European Working Session on Learning*.
7. Michie, D. (1993). Knowledge, learning and machine intelligence. In L. S. Sterling (ed.) *Intelligent Systems*. Plenum Press, New York.
8. Quinlan, J. and Cameron-Jones, M. (1993). FOIL: A midterm report. In *Proc. Sixth European Conference on Machine Learning*.
9. Urbančič, T. and Bratko, I. (1994). Reconstructing human skill with machine learning. In *Proc. Eleventh European Conference on Artificial Intelligence*.

Simplifying Decision Trees by Pruning and Grafting: New Results
(Extended Abstract)

Floriana Esposito, Donato Malerba and Giovanni Semeraro

Dipartimento di Informatica - Università degli Studi di Bari - via Orabona 4, 70126 Bari, Italy
{esposito I malerbad I semeraro}@vm.csata.it

Abstract. This paper presents some empirical results on simplification methods of decision trees induced from data. We observe that those methods exploiting an independent pruning set do not perform uniformly better than the others. Furthermore, a clear definition of bias towards overpruning and underpruning is exploited in order to interpret empirical data concerning the size of the simplified trees.

1 Introduction

A major problem in top-down induction of decision trees (TDIDT) is the determination of the leaves [1]. One way to cope with it consists in keeping on growing a tree T_{max} in any case, and then retrospectively removing those branches that seem superfluous with respect to predictive accuracy. The final effect is that in this way the intelligibility of a decision tree is improved, without really affecting its predictive accuracy. Many methods have been proposed for simplifying decision trees; in [3] a review of some of them that employ *pruning* operators is presented. Informally, a pruning operator cuts a branch at a node t and removes the descendants of t itself. However, another complementary simplification operator, that we named *grafting*, has been employed in a well-known TDIDT system: C4.5 [9]. Briefly, a grafting operator substitutes a sub-branch of a node t onto the place of t iself, thus removing only some of the nodes of the subtree rooted in t. Simplification methods that use pruning and grafting operators are denoted with the general term of *pruning methods*.

In this paper we present the results of a wide experimentation on nine different pruning methods. In this empirical study, eleven databases taken from the UCI machine learning repository are considered. In order to detect possible biases of the methods towards underpruning or overpruning, we generate the smallest optimally pruned grown/trained tree for each experiment, and we compare the size of optimally pruned trees with the size of trees returned by the pruning method.

2 Experimental Design

The need of repeating experiments on some pruning methods arises from the fact that the experimental procedure designed by Mingers [6] to compare several pruning methods, in our opinion, presents some problems (see [3] for a detailed discussion).

In Table 1, the main characteristics of the data sets considered in our experiments are reported. Some of them have already been used to compare different pruning methods [6,8]. The database Heart is actually the join of four data sets on heart diseases, with the same number of attributes but collected in four distinct places (Hungary, Switzerland,

Table 1. Main characteristics of the databases used for the experimentation.

database	No. Cases	No. Classes	No. Attributes	Continuous attributes	Multi-valued attributes	Null values	% Base Error	Noise level	Uniform distrib.
Iris	150	3	4	4	0	no	66.67	low	yes
Glass	214	7	9	9	0	no	64.49	low	no
Led	1000	10	7	0	0	no	90	10%	yes
Hypo	3772	4	29	7	1	yes	7.7	no	no
P.-gene	106	2	57	0	57	no	50	no	yes
Hepat.	155	2	19	6	0	yes	20.65	no	no
Cleveland	303	2	14	5	5	yes	45.21	low	yes
Hungary	294	2	14	5	5	yes	36.05	low	no
Switzerland	123	2	14	5	5	yes	6.5	low	no
Long Beach	200	2	14	5	5	yes	25.5	low	no
Heart	920	2	14	5	5	yes	44.67	low	yes

Cleveland and Long-Beach). Only 14 out of the 76 original attributes have been selected, since they are the only ones deemed useful for the classification task. Moreover, examples have been assigned to two distinct classes: *no presence* (value 0 of the target attribute) and *presence* of heart diseases (values 1, 2, 3, 4).

In Table 1, columns headed "Continuous" and "Multi-valued" concern the number of attributes that are treated as real-valued and multi-valued discrete attributes respectively. All other attributes are binary. In the column "Null values", we simply report the presence of null values in at least one attribute of any observation. In fact, the system C4.5 used for building decision trees in our experiments provides us with a way of managing null values [9]. The column on base error refers to the percentage error obtained if the most frequent class is always predicted. We expect that good decision trees show a lower error rate than the base error. The last column states whether the distribution of examples per class is uniform or not.

In our experimental setup, each data set is randomly split into three subsets, according to the following criterion: *growing* set (49%), *pruning* set (21%) and *test* set (30%). The union of the growing and pruning set is called *training* set, and its size is just 70% of the whole data set. The growing set contains the 70% of cases of the training set, while the pruning set the remaining 30%. The growing set and the training set are used to learn two decision trees, which are called *grown* tree and *trained* tree respectively. The former is used by those methods that need an independent set in order to prune a decision tree, namely the reduced error pruning (REP) [8], the minimum error pruning (MEP) [2,7], the critical value pruning (CVP) [5], as well as those versions of the error complexity pruning based on a pruning set and adopting the 1SE rule (1SE) or not (0SE) [1]. Conversely, the trained tree is used by those methods that exploit the training set only, such as pessimistic error pruning (PEP) [8], error-based pruning (EBP) [9], as well as the cost-complexity pruning based on 10 cross-validation sets and adopting either the 0SE rule (CV-0SE) or the 1SE rule (CV-1SE). The evaluation of the error rate is always made on the test set.

For each data set employed, 25 trials are repeated by randomly partitioning the data set into three subsets. Moreover, for each trial two statistics are recorded: the number of leaves (*size*) of the resultant tree, and the error rate (*e.r.*) of the tree on the test set. This is done for pruned, grown and trained trees, so that a two-tailed paired t-test can be used to evaluate the significance of the error rate and size differences between trees.

As to MEP, the following m values have been chosen: 0.5, 1, 2, 3, 4, 8, 12, 16, 32, 64, 128, 512 and 1024. Experiments on the CVP are made by setting a maximum critical value equal to 1.0 and a step equal to 0.01. The only selection measure considered is the gain ratio [9].

3 Results and Conclusions

In order to study the effect of pruning on predictive accuracy of decision trees, we compare the error rates of the pruned trees with those of the corresponding trained trees. In practice, we compare two tree induction strategies: a *sophisticated* strategy that, in a way or another, prunes a large tree T_{max} constructed through recursive splitting, and a *naive* strategy that simply returns T_{max}. The main goal of this comparison is that of understanding whether tree simplification techniques are beneficial or not, at least for various databases considered in our experiments. Table 2 reports the results of the t-tests with a 0.1 confidence level. A (+) means that the application of the pruning method actually improves, on average, the predictive accuracy of the decision tree, while a (-) indicates a significant decrease in predictive accuracy. When the effect of pruning is neither good nor bad, a **0** is reported. It is easy to see that pruning does not generally decrease predictive accuracy. The only exception is represented by the application of the 1SE rule with cross-validation sets. Moreover, there is no clear indication that methods exploiting a pruning set perform definitely better than the others, as claimed in [5].

Another interesting characteristic of pruning methods is their tendency to overprune decision trees. In order to study such a problem, we produced two decision trees for each experiment, called *optimally pruned grown-tree* (OPGT) and *optimally pruned trained-tree* (OPTT) respectively. The former is a grown tree that has been pruned by using the reduced error pruning on the test set. Thus, it is the best pruned tree we could produce from the grown tree because of a property of optimality of the reduced error pruning [3]. Similarly, the OPTT is the best tree we could obtain by pruning some branches of the trained tree. Obviously, OPGTs are suitable to compare trees obtained with pruning methods that *do* use an independent pruning set, while OPTTs are more appropriate to compare results of pruning methods that *do not* need a pruning set. Therefore, by comparing the size of trees produced by a pruning method with the size of the corresponding optimal tree, we can have an indication of the tendency of each method. In Table 3, a summary

Table 2. Error rate variations for different pruning methods (significance level: 0.10)

Table 3. Tree size variations for different pruning methods (significance level: 0.10)

database	REP	MEP	CVP	OSE	1SE	PEP	CV 6SE	CV 1SE	EBP
Iris	0	0	0	0	0	0	0	-	0
Glass	-	0	0	0	-	0	-	-	0
Led	-	-	-	0	-	0	0	-	0
Hypo	+	+	0	+	0	+	+	-	+
P. gene	0	0	0	0	0	0	0	0	0
Hepatitis	0	0	0	0	0	0	0	0	0
Cleveland	0	0	0	0	0	0	0	-	0
Hungary	+	+	0	+	+	+	+	+	+
Switzerland	+	0	+	+	+	+	+	+	+
Long Beach	+	+	+	+	+	+	+	+	+
Heart	0	0	0	0	0	+	0	-	+

database	REP	MEP	CVP	OSE	1SE	PEP	CV 6SE	CV 1SE	EBP
Iris	-	-	u	-	-	-	-	0	u
Glass	-	u	u	-	0	u	-	0	u
Led	-	u	u	u	0	0	u	0	u
Hypo	0	u	u	-	0	-	-	0	u
P. gene	0	u	u	-	0	0	-	0	u
Hepatitis	-	u	-	-	0	-	0	0	u
Cleveland	-	-	u	-	0	u	0	0	u
Hungary	0	-	u	0	0	-	-	0	u
Switzerland	-	u	-	-	-	-	-	-	-
Long Beach	-	u	-	-	0	-	-	0	u
Heart	-	-	u	-	0	0	0	0	-

of the two-tailed paired t-tests at a significance level 0.1 is shown. Here, (u) stands for significant underpruning, (o) for significant overpruning, while (-) means no significant difference. At a glance, we can immediately conclude that MEP, CVP and EBP tend to underprune, while REP, 1SE and CV-1SE tend to overprune. We would be tempted to conclude that the predictive accuracy is improved whenever a pruning method does not produce trees with significant difference in size from the corresponding optimally pruned tree. However, this is not true for two reasons. First of all, it is not always true that an optimally pruned tree is more accurate than the corresponding grown/trained tree. In other words, pruning may help to simplify trees without improving its predictive accuracy. Secondly, tree size is a global feature that can provide us with an idea of what is happening, but it is not detailed enough to guarantee that only over or underpruning occurred. For instance, if a method overprunes a branch but underprunes another one, then it is actually increasing the error rate with respect to the optimal tree, but not necessarily the size. This problem can be observed with the database Glass and the method CV-0SE. Indeed, in this case there is a decrease in accuracy (see Table 2) but the size of pruned trees is close to the optimal value (see Table 3).

By ideally superimposing Tables 2 and 3 it is also possible to draw some other interesting conclusion. For instance, in some databases, such as Hungary and Heart, overpruning produces better trees than underpruning. This latter surprising result confirms Holte's observation that even simple rules perform well on most commonly used data sets in the machine learning community [4]. In any case, we have also indications that overpruning may have undesirable effects when too extremist, as in the case of the application of the rule 1SE.

References

1. Breiman, L., Friedman, J., Olshen, R., & C. Stone, *Classification and regression trees*, Belmont, CA: Wadsworth International, 1984.
2. Cestnik, B., & I. Bratko, On estimating probabilities in tree pruning. In Y. Kodratoff (Ed.), *Machine Learning - EWSL-91*, Lecture Notes in Artificial Intelligence, Berlin: Springer-Verlag, 138-150, 1991.
3. Esposito, F., Malerba, D., & G. Semeraro, Decision tree pruning as a search in the state space. In P. Brazdil (Ed.), *Machine Learning: ECML-93*, Lecture Notes in Artificial Intelligence, Berlin:Springer-Verlag, 165-184, 1993.
4. Holte, R.C. , Very simple classification rules perform well on most commonly used datasets. *Machine Learning*, 11, 63-90, 1993.
5. Mingers, J., Expert systems - rule induction with statistical data. *Journal of the Operational Research Society, 38*, 39-47, 1987.
6. Mingers, J., An empirical comparison of pruning methods for decision tree induction. *Machine Learning, 4*, 227 - 243, 1989.
7. Niblett, T., & I. Bratko, Learning decision rules in noisy domains. *Proceedings of Expert Systems 86*, Cambridge: Cambridge University Press, 1986.
8. Quinlan, J.R., Simplifying decision trees. *International Journal of Man-Machine Studies, 27*, 221-234, 1987.
9. Quinlan, J.R., *C4.5: Programs for machine learning*. San Mateo, CA: Morgan Kaufmann, 1993.

A Tight Integration of Pruning and Learning (Extended Abstract)

Johannes Fürnkranz

Austrian Research Institute for Artificial Intelligence
Schottengasse 3, A-1010 Vienna
E-mail: juffi@ai.univie.ac.at

Abstract. This paper outlines some problems that may occur with *Reduced Error Pruning* in rule learning algorithms. In particular we show that pruning complete theories is incompatible with the *separate-and-conquer* learning strategy that is commonly used in propositional and relational rule learning systems. As a solution we propose to integrate pruning into learning and examine two algorithms, one that prunes at the clause level and one that prunes at the literal level. Experiments show that these methods are not only much more efficient, but also able to achieve small gains in accuracy by solving the outlined problem.

1 Introduction

Most rule learning algorithms deal with noise in the data during learning, i.e. they employ *pre-pruning*. In relational learning systems like FOIL [Quinlan, 1990] pre-pruning is commonly used in the form of so-called *stopping criteria*. An alternative way for dealing with noise — *post-pruning* — is to first learn a theory that overfits the data and then prune this theory to an appropriate level of generality.

2 REP

The most common post-pruning algorithm, *Reduced Error Pruning (REP)*, has been adopted from propositional decision tree learning to relational rule learning [Brunk and Pazzani, 1991]. After splitting the training set into a growing and a pruning set according to some user-specified ratio, a concept description that covers all of the positive and none of the negative examples of the growing set is learned with a separate-and-conquer rule learning algorithm like the propositional learner CN2 or the relational learner FOIL. This intermediate theory is then simplified by deleting literals and clauses until any further deletion would lead to a decrease of accuracy on the pruning set.

The major shortcomings of this straightforward adaptation of REP for rule learning are its inefficiency and its incompatibility with the separate-and-conquer search strategy that is commonly employed in propositional and relational rule learning algorithms. REP is very inefficient, because the overfitting theory it generates in its first pass can be much more complex than the final theory that is left after the post-pruning phase. A lot of work is wasted in learning and subsequently pruning superfluous literals and clauses. This argument has been formalized in [Cohen, 1993], where it was shown that the growing phase of REP has a time complexity of $\Omega(n^2 \log n)$ and that its pruning phase has a time complexity of $\Omega(n^4)$ (where n is the size of the training set).

[Fürnkranz and Widmer, 1994] point out another problem with REP that is caused by the differences between the *divide-and-conquer* approach used for decision tree learning and the *separate-and-conquer* strategy commonly used for rule learning. Although the two approaches share many similarities, there is one important difference: Pruning of branches in a decision tree will never affect the neighboring branches, whereas pruning of literals of a rule will affect all subsequent rules. One way of looking at this problem may be to view a PROLOG program as a binary decision tree that allows conjunctive tests at each interior node, and where at least one of the two successors of each node is a leaf. The body of each clause of the program corresponds to a node in the decision tree. If the body is true, the head is proven and we arrive at a leaf node. Otherwise we try the next node in the tree, i.e. the next clause in the program. Classical decision tree pruning would only allow to prune the nodes bottom up, i.e. only allow to delete clauses from the end of the program. REP, however, not only allows to prune any (instead of only the last) node, but also to prune the conditions of the rules associated with each node by deleting literals. Changing the test associated with a node in a decision tree will in general change the split it induces on the examples and thus could lead to the generation of different subtrees for its children. However, as the test is changed at pruning time (*after* learning), REP has to keep the subtree that has been previously learned from a different set of examples, although there might be a better subtree to explain this new set of examples.

3 I-REP

Incremental Reduced Error Pruning (I-REP) [Fürnkranz and Widmer, 1994] was motivated by the observation that REP is incompatible with the separate-and-conquer learning strategy as we have discussed in Sect. 2. Its basic idea is that instead of first growing a complete concept description and pruning it thereafter, each individual clause will be pruned right after it has been generated. This ensures that the algorithm can remove the training examples that are covered by the pruned clause before subsequent clauses are learned. Thus it can be avoided that these examples influence the learning of the following clauses.

Before learning a clause, the current set of training examples is split into a growing (usually 2/3) and a pruning set (usually 1/3) as in many post-pruning algorithms. After learning a clause from the growing set, literals will be deleted from this clause in a greedy fashion until any further deletion would decrease the accuracy of this clause on the pruning set. The resulting rule will then be added to the concept description and all covered positive and negative examples will be removed from the training — growing *and* pruning — set. The remaining training instances are then redistributed into a new growing and a new pruning set to ensure that each of the two sets contains the predefined percentage of the remaining examples. From these sets the next clause will be learned. When the predictive accuracy of the pruned clause is below the predictive accuracy of the empty clause (i.e. the clause with the body `fail`), the clause will not be added to the concept description and I-REP returns the learned clauses.

Most of the efficiency of the I-REP algorithm comes from the integration of pre-pruning and post-pruning by this definition of a stopping criterion based on the accuracy of the pruned clause on the pruning set. Thus I-REP does not need REP's `delete-clause` operator [Brunk and Pazzani, 1991], because the clauses of the final theory are constructed directly and learning stops when no more useful clauses can be found. However, this may also cause problems: Whenever the pruned clause does not have an accuracy above the accuracy of the empty clause, no more clauses will be learned. If this accuracy is not estimated accurately, either because there are not enough remaining examples or because of a bad split, I-REP will be prone to over-generalization.

4 I²-REP

I-REP still has to learn overfitting clauses which we tried to avoid with a new algorithm. Just as I-REP improves upon REP by pruning on the clause level instead of the theory level, we tried to improve I-REP by pruning on the literal level instead of the clause level.

As in pre-pruning algorithms I²-REP tries to select only the right literals in the first place and to decide when to stop adding literals to the theory. However, it uses a typical post-pruning method (evaluation on a separate pruning set) to do so. For this purpose the set of training examples is split into two subsets of equal size. A literal that maximizes some heuristic function is found for each of the two sets. These two literals are then compared and the one that has a higher accuracy on the entire set of examples is chosen to extend the current clause. This is repeated until the clause covers no negative examples in one of the two sets or until the chosen literal does not improve the accuracy of this clause. In that case the learned clause is compared to the clause with the body `fail` and if its accuracy is higher, it will be added to the theory and the next clause will be learned from the examples that are not yet covered. If the current clause cannot improve upon the empty clause, learning stops as in I-REP.

One of the problems with I-REP is that a bad split of the training examples into a growing and a pruning set can cause over-generalisation, because I-REP would either learn an incorrect clause from a bad growing set or evaluate a correct clause on a bad pruning set. In both cases the learned clause may appear worse than the empty clause and I-REP will stop. This can lead to the learning of over-general domain theories, in particular in domains with only a limited amount of noise or domains with low example set sizes. I²-REP having two literals to chose from, will hopefully be less likely to prematurely stop learning if one of them is a bad choice or a good choice that is badly evaluated. Besides, I²-REP's procedure for selecting a literal is very similar to 2-fold cross-validation which has recently been shown to be a reliable procedure for comparing classifiers, in particular at low training set sizes [Weiss and Indurkhya, 1994]. Therefore we hope that I^2-REP will be able to improve upon I-REP in these cases.

5 Results

We have tested REP, I-REP, and I^2-REP on the relational KRK chess endgame domain and on several propositional domains from the UCI repository of Machine Learning databases. The results can be found in [Fürnkranz, 1995] which is available via anonymous ftp from ftp.ai.univie.ac.at. I-REP and I^2-REP are both significantly faster than REP. In the KRK domain they also learn significantly better theories, in particular at high training set sizes. In addition, I^2-REP improves upon I-REP on small training set sizes. The price that has to be paid for this is that I^2-REP is a little slower than I-REP. Nevertheless the experiments showed that both algorithms have about the same subquadratic asymptotic time complexity, while REP's asymptotic time complexity has been confirmed to be $\Omega(n^4)$.

Acknowledgements

This research is sponsored by the Austrian *Fonds zur Förderung der Wissenschaftlichen Forschung (FWF)* under grant number P10489-MAT. I would like to thank Gerhard Widmer and Bernhard Pfahringer for many helpful comments and discussions. Thanks are also due to William Cohen, Mike Cameron-Jones and Ross Quinlan for some valuable suggestions.

References

[Brunk and Pazzani, 1991] Clifford A. Brunk and Michael J. Pazzani. An investigation of noise-tolerant relational concept learning algorithms. In *Proceedings of the 8th International Workshop on Machine Learning*, pages 389–393, Evanston, Illinois, 1991.

[Cohen, 1993] William W. Cohen. Efficient pruning methods for separate-and-conquer rule learning systems. In *Proceedings of the 13th International Joint Conference on Artificial Intelligence*, pages 988–994, Chambery, France, 1993.

[Fürnkranz and Widmer, 1994] Johannes Fürnkranz and Gerhard Widmer. Incremental Reduced Error Pruning. In *Proceedings of the 11th International Conference on Machine Learning*, pages 70–77, New Brunswick, NJ, 1994.

[Fürnkranz, 1995] Johannes Fürnkranz. A tight integration of pruning and learning. Technical Report OEFAI-TR-95-03, Austrian Research Institute for Artificial Intelligence, 1995.

[Quinlan, 1990] John Ross Quinlan. Learning logical definitions from relations. *Machine Learning*, 5:239–266, 1990.

[Weiss and Indurkhya, 1994] Sholom M. Weiss and Nitin Indurkhya. Small sample decision tree pruning. In *Proceedings of the 11th Conference on Machine Learning*, pages 335–342, Rutgers University, New Brunswick, NJ, 1994.

Decision-Tree Based Neural Network (Extended Abstract)

Irena IVANOVA[1] and Miroslav KUBAT[2]

1 Department of Medical Informatics, Graz University of Technology, Brockman-ngasse 41, A-8010 Graz, Austria—on leave from the Bulgarian Academy of Sciences, Institute for Information Technologies, Acad. G. Bonchev Str., Bl. 29A, 1113 Sofia, Bulgaria, e-mail: irena@iinf.bg

2 Institute of Systems Sciences, Johannes Kepler University, Altenbergerstr.69, A-4040 Linz, Austria, e-mail: mirek@cast.uni-linz.ac.at

1 Introduction: The Algorithm TBNN

The system TBNN (Tree-Based Neural Net) maps decision trees to neural networks trained by the backpropagation algorithm. This idea is not new. In Sethi (1990), the tree is mapped to a network with 2 hidden layers. Park (1994) shows a mechanism for mapping multivariate decision trees to networks with one or two hidden layers. TBNN differs from its predecessors in 1) *fully interconnecting* all adjacent layers, 2) redescribing the examples in terms of interval-membership functions, and then 3) using its own mechanism to *fuzzify these functions*.

The algorithm of TBNN is summarized in Table 1. For the induction of the decision tree we re-programmed the system ID3 (Quinlan, 1986) and used for the treatment of numeric attributes the binarization technique suggested by Fayyad and Irani (1992). The decision tree encodes one DNF for each class: the conditions along a branch are conjuncted and the individual branches are disjuncted. In the network, each branch is mapped to one hidden neuron and each class is mapped to one output neuron. Input neurons represent intervals imposed on the attributes by the tests in the internal nodes of the tree. For instance, if the tests on a_1 appeared in two places as $a_1 < 0.3$ and $a_1 < 0.7$, then there will be 3 input neurons representing the intervals $[0; 0.3), [0.3; 0.7)$, and $[0.7; 1]$ (provided a_1 is normalized to the interval $[0, 1]$).

At this point, the network is partially connected—it contains only *principal links* determined by the logic of the decision tree. The weights along the principal links are set only after the supplementation of *additional links* (with very small random weights) that make the network fully connected. The weights along the principal links are calculated from the additional weights and from the logic encoded in the decision tree so that the network closely emulates the classification behavior of the tree (the necessary formulae and their derivation can be found in Ivanova and Kubat, 1995).

To *soften* the interval-membership function, TBNN first determines the closeness of the attribute value to the interval center: $C_i = (R_i - 2 \, |\mu_i - x_j|)/(2R_i)$, where μ_i is the center of the i-th interval, R_i is the size of the interval, and x_j is the actual value of the related attribute. Closeness C_i is then subjected to the sigmoid function $m_i = 1/(1 + e^{-hC_i})$ of the input neurons.

Table 1: Algorithm of the system TBNN

1. Take a *subset* of the examples and induce from them a decision tree;
2. Transform attribute values into interval-membership functions, and thus define input neurons. Turn the tree into a neural network with only those links (referred to as *principal*) that were derived from the tree;
3. Fully interconnect the adjacent layers (the new links are referred to as *additional*). Assign to the new links small initial weights;
4. Calculate the weights along the principal links so that the network emulates the decision-tree classifications;
5. Slightly perturb all weights and train the network by the backpropagation algorithm using *all* training examples.

Table 2: Classification accuracy achieved on the glass, diabetes, and breast-cancer data.

file	C4.5	C4.5-rules	LVQ	ID3	TBNN
glass	64.2 ± 3.3	62.1 ± 1.8	62.4 ± 5.3	60.9 ± 5.6	70.0 ± 2.4
diabetes	87.6 ± 3.1	87.6 ± 3.1	95.1 ± 2.1	89.0 ± 3.0	94.1 ± 2.5
cancer	94.0 ± 0.7	94.8 ± 0.6	84.5 ± 2.4	94.6 ± 0.7	96.2 ± 0.5

2 Experiments

• To test the overall performance of TBNN, we ran the program on three benchmark files representing examples by numeric attributes: *glass*, *diabetes*, and *breast-cancer* data. Missing values in the breast-cancer file were filled with the most frequent values. For performance estimation we applied the random-subsampling strategy for 10 different training/testing splits. Table 2 shows the results achieved by TBNN and compares them to some more traditional systems.

• The original idea of the algorithm was that a *subset* S_I of examples would be used for the tree induction and then a superset $S_T \supseteq S_I$ (*all* training examples) would be used for the backpropagation training. The next experiment shows to what extent the size of S_I (by fixed S_T) affects the quality of the network after the tree-to-net mapping. The results shown in Figure 1 confirm the intuition that the more examples are used for the tree induction, the better the starting point of the backpropagation algorithm.

• TBNN's potential to attack a really difficult medical task (automatic sleep classification) was tested on three subjects, BR, KR, and RA, with file sizes 920, 920, and 770 examples, respectively. Examples were described by 15 numeric attributes and categorized into 7 possible classes. There were no missing values but attributes were somewhat noisy and the classifications were inconsistent. To prevent overtraining, the backpropagation part of TBNN used a subset of the training examples as the 'training test set'—the training stopped when the accuracy on this set leveled off.

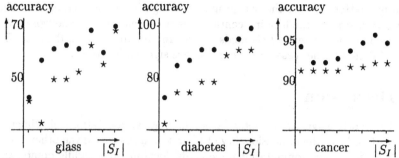

Fig.1 Effect of the size of the set S_I of examples used for generation of the tree on the performance of ID3 (⋆) and TBNN (•)

Table 3: Classification accuracy achieved by various systems on the sleep data. All systems were run on the same training examples (600 in the case of BR and KR, and 450 in the case of RA) and tested on the same 320 testing examples.

file	MLP	C4.5	LVQ	ID3	TBNN
BR	60.0 ± 2.8	78.1 ± 1.8	81.0 ± 1.5	77.3 ± 3.0	85.5 ± 3.6
KR	39.7 ± 5.3	61.7 ± 3.8	66.5 ± 2.5	64.0 ± 1.6	68.3 ± 4.9
RA	68.3 ± 11.0	76.8 ± 1.9	78.5 ± 2.5	77.5 ± 1.5	80.8 ± 0.6

Table 3 summarizes the classification accuracies achieved on these data files by various learners. MLP used 10 hidden units and the same overtraining-prevention strategy as TBNN. The positions of the code vectors in LVQ were determined by the k-means algorithm with $k = 2$. TBNN consistently provided the best classification accuracy. Moreover, its computational requirements (several epochs) were much lower than those of MLP (thousands of epochs).

Table 4 shows the impact of the individual aspects of TBNN: the backpropagation algorithm (B), additional links (A), and the input fuzzification (F). The dashes in the headings of columns 3 and 4 mean that the same results were ob-

Table 4: Performance of various configurations of TBNN on the sleep data

	F	F	not F	not F	not F ⋆	not F	F
	A	not A	not A	A	not A ⋆	A	A
	not B	—	—	not B	not B ⋆	B	B
BR	67.0	67.0	71.6	72.4	72.0	77.0	85.5
KR	47.6	49.3	51.5	51.7	55.6	60.1	68.3
RA	46.5	48.0	63.8	64.3	71.2	74.1	80.8

tained no matter whether the backpropagation algorithm was used or not. The column with stars in the heading contains the performance of the network with the step functions instead of sigmoids. These results are equal to those of ID3 run on S_I. In all other cases, the neurons have sigmoid functions.

3 Discussion

Neural networks have strong potential for finding representations of 'difficult' concepts thanks to the dimensionality of their search space. On the other hand, they suffer from high computational demands, local minima, saddle points, the danger of overtraining, network paralysis, strong reliance on the architecture, and the need for many training examples.

One possibility how to reduce the impact of these shortcomings is to begin with some initial approximation of the concept, provided by mapping a decision tree on a network architecture. The network training then starts from a point that is already close to the global minimum or, at least, to some good local minimum. This dramatically reduces computational requirements and helps avoiding local minima.

The research reported here studied the properties of the system TBNN that builds on these conjectures. It turns out that mere backpropagation algorithm is not enough. Only fully connected network with softened inputs will provide maximum performance.

TBNN offers the following advantages: high classification accuracy, ability do achieve high performance with modest number of learning examples, and acceptable computational requirements.

Acknowledgement

The medical data (sleep classification) used in the case study had been recorded and classified under a grant sponsored by the agency 'Fonds zur Förderung der wissenschaftlichen Forschung' (Project $S49/03$).

References

U.M. Fayyad and K.B. Irani (1992). On the Handling of Continuous-Valued Attributes in Decision-Tree Generation. *Machine Learning*, 8:87–102

I. Ivanova and M. Kubat (1995). Initialization of Neural Networks by Means of Decision Trees. *Knowledge Based Systems* 8(4), in press

Y. Park (1994). A Mapping from Linear Tree Classifiers to Neural Net Classifiers. *Proceedings of IEEE International Conference on Neural Networks*, Orlando, Florida, June–July, Vol. I, 94–100

J.R. Quinlan (1986). Induction of Decision Trees. *Machine Learning*, 1:81–106

I.K. Sethi (1990). Entropy Nets: From Decision Trees to Neural Networks. *Proceedings of the IEEE* 78:1605–1613

Learning Recursion with Iterative Bootstrap Induction
(Extended Abstract)

Alípio Jorge and Pavel Brazdil

LIACC, University of Porto, Rua do Campo Alegre, 823, 4150 PORTO, Portugal
Tel. +351 2600 1672. Fax. +351 2600 3654. Email: {amjorge,pbrazdil}@ncc.up.pt

Abstract. In this paper we are concerned with the problem of inducing recursive Horn clauses from small sets of training examples. The method of iterative bootstrap induction is presented. In the first step, the system generates simple clauses, which can be regarded as properties of the required definition. Properties represent generalizations of the positive examples, simulating the effect of having larger number of examples. Properties are used subsequently to induce the required recursive definitions. This paper describes the method together with a series of experiments. The results support the thesis that iterative bootstrap induction is indeed an effective technique that could be of general use in ILP.

1. Introduction

One potential usage of ILP systems is in algorithm synthesis. However most ILP systems still require relatively large example sets which is rather impractical. Several people have proposed a solution (e.g. [1], [4], [6]). The solution described in [1] and incorporated in CRUSTACEAN exploits common substructures in the examples. Although encouraging results have been achieved, the method seems to be difficult to extend and integrate into a general purpose inductive system.

In this paper we investigate another method called *iterative bootstrap induction*, which represents an alternative approach to this problem. This method can be seen as a special case of the closed-loop learning strategy [5]. An implementation of this method proved experimentally to be able to induce recursive definitions from small sets of positive examples even if these were generated at random.

The system of Zelle et al. [7], CHILLIN, also employs the idea of closed loop learning to overcome incomplete example sets. However, CHILLIN uses a FOIL-like heuristic to guide the search and still needs relatively large example sets.

System SKIL

We adapted the system SKIL [2], which performs induction by refining algorithm sketches, to incorporate the iterative bootstrap induction method. SKIL takes as input positive and negative examples and optionally algorithm sketches. Background predicates are defined either extensionally or intensionally. The concept language is described by means of a definite clause grammar (DCG) similar to [3].

SKIL is a top-down covering system. For each positive example, SKIL looks for a sequence of ground facts that obtain the output arguments from the inputs. Each of those facts needs to either be proved from the background knowledge, or represent a positive example. Each sequence can give rise to a different candidate clause which is accepted as long as it does not cover negative examples. This process is similar to relational pathfinding described in [8].

2. Iterative Bootstrap Induction

The method presented constructs theories in a stepwise manner. In each step a tentative theory is produced which can be reused in the next cycle of the induction process. If certain stopping criteria are satisfied, the process terminates.

Let us see an example. Suppose the aim is to induce a definition of member on the basis of two positive examples (see Table 1) plus appropriate negative examples and background knowledge. If these are presented to SKIL it generates the theory T1. The two clauses generalize the positive examples and express in fact properties of the member relation. They are valid for the examples without necessarily being part of the target theory. If we add these two properties to the background knowledge and call SKIL again, we obtain theory T2. This is a correct definition, although more specific than the usual one.

Why does the method work? To generate the recursive clause in T2 that covers example *member(3,[4,1,3])*, SKIL needs the fact *member(3,[1,3])* corresponding to the recursive call. Although this fact does not appear among the examples, it is implied by the property *member(A,[C,A/E])* in T1.

T0: positive examples:	T1: first step theory, the properties:	T2: second step theory: (T1 is background knowledge)
member(2,[1,2,3])	*member(A,[C,A/E]).*	*member(A,[C,A/E]).*
member(3,[4,1,3])	*member(A,[C,E,A/G]).*	*member(A,[C/D]):-member(A,D).*

Table 1: Iterative bootstrap induction on the member example.

In general, the method proceeds as follows. Given positive and negative examples, we start by inducing a theory T1 invoking SKIL. If this theory performs well enough on a test set it is considered final, and it is output as the solution theory. Otherwise T1 is kept and added to the background. Then we proceed to induce T2 (invoking SKIL again). The original theory T1 is used to enhance the introduction of literals in the clauses of T2.

The performance of T2 is monitored on a test set. If it is worse than T1´s, we may have reached a stable (possibly sub-optimal) point and cannot proceed. If the performance has however improved, T2 is added to the background and the process is repeated. The process stops once the given performance has been achieved.

3. Experiments

We have set out to run SKILit on a set of benchmark problems. These are simple definitions with one recursive clause and one base clause. The positive examples given need not necessarily be on the same resolution chain.

Manually selected input

Following a similar demonstration in [1], we provided SKILit with manually chosen small sets of positive and negative examples of 10 predicates, namely *append/3*, *member/2, delete/3, noneiszero/1, plus/3, extractNth/3, factorial/2, rv/2, last_of/2, split/3,* and in addition also *insertion_sort/2* and *quick_sort/2.* In all of these experiments the recursive definition was successfully generated. Table 2 summarizes the results of some of these experiments.

Input:
mode(delete(+,+,-)).
+delete(3,[1,2,3,4],[1,2,4]).
+delete(5,[6,5],[6]).
(-delete(3,[1,2,5],[1,2,5])).
(-delete(7,[7,9],[7])).
 	
Definition obtained:
delete(A,B,C):-
    dest(B,D,E),delete(A,E,F),const(C,D,F).
delete(A,B,C):-
    dest(B,D,E), dest(E,A,F),const(C,D,F).
	mode(extNth(+,+,-)).
	+extNth(s(0),[6,5,3,4],6).
	+extNth(s(s(0)),[1,2],2).
	(-extNth(s(s(0)),[1,2],1)).
	(-extNth(s(0),[2,1],1)).
	(-extNth(s(0),[2,1,3],1)). (-extNth(0,X,Y)).
	(-extNth(s(s(0)),[2,1,3],2)).
	(-extNth(s(s(s(0))),[1,2],2)).
	(-extNth(s(s(0)),[1],1)). (-extNth(0,X,Y)).
	extNth(A,B,C):-
	    dest(B,C,D),pred(A,E),zero(E).
	extNth(A,B,C):-
	    dest(B,D,E),pred(A,F),extNth(F,E,C).

mode(rv(+,-)).
+rv([1,2,4],[4,2,1]).
+rv([3,1],[1,3]).
(-rv([1,2],[1])).
Definition obtained:
rv(A,B):-
    dest(A,C,D),addlast(D,C,B).
rv(A,B):-
    dest(A,C,D),
    rv(D,E),
    addlast(E,C,B).
	mode(qsort(+,-)).
	+qsort([3,5,2,4,1],[1,2,3,4,5]).
	+qsort([],[]). +qsort([3,1],[1,3]).
	(-qsort([2,1],[2,1])). (-qsort([1,2],[2,1])).
	(-qsort([3,1,2],[1,3,2])).
	(-qsort([3,2,1],[2,1,3])).
	qsort(A,B):-
	    dest(A,C,D), part(C,D,E,F),
	    qsort(E,G), qsort(F,H),
	    const(I,C,H), append(G,I,B).
	qsort(A,B):- null(A), A=B.

Table 2. Some results of SKILit with manually selected examples

Note that SKILit does not impose any constraints on the number of clauses to be generated or on the number of recursive literals, as in CRUSTACEAN. Despite this, our simple strategy permits to obtain results which are comparable to this system.

Randomly selected inputs
We also examined the ability of SKILit to synthesise theories from random sets of examples without assuming a priori knowledge of the solution.

We followed the evaluation methodology described in [1]. For each predicate we sampled positive examples from a universe of facts involving lists and peano integers. The depth of those terms varies from 0 to 4 with uniform distribution. List elements were drawn from a universe of 10 digits (0 to 9) with uniform distribution.

For each predicate, we varied the number of input positive examples from 2 to 5. The number of negative examples was kept constant. The results shown in Table 3 represent averages over 5 runs. The accuracy values were obtained by the generated definitions on relatively large independent test sets. The table also shows the percentage of output theories that contained correct recursive clauses. The last two columns give accuracies obtained by CRUSTACEAN under similar circumstances.

	Accuracy (SKILit)			% of defs with recursion			CRUSTACEAN	
predicate	2 ex.+	3 ex.+	5 ex.+	2 ex.+	3 ex.+	5 ex.+	2 ex.+	3 ex.+
append/3	0.760	0.802	0.888	0	20	40	0.630	0.738
delete/3	0.754	0.880	1.000	0	100	100	0.617	0.713
rv/2	0.664	0.848	0.868	40	40	40	0.805	0.855
member/2	0.700	0.886	0.952	60	100	100	0.652	0.762
last of/2	0.714	0.722	0.944	40	40	100	0.744	0.884

Table 3. Some results of SKILit on randomly selected examples

We see that with random examples, SKILit got somewhat better results than the ones obtained by CRUSTACEAN. However, we believe that iterative bootstrap induction provides a more general solution which is applicable to larger classes of programs. It is potentially useful not only to learn recursion but in a more general setting of multi-predicate learning.

4. Conclusion

Iterative bootstrap induction provides a strategy for the induction of recursive theories from small sets of positive examples. The system SKILit obtained by incorporating a special case of iterative bootstrap induction within SKIL, was able to induce recursive definitions for predicates representative of an important class of logic programs.

The method presented finds regularities within the positive and expresses them in terms of the available background knowledge. Background knowledge may contain definitions of structure handling predicates, test predicates and other more complicated predicates. This fact allows SKILit to express the regularities in a richer language than in [1], enabling it to handle larger classes of problems.

References

[1] Aha D W, Lapointe S, Ling C X, Matwin S (1994): "Inverting Implication with Small Training Sets", in *Proceedings of the European Conference on Machine Learning, ECML-94*, ed. F. Bergadano and L. de Raedt, Springer Verlag.

[2] Brazdil P, Jorge A. (1994): "Learning by Refining Algorithm Sketches", in *Proceedings of ECAI-94*, T. Cohn (ed.), Amsterdam, The Netherlands.

[3] Cohen W W (1993): "Rapid prototyping of ILP systems using explicit bias" in *Proceedings of 1993 IJCAI Workshop on ILP*.

[4] Idestam-Almquist P (1993) "Generalization under implication by recursive anti-unification", in *Proceedings of ILP-93*, Jozef Stefan Institute, technical report.

[5] Michalski R S, (1994): "Inferential Theory of Learning: Developing Foundations for Multistrategy Learning", in *Machine Learning, A Multistrategy Approach, Volume IV*, ed.by Ryszard Michalski and Gheorghe Tecuci, Morgan Kaufmann.

[6] Muggleton S. (1993): "Inductive Logic Programming: derivations, successes and shortcomings" in *Proceedings of ECML-93*, P.Brazdil (ed.), Springer-Verlag.

[7] Zelle J M, Mooney R J, Konvisser J B, (1994):"Combining Top-down and Bottom-up Techniques in Inductive Logic Programming" in *Proceedings of the Eleventh International Conference on Machine Learning ML-94*, Morgan-Kaufmann.

[8] Richards B, Mooney R (1992): "Learning relations by pathfinding" in *Proceedings of the Tenth National Conference on Artificial Intelligence*, Cambridge, MA, MIT Press.

Patching Proofs for Reuse (Extended Abstract)

Thomas Kolbe and Christoph Walther

FB Informatik, TH Darmstadt, Alexanderstr. 10, D-64283 Darmstadt, Germany.
Email: {kolbe|walther}@inferenzsysteme.informatik.th-darmstadt.de

1 Introduction

We investigate the application of machine learning paradigms [2, 4, 3] in auto-mated reasoning for improving a theorem prover by reusing previously computed *proofs* [7]. Assume that we have already computed a proof P of a conjecture

$$\varphi := \big(\forall u \; \text{plus}(\text{sum}(x), \text{sum}(u)) \equiv \text{sum}(\text{append}(x, u))\big)$$
$$\rightarrow \text{plus}(\text{sum}(\text{add}(n, x)), \text{sum}(y)) \equiv \text{sum}(\text{append}(\text{add}(n, x), y))$$

from a set of axioms AX. The schematic conjecture $\Phi := \mathbf{H} \rightarrow \mathbf{C} :=$

$$\big(\forall u \; F(G(x), G(u)) \equiv G(H(x, u))\big) \rightarrow F(G(D(n, x)), G(y)) \equiv G(H(D(n, x), y))$$

is obtained from φ via the generalization {plus $\mapsto F$, sum $\mapsto G$, append $\mapsto$ H, add $\mapsto D$} of function *symbols* plus, sum, ... to function *variables* $F, G, \ldots$ In the same way a *schematic catch*, i.e. a set of schematic axioms $AX' = \{(1), (2), (3)\}$ is obtained from AX where e.g. (1) stems from the axiom $\text{sum}(\text{add}(n, x)) \equiv \text{plus}(n, \text{sum}(x))$. The generalization of P finally yields a sche-matic proof P' of Φ in which the

$$G(D(n, x)) \equiv F(n, G(x)) \qquad (1)$$

schematic conclusion C is modified in

$$H(D(n, x), y) \equiv D(n, H(x, y)) \qquad (2)$$

a backward chaining style:

$$F(F(x, y), z) \equiv F(x, F(y, z)) \qquad (3)$$

$F(G(D(n, x)), G(y))$	$\equiv G(H(D(n, x), y))$	C
$F(\underline{F(n, G(x))}, G(y))$	$\equiv G(H(D(n, x), y))$	Replace (1)
$F(F(n, G(x)), G(y))$	$\equiv G(\underline{D(n, H(x, y))})$	Replace (2)
$F(F(n, G(x)), G(y))$	$\equiv \underline{F(n, G(H(x, y)))}$	Replace (1)
$F(F(n, G(x)), G(y))$	$\equiv F(n, \underline{F(G(x), G(y))})$	Replace (H)
$\underline{F(n, F(G(x), G(y)))}$	$\equiv F(n, \underline{F(G(x), G(y))})$	Replace (3)
TRUE		Reflexivity

The key idea of our reuse procedure is to *instantiate* such a schematic proof with a second-order substitution π obtained by matching Φ with a new conjecture ψ which is (formally) similar to φ, i.e. $\psi = \pi(\Phi)$. As long as the matcher π only replaces function variables with function symbols, the instantiated schematic proof $\pi(P')$ is a proof of ψ from the axioms $\pi(AX')$ because the structure of P' is preserved. However, the success of the method is limited by such a restric-tion. Therefore function variables are also replaced using general second-order substitutions[1] like $\pi := \{F/w_2, G/\text{minus}(w_1, w_1), H/\text{plus}(w_1, w_2), D/\text{succ}(w_2)\}$ obtained by matching Φ with the new conjecture $\psi := \pi(\Phi) = \pi(\mathbf{H} \rightarrow \mathbf{C}) =$

---

[1] A second-order substitution replaces a n-ary function variable V with a (first-order)

$$\bigl(\forall u \; minus(u, u) \equiv minus(plus(x, u), plus(x, u))\bigr)$$
$$\rightarrow minus(y, y) \equiv minus(plus(succ(x), y), plus(succ(x), y)).$$

AX' is instantiated yielding the set of axioms $\pi(AX') = \{\pi(1), \pi(2), \pi(3)\}$:

$minus(succ(x), succ(x))$	$\equiv$ $minus(x, x)$	$\pi(1)$
$plus(succ(x), y)$	$\equiv$ $succ(plus(x, y))$	$\pi(2)$
z	$\equiv z$	$\pi(3)$

If the proof P shall be reused for proving ψ from the set of axioms $\pi(AX')$ by instantiating the schematic proof P' with π, we obtain $\pi(P')$ as

$minus(y, y)$	$\equiv$ $minus(plus(succ(x), y), plus(succ(x), y))$	$\pi(\mathrm{C})$
$minus(y, y)$	$\equiv$ $minus(plus(succ(x), y), plus(succ(x), y))$	Replace ($\pi(1)$)
$minus(y, y)$	$\equiv$ $minus(succ(plus(x, y)), succ(plus(x, y)))$	Replace ($\pi(2)$)
$minus(y, y)$	$\equiv$ $\underline{minus(plus(x, y), plus(x, y))}$	Replace ($\pi(1)$)
$minus(y, y)$	$\equiv$ $\underline{minus(y, y)}$	Replace ($\pi(\mathrm{H})$)
$\underline{minus(y, y)}$	$\equiv$ $minus(y, y)$	Replace ($\pi(3)$)
	TRUE	Reflexivity

But $\pi(P')$ is *not* a proof: Although each statement is implied by the statement in the line below, the *justifications* of the inference steps are not valid. E.g. the first *replace*($\pi(1)$)-step is illegal because the *position* of the replacement (the former first argument of F) does not exist in $\pi(\mathrm{C})$. Also the *replace*($\pi(2)$)-step is illegal, as it actually consists of *two* replacements which have to be performed separately at different positions. Finally, the *replace*($\pi(3)$)-step is redundant and should be omitted. Thus $\pi(P')$ has to be *patched* for obtaining a proof of ψ.

Such a machine-found proof can be processed subsequently, e.g. by translating it into natural language to obtain a proof similar to those found in mathematical textbooks [5]. Furthermore proofs can be worked up for planning or synthesis tasks if plans or programs should be extracted form proofs [1]. These applications require a *specific* proof, i.e. it is not enough to know that *some* proof exists.

2 An Algorithm for Patching Proofs

We first illustrate the patching of a single replacement step: Let t be a schematic term (containing function variables) which can be modified by *one* replacement step with a certain schematic equation $l \equiv r$ at a certain position p (i.e. $t|_p = l$) yielding another schematic term $t' = t[p \leftarrow r]$ as the result. The function call *patch_positions*(t, p, π) yields for an arbitrary second-order substitution π a list of positions $[p_1, ..., p_k]$ such that the instance $\pi(t)$ can be modified by a (possibly empty) *sequence* of k replacement steps with the instantiated equation $\pi(l) \equiv \pi(r)$ at the positions $p_1, ..., p_k$ such that the instance $\pi(t')$ is obtained.

$$
\begin{array}{ccc}
t & \xrightarrow{\;\; l \equiv r \;\;}_{1} & t' \\
{\scriptstyle \pi}\Big\downarrow & & \Big\downarrow{\scriptstyle \pi} \\
\pi(t) & \xrightarrow{\;\; \pi(l) \equiv \pi(r) \;\;}_{k} & \pi(t')
\end{array}
$$

term where special *argument variables* $w_1, \dots, w_n$ serve as the formal parameters of V. For instance π replaces the binary function variable D with the function symbol succ, where the first argument w_1 of D is ignored.

function *patch_positions* $(t,\ p,\ \pi)$: *list of positions in* $\pi(t)$
if $p = \epsilon$ **then return** $[\epsilon]$
else let $p =: ip'$; $t =: X(t_1, ..., t_n)$; $[p_1, ..., p_k] := patch\_positions(t_i, p', \pi)$
   if $X \in dom(\pi)$ **then** $s := \pi(X)$; $[q_1, ..., q_m] := \{q \in Pos(s) \mid s|_q = w_i\}$
      return $[q_1 p_1, ..., q_1 p_k, ..., q_m p_1, ..., q_m p_k]$
   else return $[ip_1, ..., ip_k]$ **fi fi**

Theorem 1. [6] *Let* t, l, r *be schematic terms,* p *a position in* t *and* π *a second-order substitution. If* $t|_p = l$ *then the call* $patch\_positions(t, p, \pi)$ *terminates yielding a list of positions* $[p_1, ..., p_k]$ *in* $\pi(t)$ *such that for* $i, j \in \{1, ..., k\}$
1) if $i \neq j$ *then there is no* $p \in \mathbb{N}^*$ *such that* $p_i = p_j p$ *or* $p_j = p_i p$,
2) $\pi(t)|_{p_j} = \pi(l)$ *and* $\pi(t)[p_1, ..., p_k \leftarrow \pi(r)] = \pi(t[p \leftarrow r])$.

The goal of a (schematic) proof is a so-called *sequent* $H \to C$ with a conjunction H of hypotheses each of which is of the form $\forall u^*\ t_1 \equiv t_2$ and a conclusion C of the form $s_1 \equiv s_2$. A *proof* of $H \to C$ (from a set of axioms AX) is a list $[S_0, j_1, S_1, j_2, ..., S_n]$ of sequents S_i (with $S_0 = H \to C$) and *justifications* j_i, where the latter contain the information how the next sequent is derived. A proof is constructed by applying the following inference rules,[2] where σ is a first-order substitution, p is a position in C and $m \in \{"AX", "H"\}$:

Reflexivity
$$\frac{}{[H \to t \equiv t]}$$

Replacement
$$\frac{[H \to C[p \leftarrow \sigma(r)] \mid L]}{[H \to C[p \leftarrow \sigma(l)], \langle p, \sigma, u^*, l, r, m \rangle, H \to C[p \leftarrow \sigma(r)] \mid L]}$$

    if either $\forall u^*\ l \equiv r \in AX$ and $m = "AX"$
      or $\forall u^*\ l \equiv r \in H$, $dom(\sigma) \subseteq u^*$ and $m = "H"$.

function *patch_proof* $(P',\ \pi)$: *proof*
if $P' = [H \to C]$ **then return** $[\pi(H) \to \pi(C)]$
else let $P' =: [H \to C, \langle p, \sigma, u^*, l, r, m \rangle, H \to C' \mid L]$
  $P_\pi := patch\_proof([H \to C' \mid L],\ \pi)$
  if $\pi(C) \neq \pi(C')$ **then** $[p_1, ..., p_k] := patch\_positions(C, p, \pi)$
    $\sigma_\pi := \{v/\pi(\sigma(v)) \mid v \in dom(\sigma)\}$; $C_k := \pi(C')$
    for $j := k$ **downto** 1 **do** $C_{j-1} := C_j[p_j \leftarrow \sigma_\pi(\pi(l))]$
      $P_\pi := [\pi(H) \to C_{j-1}, \langle p_j, \sigma_\pi, u^*, \pi(l), \pi(r), m \rangle \mid P_\pi]$ **od fi**
  return P_π **fi**

In a replacement step an *instance* $\sigma(l) \equiv \sigma(r)$ of an equation $l \equiv r$ is applied, but in the patched proof only (instances of) the equation $\pi(l) \equiv \pi(r)$ are available. However, we can use the first-order substitution $\sigma_\pi := \{v/\pi(\sigma(v)) \mid v \in dom(\sigma)\}$ in *patch_proof* because $\pi(\sigma(u)) = \sigma_\pi(\pi(u))$ holds for each (schematic) term u.

Now we can compute $P_\pi := patch\_proof(P', \pi)$ to obtain a patched proof for

---

[2] Proofs can be extended to deal with arbitrary formulas instead of equations only if we define further inference rules. Then H may also contain additional conditions.

the conjecture $\psi = \pi(\mathrm{H}) \to \pi(\mathrm{C})$ from Section 1:

$$
\begin{array}{ll}
\mathsf{minus}(y,y) \equiv \mathsf{minus}(\mathsf{plus}(\mathsf{succ}(x),y),\mathsf{plus}(\mathsf{succ}(x),y)) & \pi(\mathrm{C}) \\
\mathsf{minus}(y,y) \equiv \mathsf{minus}(\underline{\mathsf{succ}(\mathsf{plus}(x,y))},\mathsf{plus}(\mathsf{succ}(x),y)) & \text{Replace } (\pi(2)) \\
\mathsf{minus}(y,y) \equiv \mathsf{minus}(\mathsf{succ}(\mathsf{plus}(x,y)),\underline{\mathsf{succ}(\mathsf{plus}(x,y))}) & \text{Replace } (\pi(2)) \\
\mathsf{minus}(y,y) \equiv \mathsf{minus}(\underline{\mathsf{plus}(x,y),\mathsf{plus}(x,y)}) & \text{Replace } (\pi(1)) \\
\mathsf{minus}(y,y) \equiv \underline{\mathsf{minus}(y,y)} & \text{Replace } (\pi(\mathrm{H})) \\
\hspace{2.5cm} \textbf{TRUE} & \text{Reflexivity}
\end{array}
$$

Compared to the schematic proof P from Section 1, the first *replace*(1)-step is eliminated while the *replace*(2)-step is doubled. The test $\pi(C) \neq \pi(C')$ in *patch_proof* is merely an optimization to avoid redundant steps like $replace(\pi(3))$, cf. Section 1.

Theorem 2. [6] *Let P' be a proof of the sequent $H \to C$ from the set of axioms AX. Then for each second-order substitution π, the call patch_proof(P', π) terminates and yields a proof P_π of $\pi(H) \to \pi(C)$ from $\pi(AX)$.*

Summing up, we have presented an algorithm that constructs a proof for the instantiated conjecture from a schematic proof of a schematic conjecture and a second-order substitution. This allows us to exploit the full flexibility of second-order instantiations for the reuse procedure developed in [7]. Thus more conjectures are (formally) similar than by just instantiating function variables with function symbols, i.e. the applicability of a schematic catch is increased. Furthermore the obtained proofs may be more flexible, i.e. the reusability of a schematic catch is increased.

Acknowledgements. This work was supported under grants no. Wa652/4-1,2,3 by the DFG within the focus program "Deduktion". We thank Jürgen Brauburger, Stefan Gerberding, Jürgen Giesl and Martin Protzen for helpful comments and discussions.

References

1. J. L. Bates and R. L. Constable. Proofs as Programs. *ACM Transactions on Programming Languages and Systems*, 7(1):113–136, 1985.
2. T. Ellman. Explanation-Based Learning: A Survey of Programs and Perspectives. *ACM Computing Surveys*, 21(2):163–221, 1989.
3. F. Giunchiglia and T. Walsh. A Theory of Abstraction. *Artificial Intelligence*, 57:323–389, 1992.
4. R. P. Hall. Computational Approaches to Analogical Reasoning: A Comparative Analysis. *Artificial Intelligence*, 39:39–120, 1989.
5. X. Huang. PROVERB: A System Explanining Machine-Found Proofs. In *Proc. of 16th Annual Conference of the Cognitive Science Society*, Atlanta, Georgia, 1994.
6. T. Kolbe and C. Walther. Patching proofs for reuse. Technical report, Technische Hochschule Darmstadt, 1994.
7. T. Kolbe and C. Walther. Reusing Proofs. In A. Cohn, editor, *Proceedings of the 11th European Conference on Artificial Intelligence, Amsterdam*, pages 80–84. John Wiley & Sons, Ltd., 1994.

Adapting to Drift in Continuous Domains (Extended Abstract)

Miroslav Kubat[1] and Gerhard Widmer[2]

[1] Institute for Systems Sciences, Johannes Kepler University Linz,
A-4040 Linz, Austria
[2] Department of Medical Cybernetics, University of Vienna, and
Austrian Research Institute for Artificial Intelligence, A-1010 Vienna, Austria

1 Introduction: The Algorithm FRANN

Perhaps the first systems capable of tracking concept drift in supervised incremental learning were STAGGER (Schlimmer and Granger, 1986), FLORA (Kubat, 1989), and IB3 (Aha et al., 1991). Learning in time-varying environments has also been studied in the framework of genetic algorithms (Smith, 1987) and in adaptive-control applications of neural networks (Narendra & Parthasarathy, 1990). The latest descendant of the FLORA family is FLORA4 (Widmer, 1994).

Whereas most drift-tracking algorithms were oriented towards learning with symbolic attributes, the system FRANN, to be briefly described here, was developed for *numeric* domains with complex decision boundaries. Its algorithm is summarized in Table 1: a time window slides over a series of examples. From the window examples, a *radial-basis function (RBF) network* is created. At each step, N new examples are added to the window. Concept drift is recognized by decreased classification accuracy, as measured on the last M incoming examples.

Like the FLORA systems, FRANN possesses a *window-size* heuristic which decides about the potential need for shrinking the window (i.e., deleting from it some of the oldest examples) when concept drift is suspected. It combines two variables: the current window size and the number of erroneous classifications on the last M examples. Basically, old examples are deleted when the window is too large and/or when the number of errors grows (signalling concept drift).

2 Experimental Design

To assess the performance of FRANN, we compared its classification accuracy to that of FLORA4 (Widmer, 1994) on several artificial data sets, all of which simulate more or less extreme forms of concept drift. For FRANN, symbolic attributes are turned into numeric ones by replacing each attribute-value pair with a boolean variable and substituting 0 for *false* and 1 for *true*. To be able to deal with numeric attributes, FLORA4 was extended with a simple generalization operator that implements Michalski's *closing interval rule*. FLORA4 thus approximates numeric concepts by axis-parallel hyperrectangles.

Below is the characterization of the test domains. For each of them, 10 training sequences of 200 random examples were generated; the underlying concept

Table 1. Algorithm of the system FRANN

---

1. Put N new examples in the window;
2. Apply hill-climbing search to find the best subset of the examples in the window, and create an RBF network from them; determine the output-layer weights;
3. Use the network for the classification of both training and testing data and collect the respective statistics;
4. Use the window-size heuristic to decide about deletions of older examples from the window, carry out the deletions and return to step 1.

---

was made to change after every 50 examples. Predictive accuracy was tested after every learning step on a set of 100 independent test examples. The reported results are averages over the 10 sequences. To ensure a stable learning environment, the positive and negative examples in the training sets alternated.

1. SINE. *Abrupt concept drift, noise-free examples.* The examples were uniformly distributed in the 2-dimensional unit square $[0,1] \times [0,1]$, with coordinates $[x, y]$. In the first context, all points lying below the curve $y = \sin(x)$ are classified as positive and the rest as negative. In the second, the classification is reversed;

2. CIRCLES. *Gradual concept drift, noise-free examples.* Four contexts are determined by four circles partially overlapping each other. Points inside the circles are positive and the points outside the circles are negative;

3. GAUSS. *Abrupt concept drift, noisy examples.* Positive examples from the domain $R \times R$ are normally distributed around the center $[0,0]$ with standard deviation 1. Negative examples are normally distributed around $[2,0]$ with standard deviation 4. The overlap of the two classes models noise. At each point of context change, the classification is reversed;

4. SYMBOLIC. *Abrupt concept drift, symbolic noise-free examples.* Here we used the series of symbolic concepts from Schlimmer and Granger (1986);

5. MIXED. *Abrupt concept drift, mixed boolean/numeric noise-free examples.* The examples are described by two boolean attributes and two numeric attributes from the domain $[0, 1]$. After each context change, the classification is reversed.

3 Results

Figures 1 through 5 compare the accuracies of FRANN vs. FLORA4 in the above domains. Points where the target concept changes are marked by vertical lines. Figures 4 and 5 give the results of different versions of FRANN: the curves marked *FRANN 1/3* represent the accuracy of FRANN when the number of hidden units in the RBF is 1/3 of the current window size; *FRANN 2/3* and *FRANN 3/3* are to be interpreted analogously. All other figures plot *FRANN 1/3*. FRANN is superior to FLORA4 in most of the numeric problems because FLORA4 approximates numeric concepts by axis-parallel hyperrectangles, while FRANN's RBF networks represent concepts by a set of weighted prototypes.

In the noisy GAUSS experiment, FLORA4 scores well in the first context, but worse in the second; this is probably because the first concept—positive examples

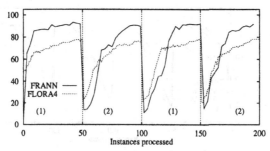

Fig. 1. Experiment 1 — Abrupt drift, noise-free examples.

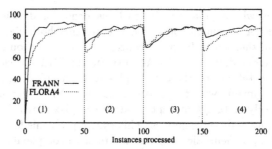

Fig. 2. Experiment 2 — Gradual drift, noise-free examples.

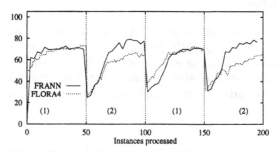

Fig. 3. Experiment 3 — Abrupt drift, noisy examples.

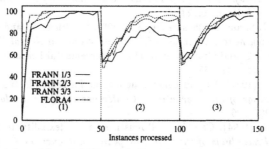

Fig. 4. Experiment 4 — Abrupt drift, symbolic noise-free examples.

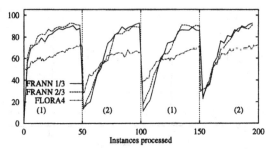

Fig. 5. Experiment 5 — Abrupt drift, mixed symbolic-numeric examples.

around a center with standard deviation 1—is 'denser' and easier to represent in closed form. FRANN, on the other hand, represents both classes explicitly via prototypes and thus learns both the concept and its inversion equally easily.

In the symbolic domain, FLORA4 outperforms FRANN because of its crisp concept representation and the more sophisticated windowing mechanism.

In the experiments with the 'mixed data', FRANN is significantly superior. Here, the underlying target concept is rather complex in relation to the number of attributes and training examples. This causes problems for FLORA4, whose window adjustment heuristic considers the relative complexity of hypotheses.

4 Conclusion

The experiments demonstrate that FRANN compares favourably with FLORA4 in the presence of concept drift. Learning is possible from examples described by symbolic as well as by numeric attributes, and because of its representation formalism (RBF networks, which realize a kind of prototype weighting scheme) FRANN is particularly effective in capturing concepts with nonlinear boundaries.

References

Aha, D., Kibler D., and Albert, M.K (1991). Instance-Based Learning Algorithms. *Machine Learning* 6:37–66.

Kubat, M. (1989). Floating Approximation in Time-Varying Knowledge Bases. *Pattern Recognition Letters*, 10:223–227.

Narendra, K.S. and Parthasarathy, K. (1990). Identification and control of dynamical systems using neural networks. *IEEE Transactions on Neural Networks* 1:4–27.

Schlimmer, J.C. and Granger, R.H. (1986). Incremental Learning from Noisy Data. *Machine Learning* 1, 317–354.

Smith, R.E. (1987). Diploid genetic algorithms for search in time varying environments. *Proceedings of an International Conference on Genetic Algorithms and their Applications*, 202–206.

Widmer, G. (1994). Combining Robustness and Flexibility in Learning Drifting Concepts. In *Proceedings of the 11th European Conference on Artificial Intelligence, ECAI94*, Amsterdam. Chichester: Wiley & Sons.

Parallel Recombinative Reinforcement Learning (Extended Abstract)

Aristidis Likas, Konstantinos Blekas and Andreas Stafylopatis

Computer Science Division
Department of Electrical and Computer Engineering
National Technical University of Athens
157 73 Zographou, Athens, Greece

1 Introduction

This paper presents a population-based technique that is suitable for function optimization in high-dimensional binary domains. The method allows an efficient parallel implementation and is based on the combination of genetic algorithms and reinforcement learning schemes. More specifically, a population of probability vectors is considered, each member corresponding to a reinforcement learning optimizer. Each probability vector represents the adaptable parameters of a team of stochastic units whose binary outputs provide a point of the function state space. At each step of the proposed technique the population members are updated according to a reinforcement learning rule and then recombined in a manner analogous to traditional genetic algorithm operation. Special care is devoted to ensuring the desirable properties of sustained exploration capability and sustained population diversity. We shall denote the proposed population-based approach as *Parallel Recombinative Reinforcement Learning (PRRL)*.

2 Genetic Algorithms and Reinforcement Learning

Genetic algorithms in their traditional formulation assume a population of binary strings and at each generation step new members are created by applying genetic operators to appropriately selected strings. Following the principle of 'survival of the fittest', strings are selected for reproduction with probability proportional to their corresponding fitness (function value). The selected strings (usually two) can be combined using the single-point crossover or the uniform crossover operator. In addition, the basic genetic algorithm employs a mutation operator which introduces randomness in the search process by randomly flipping some bit values in the population strings. The main problem with simple genetic algorithms is that they exhibit a fast convergence behavior, mainly due to the effects of the selection scheme and the crossover operator. Population diversity can be introduced only through mutation but its effectiveness is rather limited [?]. This property of gradual decrease of diversity in the population limits the sustained exploration capabilities of simple genetic algorithms, since it inhibits continuing search which is necessary in solving difficult problems.

In the reinforcement learning approach to function optimization [?, ?] a point in the function space is generated according to a probabilistic distribution, and the corresponding function value which is called *reinforcement* is provided to the system. The parameters of the distribution are updated so as to direct the search towards the generated point (high reinforcement), or make the point less probable to be sampled again in the upcoming trials (low reinforcement). In applications to problems defined on binary domains, the simplest reinforcement learning scheme considers that the point $y = (y_1, \ldots, y_n)$ $(y_j \in \{0, 1\})$ to be evaluated at each step is generated by a team of *Bernoulli units*. Each Bernoulli unit j determines the component y_j of the output vector through a Bernoulli selection with probability $p_j = f(w_j)$, where $W = (w_1, \ldots, w_n)$ is the vector of adjustable parameters (weights) and f is a sigmoid function of the form

$$p_j = f(w_j) = 1/(1 + \exp(-w_j)) \tag{1}$$

REINFORCE algorithms [?] constitute an important class of reinforcement learning algorithms. We shall consider the application of a REINFORCE algorithm to a team of Bernoulli units. At each step, the weights are updated as follows:

$$\Delta w_j = \alpha_j(r - \bar{r})(y_j - p_j) - \delta w_j \tag{2}$$

where α_j is the learning rate factor, r is the reinforcement signal delivered by the environment and $\bar{r}$ is a standard of comparison. The latter is computed as a trace of past reinforcement values $\bar{r}(t) = \gamma\bar{r}(t-1) + (1-\gamma)r(t)$, the parameter γ being a decay rate positive and less than 1 (taken equal to 0.9 in our experiments). The decay term $-\delta w_j$ $(0 < \delta < 1)$ in (2) provides sustained exploration capability.

In our scheme the vectors of probabilities $P_i = (p_{i1} \ldots, p_{in})$ constitute the members of the population. For this reason the weights w_j have been discarded and the necessary updates are performed directly on the probability values, according to the following equation which is derived from (1) and (2):

$$p_{ij} := f\left((1 - \delta)\ln\frac{p_{ij}}{1 - p_{ij}} + \alpha_{ij}(r_i - \bar{r}_i)(y_{ij} - p_{ij})\right) \tag{3}$$

3 The Recombinative Scheme

According to the PRRL approach, each population member i is a vector P_i of probabilities p_{ij} $(i = 1, \ldots, p, \ j = 1, \ldots, n)$ that constitute the state of a reinforcement learning optimizer. At each step, first a reproduction procedure combines the probability vectors and a new generation of vectors is created. Then a sampling procedure is performed and p points $Y_i = (y_{i1}, \ldots, y_{in})$ $(i = 1, \ldots, p)$ of the function space are generated with Bernoulli selection using the corresponding probabilities p_{ij}. The fitness r_i of each point Y_i is evaluated and a reinforcement update of the probabilities takes place using equation (3) so that the search is guided towards promising regions of the space. At each generation step, the p new population members are created as follows: for each current member i we apply crossover with probability p_c. In this case, another member

k is randomly selected and a single-point crossover is performed between the two probability vectors. The crossover point t $(1 \leq t \leq n-1)$ is randomly selected. In order to retard the decrease of population diversity, the new probability vector P_l is constructed so as to remain as close as possible to the vector P_i: if $t \leq \lceil n/2 \rceil$, then we set $p_{lj} = p_{kj}$ for $j = 1, \ldots, t$ and $p_{lj} = p_{ij}$ for $j = t+1, \ldots, n$, otherwise, we set $p_{lj} = p_{ij}$ for $j = 1, \ldots, t$ and $p_{lj} = p_{kj}$ for $j = t+1, \ldots, n$.

Reproduction is followed by the sampling (based on the new probability vectors) and evaluation phase for the p population members. Then, the reinforcement update takes place for each population member according to the learning rule of equation (3). The reinforcement comparison $\bar{r}_i$ is computed seperately for each population slot i as a weighted average of prior reinforcement values r_i. At the beginning of the genetic search, all the components of the probability vectors are set equal to 0.5, i.e., no initial knowledge is provided to the learning system. Sustained exploration is achieved with the introduction of the decay term, but we still have a lack of *sustained diversity* due to the effects of crossover.

In order to avoid *genetic drift* we have not employed the 'survival of the fittest' principle, but a uniform random selection scheme concerning all population members. Also, as already mentioned, each current population member is replaced by the closest of the two generated children, so as to avoid a serious disruption of the states of local optimizers. A third technique that has proved very effective in maintaining population diversity is based on the notion of *apathy* [?]. According to the latter approach, some population members remain apathetic for some generations, in the sense that they cannot be selected for recombination. Apathetic members cannot change their state through crossover, but can be chosen for crossover by other members of the population. We put a member into apathy whenever it generates a point of the state space of higher fitness than the best value achieved so far. If for a specified number of steps no better solution is obtained the member is brought back to the active state.

4 Experimental Results

The test problems that were selected for evaluating the effectiveness of our approach are versions of the order-3 deceptive problem, the same as in [?]. The problems considered assume eight subfunctions of the type described in the table below, thus the dimension of the binary space is 24. The fitness of each 24-bit string results from the sum of the corresponding values of the eight subfunctions.

x	000	001	010	011	100	101	110	111
$f(x)$	28	26	22	0	14	0	0	30

The first of the examined problems (called the *tight problem*) is a concatenation of eight subfunctions, where the first three bits of the string are the domain of the first subfunction, the next three bits are the domain of the second subfunction and so on. In the second problem (called the *loose problem*) bits 0, 8, and 16 constitute the domain of the first subfunction, bits 1, 9 and 17 are the domain of the second subfunction and so on. Both problems have 255 local maxima and only one global maximum with value 240. In all experiments the algorithm was terminated when the global maximum was found or when 5000 generations had been performed concidering different sizes of the population p. In the latter case the result was the best solution found during the search. For each population size 30 experiments were performed using different seed values for the random number generator. The values of the parameters were $\alpha = 0.05$ and $\delta = 0.02$, whereas the crossover probability was $p_c = 1$ and the maximum allowed value for the apathy counter was set equal to 150.

	p	PRRL		PRL	
		Success (%)	Avg. nb. steps	Success (%)	Avg. nb. steps
	8	46.6	1900	20.0	
Tight	16	80.0	1019	46.6	1133
problem	32	100.0	640	93.3	1097
	64	100.0	530	100.0	1143
	8	33.3	2746	28.0	3287
Loose	16	62.0	1896	49.3	3010
problem	32	88.3	1465	75.0	2559
	64	100.0	1249	93.3	1973

The results summarized in the table illustrate the performance of PRRL in comparison with a Parallel Reinforcement Learning (PRL) scheme, that considers a population of independent reinforcement learning optimizers operating without crossover. The results represent the percentage of cases in which the global maximum was found, as well as the average number of generation steps required to find it. Experiments were also carried out using a simple genetic algorithm that was successful in very few cases. Our results show that the proposed technique offers clear advantage over both conventional genetic algorithms and parallel reinforcement learning. It is clear that the PRRL algorithm is characterized by a high degree of parallelism since all operations can be performed simultaneously for all members of the population.

References

1. Ackley, D. H., *A Connectionist Machine for Genetic Hillclimbing*, Kluwer Academic Publishers, 1987.
2. Kontoravdis, D., Likas, A. and Stafylopatis, A. *A Reinforcement Learning Algorithm for Networks of Units with Two Stochastic Levels*, Proceedings ICANN-92, vol. I, pp. 143-146, Brighton, United Kingdom, 1992.
3. Mahfoud, S. W. and Goldberg, D. E., *Parallel Recombinative Simulated Annealing: A Genetic Algorithm*, IlliGAL Tech. Report No. 92002, Univ. of Illinois at Urbana-Champaign, July 1993.
4. Williams, R.J. and Peng, J., *Reinforcement Learning Algorithms as Function Optimizers*, Proceedings of the International Joint Conference on Neural Networks, Washington DC, vol. II, pp. 89-95, 1989.

Learning to Solve Complex Tasks for Reactive Systems
(Extended Abstract)

Mario Martin and Ulises Cortés

Dept. Llenguatges i Sistemes Informàtics
Universitat Politècnica de Catalunya
Pau Gargallo 5, 08028, Barcelona (Catalunya), Spain

1 Introduction

One important issue in reactive systems research is the learning ability to solve complex tasks. There has been several mechanisms proposed to make reactive systems learn, for instance [4] [5] (for a review see [2]). These mechanisms consist in obtaining, usually by means of a trial and error process guided by a reinforcement signal, a mapping between the set of possible perceptions and the set of actions, that describes an adequate behavior.

Unfortunately, these methods are not well suited to learn how to solve complex tasks. A task whose solution is formed by a long chain of actions can be roughly considered as complex. It is hard to solve by trial and error these tasks because the number of possible chains of actions to consider grows exponentially with the length of the chain solution.

We propose that this limitation can be overcome by previously learning to solve more simple but general tasks, useful to solve the initial problem. This approach implies a *constructivist* or *developmental* learning process in which the system steps over different stages. In each stage, characterized by the set of actions the system knows, it learns new behaviors that can be used as new complex actions to solve more complex tasks in a higher stage.

This article develops this proposal with a new reinforcement learning algorithm. The new algorithm is necessary due to the inadequacy of other known algorithms in learning general behaviors in our framework.

2 Learning to Solve Complex Tasks

In this section, the features for a good learning method to solve complex tasks are discussed and considered in order to build our learning mechanism.

When trying to develop a mechanism for learning to solve *complex tasks* by reinforcement, we must understand the difficulties they present. The complexity of a task is mainly conditioned by the number of actions that composes the solution (actions executed until a positive or negative reinforcement is obtained) and by the number of perceptual states the system must deal with.

Without any initial knowledge, the reactive system has only the trial and error procedure for trying to solve any problem. It is known that it is very hard *learn by trial and error how to accomplish goals which imply a long sequence of actions.* Then, the complexity of the task comes from the adequacy of the actions the system can take to solve it: an adequate set of general actions lets solving the problem in a few steps. The system, built with a set of primitive actions can find some tasks too difficult to be learnt from the beginning just with it. In our approach, the system solves this impasse learning to solve more general actions which will let it improve its skills. In order to learn these new actions, the system will try to learn how to solve intermediate general tasks. The behaviors learnt to solve these tasks can be included as new available actions to the initial set. The intermediate tasks the system must learn in order to solve a complex task will be given opportunely to the system by a teacher.

On the other hand, it is known from the debate Ginsberg-Chapman [1] that, for solving complex tasks, it is necessary to *generalize* situations. In complex tasks, the number of different situations is too large to consider a response for each of them. Chapman [1] shows that a limited world perception by means of "deictic" sensors can be indicated for reactive systems solving complex tasks, producing a very profitable generalization process. This limited perception implies that the information of the environment the system has, is always partial, *incomplete and ambiguous.* Most learning mechanisms, for instance Q-learning [5], suppose the system having complete information about its environment. When these methods have to deal with incomplete information or ambiguities, the problem of "perceptual aliasing" [6] appears, disabling the learning process. Then, an important feature that our learning process must show is the ability for learning with limited world perception in order to solve complex tasks.

Finally, the reinforcement is given to solve a concrete problem, but an important feature the learning mechanism must show is the ability of learning *general behaviors* (not particular solutions) to solve problems. Problems with the same general goal ought to be solved with the same learnt method. This feature is not usually fulfilled in reinforcement learning mechanisms. They usually learn how to solve a problem in a concrete environment.

3   A new learning mechanism

In this section, we expose the basic learning mechanism developed according to the requirements obtained in the previous section. This mechanism must be able to learn general behaviors and to deal with incomplete information. In order to build a hierarchy of behaviors, it also must show a good performance in learning *reliable* behaviors from a crisp reinforcement signal.

The architecture developed by the learning process consists in an indexed table. The entries of the table are formed by the state of the sensors (situation). The output consists in statistical information to compute the "probability" to obtain, for each executable action, a positive reinforcement. This statistical information is composed of the number of successes and failures occurred depending on the execution or not execution of each action in that situation.

The probability to get a positive reinforcement when executing an action a, given the actual situation s, is estimated as follows [1]:

$$P(s,a) = \frac{S\_A(s,a)}{S\_A(s,a) + F\_A(s,a)} - \frac{S\_NA(s,a)}{S\_NA(s,a) + F\_NA(s,a)}$$

$S\_A(s,a)$ is the number of successes when action a has been executed in situation s, $S\_NA(s,a)$ is the number of successes obtained when the action has not been executed, $F\_A(s,a)$ is the number of failures when the action has been executed, and $F\_NA(s,a)$ is the number of failures when the action has not been executed.

With all this considerations, the algorithm for learning behaviors will consist in the execution of the best action (defined as the one with a higher probability of leading to a positive reinforcement) for every situation faced until there's an error or a success. When this process has finished, the learning consists in to actualize and weight the statistics involved in the choosing of actions (see details in [3]). The learning stops when the system does not learn anything in a predetermined number of new problems presented. In this case, the knowledge of how to solve the task is kept in a policy table which will be used to increase the system's set of actions and to achieve solving more complex problems.

The proposed basic algorithm presents several differences respect to other well known reinforcement learning mechanisms, specially with the TD family ([4], [5]), mainly in the learning of reliable and general behaviors under perceptual aliasing (see details in [3]).

According to section 2, the possibility of learning to solve a complex task is subordinated to the set of actions available to the system. In order to achieve the needed skills for facing complex tasks, a teacher must guide the learning process giving a sequence of general tasks to be learnt.

For every task the teacher must know the following information: the objective state (when the positive reinforcement signal must be given), when an error has occurred (i.e. the maximum number of actions to be taken to solve a problem and the dangerous states) and finally, the set of useful actions to solve a task from the whole set of possible actions, as well as the subset of sensors.

From this knowledge, a hierarchy of behaviors is built up until the system can solve the desired complex task. An example of this construction is exposed in the next section.

4 Experiences

A set of experiments have been performed in order to test the performance of the learning mechanism. The environment selected is the "blocks world", that fulfills the required conditions of complexity: incrementally complex tasks can be proposed, the perceptual system gives incomplete or ambiguous reports, the

---

[1] This measure has been compared with other ones and presents a more successful performance. Particularly, this measure uses information about the number of successes when the action has not been activated, given a estimation more similar to a correlation that a conditional probability.

initial set of actions is too simple to solve complex tasks, etc. This environment has also been used previously by Chapman [1] and Whitehead and Ballard [6] to show the possibilities and drawbacks of reactive systems in complex domains.

The system has been designed for this environment with a set of sensors that reports ambiguous information of the world, and a very simple set of actions. The sensory system is composed of: foveal vision, peripheral vision, visual memory, proprioceptive sensors and tactile sensors. The initial set of actions of the system is composed of very primitive actions over the visual focus and over a mechanical hand (see details in [3]).

The complex task the system must solve consists in putting an unlocalized block of a given color in the position where a mark lies. Initially, the system only has the mentioned set of actions and sensors. Then, a solution to the problem will be composed of a large chain of actions that, as we have seen in section 2, is the main problem that prevents learning from a trial and error procedure.

In order to solve the problem with our method, we will suppose that the teacher provides a set of general subtasks to learn which allows to solve the initial problem. In our case, the teacher proposes to learn the following general tasks: Searching for a block, Moving the hand to the visual focus, Removing the top of a stack and Grasping a block. The learning process for each of these tasks generates a behavior that can be considered as a new general action. These new actions increase the repertory of actions of the system and can be used for solving more complex problems.

The experimental results (see details in [3]) are positive for the proposed task and indicates that complex tasks as the "fruitcake" problem [1] can be solved in this way.

5   Conclusions

This research has lead us to show that it is possible, for reactive systems, to learn how to solve complex tasks. The task proposed in the "blocks world", considering the initial set of actions the system knows, is not currently resolvable by any other direct learning method. The success of our proposal is due to the use of a learning mechanism robust to ambiguous information, that can improve the abilities of the system, learning new behaviors to solve general tasks.

References

1. D. Chapman. Penguins can make cake. *AI Magazine*, 10:45–50, winter 1989.
2. L.P. Kaelbling. *Learning in Embedded Systems*. MIT Press, 1993.
3. M. Martin. Learning to solve complex tasks by reinforcement: A new algorithm. Technical report, Universitat Politècnica de Catalunya, 1995.
4. R.S. Sutton. Learning to predict by the methods of temporal differences. *Machine Learning*, 3(1):9–44, 1988.
5. C. Watkins. *Learning from delayed rewards*. PhD thesis, Cambridge Univ., 1989.
6. S.D. Whitehead and D.H. Ballard. Learning to percive and act by trial and error. *Machine Learning*, 7:45–83, 1991.

Co-operative Reinforcement Learning By Payoff Filters
(Extended Abstract)

Sadayoshi Mikami[1][2], Yukinori Kakazu[1], and Terence C. Fogarty[2]

[1] Hokkaido University, Kita-13, Nishi-8, Sapporo, 060, Japan
[2] University of the West of England, Coldharbour Lane, Frenchay, Bristol, BS16 1QY, UK

Abstract. This paper proposes an extension of Reinforcement Learning (RL) to acquire co-operation among agents. The idea is to learn filtered payoff that reflects a global objective function but does not require mass communication among agents. It is shown that the acquisition of two typical co-operation tasks is realised by preparing simple filter functions: an averaging filter for co-operative tasks and an enhancement filter for deadlock prevention tasks. The performance of these systems was tested through computer simulations of n-persons prisoner's dilemma, and a traffic control problem.

1 Introduction

Reinforcement Learning (RL) is widely used in robot learning fields [1][2]. One reason for the feasibility to robotic applications is that it requires minimum information to develop policies; only state observation and real-valued payoff feedback are necessary, and these two types of information are always guaranteed in real-world robotic applications. This paper is aiming at extending single RL to acquire co-operation among multiple-agents, preserving the simplicity of RL that it can learn from minimal information.

The approach is to acquire global co-operation from locally exchanging payoff signals. Since communication of payoff is realised by asynchronously broadcasting and listening to scalar values, it is a minimal realistic way of co-ordinating co-operation. The main idea proposed here is to apply a filter to gathered payoffs to generate a payoff that will guide the agent to behave co-operatively. It is shown that spatial averaging and enhancement filters will give global co-operation over agents, and that the type of acquired co-operation is predicted by the type of the filter.

2 Related Works

Achieving co-operation among robots is actively studied in the field of Decentralised AI (for example[3]) and Artificial Life (for example [4]). Although there are some works that use RL to acquire robot co-operation (for example [5][6]), these works do not include communication amongst agents, which is necessary to learn complicated interactions, or they require huge real-time communication capabilities so that physical implementation into distributed robots is difficult. This paper is the first attempt to realise communication-based co-operative RL under realistic constraints.

The idea of applying filter to payoff has been widely used in RL Temporal filters, such as TD algorithms [1], are well studied. However, spatial filters amongst agents, such as the one proposed in this paper, have not been investigated. The learning of an iterated N-persons prisoner's dilemma game is employed for testing co-operative RL, since it is one of the commonly used co-operative problems and there are many GA based approaches to acquire co-operation such as [7].

3 Payoff Filters

We define a minimal co-operative agent (robot) as the one that performs the following trial-communication-learn cycle:

1. get sensory data as a state vector,
2. perform an action according to the state,
3. evaluate immediate local payoff r_i , where i is the index of an agent,
4. broadcast the normalised payoff to neighbours,
5. monitor the broadcasted message, and
6. apply filter to the broadcasted message, and invoke RL by using the filtered payoff.

The objectives of co-operation are generally classified into two types: one is to maximise one common objective function, and another is to maximise each objective function where they interfere with each other as the result of sharing an environment.

For the former type of co-operation, we consider the case where the global objective function is a summation of local payoffs $\sum_{\forall i} r_i$ and where each agent has an identical local payoff at the state where the global function is maximised. In this case, the payoff filter should easily be implemented by averaging local payoffs as

$$r' = \sum_{\forall j} r_j / N,\qquad(1)$$

where r' is the payoff given to RL and N is the number of neighbouring agents. It is proven that if neighbours of agents overlap with each other, the filter maximises the global objective function.

A more important case is the latter type of co-operation. We deal with the case where each agent's objective is to achieve its goals one after another, that are specified as the tops of a payoff landscape. In this case, a dead-lock over many agents may take place at states where climbing up directions for payoff functions differs for each agent (Fig.1). Thus, to co-operate corresponds to exiting this dead-lock situation. This is achieved by encouraging one agent to achieve its goal, and the other agents to give way. Representing this strategy into a payoff filter, it should be written as the following spatial enhancement filter:

$$r' = \begin{cases} r + \alpha|r|, & \text{if } (\sum_{\forall j} r_j / N) \le r; \\ r - \alpha|r|, & \text{otherwise,} \end{cases} \qquad (2)$$

where α is a positive enhancement factor.

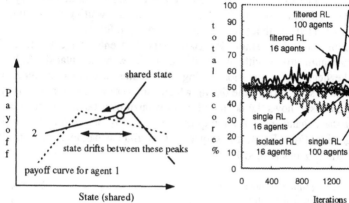

Fig. 1. Deadlock on two agents.   Fig. 2. Score curve by the simulation 1.

4   Simulation 1: Learning N-Persons Prisoners Dilemmaa

This experiment was conducted to illustrate the effect of an averaging filter (Eq.1). Each agent is allocated a cell in a NxN lattice. Each agent performs either an action 0 (co-operative) or 1 (selfish). Action 0 gives score $10/N^2$ to the agent whereas action 1 gives score $30/N^2$ to the agent and subtracts score $10/N^2$ from all the agents. The objective is to maximise the total scores over agents.

Three simulations were conducted: (1) single agent RL, (2) average filtered RL with 4 overlapping neighbours, and (3) average filtered RL with 4 isolated neighbours. TD(0) was used for the RL algorithm and its learning parameter was set to 0.02. Fig.2 shows the percentage of the global score plotted against iteration times. It is shown that the overlapping average filtered RL could achieve co-operation. It should be pointed out that the convergence speed will be faster if the size of the scope of the neighbourhood is relatively bigger.

5   Simulation 2: Conflict Resolution in Traffic Signal Control

To test the enhancement filter (Eq.2), a simple traffic control simulation was employed, where each traffic signal was controlled by RL. It should be noted that an optimisation of the traffic flow at a junction may sometimes cause congestion at the other junctions. This is the typical deadlocking situation and it is therefore a good example of testing the ability of conflict resolution.

The simulation contains 3x3 lattice roads. A car arrives at the edge of randomly chosen road approximately once every 2 seconds, and it runs 33km/h. At a junction, it decides its new direction according to the probability associated with that junction.

The number of cars that are allowed to stay on the roads is limited, by which we can specify the traffic density. More precise descriptions are found in [7].

Each junction is associated with an agent that controls two phases (go or stop) of its 4 signals. At each unit time (around every 15 seconds), it decides whether to change its signal phase or not, according to the output from RL. The state provided to RL is the signal phases of its 4-neighbouring junctions. Immediate local payoff is provided by the multiplication of -1 by the number of cars waiting at the junction during a unit time. TD(0) with learning factor 0.5 was used for RL.

Pure random controllers, single RL controllers, and enhancement filtered RL controllers communicating with 4 neighbourhood, were simulated. Table 1 summarises the degree of congestion during 40 minutes in simulation time. The number in the table shows total time during which cars were waiting for signals. The number in parenthesis shows the degree of improvement over random controllers. It is shown that the enhancement filter improved the quality of control over a wide range of congestion. From Fig.3, it is shown that the filter is parameter α sensitive, and the appropriate α lies around 1.5.

Table 1. Total waiting time (minutes) over 40 minutes simulation.

Maximum cars	Random	Single RL (%)	Filtered RL (%)
10	108	79 (137)	78 (138)
30	343	213 (161)	200 (171)
50	551	346 (159)	329 (167)
60	654	405 (162)	391 (168)

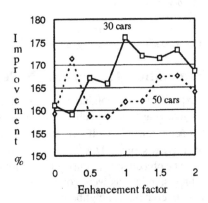

Fig. 3. Performance improvement against enhancement parameter.

References

1. Sutton, R.S., ed.: Reinforcement Learning, Kluer Academic (1993)
2. Connell, J.H., Mahadevan, S.: Robot Learning, Kluer Academic (1993)
3. Steels. L.: Co-operation between Distributed Agents through Self-Organisation, Decentralised AI, North-Holland (1990)
4. Arkin, R.C.: Integration of Reactive and Telerobotic Control in Multi-agent Robotic System, From Animals to Animats 3, MIT Press (1994) 473 478
5. Mataric, M.J.: Learning to Behave Socially, From Animals to Animats 3, MIT Press (1994) 453 462
6. Tan, M.: Multi-Agent Reinforcement Learning, Proc. Machine Learning (1993) 330 337
7. Fogel, D.B.: Evolving Behaviors in the Iterated Prisoner's Dilemma, Evolutionary Computation, 1 1 (1993)
8. Mikami, S., Kakazu, Y.: Genetic Reinforcement Learning for Co-operative Traffic Signal Control, IEEE World Congress on Computational Intelligence (1994) 223 228

Automatic Synthesis of Control Programs by Combination of Learning and Problem Solving Methods (Extended Abstract)

Wolfgang Müller and Fritz Wysotzki

Fraunhofer-Institute for Information and Data Processing
Branch Lab for Process Optimization
Kurstr. 33, D-10117 Berlin, email: wmueller@epo.iitb.fhg.de

1 Introduction

An especially important field of today's research in Machine Learning is the control of complicated dynamical processes in environment and technology which cannot (or only partly) be modelled mathematically. Seen from the cognitive point of view there are close similarities to the problem of skill acquisition.

A series of learning methods for generating control trajectories – in the state space of a process – for real time applications have been investigated in AI and Neural Information Technology in recent years (e.g. BOXES [3, 5], CART [2], ASE/ACE [1]). In general, these approaches have disadvantages in real time applications and their complexity may increase dramatically if more than two different control actions are to be applied. Furthermore an apriori splitting of the state space is needed for some of them.

This article outlines an approach for generating a series of optimal control actions by combining learning with simple problem solving methods, which has a suitable real time behaviour and can handle a larger number of different discrete control actions.

2 Control of dynamic processes based on classification learning (learning control)

This approach tackles the splitting problem of the state space into boxes as a task of classification learning. As class an optimal control action will be attached to points in the state space assuming a set of discrete ones to be available. Generally, the approach proposed in this paper consists of the following steps: (a) generation of a training data set: the optimal control action is *not determined by an expert* [8] but by a problem solver using an empirical evaluation function for process states having its extremum at the target (goal) area; (b) splitting the state space automatically into subareas with unique control actions attached by learning: this way one obtains a classifier which is able to assign an optimal control action to any point of the state space in extremely short execution time (the steps (a) and (b) can be carried out off-line, where time is not critical); (c) automatic generation of control trajectories in real time by applying the classifier recursively (see also [8, 4]).

As an *example control problem* the roll axis stabilization (as reaction to disturbances) of a communication satellite in orbit with respect to its position to the earth axis was taken. Here the real control process was substituted by an appropriate simulator developed by MBB Munich within the ESPRIT- project Statlog [9] (see also [4]). The position manoeuvres are carried out by thruster torques delivering a set of discrete control actions the application of which consumes fuel. Therefore the control task is to hold the satellite axis in a certain small target interval of its attitude angle consuming as little fuel as possible (i.e. performing a small number of small control actions). The state space of the process is defined by the attitude angle ϕ of the satellite and its rate $\dot{\phi}$. The target area of control is some region around $\phi = 0$ and $\dot{\phi} = 0$ (some maximal value of $|\phi|$ is given which must not be exceeded). There are additional variables $q_1, q_2, \dot{q}_1, \dot{q}_2$ describing oscillations of the two solar generators of the satellite which influence the process states especially the rate $\dot{\phi}$. They are treated as "hidden parameters" and their influence could be considered as noise or taken into account by including a history of preceding states in the definition of current state.

As a *training set* a set of n points $m_j \in M, j = 1, 2, ..., n, m_j = (\phi_j, \dot{\phi}_j)$ in the two dimensional state space, was selected at random and to each of them an "optimal" control action $f_{j\,opt}$ assigned. This action was chosen automatically from a given (finite) set of executable control actions $P_f = \{f_1, f_2, ..., f_q\}$ by an empiric evaluation function $F : X \longrightarrow R$, which maps the state space X into the set of real numbers. The applied control actions f_i produce for each point m_j a set $\overline{M}_j$ of temporary successor points

$$\overline{m}_{j,i} = g(m_j, f_i), \ \overline{m}_{j,i} \in \overline{M}_j, \ i = (1, 2, ..., q). \tag{1}$$

$\overline{M}_j$ is computed by the simulator, and must be found by experimentation with the process if no model is available. The optimal control action f_{opt} for point m_j is that f_i for which the evaluation function at the next state generated by applying this action becomes a minimum:

$$F(\overline{m}_{j\,opt}) = \min_{i \in \{1,...,q\}} F(\overline{m}_{j,i}) = \min_{i \in \{1,...,q\}} F(g(m_j, f_i)) = F(g(m_j, f_{j\,opt})) \tag{2}$$

By carrying out this procedure for all $m_j \in M$ a learning data set $M' = \{m_j, f_{j\,opt}\}, \ j = 1, 2, .., n$ is formed. This is gradient descent, known to give a local optimal solution in general but a global optimal solution, too, in the case of a convex evaluation function having exactly one extremal point (greedy behaviour).

For the current process a convex F can be chosen. The simplest is

$$F(\phi, \dot{\phi}, f) = \phi^2 + \kappa\dot{\phi}^2 + \varepsilon \mid f \mid, \tag{3}$$

the sum of a weighted (squared) Euclidean distance from the origin and a weighted penalty function. $\mid f \mid$ stands for the value of the control torque and is proportional to the amount of fuel consumption. The weights κ and ε were optimized due to some criteria for achieving a good control performance (i.e. small amount of fuel consumption and some desirable properties of control curves). A satisfying parameter combination found after systematic experimentation is $\kappa = 10^{-2}, \varepsilon = 8.10^{-10}$. These parameter values were also confirmed by theoretical considerations using a simple process model based on the equations of motion for ϕ and $\dot{\phi}$.

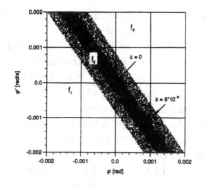

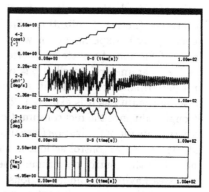

Fig.1. State space split into three subareas of different control actions, $f_1 = 20Nm$, $f_2 = 0Nm$, $f_3 = -20Nm$

Fig.2. Plot over time of satellite's behaviour. 5 control torques ($\pm$ 5, $\pm$ 2.5, 0 Nm) used. Tex is the sum of disturbance and control torque

Figure 1 is the graphical representation of the state space after assigning an optimal control action to each point assuming three different control actions available[1]. The state space contains three homogeneous subareas due to different optimal control actions. Two different evaluation functions ($\varepsilon = 0$, $\varepsilon = 8.10^{-10}$) are presented to demonstrate the effect of the penalty function. To the constructed training set the classification algorithms CAL5 and DIPOL [3, 6, 7] were applied to *develop optimal decision functions*. There were no significant differences in control performance. Of course other methods of classification learning can be applied, too. A learned classification function ψ now delivers an optimal control trajectory from any state s into the set of target states S_{goal} by means of the recursion equation $\Psi(s) = $ if $s \in S_{goal}$ then s else $\Psi(\psi_s(s))$, where ψ_s is the output (optimal control action) of the classifier ψ for input state s and $\psi_s(s)$ the result of appplication of ψ_s to s (the next state).

The classifiers developed by CAL5 and DIPOL were built into the simulator instead of the original PD-controller and the simulation results were compared with those of the original controller.

3 Results

An example of simulated satellite's behaviour is shown in figure 2. The applied disturbance was 0.05 Nm per 50 sec. The system is stabilisized by a decision tree controller developed by CAL5 immediately after the disturbance has disappeared. The main results of a number of experiments (varying the type of F and the generalization level of the classifiers) are: 1) The above introduced control method using learned classifications of process states by optimal control

---

[1] Note that applying a "control action" $f = 0Nm$ (i.e. doing nothing) corresponds to leaving the system move according to its inherent dynamics governed by the equations of motion.

actions shows better results in most cases than an appropriate "classical" PD
-controller (better stabilization, smaller number of control actions, i.e. less fuel
consumption). Experiments in which a state history of length 4 was included
in the definition of a state and performed to take into account the influences of
"hidden parameters" (oscillations of solar arrays) resulted in even better control performance of the classifier. Errors of the classifiers lead to some amount
of suboptimality as it is expected. 2) The parameters of the evaluation function
strongly influence the fuel consumption and the control performance. At present,
experiments for optimization (learning) of these parameters are performed in our
lab. 3) The more control actions in the range from +20Nm to -20Nm were used
the better the control performance became. 4) In the case of more complicated
processes having "forbidden regions" in the state space the definition of a convex evaluation function is no longer possible and more general problem solving
methods have to be applied. This will be a topic of future research.

Acknowledgements: Thanks are due to C. Bruehe for carrying out the experiments.

References

1. Barto, A. G, Sutton, R. S.,Anderson, C. W.: Neuronlike Adaptive Elements That
   Can Solve Difficult Learning Control Problems, IEEE Transactions on Systems,
   Man and Cybernetics, Vol. SMC-13, Number 5, pp 835 - 846, 1983
2. Connell, M. G./Utgoff, P. E.: Learning to Control a Dynamic Physical System,
   AAAI 87, Seattle, pp 456 - 460, 1987
3. Michie, D.; Spiegelhalter, D.J.; Taylor, C.C.: Machine Learning, Neural and Statistical Classification. Ellis Horwood, Hertfordshire, U.K., 1994
4. Michie D. : Experiments in Rule Based Control, Beyond the Neural Pradigm for
   Machine Learning. Proc. of JSAI meeting, Tokyo, June 1991
5. Michie, D.,Chambers, R. A.: BOXES as a Model of Pattern-formation, Towards
   a Theoretical Biology, Vol. 1, Prolegomena, C. H. Waddington (Ed.), Edinburgh:
   Edinburgh Univ. Press, pp 206 - 215, 1968
6. Mueller,W.; Wysotzki,F.: Automatic Construction of Decision Trees for Classification in Annals of Operation Research 92,Moser, K.,Schader M. (Eds) J.C. Baltzer
   AG Science Publishers, Wijdenes, Netherlands, 1994, pp.231-247
7. Schulmeister, B.; Wysotzki, F.: Piecewise Linear Classifier DIPOL92, Proc. of the
   ECML 94, 7th European Conference on ML, 1994
8. Sammut, C,; et al : Learning to fly. Machine Learning, Proc. of the Ninth International Workshop ML 92, Morgan Kaufmann Publishers,San Mateo, CA
9. Statlog Deliverable 2.2 : Description and Specification of the Simulation Program
   of Spacecraft-Dynamics, ESPRIT Project 2170, Statlog (Comparative Testing of
   Statistical and Logical Learning), Munich, 1991

Analytical Learning Guided by Empirical Technology: An Approach to Integration (Extended Abstract)

Nikolay I. Nikolaev[1] and Evgueni N. Smirnov[2]

[1] Department of Computer Science, American University in Bulgaria
Blagoevgrad 2700, Bulgaria, e-mail: nikolaev@nws.aubg.bg
[2] Institute for Information Technologies, Bulgarian Academy of Sciences
Acad.G.Bonchev Str.,blok 29A,Sofia 1113,Bulgaria,e-mail: smirnov@iinf.bg

Abstract. An approach to integration of the analytical and empirical learning strategies for solving the theory-based concept specialization problem is proposed. The emphasis is on learning correct concepts within conjunctive description language isolated from supplied domain theory. In order to overcome expressive limitations of such language, the analytical learning component is guided by a specific empirical version space technology. The approach learns incrementally a correct pure conjunctive or DNF concept definition in dependance on the domain theory.

1 Introduction

The theory-based concept specialization problem (TBCS), defined in [1] and [5], requires a more general formulation for practical applications. There are given: (1) a first order domain theory DT from DNF rules with consequents from one predicate; (2) a goal concept GC defined by the domain theory; (3) a finite set TS of examples described in pure conjunctive first order language, which are positive examples of the concept GC, and are positive and negative examples of an unknown concept under study SC (SC is specialization of GC). The task is to find a complete and consistent definition of the concept under study SC, described in DNF first order language, that is implied by the positive and not by the negative examples in context of the domain theory.

Most of the previous works deal only with specific cases of the above TBCS problem and solve these cases by integrated empirical-after-analytical learning approaches: IOE [1], MECEA [5]. They produce a complete and consistent pure conjunctive concept definition of SC when the domain theory determines a sufficiently expressive concept description language. When the language expressivenes is insufficient (i.e., the definition of SC is DNF), these approaches fail. This situation arises when in the process of incremental learning either of the two anomalies occurs [4]; (1) incompleteness: a positive example is encountered, but the current concept definitions cannot be generalized to admit it without admitting negative training; (2) inconsistency: a negative example is encountered, but the current concept definitions cannot be specialized to reject it without also rejecting positive training.

This paper proposes an improved approach, called Multiple Explanation-based learning guided by the Space Fragmenting Algorithm (MESFA), for solving the TBCS problem. The idea is to direct the analytical learning with a specific empirical technology that allows the production of correct concepts regardless of the expressiveness of the concept description language isolated from domain theory. The novelty is that all hypothetical concept definitions within the language are considered as a disjunctive version space. The disjunctive version space is representable by its boundary sets and admits incremental learning with the Space Fragmenting algorithm [4] Space Fragmenting forms a correct, complete and consistent, pure conjunctive or DNF definition of the concept under study.

2 Representation and Ordering of the Concepts

The concept definitions in MESFA are expressed in a concept description language (CDL_{DT}) isolated from supplied domain theory DT:

Definition 1. *The concept description language is a finite set of concept definitions:* $CDL_{DT} =\{ c \mid E \in P(TS), DT \cup E \vdash c$ *such that* $DT \cup c \vdash GC \}$, *where* $P(TS)$ *is powerset of the training set TS and the examples E are subset of TS.*

The finiteness of CDL_{DT} is achieved by a proper theorem prover. Between the elements of CDL_{DT} a relation generalized concept ordering holds. The generalized concept ordering is reflexive, anti-symmetric tautologic and transitive:

Definition 2. *A concept c_2 ($c_2 \in CDL_{DT}$) is more general than or equally general to another concept c_1 ($c_1 \in CDL_{DT}$), written $c_2 \succeq c_1$, in the context of the domain theory DT if and only if the entailment $DT \cup c_1 \vdash c_2$ holds.*

It is proven[1] that all subsets C of CDL_{DT} possess the properties convexity and definiteness [2]. Therefore, the subsets of CDL_{DT} are representable by boundary sets and admit version space learning. MESFA distinguishes by supporting all hypothetical concept definitions in form of a disjunctive version space:

Definition 3. *The set C is a disjunctive version space (DVS_{SC}) of the concept under study SC if and only if it consists of all concept definitions c ($c \in CDL_{DT}$) that are not implied by the negative examples E_N of SC in context of the domain theory:* $C = (DVS_{SC})$ *iff* $C = \{ c \in CDL_{DT} \mid DT \cup E_N \nvdash c \}$.

With regard to the TBCS problem, definitions 1 and 2 suggest that the disjunctive version space consists of conjunctive concept definitions. Each conjunctive definition summarizes some positive training (*relaxed completeness*) while remaining consistent with all of the negative training (*strict consistency*). The disjunctive concept definitions are built of conjunctive ones that are: first, not mutually related by generalized concept ordering; and second, the conjunctive definitions together satisfy the completeness requirement.

---

[1] The complete paper with proofs and examples is available from the authors.

The disjunctive version space $\mathcal{DVS}_{SC}$ of the concept under study SC is represented by its maximal and minimal boundary sets G and S:

$$\mathcal{DVS}_{SC} \langle G,S \rangle = \{\ c \in CDL_{DT} \mid \exists s_i \in S,\ \exists g_i \in G \text{ such that } s_i \preceq c \preceq g_i\ \}$$

The set G is the set of maximally general concept definitions in CDL_{DT}, which are not implied by the negative examples E_N of the concept SC:

$$G = \{\ g_i \in CDL_{DT} \mid DT \cup E_N \nvdash g_i \text{ such that } \neg\exists g \in CDL_{DT}: g_i \prec g,\ DT \cup E_N \nvdash g\ \}$$

The set S consists of elements s_i that are more specific than some corresponding g_i. Every s_i is the minimally specific concept definition implied by all elements of its set S_i. Every S_i is a set of minimally specific concept definitions s_{ik} implied by the positive examples E_{Pi} of SC that also imply g_i:

$$S_i = \{\ s_{ik} \in CDL_{DT} \mid DT \cup E_{Pi} \vdash s_{ik},\ g_i \succeq s_{ik} \text{ such that } \neg\exists s: s \prec s_{ik},\ DT \cup E_{Pi} \vdash s\ \}$$
$$S = \{\ s_i \in CDL_{DT} \mid DT \cup S_i \vdash s_i,\ g_i \succeq s_i \text{ such that } \neg\exists s: s \prec s_i,\ DT \cup S_i \vdash s\ \}$$

For some g_i ($g_i \in G$) the sets of positive examples E_{Pi} implying them may be empty. The corresponding s_i to these g_i are specified with the symbol $\perp$ (a bottom element implying all elements in the ordered CDL_{DT}), which is an empty definition that classifies every example as negative.

3 Scenario for Learning with MESFA

MESFA is developed employing the Space Fragmenting algorithm. The Space Fragmenting algorithm supports a disjunctive version space of all hypothetical concept definitions of SC. It carries out efficient incremental learning by manipulating only the boundary sets G and S.

Initialize: $G = \{\ (\text{ antecedent of } GC\ )_1\ \}$ $\qquad S = \{\ (\perp)_1\ \}$

For each next example update $\mathcal{DVS}_{SC} \langle G,S \rangle$ into a new one $\mathcal{DVS}'_{SC} \langle G',\ S' \rangle$:

In case of a positive example e_p :

$G' = G$

$S' = \{\ s'_i \in CDL_{DT} \mid DT \cup S'_i \vdash s'_i,\ g'_i \succeq s'_i \text{ such that} \neg\exists s: s \prec s'_i,\ DT \cup S'_i \vdash s\ \}$

where for each i:

if $g_i \succeq e_p$ then $S'_i = \{\ s'_{ik} \in CDL_{DT} \mid DT \cup \{s_i\} \cup \{e_p\} \vdash s'_{ik},\ g'_i \succeq s'_{ik}$
$\qquad\qquad\qquad$ such that $\neg\exists s: s \prec s'_{ik},\ DT \cup \{s_i\} \cup \{e_p\} \vdash s\ \}$

if $g_i \nsucceq e_p$ then $S'_i = \{s_i\}$

In case of a negative example e_n :

$G' = \{\ g'_i \in CDL_{DT} \mid DT \cup \{e_n\} \nvdash g'_i,\ DT \cup \{g'_i\} \vdash g_i$
$\qquad\qquad$ such that $\neg\exists g \in CDL_{DT}: g'_i \prec g,\ DT \cup \{e_n\} \nvdash g,\ DT \cup \{g\} \vdash g_i\ \}$

$S' = \{\ s'_i \in CDL_{DT} \mid DT \cup \{s'_i\} \vdash s_i,\ s'_i \preceq g'_i$
$\qquad\qquad$ such that $\neg\exists s: s \succ s'_i,\ DT \cup \{s\} \vdash s_i,\ s \preceq g'_i\ \}$

MESFA always terminates when the explanations of the positive examples are different from the explanations of the negative ones. This is due to the avoidance of the incompleteness and inconsistency anomalies. Two terminations of the learning process are possible. First, when the elements g_i of G are identical with their corresponding s_i of S, a *completely learned definition* of the concept SC is generated. Second, when the boundary sets are not focused, *an incompletely learned definition* of the concept SC is generated. Depending on the power of the set S, the resulting concept definition is pure conjunctive or DNF.

4 Comparisons and Relevance to Other Works

MESFA and IOE [1] are two approaches to solving the TBCS problem. IOE uses domain theory to build an explanation only from the positive examples and forms definitions of SC by an empirical technique over the explanation. A shortcoming of IOE is that it is not capable of learning from negative examples, and therefore it cannot be applied in real domains where the concepts are DNF rather than pure conjunctive.

MESFA is close to the Hirsh's combination of empirical and analytical learning with IVSM [3]. His integrated approach syntactically processes analytically generalized definitions of the examples. This and the kinds of learned concept definitions suggest that MESFA proposes a more general form of learning.

5 Conclusion

A novel approach, called Multiple Explanation-based learning guided by the Space Fragmenting Algorithm (MESFA), was presented. The main advantage of MESFA is that it generates a pure conjunctive or DNF concept definition in an incremental manner in dependence on the provided first order domain theory.

The MESFA approach allows careless design of the domain theory, requires a small number of examples and few computation resources, and may construct a correct definition for several unknown concepts SC.

References

1. N.S.Flann and T.G.Dietterich, A Study of Explanation-Based Methods for Inductive Learning, *Machine Learning*, 4(2):187-226, 1989.
2. H.Hirsh, Theoretical Underpinnings of Version Spaces, In *Proc. of the Twelfth Int. Joint Conf. on Artificial Intelligence*,IJCAI-91, pp.665-670, Sydney, Australia,1991.
3. H.Hirsh, Generalizing Version Spaces, *Machine Learning*, 17(1):5-46, 1994.
4. E.N.Smirnov, Space Fragmenting– A Method For Disjunctive Concept Acquisition, In B.duBoulay and V.Sgurev, eds., *Artificial Intelligence V– Methodology, Systems, Applications*, pp.97-104, Elsevier Science Publishers, 1992.
5. E.N.Smirnov and N.I.Nikolaev, Multiple Explanation-Based Learning Guided by the Candidate Elimination Algorithm, In P.Jorrand and V.Sgurev, eds., *Artificial Intelligence VI– Methodology, Systems, Applications*, pp.247-256, World Scientific Publ., Singapore, 1994.

A New MDL Measure for Robust Rule Induction (Extended Abstract)

Bernhard Pfahringer *

Austrian Research Institute for Artificial Intelligence
Schottengasse 3, A-1010 Vienna, Austria
E-mail: bernhard@ai.univie.ac.at

Abstract. We present a generalization of a particular Minimum Description Length (MDL) measure that so far has been used for pruning decision trees only. The generalized measure is applicable to (propositional) rule sets directly. Furthermore the new measure also does not suffer from problems reported for various MDL measures in the ML literature. The new measure is information-theoretically plausible and yet still simple and therefore efficiently computable. It is incorporated in a propositional FOIL-like learner called KNOPF.

1 Introduction

The *Minimum Description Length (MDL) Principle* [Rissanen 78], sometimes also called the *Minimum Message Length (MML) Principle*, has been successfully applied in Machine Learning, both for inducing decision trees [Quinlan 93, Forsyth 93], for constructing new attributes [Pfahringer 94a], and in ILP [Muggleton et al. 92]. But recently also some problems with MDL were discovered [Quinlan 94]. Section 2 will describe these problems. A new MDL measure applicable to propositional rule learning aimed at overcoming these problems will be introduced in section 3. Section 4 very briefly discusses a propositional FOIL-like learning algorithm using this new MDL measure as both a stopping criterion for rule induction and as a criterion to choose between different rule sets, especially to choose between sets of pruned rules and sets of unpruned rules. Section 5 lists open problems and further research directions.[2]

2 MDL in Rule Learning and its Problems

Empirical induction is always faced with the problem of *overfitting* the data, especially in the presence of noise or irrelevant attributes. The MDL principle is a possible solution as it measures both the simplicity and the accuracy of a particular rule set in a common currency, namely in terms of the number of

---

* Financial support for the Austrian Research Institute for Artificial Intelligence is provided by the Austrian Federal Ministry of Science and Research. I would like to thank Gerhard Widmer and Johannes Fürnkranz for help with this paper.

[2] For a long version of this paper including empirical results see [Pfahringer 94b].

bits needed for encoding. The precise MDL formula used by [Quinlan 93] for simplifying rule sets is:

$$Cost = TheoryCost + log_2 \left(\binom{C}{FP} \right) + log_2 \left(\binom{NC}{FN} \right)$$

In this formula $TheoryCost$ is an estimate for the number of bits needed to encode the theory. C is the total number of training examples covered by the theory, FP is the number of false-positive examples, NC is the total number of training examples not covered by the theory, and FN is the number of false-negative examples.

So what are the problems with that formula? [Quinlan 94] states two and we would like to add an additional one: (1) the formula for computing exception cost is symmetric; (2) if the class to be learned is significantly in the majority (minority), induced theories tend to under-generalize (over-generalize), especially in the presence of noise and with small numbers of learning examples; (3) when learning from lots of examples in the presence of noise, there is still a tendency to fit the noise.

All these problems with the above formula stem from the fact that this formula is just an approximation of the generic MDL principle as defined above. It does not estimate encoding cost of *all* examples with respect to a given theory but instead computes a kind of penalty for wrong classifications only! So the remedy would be to look for a formula that is more faithful to the MDL principle.

3 An alternative MDL formula

[Forsyth 93] introduces a well-performing formula for encoding decision trees:

$$cost(tree) = \Sigma cost(leaf_i)$$
$$cost(leaf_i) = d_i + e_i * n_i$$

where d_i is the depth of the leaf in the tree, n_i is the number of examples covered by the leaf, and e_i is average entropy of the outcome at that leaf defined by:

$$e_i = -(p * log(p) + (1 - p) * log(1 - p))$$

where p is the proportion of positive examples covered by $leaf_i$.[3] Note that $e_i * n_i$ is the number of bits needed by an optimal or 'Huffman' coding of the classifications at $leaf_i$ in terms of the relative frequencies of positive and negative examples at $leaf_i$.

We have modified this formula for coding sets of propositional rules. The essential differences are a cost estimate for examples not covered by the rule set and an information-theoretically plausible encoding cost for the rules themselves. Note that the ordering of rules is significant in this encoding, meaning that an example is covered by the first of all the rules matching it. We define the cost of a rule set as follows:

---

[3] $0 * log(0)$ is defined to equal 0.

$$cost(ruleset) = n_{nc} * e_{nc} + \Sigma cost(rule_i)$$
$$cost(rule_i) = rc_i + e_i * n_i$$

where n_{nc} is the total number of examples not covered by the rule set and e_{nc} is the according entropy of this set. The complexity of a single rule is accounted for by rc_i. This is an estimate of the coding cost for the body of the rule. Assuming a total number N_{pt} of tests that could possibly be used by a rule and adopting Quinlan's idea for encoding exceptions we can define the cost for encoding the body of a rule as follows. The cost for choosing $Length_i$ tests out of N_{pt} possible can be estimated as:

$$rc_i = log_2 \left(\binom{N_{pt}}{Length_i} \right)$$

The new estimate certainly solves problem 3 as coding cost for *all* examples is estimated (remember that the entropy of a rule e_i is multiplied by the total number of examples covered by that rule n_i as part of the cost of a rule). Problem 2 is only partially solved as errors are penalized in a totally different way. We do not get consistently over- or under-generalizing behavior, but with too small training sets the empty theory can result from induction. But this is a consequence of using MDL itself: enough positive data has to support a rule, otherwise the intrinsic cost of the rule will outweigh the classification advantage gained by this rule. Regarding the so-called problem 1, the new formula is even more symmetric in the sense that in principle positive and negative rules could be freely mixed in an induced theory. For practical reasons one would have to add one more bit per rule for encoding the decision part (positive or negative) of each rule, if one wanted to take advantage of that property.

To summarize, the new formula measures cost for encoding all the training examples in terms of the theory (the single rules), classification errors are accounted for at a per-rule basis using local entropies, and complexity of rules is estimated in an information-theoretically plausible way. Furthermore this formula still is symmetric with respect to *negative* theories.

4 Algorithmic Usage of the new Formula

For empirical testing of the new formula we have implemented a kind of propositional FOIL [Quinlan & Cameron-Jones 93] called KNOPF. Right now KNOPF is restricted to purely symbolic 2-class learning problems. It is completely free of user-settable parameters. The MDL principle is used in two ways: firstly as a stopping criterion when inducing a single rule set and secondly for choosing the final rule set out of a number of induced rule sets.

The first pruning strategy is *correctness preserving*: the pruned rule will not cover more negative examples than the unpruned rule. The second strategy just maximizes the difference $p - n$ of positive and negative examples covered by the rule. MDL also implicitly judges the presence of noise: When a set of correctness preservingly pruned rules is chosen as the final result, we can assume noise-free data and vice versa.

5 Conclusions, Related Work, and Further Research

We have defined a new MDL measure for rule sets and incorporated it into the inductive learner KNOPF. This new measure is information-theoretically plausible in the way it encodes the theory and the examples and it also gives good experimental results. But there are still a lot of open questions and opportunities for improvement, e.g. finding better coding schemas, improving search, generalize the formula, so that it will be applicable to numbers and variables, and take into account new attributes produced by constructive induction.

In summary, the new MDL measure proposed in this paper is a generalization of the formula given in [Forsyth 93] applicable to sets of rules, it overcomes the deficiences of the formula used in C4.5, and it is simpler (and may also be more reliable for small training sets) than the coding scheme used by [Muggleton et al. 92].

References

[Forsyth 93] Forsyth R.S.: Overfitting Revisited: An Information-Theoretic Approach to Simplifying Discrimination Trees, in JETAI 6(3), 1994.

[Muggleton et al. 92] Muggleton S., Srinivasan A., Bain M.: Compression, Significance, and Accuracy, in Sleeman D. and Edwards P.(eds.), Machine Learning: Proceedings of the Ninth International Workshop (ML92), Morgan Kaufmann, San Mateo, CA, pp.338-347, 1992.

[Pfahringer 94a] Pfahringer B.: CiPF 2.0: A Robust Constructive Induction System, Proceedings of the Workshop on Constructive Induction and Change of Representation, 11th International Conference on Machine Learning (ML-94/COLT-94), New Brunswick, New Jersey., 1994.

[Pfahringer 94b] Pfahringer B.: A New MDL Measure for Robust Rule Induction, Österreichisches Forschungsinstitut für Artificial Intelligence, Wien, TR-94-29, 1994. (also available electronically as ftp://ftp.ai.univie.ac.at/papers/oefai-tr-94-29.ps.Z)

[Quinlan & Cameron-Jones 93] Quinlan J.R., Cameron-Jones R.M.: FOIL: A Midterm Report, in Brazdil P.B.(ed.), Machine Learning: ECML-93, Springer, Berlin, pp.3-20, 1993.

[Quinlan 93] Quinlan J.R.: C4.5: Programs for Machine Learning, Morgan Kaufmann, San Mateo, CA, 1993.

[Quinlan 94] Quinlan J.R.: The Minimum Description Length Principle and Categorical Theories, in Cohen W.W. and Hirsh H.(eds.), Machine Learning: Proceedings of the Eleventh International Conference (ML94), Morgan Kaufmann, San Mateo, CA, 1994.

[Rissanen 78] Rissanen J.: Modeling by Shortest Data Description, in Automatica, 14:465-471, 1978.

Class-Driven Statistical
Discretization of Continuous Attributes
(Extended Abstract)

M. Richeldi and M. Rossotto

CSELT (Centro Studi e Laboratori Telecomunicazioni) - Torino, ITALY

Abstract. Discretization is a pre-processing step of the learning task which offers cognitive benefits as well as computational ones. This paper describes StatDisc, a statistical algorithm that supports supervised learning by performing class-driven discretization. StatDisc provides a concise summarization of continuous attributes by investigating the data composition, i.e., by discovering intervals of the numeric attribute values wherein examples feature distribution of classes homogeneous and strongly contrasting with the distribution of other intervals. Experimental results from a variety of domains confirm that discretizing real attributes causes little loss of learning accuracy while offering large reduction in learning time.

1. Introduction

Discretization is a pre-processing step of the learning task. It is performed by dividing the values of a continuous attribute into a small number of intervals, where each interval is mapped to a discrete symbol. The discretization process constructs an abstraction space over the continuous attributes. Learning in this new abstraction space has several advantages. First, it allows for effective feature construction. Second, dependence analysis between continuous and nominal attributes can be performed. Finally, discretization results in substantial speed-up for the inductive process, i.e., it cuts down the computational cost of the learning task [1].

Simple methods for discretizing a continuous attribute have appeared in the statistical literature. [2] compares three techniques: the *equal-width discretization*, the *equal-frequency discretization*, and the *maximum marginal entropy discretization*. methods. They all require the user to specify the number of intervals into which each attribute will be partitioned. These methods are easy to implement but performs poorly in many situations. The main reason for their failure is their inherent "class-blindness", i.e., they ignore the class of examples when partitioning the training set. A classification algorithm will be no longer able to separate examples of different classes that have been grouped into the same interval. Conversely, a discretization that takes into account class distribution of examples, termed a *class-driven discretization technique*, will retain examples of different classes into different intervals and produce the right partitions.

2. Class-driven discretization techniques

Class-driven methods achieve a good discretization by approximating the class distribution of the continuous attribute. True class distributions are estimated by relative class frequencies. Training examples are first sorted according to their value of the attribute being discretized. Each training example is regarded as a single-element interval. Then, an association measure is applied continuosly to ascertain whether adjacent intervals feature dissimilar relative class frequencies. If they do not, intervals are merged. As a result, the method yields high intra-interval uniform and high inter-interval different partitions.

Different association measures can be used to compare relative class frequencies of adjacent intervals. Catlett's D2 [1] exploits information gain ratio and results are quite reasonable. A more effective approach has been introduced by Kerber in [3]. Kerber proposes the statistical measure χ^2 to evaluate the similarity of relative class frequencies of adjacent intervals. The χ^2 statistic is used to compare the class distribution of each single interval (observed distribution) with the class distribution that would be expected if the pair of intervals were independent of the class attribute (hypotethical, or expected distribution). If the hypothesis of independence is confirmed, the intervals should be merged, since their relative class frequencies are very similar. Conversely, the difference in the class distribution of the two intervals is statistically significant, and the intervals should remain separated.

Chi-Merge is robust with respect to class-blind methods but suffers a major shortcoming: it is inclined to produce more intervals when there are more examples. When the observed distribution is fixed, the χ^2 value augments proportionally to the increase in the number of examples. Consequently, the algorithm produces a very high number of intervals for medium or large data sets (see experimental results relating to Segment dataset in section 4). Further limitations are: First, it examines pair of adjacent intervals only, ignoring other surrounding intervals. Thus, it is possible that the formation of large, uniform intervals is prevented by this restricted local analysis. Second, it produces a fixed partition of the attribute values. Lastly, the algorithm can separate adjacent examples of the same class by assigning them to two different intervals. This is highly undesirable: a poor class separation obtained by the discretization algorithm makes the learning process harder.

3. The StatDisc Algorithm

StatDisc (*Stat*istical *Disc*retization) overcomes most of the undesirable properties of the techniques described in section 2. It consists of three phases: initialization; interval hierarchy creation; selection of the best discretization.

1. The initialization phase. StatDisc is initialized by sorting the training examples according to their value for the attribute being discretized. The initial discretization is obtained by grouping adjacent examples labelled by the same class value in the same interval. Thus, no time is wasted to merge examples which are known to belong to the same concept. Conversely, ChiMerge always applies the merging process on all examples, even if it is not necessary.

2. The creation of the interval hierarchy. StatDisc's merge process creates a hierarchy of intervals. Each level of the hierarchy represents a discretization of the continuous attribute. The construction of the tree proceeds bottom-up. Intervals that were created in the initialization phase are associated to leaf nodes. StatDisc repeatedly selects a set of adjacent intervals to merge by using the *merge criterion* that will be described later on. A new non-leaf node is added to the tree whenever a merge occurs. This node, associated to the new interval, is connected to the nodes that represent the intervals that have been merged. The root of the tree is associated to the number line. All the training examples belong to this interval. When the merging process is over, the interval hierarchy is explored and a discretization automatically selected according to the characteristic of the data (selection of the best discretization phase). However, one can decide to select a different discretization from the one suggested by the algorithm. The hierarchy provides an insight into the data composition.

Changing the scope of the merging process. The user can select the maximum number N of adjacent intervals that are examined to perform a merge step. By enlarging the scope of the merging process, we moderately slow down the algorithm but strongly decrease the likelihood of missing to form large, uniform intervals.

Statistics for measuring interval similarities. We surveyed most of the statistics in the two-way tables [5] to find out an effective and statistically sound criterion for merging adjacent intervals. χ^2, Fisher's exact test, and measures related to χ^2, e.g. Cramer's V test, the contingency coefficient P, and Φ (Phi), can be used to compare relative class frequencies of adjacent intervals. The considerations below drew us to the conclusion that Φ is the association measure most appropriated for the merge task. First, χ^2 yields different results when comparing the same distributions for different sample sizes. Second, Φ overcomes the shortcomings of χ^2, as it is truly independent of the cardinality of intervals. Third, it can be shown that Cramer's V is equivalent to $\sqrt{2\Phi}$ and P is equivalent to $\sqrt{\Phi^2/(1+\Phi^2)}$ when used to test similarities of class fequencies. Lastly, Fisher's exact test is sometimes moderately more precise of Φ but it is very much computationally expensive.

The merge criterion. The merging process contains two phases, repeated continously. In the first one, StatDisc computes the Φ statistic for any N-uple of adjacent intervals. In the second phase, it merges the N-uples with the lowest Φ value. Merging continues until all N-uples of intervals have a Φ value greater than $\Phi_{v,\alpha}(\eta)$. $\Phi_{v,\alpha}(\eta)$ denotes the value of the Φ distribution at the desired level of significance α and degrees of freedom v for a sample of size η. A two-steps heuristic is then applied to force the merging process to continue until a one-interval partition is obtained.

3. Selection of the best discretization. StatDisc seeks the largest partition that was obtained before decreasing the significance level α. If this search fails, it returns the partition which, on average, contains the largest adjacent intervals whose relative class frequencies are the most dissimilar.

4. Results of experiments

To test StatDisc on classification accuracy, we ran the following experiment on six domains with real-valued attributes. The domains were obtained from LIACC, University of Port [6]. They are: Australian (690 cases); Diabetes (768 cases); Hypertyroid (3772 cases); Segment (2310 cases); Vehicle (846 cases); Glass (214 cases). As StatDisc is not a classification algorithm itself, it was used to create intervals for C4.5 [4]. We averaged the results of three 10-fold cross validation test trials for each domain. We ran C4.5 on raw continuous data, then discretized the dataset using equal-width discretization (EW), equal-frequency discretization (EF), D2, Chi-Merge (CM) where possible, StatDisc (SD), and ran C4.5 on discretized data. Equal-width, equal-frequency, and D2 were forced to create 5- and 10-interval discretizations. Next tables show the results of the comparison experiments. Cell entries report mean error rate on the test set in percentage.

Dataset	raw data	EF (5)	EF (10)	EW (5)	EW (10)	D2 (5)	D2 (10)	CM [α]	SD
Australian	15.5	14.9	14.0	15.8	14.9	14.8	14.5	15.2 [0.01]	13.6
Diabetes	27.9	27.2	28.9	24.8	25.6	24.1	25.3	23.8 [0.005]	23.3
Hypertyroid	0.5	6.7	6.7	7.1	6.6	0.7	0.7	0.4 [0.001]	0.4
Segment	4.0	6.3	5.0	7.2	5.0	6.9	4.6	---	3.7
Vehicle	28.8	31.7	28.3	33.1	29.7	28.7	29.2	28.9 [0.005]	26.8
Glass	32.9	36.3	31.6	38.1	34.2	29.8	27.8	26.8 [0.05]	25.2

Table 1. Results of experiments.

Some comparisons with class-blinded methods showed that their performance is quite unpredictable. Furthermore, their performance is nearly always inferior to the one of class-driven techniques. All the domains were improved by discretization. Our results confirm experiments reported in [1]. Two are the possible explanations. First, discretized trees are smaller than trees on original data. Second, discretization can accurately approximate class distribution from the full data set.

Chi-Merge could not produce a discretization with less than 50 intervals in the Segment domain. It could hardly discretize Diabetes and Hypertyroid domains as well. Partitions with less than 20 intervals could be obtained only by decreasing the level of significance [α] to the limit. However, the performance of Chi-Merge on these two last datasets was close to the one of StatDisc. This result was expected, since both algorithms base on chi-squared related statistics.

Two-sided t-test at the 5% level confirmed that StatDisc showed a significant improvement in performance in regard to the other algorithms. StatDisc seems to provide a more concise and effective summarization of continuous attributes.

Comparison of learning time showed that C4.5 took half the time to process discretized dataset. We can safely conclude that discretization can speedup the learning task with very little, if any, loss of accuracy.

5. References

[1] J. Catlett. "On Changing Continuous Attributes into Ordered Discrete Attributes," *Proc. of the EWSL-91*, 164-177, 1991.
[2] D. Chiu, A. Wong, et al. "Information Discovery through Hierarchical Maximum Entropy Discretization and Synthesis," *Knowledge Discovery in Databases*, The AAAI Press, 1991.
[3] R. Kerber. "ChiMerge: Discretization of Numeric Attributes," *Proc. of the AAAI-92*, 1992.
[4] J. Quinlan. "C4.5: Programs for Machine Learning," Morgan Kaufmann Publ., 1993.
[5] M. Kendall and A. Stuart. "The Advanced Theory of Statistics," Griffin London, 1973.
[6] P. Brazdil, J. Gama, and B. Henery. "Characterizing the Applicability of Classification Algorithms Using Meta-Level Learning," *ECML-94*, Springer Verlag, 1994.

Generating Neural Networks Through the Induction of Threshold Logic Unit Trees (Extended Abstract)

Mehran Sahami

Computer Science Department, Stanford University, Stanford, CA 94305, USA
Email: sahami@CS.Stanford.EDU

Abstract. We investigate the generation of neural networks through the induction of binary trees of threshold logic units (TLUs). Initially, we describe the framework for our tree construction algorithm and how such trees can be transformed into an isomorphic neural network topology. Several methods for learning the linear discriminant functions at each node of the tree structure are examined and shown to produce accuracy results that are comparable to classical information theoretic methods for constructing decision trees (which use single feature tests at each node). Our TLU trees, however, are smaller and thus easier to understand. Moreover, we show that it is possible to simultaneously learn both the topology and weight settings of a neural network simply using the training data set that we are given.

1 Introduction

We present a non-incremental algorithm that learns binary classification tasks by producing decision trees of threshold logic units (TLU trees). While similar to the decision trees produced by algorithms such as ID3 [QU, 1986], TLU trees promise more generality as each node in our tree implements a linear discriminant function as opposed to testing only one feature of the instance vector. Thus, if the data to be classified does not align closely with the principle axes of the instance space, a large number of single feature tests may be required to properly separate the data set, while just a few *oblique* separating functions could perform just as well. Such *multivariate* decision trees have only very recently begun to attract the attention of researchers in the machine learning community [BU, 1992; 1994].

Furthermore, we show how any such TLU trees can be mechanically transformed into a three-layer neural network as first suggested by Brent [BR, 1990] and developed by Sahami [SA, 1993]. In our investigation, we compare several different methods for learning the linear discriminant at each node of the tree and compare these with ID3's univariate approach and a naive Bayesian method for learning multivariate tests.

2 The TLU Tree Algorithm

The tree building algorithm is non-incremental requiring that the set of all training instances, S, be available from the outset. We begin with the root node of the tree and induce a hyperplane to separate the training set into the sets S_0 and S_1, where S_i ($i = 0, 1$) indicates the set of instances classified as i by the separating hyperplane. If S_0 contains instances labeled 1 we create a left child and recursively apply the algorithm to it using S_0 as the training set. Similarly, if S_1 contains instances labeled 0 we create a right child and again recursively apply our algorithm to it using S_1 as the training set. Thus the algorithm normally terminates when all of the instances in the original training set, S, are correctly classified by the tree. In our experiments, we stop growing a branch if a child produces no better split than its parent or the number of errors at the leaf is less than some prespecified level of error, E, to prevent overly complex trees — an application of Occam's Razor.

3 Creating Networks From TLU Trees

The trees which are produced by the TLU tree algorithm can be mechanically transformed into three-layer connectionist networks that implement the same functions. Given an TLU tree, T, with m nodes we can construct an isomorphic network containing the m nodes of the tree in the first hidden layer (each fully connected to the inputs). The second hidden layer consisting of a node (*AND* gate) for each possible *distinct* path between the root of T and a fringe node (any node without two children). Finally, the output layer is merely a single *OR* gate connected to all nodes in the previous layer. The connections between the first and second hidden layers are constructed by traversing each possible path from the root to a fringe node in T, and recording which nodes lie along such paths. Thus, each node in the second hidden layer represents a single distinct path through T by being connected to those nodes in the first layer which correspond to the nodes that were traversed along the given path. Since the nodes in the second hidden layer are merely *AND* gates, the inputs coming from the first hidden layer must first be inverted if a left branch was traversed at the node corresponding to a given input from the first hidden layer.

4 Experimental Results

4.1 Experimental Considerations

In our experiments we compare a number of methods for partitioning the instance space at each node of the tree. We consider our own variation of the ID3 algorithm in which single feature tests are selected based on minimizing entropy. The second method uses a naive Bayesian classifier to find an optimal separating hyperplane that minimizes the probability of error at each node *assuming the features of the instance are statistically independent*. Comparatively, we examine a number of adaptive techniques for finding hyperplanes: (i) the Perceptron error-correction rule [NI, 1965] employing the Pocket algorithm [GA, 1986], (ii) the Least Mean Square (LMS) algorithm [WW, 1988] with an annealled learning rate, and (iii) Back-propagation [RHW, 1986] applied to one neuron and then hard-thresholded *after* learning.

4.2 Learning Simple Boolean Functions

3 bit - 1 corner: $X \in \{0,1\}^3$ — class 1 if $\sum_{i=1...3} x_i = 3$, else class 0

3 bit - 2 corners: $X \in \{0,1\}^3$ — class 1 if $\sum_{i=1...3} x_i = 0$ or 3, else class 0

5 bit - 1 corner: $X \in \{0,1\}^5$ — class 1 if $\sum_{i=1...5} x_i \leq 1$, else class 0

5 bit - 2 corners: $X \in \{0,1\}^5$ — class 1 if $\sum_{i=1...5} x_i \leq 1$ or $\sum_{i=1...5} x_i \geq 4$, else class 0

We first examine tasks where all instances in the instance space are presented to the algorithm during learning. Here, functions are especially chosen to capture the inherent characteristics of different distributions of vectors in the instance space. We chose both linearly separable and non-linearly separable functions and also compared conjunctive versus k-of-n threshold concepts, as the former tend to be closely aligned with the principle axes of the instance space whereas the latter are not.

The three adaptive algorithms were trained using 10,000 instance presentations (drawn randomly) at each node of the tree during construction. Both the Bayes and ID3 algorithms were given an exhaustive enumeration of the instance space of the function to be learned. The error toleration parameter, E, was set to 0% as there was no noise in the training instances. We averaged the algorithms over 10 runs. The accuracy and standard deviation when tested on the entire instance space is reported in Table 1. The average size of the trees produced is also shown in parentheses. Note that the non-adaptive schemes always induce the same decision tree given the same training data.

Algorithm	3 bit-1 corner	3 bit-2 corners	5 bit-1 corner	5 bit-2 corners
Perceptron	100.0±0.0 (1.0)	100.0±0.0 (2.0)	100.0±0.0 (1.0)	96.3±11.3 (4.7)
LMS	96.3±5.7 (1.7)	92.5±11.5 (2.4)	96.9±3.4 (3.9)	97.2±3.3 (12.2)
Back-Prop	100.0±0.0 (1.0)	100.0±0.0 (2.0)	100.0±0.0 (1.0)	100.0±0.0 (2.0)
N. Bayes	100.0±0.0 (1.0)	75.0±0.0 (2.0)	84.4±0.0 (3.0)	65.6±0.0 (3.0)
ID3	100.0±0.0 (3.0)	100.0±0.0 (5.0)	100.0±0.0 (14.0)	100.0±0.0 (23.0)

Table 1. Results on the function approximation tasks.

The results of these experiments show that not only do the adaptive learning methods equal or surpass the accuracy of classical methods for inducing decision trees, but these trees are also much smaller in size. The trees generated by Back-Propagation are not only perfectly accurate, but they reflect the minimum number of hyperplanes required to separate the instance space. Since these trees can now be tranformed into neworks, we see that it is possible to simultaneously learn both the topology of a network needed to learn a function and to learn the function itself. Moreover, we can use the TLU tree algorithm as an initial step in neural network design to give us an idea as to how large a network should be to learn a given function. We can first generate the appropriate TLU tree, transform it into a network with "informed" initial weights and then train the network using any network training method we wish.

4.3 The Monks Problems

For further learning experiments, we use a standard test-bed for learning tasks known as the Monk's Problems [TH, 1991]. This set of three learning tasks has been well studied on a number of different machine learning algorithms and includes standard training and test sets to help make fair comparisons between learning methods. For our learning algorithms we encoded these problems into a 17 dimensional boolean space using a local encoding scheme. As above, we used 10,000 samples drawn randomly with replacement from the training set to train the nodes of our TLU trees for the adaptive learning methods. The statistical learning methods had the entire training set available from which to compute frequency statistics. Since the first two Monks Problems are noise free and the third contains noise, we ran the tree induction algorithm using an error toleration parameter, E, of 0% for problems 1 and 2 and 10% for problem 3. Each experiment involved running each algorithm 10 times. Table 2 shows the accuracy and standard deviation of the induced TLU trees being tested on the entire instance space (much of which has not been seen before) as a test set. The avererage tree size is shown in parentheses.

Algorithm	Monk 1 (E = 0%)	Monk 2 (E = 0%)	Monk 3 (E = 10%)
Perceptron	83.9±6.3 (11.0)	75.5±5.3 (23.9)	95.9±1.6 (1.7)
LMS	92.2±3.5 (13.3)	76.9±6.5 (42.2)	94.2±2.5 (5.0)
Back-Prop	100.0±0.0 (3.0)	94.0±3.7 (7.4)	94.5±1.0 (1.1)
Naive Bayes	70.8±0.0 (5.0)	67.1±0.0 (2.0)	97.2±0.0 (1.0)
ID3	92.6±0.0 (20.0)	86.6±0.0 (45.0)	97.2±0.0 (2.0)

Table 2. Results on the Monks Problems learning tasks.

In considering the first two Monks Problems, we find that the TLU trees produced using Back-propagation seem to clearly outperform the non-adaptive methods when considering a combination of accuracy and tree size. On Monk 3 the results are a bit more inconclusive as all the learning methods seem to fare comparably in size and accuracy (possibly due to the error toleration parameter and noise in the training set). Interestingly, the trees induced using Perceptron and LMS are not nearly as small as expected, and their accuracy also seems to suffer as a result of not being able to learn a parsimonious multivariate shattering of the instance space. We conjecture that this problem results from these algorithms inability to converge properly when presented with non-linearly separable data, further complicated by the high dimensionality of the instance space, as we did not see this problem arise as severely when learning simple boolean functions. Nevertheless, the adaptive methods still fare well, led by Back-propagation which produces small and accurate (often the best) trees, especially in Monk 2 where the Back-propagation TLU trees are most accurate and yet 5 times smaller than trees induced with ID3.

5   Conclusions

We have shown the TLU tree algorithm to be a viable learning method capable of inducing small, yet accurate, decision trees by allowing each node to test more than one attribute. Not only can the TLU tree algorithm be used as a stand-alone learning algorithm, but the trees produced by it can be transformed into neural networks to determine a rough approximation of the topology necessary to properly learn a given data set. Moreover, by inducing a TLU tree, we can produce an initial set of weights for a network which we can further train incrementally as new training data becomes available.

Acknowledgments   We are indebted to Nils Nilsson for providing the initial guidance and support to pursue this line of research. Discussions with George John and Pat Langley have also been useful. The author is supported by a Fred Gellert Foundation ARCS fellowship.

References

[BR, 1990]   Brent, R.P. 1990. Fast training algorithms for multi-layer neural nets. Numerical Analysis Project Manuscript NA-90-03, Computer Sci. Dept, Stanford.

[BU, 1992]   Brodley, C.E., and Utgoff, P.E. 1992. Multivariate Versus Univariate Decision Trees. COINS Technical Report 92-8, Computer Science Dept., UMass.

[BU, 1994]   Brodley, C.E., and Utgoff, P.E. 1994. Multivariate Decision Trees. To appear in *Machine Learning*.

[GA, 1986]   Gallant, S.I. 1986. Optimal Linear Discriminants. In *Eighth International Conference on Pattern Recognition*, 849-852. New York: IEEE.

[NI, 1965]   Nilsson, N.J. 1965. *Learning machines*. New York: McGraw-Hill.

[QU, 1986]   Quinlan, J.R. 1986. Induction of decision trees. *Machine Learning* 1:81-106.

[RHW, 1986]   Rumelhart, D.E.; Hinton, G. E.; and Williams, R.J. 1986. Learning internal representations by error propagation. *Parallel Distributed Processing, Vol. 1*, eds. D. E. Rumelhart and J. L. McClelland, 318-62. Cambridge, MA: MIT Press.

[SA, 1993]   Sahami, M. 1993. Learning Non-Linearly Separable Boolean Functions With Linear Threshold Unit Trees and Madaline-Style Networks. In *Proceedings of the 11th National Conference on Artificial Intelligence*, 335-41. Menlo Park, CA: AAAI Press.

[TH, 1991]   Thrun, S.B., and 23 co-authors. 1991. The monk's problems: a performance comparison of different learning algorithms. TR CMU-CS-91-197, Carnegie Mellon.

[WW, 1988]   Widrow, B., and Winter, R.G. 1988. Neural Nets for Adaptive Filtering and Adaptive Pattern Recognition. *IEEE Computer, March*:25-39.

Learning Classification Rules Using Lattices (Extended Abstract)

Mehran Sahami

Computer Science Department, Stanford University, Stanford, CA 94305, USA
Email: sahami@CS.Stanford.EDU

Abstract. This paper presents a novel induction algorithm, Rulearner, which induces classification rules using a Galois lattice as an explicit map through the search space of rules. The Rulearner system is shown to compare favorably with commonly used symbolic learning methods which use heuristics rather than an explicit map to guide their search through the rule space. Furthermore, our learning system is shown to be robust in the presence of noisy data. The Rulearner system is also capable of learning both decision lists and unordered rule sets allowing for comparisons of these different learning paradigms within the same algorithmic framework.

1 Introduction

Research in rule induction by means of search [MC, 1969; MI, 1982; CN, 1989] has been on-going for some time. While some systems, such as Version Spaces, make direct use of the data to be learned during rule induction, such methods are highly sensitive to noisy data. In other systems, the search through the space of rules is guided by heuristics as opposed to using the data to build an explicit map through the space of rules to induce. In this capacity, such algorithms are only *data-driven* to the extent that the heuristics employed in them make use of the data to be learned.

We present the Rulearner system which seeks to combine both the direct use of data with robustness in the presence of noise during the rule induction process. Since the algorithm uses a Galois lattice constructed from training data [OO, 1988] as an explicit guide through the rule space, the algorithm is directly *data-driven* as it does not simply heuristically fit the training data. Our system is also capable of inducing both an unordered set of classification rules as well as a decision list [RI, 1987]. This allows for the Rulearner system to be used in making direct comparisons between these two learning paradigms within a single algorithmic framework.

Several experiments with the Rulearner system are presented comparing it with the commonly used symbolic learning systems C4.5 [QU, 1993] and CN2 [CN, 1989].

2 Lattice Definitions

A lattice is defined to be a directed acyclic graph in which any two nodes, u and v, have a unique *join* (a node "higher" in the graph to which a u and v are connected by minimal length paths) and a unique *meet* (a node "lower" in the graph which is connected to u and v by minimal length paths) — referred to respectively as *least upper bounds* and *greatest lower bounds* in formal mathematics. We also define:

Definition 1. The *upward closure* of node u, denoted UC(u), is the set of all nodes, including u, that can be reached from u following upward arcs in the lattice.

Definition 2. The *downward closure* of a node u, denoted DC(u), is the set of all nodes which contain u in their upward closure.

Definition 3. The *cover* of a node u, denoted Cover(u), is the number of instance nodes in DC(u).

Our lattices are defined by representing each training instance by a single node (referred to as an *instance node*) in the "lowest" level of the lattice. In the "greatest" level of the lattice we create a node for every possible feature that an instance in the training set may have (referred to as *feature nodes*). These two sets of nodes uniquely define a set of internal arcs and nodes which comprise the complete lattice. We use the GRAND algorithm [OO, 1988] for lattice construction in our experiments.

3 The Rulearner Algorithm

The Rulearner algorithm takes as input (i) a lattice, L, (ii) a set of instance classification labelings, C, which correspond to the instance nodes in L, and (iii) a noise parameter, N, indicating a percentage by which each induced rule can misclassify some portion of the training instances to which it applies. The algorithm produces a set of symbolic classification rules as output. Furthermore, the user can configure the system to induce either a decision-list or an unordered set of rules, and can also decide whether the rules induced should only classify one (ie. positive) or all given labelings. While the algorithm is general enough to deal with more than two classification labelings, we present the algorithm here as a binary classifier for easier understanding.

The algorithm first labels all instance nodes (whose labelings are given in C) and then filters these labelings up the lattice. A node u is given a particular label, say POSITIVE, if the instance nodes in DC(u) are all of the class POSITIVE (allowing for some percentage of mislabelings given by the noise parameter N). If there are insufficient instance nodes of any given class in DC(u) to give u a particular label, then it is labeled MIXED. Each node is initially marked "active," and each time a rule is induced using a node u, all the nodes in DC(u) are marked "inactive". As long as "active" nodes remain in the lattice, there are still candidate nodes for rule induction and hence new rules are induced. The rule induction process simply finds a non-MIXED "active" node in the lattice which covers the most previously uncovered instance nodes and forms a rule. If several nodes have the same number of instances in their downward closures, we prefer the node which has the fewest features in its upward closure — an application of Occam's Razor. Intuitively, this corresponds to finding a minimal set of features that covers a large portion of the instance space with a given labeling. An important factor in this minimal set of features is that it is directly derived from commonalties in the underlying data and hence the antecedent of the rule induced is directly driven by the data in the training set.

```
PROCEDURE Rulearner(L, C, N)
    Initialize all nodes in the lattice to be "active"
    Label all nodes in the lattice (using the noise parameter N)
    WHILE (there are still "active" nodes in the lattice)
        u ← node with greatest cover and non-MIXED labeling
        Output rule: "feature nodes in UC(u) implies label of node u"
        FORALL (v ∈ DC(u) where v is an instance node)
            FORALL (w ∈ UC(v))
                Decrement the cover of w
                IF (cover of w ≤ 0) mark w "inactive"
            Mark v as "inactive"
        IF (Decision-List) re-label "active" nodes (using the noise parameter N)
END
```

Fig. 1. Pseudo-code for the Rulearner algorithm.

4 Experimental Results

The Rulearner system was first tested on the Monk's Problems [TH, 1991]. As a comparison, we tried several configuration of other induction systems to capture the *best* performance of those systems compared to Rulearner. For the first two Monk problems, we test three basic configurations of the Rulearner system: (i) decision-lists, (ii) unordered rule sets, and (iii) rule sets to classify only the positive instances, predicting negative as a default rule. The noise parameter, N, was set at 0%.

Algorithm	Monk 1	Monk 2
CN2 (decision-list)	100.0%	72.9%
CN2 (unordered rules)	98.6%	75.7%
C4.5 (unpruned tree)	76.6%	65.3%
C4.5 (pruned tree)	75.7%	65.0%
C4.5 -s (unpruned tree)	94.4%	69.0%
C4.5 -s (pruned tree)	100.0%	70.4%
Rulearner (decision-list)	100.0%	74.5%
Rulearner (unordered rules)	100.0%	74.8%
Rulearner (pos rules only)	100.0%	70.4%

Table 1. Accuracy of induction algorithms on MONK'S Problems 1 and 2.

In Monk 1, all three configurations of the Rulearner system not only performed with 100% accuracy but also learned the minimal concept description for the problem, whereas only the very best configurations of the other learning methods showed similar results. Monk 2 proves challenging to symbolic learning systems since the concept is not easily representable in DNF. Here we find that all the symbolic learning methods hover close to 70% in their accuracy and produce lengthy rule sets, reflective of the checkerboard distribution of classes in the instance space. These experiments show that symbolic learning methods must integrate a bias for more than just functions easily representable in DNF to fare well on a wide range of problems.

Algorithm	Monk 3
CN2 (DL, chi-sq=0.0)	93.3%
CN2 (unord., chi-sq=0.0)	90.7%
CN2 (DL, chi-sq=4.0)	94.4%
CN2 (unord., chi-sq=4.0)	87.5%
C4.5 (unpruned, CF=15%)	92.6%
C4.5 (pruned, CF=15%)	97.2%
C4.5 (unpruned, CF=25%)	92.6%
C4.5 (pruned, CF=25%)	97.2%
Rulearner (DL, N=5%)	94.4%
Rulearner (unord, N=5%)	94.0%
Rulearner (DL, N=10%)	94.4%
Rulearner (unord, N=10%)	95.1%

Algorithm	Breast Can.
Default Rule (majority)	71.7±7.2%
CN2 (DL, chi-sq=4.0)	73.3±6.0%
CN2 (unord., chi-sq=4.0)	71.3±4.5%
CN2 (DL, chi-sq=8.0)	72.1±4.0%
CN2 (unord., chi-sq=8.0)	72.9±5.3%
C4.5 (unpruned, CF=15%)	67.7±9.8%
C4.5 (pruned, CF=15%)	75.2±7.6%
C4.5 (unpruned, CF=25%)	67.7±9.8%
C4.5 (pruned, CF=25%)	73.3±4.5%
Rulearner (DL, N=30%)	74.9±5.8%
Rulearner (unord, N=30%)	74.1±6.4%
Rulearner (DL, N=40%)	74.8±6.6%
Rulearner (unord, N=40%)	73.6±7.8%

Table 2. Accuracy on Monk 3.   **Table 3.** Accuracy on Breast Cancer.

We also compared Rulearner on noisy domains: Monk 3 which contains 5% noise in the training set and the real world Yugoslavian Breast Cancer data. Again we tried a range of configurations and parameters to optimize the performance of all the algorithms in our study. In Table 2 we see that all three algorithms are clearly able to learn in the presence of noise. More importantly, however, we see the importance of pruning as reflected in the results from C4.5. Since CN2 and Rulearner currently do no pruning of their induced rules, this could be a promising venue to further increase their accuracy on noisy data, especially since Rulearner outperforms unpruned C4.5.

In the Breast Cancer domain we performed a three-fold cross-validation and report both the accuracy and standard deviation of the results. This is a very difficult problem as none of the algorithms tested perform significantly better than the majority default rule. Here, we again see the importance of pruning as the results with C4.5 clearly indicate. In spite of performing no pruning, the Rulearner system still performs on par with the pruned trees produced by C4.5 and seems to outperform both CN2 and unpruned C4.5. Comparisons of the decision-lists and unordered rule sets produced by CN2 and Rulearner point to no clear winner at this point.

5 Conclusions

It appears that Rulearner is a viable lattice-based induction algorithm. Future work will lead us to examine how rule pruning may be employed to increase accuracy and conduct more comparative studies of the decision-list and unordered rule set paradigms. Methods for automatic noise parameter selection will also be pursued.

The interested reader should also be aware of the systems CHARADE [GA, 1987] and GRAND [OO, 1988] which also make use of lattices to guide the formation of classification rules. These systems, however, differ from ours in their induction mechanisms, biases, and methods for dealing with noise.

Acknowledgments The author thanks Nils Nilsson and Deon Oosthuizen for their thought provoking discussions. Additional thanks go to Oosthuizen for providing both the GRAND lattice construction program and the breast cancer data set, and to Peter Clark for providing CN2. George John and Pat Langley also provided useful insights. The author is supported by a Fred Gellert Foundation ARCS fellowship.

References

[CN, 1989] Clark, P. and Niblett, T. The CN2 Induction Algorithm. *Machine Learning*, 3:261-83, 1989.

[GA, 1987] Ganascia, J.G. CHARADE: A Rule System Learning System. In *Proceedings of the Tenth IJCAI, Volume 1*, pp. 345-347, Milan, Italy, 1987.

[MC, 1969] Michalski, R.S. On the Quasi-minimal Solution of the General Covering Problem. In *Proceedings of the Fifth International Symposium on Information Processing*, pp. 125-128, Bled, Yugoslavia, 1969.

[MI, 1982] Mitchell, T.M. Generalization as Search. *Artif. Intel.*, 18(2): 203-226, 1982.

[NI, 1992] Nilsson, N. J. N-Cube Lattices and Their Role in Machine Learning. *Working paper*, Department of Computer Science, Stanford University, Stanford, CA, 1992.

[OO, 1988] Oosthuizen, G.D. The Use of a Lattice in Knowledge Processing. PhD Thesis, University of Strathclyde, Glasgow, 1988.

[OO, 1994] Oosthuizen, G.D. *The Application of Concept Lattices to Machine Learning*. University of Pretoria Technical Report CSTR 94/01, 1994.

[OM, 1988] Oosthuizen, G.D. and McGregor, D.R. Induction Through Knowledge Base Normalization. *Proceedings of the European Conf. on Artificial Intelligence*, 1988.

[QU, 1993] Quinlan, J.R. 1993. *C4.5: Programs For Machine Learning*. San Mateo, CA: Morgan Kaufmann.

[RI, 1987] Rivest, R.L. Learning Decision Lists. *Machine Learning*, 2:229-246, 1987.

[TH, 1991] Thrun, S.B. *et al. The MONK'S Problems*. Carnegie-Mellon University Technical Report CMU-CS-91-197, December, 1991.

Hybrid Classification: Using Axis-Parallel and Oblique Subdivisions of the Attribute Space (Extended Abstract)

Barbara Schulmeister and Mario Bleich

Fraunhofer Institute for Information and Data Processing
Branch Lab for Process Optimisation
Kurstraße 33, D-10117 Berlin, Germany
email: schulmei/bleich@epo.iitb.fhg.de

1   Introduction and Motivation

Each individual algorithm for supervised concept learning has advantages and disadvantages. This implies that no learning formalism can be the best for solving all classification tasks. The paper presents a hybrid algorithm which uses the strengths of standard decision tree algorithms and piecewise linear classifiers because at every level of learning it chooses the appropriate subdivision of the attribute space: a split with hyperplanes in general position or an axis-parallel split. Most of the decision tree algorithms can split the attribute space in axis-parallel hyperrectangles only, especially all the well-known, intensively studied and used algorithms (ID3, CART, IndCART, C4.5), initially introduced in domains with categorial attributes and later extended to numeric attributes. There are some often repeated important advantages of application of these decision tree algorithms.

But it is clear, that when the underlying concept is defined by hyperplanes in general position in the attribute space, axis-parallel splitting methods have to produce many decision nodes for the same attributes, the resulting trees are very large and generalize poorly for unobserved patterns.

Statistical methods and neural nets can produce good classifiers in such cases, but they are more concerned with performance as measured by error rate than with interpretability of the detected concept.

Another point, decision tree algorithms work well in comparison with classical statistical methods when the data are multimodal.

However, an important criterion for a classification method to qualify under the machine learning heading is that the derived rules should be meaningful to humans and evaluable in the head. On this basis, many statistical and neural net algorithms (and so the piecewise linear classifier DIPOL which is used in combination with a decision tree algorithm) would not qualify.

In this sense the introduced algorithm makes a good compromise between interpretability, compactness, and correctness of the learned concept.

There are some other developments in this direction. In the last years decision tree algorithms have been studied in which boolean combinations of attributes and more and more general combinations are applied for the split at a node.

A comprehensive review can be found in [4]. The so-called oblique decision tree algorithms use general linear combinations of the attributes and were suggested in the book of Breiman et al. [1] for the first time, but there has been only little further work on such trees until relatively recently. The successors are linear machine decision trees [6], [7]. Two other approaches use randomizing to find good oblique splits and to overcome the computational complexity of this problem: Simulated Annealing of Decision Trees (SADT, [2]) and Oblique Classifier 1 (OC1, [4]).

2 Description of the Hybrid Algorithm DIPOL-DT

The hybrid algorithm DIPOL-DT combines the piecewise linear classifier DIPOL and the decision tree algorithm CAL5. The two following subsections describe these algorithms developed in the authors department. Suppose that a finite set of classified examples with real-valued attributes is given for learning.

2.1 The Piecewise Linear Classifier DIPOL

DIPOL is a learning algorithm which constructs an optimized piecewise linear classifier for n-class problems [3].

- In the first step of the algorithm, initial positions of the discriminating hyperplanes are determined by linear regression for each pair of classes. It is well-known, that there is no guarantee to find a separating hyperplane with linear regression in the separable case. The reason of this can be found in the fact that this solution puts the emphasis on regions with high pattern density more than on the boundary region. Because of that
- the positions of the hyperplanes are optimized in the second step of the algorithm. An error criterion function is defined depending on the misclassified patterns. This function is minimized by a gradient descent procedure for each hyperplane separately. Each newly generated weight vector is compared to the existing, and only if the criterion function is improved, the weight vector is adjusted.
- The classification of patterns is defined on a symbolic level on the basis of the signs of the discriminating hyperplanes.

As an option in the case of non-convex (in particular non-singly connected) classes a clustering procedure decomposing the classes into subclasses can be applied. A standard minimum-squared-error algorithm with an initial partition depending on the sequence of presenting the patterns is used. Like hill-climbing algorithms in general, this approach guarantees local but not global optimisation. Another problem in finding an adequate clustering of a class (that means, a clustering which allows a linear discrimination from other classes resp. subclasses) is the data-based choice of an appropriate distance measure. In higher dimensions of the attribute space it is often quite impossible to find an appropriate scaling. The consequence is, that DIPOL generates more subclasses than necessary to find a situation for linear separation of classes and subclasses, and this can result in overfitting of the training data.

2.2 The Decision Tree Algorithm CAL5

CAL5 induces a decision tree using a discretisation procedure which is especially suitable for continuous attributes. The goal of the splits at the nodes of the tree is to decrease the "impurity" of the learning subsets belonging to the nodes. CAL5 works with two impurity measures: a statistical measure and the information-theoretic entropy measure [5]. The accuracy rate and complexity of the resulting decision tree depend on two parameters - the confidence level and the dominance threshold. A coarse description of the procedure at each node of the tree is given in the following:

- The node is a leaf, if the probability of one class at the node is greater than the dominance threshold.
- If the node is no leaf, for each attribute
  - an automatic, adaptive discretisation is carried out on the basis of the prechosen confidence level and the dominance threshold and
  - the value of the impurity measure related to this discretisation is determined.

  The attribute with the least value of the impurity measure is chosen for the next split.

The algorithm stops, if each node is a leaf.

Tests on several real-world data sets show that the decision trees produced by CAL5 are usually quite compact in comparison with those generated by other algorithms, see [3], where also more details of the discretisation procedure and the used pruning method can be found.

2.3 The Hybrid Algorithm DIPOL-DT

This section describes the combination of the axis-parallel decision tree algorithm CAL5 and the piecewise linear classifier DIPOL. The hybrid algorithm chooses at each node the better of the DIPOL-split and the best axis-parallel CAL5-split. The procedure is fully deterministic and can be summarized as follows:

- **If all samples at the current node belong to the same class then STOP.**
- **Use DIPOL without any clustering to construct oblique hyperplanes (one in the case of two classes or more in the case of more than two classes).**
  Use CAL5 with the entropy measure for evaluating the impurity to split the attribute space along one chosen attribute in two or more subspaces (construction of axis-parallel hyperplanes).
  - **If no split is found: use DIPOL up to a prechosen number n_c of subclasses of all classes and STOP with the best result.**

- **If one or more splits are found: evaluate the quality of the splits constructed by DIPOL and CAL5 using the entropy measure and decide in favour of the better splitting to form new branches of the tree.**

The hybrid algorithm is investigated empirically using artificial and real-world data sets. The examples confirm that the hybrid algorithm

- in general (i. e., when the underlying classification concept is defined by oblique hyperplanes) constructs compact trees in comparison with the axis-parallel decision tree algorithm CAL5 and
- substitutes the search for an adequate clustering of classes in cases, in which the classes do not allow a linear discrimination of each class from all others (when a linear discrimination of the classes is possible, DIPOL performs the classification).

Because the decision on the split at a node is made locally, the introduced algorithm (and all other known axis-parallel and oblique decision tree algorithms) does not generate the smallest possible tree, describing a given concept. But in particular real-world examples in higher than two-dimensional attribute spaces demonstrate that the algorithm DIPOL-DT generates significantly more compact classification concepts than DIPOL or CAL5 alone.

The performance of DIPOL-DT is compared to that of several other axis-parallel and oblique decision tree algorithms and will be presented by some artificial and real-world examples in the poster session.

References

1. Breiman, L., Friedman, J., Olshen R. & Stone, C. (1984). Classification and Regression Trees. Wadsworth International Group.
2. Heath, D., Kasif, S. & Salzberg, S. (1993). Learning oblique decision trees. In Proceedings of the 13th International Joint Conference on Artificial Intelligence, pp. 1002-1007. Chambery, France, Morgan Kaufmann.
3. Michie, D., Spiegelhalter, D. J. & Taylor, C. C.(1994). Machine Learning, Neural and Statistical Classification. Ellis Horwood.
4. Murthy, S. K., Kasif, S. & Salzberg, S. (1994). A System for Induction of Oblique Decision Trees. Journal of Artificial Intelligence Research, 2, pp. 1-32.
5. Quinlan, J. R.(1986). Induction of Decision Trees. Machine Learning, 1, pp. 81-106.
6. Utgoff, P. E. (1988). Perceptron Trees: A Case Study in Hybrid Concept Representation. In Proceedings of the 6th National Conference of Artificial Intelligence, pp. 601-606.
7. Utgoff, P. E. & Brodley, C. E. (1991). Linear Machine Decision Trees. Technical Report 10, University of Massachusetts at Amherst.

An Induction-based Control for Genetic Algorithms
(Extended Abstract)

Michele Sebag[1,3] and Marc Schoenauer[2,3] and Caroline Ravise[1,3]

[1] LMS, Ecole Polytechnique, 91128 Palaiseau, France
[2] CMAP, Ecole Polytechnique, 91128 Palaiseau, France
[3] LRI, Université de Paris-Sud, Bâtiment 490, F-91405 Orsay, France

Abstract. This paper presents an induction-based control of genetic algorithms:
1- examples of the behavior of the genetic operators (crossover and mutation) are gathered;
2- rules characterizing disruptive operators are induced from the gathered examples;
3- last, these rules are used to reject operators classified disruptive.
Evolution is thereby speeded up. Experimental results on the well-known Royal Road problem and on a GA-deceptive problem are presented.

1 Introduction

Genetic Algorithms (GAs) are widely known as powerful optimization algorithms [1]. As such, they have been applied in the Machine Learning community, mainly to build classifiers systems since the seminal work of Holland [3].

In contrast with using GAs to reach ML goals, we propose to use inductive learning to control and speed up GAs. The main drawback of GAs is their slowness. This slowness is partly due to the fact that most good solutions are *fleetingly discovered* [7] : genetic operators, i.e. crossover and mutation, stochastically discover promising individuals but make them disappear as well.

This paper describes an induction-based control of crossover and mutation, achieved in a 3-step process : (a) a set of examples about the behavior of operators is gathered, then (b) rules characterizing disruptive operators are induced, and last, (c) these rules are used during the next evolution steps to reject operators classified disruptive.

The reader is assumed familiar with the basic GA; we refer to [1] for the terms used throughout this paper. Section 2 briefly illustrates the difficulties encountered by GAs on two problems [6, 14]. Section 3 poses the problem of controlling a GA as an induction problem. Section 4 presents an experimental validation on the problems introduced in section 2. Section 5 discusses the induction-based approach with respect to some related works [4, 12].

2 Motivation

Let us introduce on two problems the main difficulties encountered by GAs.

The Royal Road problem. The Royal Road problem was conceived by Mitchell and Holland [6, 7]; this fitness landscape is supposedly easy for GAs because of (a) its schema structure and (b) the fact that high-order schemas are obtained by crossing over low-order schemas. However, it is *not* easy: low-order schemas must be discovered again and again before they combine.

GA-deceptive problems. The idea lying behind GA-deception, is that a GA can be misled by a particular fitness landscape [1]. If the average fitness of schema H_1 is greater than that of schema H_2, the schema theorem [2] states that H_1 will be oversampled in the genetic population compared to H_2. But if H_2 actually contains the optimum, the optimum will likely be missed. Moreover, as claimed by Whitley [14], all challenging problems are, at least partially, deceptive.

The desired control should both decrease the chances of disruptive evolution (in order to overcome fleeting discoveries) and the need for selection (in order to limit the misleading of GAs by deceptive problems).

3 Controlling a GA through Induction

Which Examples ? The only available information (when dealing with non-artificial problems) is provided by observing the course of evolution. This observation does tell how a given operator behaves on given individual(s): it behaves well if the best offspring is fitter than the best parent, badly if the best offspring is less fit than the (best) parent, otherwise it is inactive. Such behavioral examples permit an induction-based control of genetic search:
• Disruptive operators will likely be observed to behave *badly*;
• From examples of *bad* and *good* operators, rules can be induced by a classical inductive algorithm [5, 8].
• In further evolution steps, these rules allow to reject operators classified *bad*, thereby decreasing the chances of disruptive evolution.

This induction-based control thus speeds up evolution, by preventing it to go backward. Another possibility consists in rejecting operators classified *inactive*, thus preventing evolution to "get asleep". This latter heuristic was found very useful in the last stages of evolution: when population tends to be homogeneous, most operators are inactive; rejecting them brings a significant improvement [10].

How to Represent Examples ? In a binary frame, a crossover operator c can be represented by a bitstring $(c_1, ..c_N)$, termed *crossover mask* [13]. When crossing over individuals x and y, the first offspring inherits bit i from parent x iff $c_i = 1$, otherwise it inherits bit i from parent y (and symmetrically for the second offspring). Similarly, a mutation operator m can be represented by a mutation mask $(m_1, ..m_N)$: when mutating individual x, bit i is flipped iff $m_i = 1$.

An example is so composed of (a) the description of the operator and (b) the class of the operator, *bad, good* or *inactive* according to the effects of the operator w.r.t. the individual(s) it is experimented on. This representation leads to a control termed *general control*. Another possibility is to include the description of the (best) parent the operator applies on, into the example description; this leads to more consistent examples since the behavior of an operator likely depends on the individual(s) it applies on. This latter possibility leads to another kind of control, termed *dedicated control*, which cannot be discussed here for the sake of brevity; more details can be found in [11].

Coupling GA and Induction. The coupling involves the following steps:
1. *Init*. During the first M generations, a classical genetic evolution takes place.
2. *Examples Gathering*. Let P be the size of the genetic population; either

2.1 P crossover examples are gathered, by randomly generating 2-point crossover masks and applying them on the current population; or

2.2 P mutation examples are gathered, by randomly generating mutation masks and applying them on the current population.
3. *Knowledge Building*. From these behavioral examples, rules are induced.
4. *Knowledge-guided Evolution*. In the next generations, crossovers or mutations classified *bad* according to the current rule-set, are rejected.
5. *Transition*. After M generations, the population has evolved and the rule-set may be no longer accurate. Go to step 2.

4 Experiments

We used a GA based on standards [1], with selection by roulette wheel with linear fitness scaling ; the selective pressure is set to values 1.2 and 2. Two-point crossovers are performed at a rate of 0.6. Mutation is performed at a rate of 0.05 per individual : in a mutated individual, every bit is flipped with probability 0.016. Evolution stops either after 1000 generations or when the fitness is constant over the population.

We used a star-like learner called *Constraint-Based Induction* [9]. Its complexity is $\mathcal{O}(N \times P^2)$, N being the size of the problem and P the number of examples.

Reference results are provided by running a standard GA (a) without control and (b) with a GA-based control, inspired from Spears [12]. We experimented both the crossover and the mutation control (results including simultaneous control of crossovers and mutations can be found in [11]). All results are averaged on 30 independent runs.

Parameters		Royal Road				Ugly Problem			
Sel. Press.	Pop. Size	No Control	Cross. Control GA	Cross. Control ML	Mut. Control	No Control	Cross. Control GA	Cross. Control ML	Mut. Control
1.2	100	10 (32)	43 (35)	20 (38)	57 (71)	10 (8)	7 (15)	3 (10)	53 (20)
2.0	100	7 (7)	10 (12)	3 (11)	17 (46)	20 (3)	17 (3)	17 (3)	53 (9)

Table 1. Percentage of success (nb of evaluations in thousands)

Experiments consider the Royal Road problem (2) and the Ugly problem [14] composed of 10 concatened elementary GA-deceptive problems. Table 1 shows the percentage of success (hit the optimum), together with the total number of function evaluations needed to reach the optimum, for a population size 100. Partial conclusions are that: control is not useful when the population size is large; but control can significantly improves the results obtained with a small population. The control of mutation appears significantly more efficient than both kinds of crossover control, especially on the GA-deceptive problem.

5 Discussion

The crossover control has been addressed in two ways in the literature. Levenick [4] proposes to separate low-order schemas by zones of bits termed *introns*, not involved in the fitness computation. The disruptive effects of n-point crossovers can thereby be significantly limited [7]. However, such modifications of the problem representation require rather good insights in its solution (e.g. *a priori* knowledge of the position of the relevant low-order schemas) which greatly limits the method.

Spears [12] proposes to add an extra bit to the representation of individual; this extra bit rules out whether the individual is to be crossed according to a 2-point or a uniform crossover. Genetic search thus optimizes both the individual itself, and the kind of crossover most suited to this individual. Note however, that induction allows for a much more precise control: rules can tell *where* an operator should or should not intervene (depending on the individuals at hand in the case of dedicated control). Of course, a GA-based control could be similarly precise, but at the expense of doubling the size of the representation.

The cost of the induction-based control is decomposed in two parts. In terms of fitness calculations, it implies an overhead of $(M + 1)/M$, if learning is performed every M generations. Besides, it implies the learning and classification cost — that are polynomial and do not depend on the complexity of the fitness function. So, when dealing with expensive fitness functions, the extra-cost of an induction-based control should be negligible compared to the savings in terms of the number of fitness calculations needed to reach a good solution.

6 Conclusion

This paper has presented an induction-based control of GAs. On the ML side, this work is an application of induction; the difficulty consisted in posing the problem of controlling a GA as a machine learning problem.

On the GA side, it appears that induction offers powerful and flexible means to control a GA. Moreover, this approach gives unexpected insights into the roles respectively devolved to crossover and mutation along genetic search. The fact that mutation control is much more effective than crossover control is counterintuitive, since the crossover rate is much grater than the mutation rate. A tentative explanation is that nothing can counteract the disruptive effects of mutation, except control; in opposition, the sampling of the population can limit to a great extent, the disruptive effects of crossover (especially in the end of evolution). Much more experiments are needed, of course, to validate this hypothesis.

References

1. D. E. Goldberg. *Genetic algorithms in search, optimization and machine learning.* Addison Wesley, 1989.
2. J. Holland. *Adaptation in natural and artificial systems.* University of Michigan Press, Ann Arbor, 1975.
3. J. Holland. Escaping brittleness : The possibilities of general purpose learning algorithms applied to parallel rule-based systems. In R.S Michalski, J.G. Carbonell, and T.M. Mitchell, editors, *Machine Learning : an artificial intelligence approach,* volume 2. Morgan Kaufmann, 1986.
4. J. R. Levenick. Inserting introns improves genetic algorithm success rate : Taking a cue from biology. In R.K. Belew and L.B. Booker, editors, *Proceedings of the 4th International Conference on Genetic Algorithms.* Morgan Kaufmann, 1991.
5. R.S. Michalski. A theory and methodology of inductive learning. In R.S Michalski, J.G. Carbonell, and T.M. Mitchell, editors, *Machine Learning : an artificial intelligence approach,* volume 1. Morgan Kaufmann, 1983.
6. M. Mitchell, S. Forrest, and J.H. Holland. The royal road for genetic algorithms : Fitness landscapes and ga performance. In F. J. Valera and P. Bourgine, editors, *Proceedings of the First European Conference on Artificial Life-93,* pages 245–254. MIT Press/Bradford Books, 1993.
7. M. Mitchell and J.H. Holland. When will a genetic algorithm outperform hill-climbing ? In S. Forrest, editor, *Proceedings of the 5th International Conference on Genetic Algorithms.* Morgan Kaufmann, 1993.
8. J. R. Quinlan. Induction of decision trees. *Machine Learning,* 1:81–106, 1986.
9. M. Sebag. Using constraints to building version spaces. In De Raedt L. and Bergadano F., editors, *Proceedings of ECML-94, European Conference on Machine Learning,* pages 257–271. Springer Verlag, 1994.
10. M. Sebag and M. Schoenauer. Controlling crossover through inductive learning. In H.P. Schwefel, editor, *Proceedings of PPSN-94, Parallel Problem Solving from Nature.* Springer-Verlag, LNCS 866, 1994.
11. M. Sebag and M. Schoenauer and C. Ravise. A Note on the Control of GAs by Induction. Internal Report, LMS, Ecole Polytechnique, january 1995.
12. W. M. Spears. Adapting crossover in a genetic algorithm. In R.K. Belew and L.B. Booker, editors, *Proceedings of the 4th International Conference on Genetic Algorithms.* Morgan Kaufmann, 1991.
13. G. Syswerda. Uniform crossover in genetic algorithms. In *Proceedings of the 3rd International Conference on Genetic Algorithms,* pages 2–9, 1989.
14. D. Whitley. Fundamental principles of deception in genetic search. In R.K. Belew and L.B. Booker, editors, *Proceedings of the 4th International Conference on Genetic Algorithms.* Morgan Kaufmann, 1991.

FENDER: An approach to theory restructuring (extended abstract)*

Edgar Sommer

GMD — German National Research Center for Computer Science, AI Division (I3.KI), Schloss Birlinghoven, 53757 St. Augustin, Germany, email sommer@gmd.de

Theory Restructuring is an emerging research issue whose task is to transform a given knowledge base without changing coverage of a goal concept or concepts, i.e. to in some sense improve the theory's structure, without changing its inferential outcome [Sommer 94a]. In [Sommer 94b], the notion of stratification was introduced, essentially separating the inductive properties of Inverse Resolution [Muggleton/Buntine 88] from its (re-)structuring properties. Following a specific strategy, FENDER performs a number of inter- and intraconstruction steps on a given theory, restructuring by introducing new intermediate concepts, *retaining* the set of computed answers of the theory. In other words, FENDER performs inverse resolution on given clauses, without generalizing them. The result is a new inferential structure that is deeper and more modular, and possibly easier to understand and maintain. The new intermediate concepts are intensionally defined and put to immediate use; they make implied relationships explicit by exploiting similarities and differences between original clauses of the theory.

Stratification with FENDER The basic task description: take the rules of a KB; aggregate some of the premises to form new concepts; rewrite the ruleset using these concepts. As will be seen, the decisions that need to be made along the way will be guided by two intuitions: (1) new concepts that find heavy use in the KB are to be preferred, and (2) new concepts that allow the suppression of variables in the original rules are to be preferred. The first is quite straightforward and akin to the idea of compactness in DUCE and CIGOL. The second may seem out of the blue, but most strongly characterizes the approach taken here. Consider that there is natural way of classifying the variables occurring in a rule: head and non-head. Head variables are those that appear in the conclusion of the rule, non-head those occurring *only* in the premise. If we take a goal-directed view of a KB, non-head variables are of "lesser" interest and complicate the rules they appear in — they represent objects in the domain needed for certain inferences, but not needed in the final answers. The approach taken here uses this distinction to solve some basic identification problems (which variable in one rule does variable X in another rule correspond to?) and — more significantly — to decide among alternative common partial premises (CPPs), the building blocks for new intermediate concepts.

---

* Full length version available via http://nathan.gmd.de/persons/edgar.sommer.html. Less up-to-date but more detailed description of FENDER published as [Sommer 94b].

A basic stratification procedure is detailed in Fig. 1. Stratification performed in this way groups some of the conditions of a rule (step 2), interprets these as concepts (step 4a), and rewrites all affected rules in terms of these new concepts (step 4b). When the process is repeated, some of the new concepts may be combined (with others or with original premise literals) to form further concepts, yielding a deeper inferential structure. The new concepts make recurring conditions in the original rules explicit.

---

1. collect the set of rules disjunctively defining a concept
   (all subsequent operations are performed on a copy;
   only the last step (7) actually changes the knowledge base)
2. **[CPP collection]** for each rule

   (a) collect the rule variables
   (b) for each rule variable

      i. collect the premise literals it appears in
      ii. if this is a new partial premise

         A. search the other rules for occurrence of this partial premise
            (rules affected by this partial premise)
         B. remember partial premise and affected rules

3. **[CPP grouping and selection]** select desired CPPs (see next sections)
4. **[preliminary translation]** for each partial premise

   (a) construct a new concept name and define new concept
   (b) in each affected rule, replace partial premise with new concept

5. repeat (from 2) until no new partial premises are found
6. **[final modifications]** (see next sections)
7. **[actual knowledge base translation]**

Fig. 1. *A basic stratification procedure*

Decisions to be made A number of problems and pragmatic issues must be taken into consideration. These are generally valid in a folding task. Specific solutions to them as implemented in FENDER are given in the next section; they appear in the basic procedure (Fig. 1) as steps 3 and 6.

- CPPs collected in this straightforward manner may "overlap": they share some premise literals. Only one in a group of such overlapping CPPs can be applied to the affected rules.
- A CPP in some way defines an intermediate concept, a (possibly) useful relationship between variables of the original rules. Which of the many possibilities are to be preferred?
- Does the new concept necessarily concern *all* of the variables occurring in the CPP? Not all of the variables may be of interest in the next inference step, so they could be dropped from the new concept.
- The procedure does not construct disjunctive intermediate concepts. This means that the original set of goal-concept rules is transformed one-to-one into rules with shorter premises. This does not account for rules (or CPPs) that differ "only slightly". Such slight differences can be noted in the form of disjunctive definitions, yielding more meaningful concepts, and reducing the number of top-level rules.

Strategic decisions made Specific decisions made in FENDER concern steps 3 and 6 in Fig. 1. First, following the motivation at the beginning, CPPs collected around non-head variables are preferred (compare step 2). The iteration process ends when no such **non-head CPP** is found. This is motivated by the hope of being able to suppress some such variables in the rules of the KB. It also solves half of the overlap problem mentioned above. The other half is solved by preferring the most popular CPP in an overlap group, i.e. the one which occurs most often in the original rules[2]. Grouping itself is done in simple manner: all CPPs that share one or more literals form a group (of which only one can be applied to the affected rules). Of course, much more sophisticated methods — subsumption tests, for example — are conceivable. But this is efficient and guaranteed to find the most popular, non-overlapping, non-head CPP(s) in each pass over the rule set (iterations of loop steps 2 to 5 in Fig. 1).

Second, once a non-head CPP has been decided upon in this manner, each affected rule is inspected with the following question in mind: does the seed variable occur anywhere in the premise, other than in that part represented by the CPP? If not, it can be "suppressed": the new intermediate concept to be defined by the CPP will not include the seed variable in its head. The original rules, rewritten using this new concept, will be simpler (and easier to understand & modify) because they concern less variables.

Third, the individual CPPs of an overlap group are compared. All those that differ in one conjunct only are combined to form the definition of a *disjunctive* intermediate concept. This can result in further enrichment of the inferential structure (fanning-out as opposed to depth). When stratification finds no new CPPs, all rules are compared a final time (step 6). Those that differ only in a constant are reformulated in the following manner: the constants are collected to define a new unary concept; using this concept in the definitions of the affected rules has the effect that they dissolve into one, thus further simplifying and modularizing the theory.

Conclusion & related and future work The three transformation operators FENDER employs can be cast in the general framework of inverse resolution. The main operation, replacing a CPP in several rules with a new concept, can be seen as a form of *inter*construction, which is mentioned as a complement to *intra*construction in [Muggleton/Buntine 88], but not implemented. The second, using several similar CPPs in an overlap group to form the definition of a single *disjunctive* intermediate concept, can be seen as a form of *intra*construction, applied to a new concept rather than the goal. The third, combining all rules that differ only in a constant — by constructing a new unary concept that covers these constants — is similar in scope and effect to the form of *intra*construction implemented in CIGOL. The unit clause assumption made in CIGOL has the effect that intraconstruction is applied only to clauses made up of exactly the same predicate symbols, so that its (re-) structuring capabilities are quite limited in

---

[2] An interactive version of FENDER lets the user select one of the less popular CPPs in an overlap group if deemed more valuable.

practice. Furthermore, the new concepts it finds are defined by unit clauses — i.e. by instance, while FENDER's definitions are rules.

One of the main characteristics of FENDER as a whole is that more effort is put into finding CPPs; in CIGOL and LFP2 [Wirth 89], the common generalization of the given clauses is taken. If none common to *all* clauses exists, then no restructuring is possible. In FENDER, CPPs are constructed around the individual variables of the given clauses, which offers the possibility of more meaningful intermediate concepts, of using CPPs common to some rather than all clauses, of adding more than one layer of inference, and of suppressing non-head variables.

As a first approach to theory restructuring, Fig. 1 sets up a framework for experimentation with different strategies. Problems that must be addressed by them are identified, and the specific strategy implemented in FENDER, based on CPP popularity and the elimination of non-head variables, shows some promising results. FENDER reduced the size of, and introduced useful concepts and new structure into, a KB governing access to telecom switches [Sommer et al. 94]. FOIL5 was not able to learn good rules in the original representation of the telecom KB, but found perfect definitions using the new concepts.

In a step towards offering a knowledge base restructuring tool chest, a complementary *unfolding* procedure has been incorporated in MOBAL[Morik et al. 93] along with FENDER. It is able to re-derive the original KB from the one produced by FENDER. To round off the picture, MOBAL also offers operators that analyze and restructure with respect to different notions of redundancy [Sommer 94a]. A set of criteria that attempt to quantify the quality of a KB's structure with emphasis on understandability has been implemented in MOBAL [Sommer 95]. This will aid the comparison of different KB forms produced by restructuring operators. For instance, if *number of premise literals, number of (non-head) variables, number of goal-concept rules* and *theory size* are valid measures of quality, then FENDER can be shown to improve these criteria and hence theory structure.

References

[Morik et al. 93] K. Morik, S. Wrobel, Jörg-Uwe Kietz, and W. Emde. *Knowledge Acquisition and Machine Learning*. Academic Press, London, 1993.

[Muggleton/Buntine 88] Stephen Muggleton and Wray Buntine. Machine Invention of First-Order Predicates by Inverting Resolution. In *Proc. Fifth Intern. Conf. on Machine Learning*, San Mateo, CA, 1988. Morgan Kaufman.

[Sommer et al. 94] E. Sommer, K. Morik, J.M. Andre, and M. Uszynski. What On-line Learning Can Do for Knowledge Acquisition. *Knowledge Acquisition*, 6:435–460, 1994.

[Sommer 94a] E. Sommer. Restructuring in Horn clause knowledge bases. Technical report, ESPRIT Project ILP (6020), 1994. ILP Deliverable GMD 2.1.

[Sommer 94b] E. Sommer. Rulebase Stratification: an Approach to theory restructuring. In *Proc. 4th Intl. Workshop on Inductive Logic Programming (ILP-94)*, 1994.

[Sommer 95] E. Sommer. An Approach to Quantifying the Quality of Induced Theories. Technical report, GMD, 1995. (forthcoming).

[Wirth 89] Ruediger Wirth. Completing Logic Programs by Inverse Resolution. In Katharina Morik (ed.), *Proc. Fourth European Working Session on Learning (EWSL-89)*, pp. 239–250, London/San Mateo, CA, 1989. Pitman/Morgan Kaufmann.

Language Series Revisited: The Complexity of Hypothesis Spaces in ILP (Extended Abstract)

Irene Weber, Birgit Tausend and Irene Stahl

Fakultät Informatik, Universität Stuttgart, Breitwiesenstr. 20-22, D-70565 Stuttgart

Restrictions on the number and depth of existential variables as defined in the language series of CLINT [3] or the ij-determinacy constraint of GOLEM [2] are widely used in ILP and expected to produce a considerable reduction in the size of the hypothesis space (see [1] for an empirical comparison). In this paper we will show that this expectation does not hold in general.

In CLINT, language series are introduced in order to allow a dynamic extension of the hypothesis language in case that learning fails in the current hypothesis space. Based on combinatorial investigations, we argue that the language definitions chosen in CLINT are unsuitable for sensible bias shift operations. We propose alternative approaches resulting in the desired reduction of the hypothesis space and allowing for a natural integration of the shift of bias.

Problem Setting. Given a set of examples $E = E^+ \cup E^-$, the background knowledge K and a hypothesis language L_H, the task of Inductive Logic Programming is to find a logic program $H \in L_H$ that is necessary, i.e., $K \not\vdash E^+$, sufficient, i.e., $K \wedge H \vdash E^+$, and consistent, i.e., $K \wedge H \wedge E^- \not\vdash \Box$. An important point when comparing and evaluating different systems is the complexity of the hypothesis space that is searched in L_H in worst case.

Bottom-up approaches like CLINT start the learning process by constructing a starting clause that is subsequently generalized. As described in [3], CLINT computes the most specific clause $\bot$ contained in the hypothesis language L_H and then generalizes $\bot$ by the dropping condition rule until a given positive example $e^+ \in E^+$ is covered. The set of generalizations of $\bot$ covering e^+ is called the *set of justifications* $Jus(K, L, e^+)$. The clauses in $Jus(K, L, e^+)$ consistent with the negative examples are used as starting clauses. The complexity of the subsequent generalisation depends on the length and the number of starting clauses for a given positive example. In worst case, when $\bot$ covers e^+ and all body literals of $\bot$ are consistent with the negative examples, $\bot$ has to be chosen as starting clause. The most specific clause $\bot$ depends on the hypothesis language. Since the length of $\bot$ is crucial for the complexity of the hypothesis space, it is a useful measure for comparing the complexity of hypothesis spaces searched by CLINT.

CLINT offers five different language series [3], the basic form of which is

L is the set of clauses c such that
  $head(c) = p(x_1, \ldots, x_k)$ and $body(C) \subseteq B(x_1, \ldots, x_k)$, where
  $p(x_1, \ldots, x_k)$ is the predicate to be learned,
  c is linked and range restricted,
  all x_k are different.

The language series mainly differ in the definition of the set of body literals B. For each language, the most specific clause $\perp$ includes all literals in B in its body. Thus, the complexity of $\perp$ equals the number of literals in the set $B(x_1, \ldots, x_k)$. In this paper, we investigate the influence of the parameters of the language series on the complexity of the respective sets $B(x_1, \ldots, x_k)$. For convenience, the set of all predicates in the theory is denoted by *Pred*. $\mathcal{A}$ is the maximum arity of all predicates in *Pred*.

Language Series 1. The set of body literals $B_i(x_1, \ldots, x_k)$ for a language L_i of series 1 is defined as follows.

$$
\begin{aligned}
B_i(x_1, \ldots, x_k) = \{ \quad & q(y_1, \ldots, y_n) | q \in Pred \ and \\
& (1)\ |\{y_1, \ldots, y_n\} \setminus \{x_1, \ldots, x_k\}| \le i \ and \\
& (2)\ \{y_1, \ldots, y_n\} \cap \{x_1, \ldots, x_k\} \ne \emptyset \ and \\
& (3)\ each\ variable\ in\ \{y_1, \ldots, y_n\} \cap \{x_1, \ldots, x_k\}\ occurs \\
& \quad only\ once \quad \}
\end{aligned}
$$

Table 1 shows the number of literals in $B_i(x_1, \ldots, x_k)$ as a function of parameter i. (For equations and combinatorial details see the full length version of this paper or [5].) As background knowledge we assume the following set of predicates $Pred_1 = \{nil/1, atom/1, sort/2, list/3, append/3, partition/4\}$. Since the maximum arity of the predicates in $Pred_1$ is $\mathcal{A} = 4$, the parameter i can be varied from 0 to 3.

	$i=0$	$i=1$	$i=2$	$i=3$
$B_i(X,Y)$	40	100	136	144

Table 1. The number of literals in $\perp$ in Language Series 1 as a function of i.

As table 1 indicates, incrementing i results in only a small growth of $B_i(x_1, \ldots, x_k)$ when i comes close to its maximum value $\mathcal{A} - 1$. Thus, it is not sensible to use this language series in a bias shift environment as described in [3] since the languages differ too little to justify the risk of failing because of the weakness of the hypothesis language.

Language Series 2. In the languages of series 2, the parameter q controls the maximum level of existential quantification of variables [3]. The sets $B_i^q(x_1, \ldots, x_k)$ of body literals for a hypothesis language L_i^q of series 2 are defined as follows.

$$
\begin{aligned}
B_i^1(x_1, \ldots, x_k) &= B_i(x_1, \ldots, x_k) \\
B_i^q(x_1, \ldots, x_k) &= B_i(z_1, \ldots, z_l),\ where\ \{z_1, \ldots, z_l\}\ is\ the\ set\ of \\
&\quad all\ variables\ in\ B_i^{q-1}(x_1, \ldots, x_k).
\end{aligned}
$$

Table 2 shows the number of literals of $B_i^q(x_1, \ldots, x_k)$ for $i, q \in \{1, 2, 3\}$ which arise when learning a 2-ary predicate with the set of list predicates $Pred_1$.

$|B|$	$q=1$	$q=2$	$q=3$
$i=1$	100	$1.623 \cdot 10^7$	$9.096 \cdot 10^{23}$
$i=2$	136	$3.371 \cdot 10^8$	$9.8 \cdot 10^{27}$
$i=3$	144	$6.472 \cdot 10^8$	$6.94 \cdot 10^{28}$

Table 2. The number of literals in $B_i^q(x_1, \ldots, x_k)$ as a function of i and q when learning a 2-ary predicate using background knowledge *Pred*.

Our investigations of language series 2 show that parameter i has only little influence on $|B_i^q(x_1, \ldots, x_k)|$, whereas the impact of parameter q is too strong. In fact, $|B_i^q(x_1, \ldots, x_k)|$ grows super–exponentially in q [5]. So, we can conclude that the parameters i and q as used here are suitable neither for controlling the complexity of the hypothesis language nor for sensible bias shift operations.

Language Series 3. Language series 3 is a generalisation of language series 2. The set of body literals $B_{i_1, \ldots, i_{n-1}, i_n}(x_1, \ldots, x_k)$, $i_1, \ldots, i_{n-1} \in N_0$, for a language $L_{i_1, \ldots, i_{n-1}, i_n}$ of series 3 is defined as follows.

$$B_{i_1, \ldots, i_n}(x_1, \ldots, x_k) = B_{i_n}(z_1, \ldots, z_l) \text{ where } \{z_1, \ldots, z_l\} \text{ is the set of}$$
$$\text{all variables in } B_{i_1, \ldots, i_{n-1}}(x_1, \ldots, x_k).$$

Table 3 shows some values of $B_{i_1, \ldots, i_n}(x_1, \ldots, x_k)$ for the most restrictive arrangement of languages which can be defined in series 3.

	L_0	$L_{0,1}$	$L_{0,1,0}$	$L_{0,1,0,1}$	$L_{0,1,0,1,0}$	$L_{0,1,0,1,0,1}$
$|B|$	40	100	$1.526 \cdot 10^7$	$1.623 \cdot 10^7$	$9.095 \cdot 10^{23}$	$9.095 \cdot 10^{23}$

Table 3. The number of literals in the sets $B_{i_1, \ldots, i_n}(X, Y)$ of language series 3.

These results show that there is only little difference between a language $L_{\ldots, 0}$ and the next complex language $L_{\ldots, 0, 1}$, i.e., $L_0 = L_0^q$, $L_{0,1} = L_1^1 = L_1$, $L_{0,1,0} \approx L_{0,1,0,1} = L_1^2$, and so on. This means that language series 3 does not offer significant improvement compared to series 2.

An alternative language series. The literal sets $B(x_1, \ldots, x_k)$ in language series 2 and 3 grow super-exponentially because the number of variables which are newly introduced when shifting the bias depends on the number of variables already available. A method to prevent this growth is to set a fixed limit on the number of variables which are generated on each level of existential quantification as in the following language definition.

$$B_i(x_1, \ldots, x_k) = \{ q(y_1, \ldots, y_l) | q \in Pred,$$
$$\{y_1, \ldots, y_l\} \subseteq \{x_1, \ldots, x_k\} \cup \{v_1, \ldots, v_i\} \text{ and}$$
$$\{v_1, \ldots, v_i\} \text{ is a set of } i \text{ different new variables},$$
$$\text{all variables } y_i, y_j \in pred(y_1, \ldots, y_l) \text{ are different },$$
$$\{y_1, \ldots, y_l\} \cap \{x_1, \ldots, x_k\} \neq \emptyset\}$$
$$\cup \{equal(v_m, v_n) | 1 \leq n \leq i, 1 \leq m \leq i, n \neq m\}$$
$$B_i^q(x_1, \ldots, x_k) = B_i^{q-1}(x_1, \ldots, x_k) \cup B_i(z_1, \ldots, z_i) , \text{ where}$$
$$\{z_1, \ldots, z_l\} = vars(B_i^{q-1}(x_1, \ldots, x_k)) \setminus vars(B_i^{q-2}(x_1, \ldots, x_n)).$$
$$vars(B_i^0(x_1, \ldots, x_n)) := \{x_1, \ldots, x_n\}.$$

As in language series 2 of CLINT, the parameter q in this language defines the maximum level of existential quantification. However, the parameter i does not indicate the maximum number of new variables in each literal, but restricts the total number of variables on each level $1, \ldots, q$.

Table 4 shows the number of literals in the sets $B_i^q(X, Y)$ as defined here for the set of list predicates $Pred_1$. In the language series proposed here, $|B_i^q(x_1, \ldots, x_k)|$ grows linearly with parameter q.

$|B|$	$q = 1$	$q = 2$	$q = 3$
$i = 2$	87	174	261
$i = 3$	249	870	1 491
$i = 4$	556	2 894	5 232
$i = 5$	1 056	7 386	13 716

Table 4. The number of literals in the sets $B_i^q(X, Y)$ of the new language series as a function of i and q.

Predicate Invention. An alternative approach to reduce the complexity of hypothesis languages without sacrificing expressiveness is to use *predicate invention* as bias shift operation. The idea is to produce a starting clause for the target predicate in the more restricted language L_i of series 1 that covers the positive examples but might be inconsistent. If the starting clause is inconsistent, a new auxiliary predicate is introduced that discriminates between positive and negative instantiations of the clause. Then, the process continues with the new predicate as target predicate. The main advantage is that the number k of old variables for the auxiliary predicate can be reduced using methods for finding a minimal set of arguments for a new predicate [4].

Conclusions. Our results on the language series of CLINT are largely negative. The super-exponential growth of the most special clause $\perp$ for language series 2 and 3 makes learning intractable except for toy domains. Furthermore, the chosen parameters are unsuitable for sensible bias shift operations since languages discriminated by the number of existential variables scarcely differ whereas languages discriminated by the depth of existential variables differ too strongly. As a solution for these problems, we proposed a language which allows for tractable learning procedures, and discussed how predicate invention can be used to improve the shift of bias.

References

1. Adé, Hilde, Luc De Raedt und Maurice Bruynooghe. Declarative Bias for Bottom-up ILP Learning Systems, 1994. To appear in *Machine Learning*.
2. Muggleton, S. , C. Feng. Efficient Induction of Logic Programs. *Proc. of the 1st Conference on Algorithmic Learning Theory*, Tokyo, OHMSHA, 1990.
3. L. De Raedt. *Interactive Theory Revision: an Inductive Logic Programming Approach*. Academic Press, 1992.
4. I. Stahl and I. Weber. The Arguments of Newly Invented Predicates in ILP. In *Proc. of ILP-94*, 1994.
5. I. Weber. *Komplexität von Hypothesenräumen in der Induktiven Logischen Programmierung*. Diplomarbeit Nr. 1164, Universität Stuttgart, Fakultät Informatik, 1994.

Prototype, Nearest Neighbor and Hybrid Algorithms for Time Series Classification
(Extended Abstract)

Christel Wisotzki, Fritz Wysotzki

Fraunhofer-Institute for Information and Data Processing, Branch Lab for
Process Optimisation
Kurstraße 33, D-10117 Berlin, email: wisotzki@epo.iitb.fhg.de

1 Introduction

In the paper new methods of classification of time series and other curves are introduced. The classification learning of time series is very important, for example in medical and technical diagnosis, and for forecasting in the case of complicated processes which cannot (or only partly) be modelled mathematically. The presented examples of different real-world applications will give an impression of the varying availability of curve classification methods and of their performance.

The presented classification methods are "holistic" in the sense that distance or similarity measures are used but not description of the curves by feature vectors of fixed length. Three different methods will be adopted for the task of classification learning: construction of prototypes for each class, the use of a kNN classifier ([5], [6]), and a new principle which is called the generalized prototype classifier. The latter can be viewed as a hybrid of the first two methods, improving them in a substantial way. It is well known that, in general, the kNN classification has good results but the algorithm is very expensive. On the other hand, the prototype algorithm is very simple, but classes represented by non-convex regions (e. g. consisting of disjunctive subclasses without a common description) cannot be handled successfully by this method. The generalized prototype classifier keeps the advantages and overcomes the disadvantages of both algorithms.

In the paper, two general cases concerning the available measurements of the curves are considered leading to different preprocessing strategies:

- the measurement points are in the same interval for all curves, or
- the curves are measured on different time intervals.

In both cases, the curves are firstly approximated by spline functions (piecewise polynomial functions). For this a new method of finding the optimal intervals for the spline approximation based on a clustering technique has been developed ([5], [6]). Thus, the intervals where the curve is smoothly replaced, are adaptively defined by the approximation algorithm, depending on noise to be eliminated and the granularity of the approximation which can be controlled by the user.

Therefore, in the first case, distance measures in the functional space of the approximating functions will be used for classification.

In the second case where the measurements are taken from different time intervals, the curves are mapped onto symbol strings. The symbols can be generated by a discretization of spline parameters or directly as names of some specific curve segments (e. g. certain peaks, pieces with constant slope etc.) defined by experts. The description by symbol strings leads to further noise elimination, allows the definition of complex features like repetitions, groupings, and gives the best possibility of translation-invariant recognition (classification). Since syntactical methods for string matching are very sensitive to noise (e. g. missing symbols), the strings are transformed into graphs by introducing the distance between symbols in the string as relations. In the case of time series, this may correspond to the time intervals between the segments which are named by the symbols. Having done this, measures of graph similarity based on the well-known Zelinka metric for graphs will be used to evaluate the similarity of curves. Besides the advantage of reducing noise sensitivity, this method uses explicitly the distance of symbols in the string as an additional information for classification.

2 Classification Methods for the Approximating Splines, Examples

The used classification methods base on similarity measures between the objects to be classified and certain reference objects, which generalize the classes. If all curves are given in the same time interval, then all approximating functions belong to the same functional space. In this case a similarity measure based on a difference in the corresponding space of the approximating functions can be used. Such similarity measures are independent of the number of subintervals of approximation.

Three classification methods are introduced. They differ from each other by the construction of the reference objects from the training examples.

The Prototype Method: In the training phase, prototypes are generated for all classes as generalizations of the classes. A prototype of a class is the average of the approximating functions of all training objects belonging to this class ([5], [6]). Therefore, all prototypes are in the mentioned functional space of approximating functions. In the test phase, an unseen object is assigned to the class to which prototype its approximating function has the smallest distance. The computational amount is proportional to the number of classes in the test phase.

The kNN Method: The approximating functions of all training objects themselves are taken as reference objects. In the test phase, the k nearest reference objects (k nearest neighbours) are determined for a new object. The latter object is assigned to that class which is the most frequent in the set of the k nearest neighbours. The computational amount in the test phase which is proportional to the number of training examples, exceeds that of the prototype method but, as will be seen below, its performance is essentially better in many cases.

The Generalized Prototype Method: Advantages of the prototype method over the kNN method include compact representation of the training data, fast classification of unseen curves and the ability to interpret the prototypes. For these reasons a generalization of the prototype method was developed. It should overcome the disadvantages and keep the advantages of the two considered methods. The prototype classifier separates two classes by a hyperplane in the functional space of the approximating functions. Therefore a bad classification result points out that the class regions in this space are not convex (e. g. a class region consists of two subclass regions). The generalized prototype classification method is based on class separation by piecewise linear surfaces which is obtained by generating more than one prototype per class. The training phase begins with prototypes for each class, consisting of one object. Now, for a given number p, the prototypes are tought incrementally by the remaining training objects in the following way: For a new object X the set of p nearest prototypes Π is determined. If there is a prototype in Π generalizing the class of X, then this prototype is extended by X. In the other case a new prototype is opened. This procedure is repeated until the whole training set is used.

In the boundary case in which each object forms a prototype, the generalized prototype method results in the nearest-neighbor method. On the other hand, if p increases then the generalized method becomes more and more similar to the simple prototype method, i. e. there is a number p_0 for which both methods coincide.

The performance of the three classification methods is compared using some examples from different real-world applications - chemistry, physics and economics.

Example 1 (gas chromatograms [6]): In this example 44 gas chromatograms (330 points per curve), divided up into three classes (high, medium and small concentration) were given. The three-fold cross validation has been calculated.

Example 2 (TRMC signals [2]): 300 TRMC signals (500 points per curve) and two classifications (3 classes) according to the quality (Solar1) and according to the state of the measurement system (Solar2) were given. The ten-fold cross validation has been calculated.

Example 3 (Dollar Exchange Rates): 63 curves of the measured daily changes of the exchange rates of the US-Dollar over a year were given. The task was to decide wether the average of the following quarter will increase (class +) or decrease (class -). The training set consists of the first 40 and the test set of the last 23 curves.

Discussion of Results: For the described data cross validation (with the exception of Dollar) has been calculated by the NN method, the generalized prototype method (GPMp) for $p = 1, 2, 3$ and by the simple prototype method (PM). The mean success rates (performance) and the mean numbers of prototypes (computational amount) are represented in the following table.

Method	NN		GPM1		GPM2		GPM3		PM		default
	num	rate	num	rate	num	rate	num	rate	num	rate	rate
Chrom	29.3	1.00	5.3	0.98	4	0.93	3	0.86	3	0.86	0.68
Solar1	270	0.99	27.3	0.97	15.2	0.89	3	0.62	3	0.62	0.37
Solar2	270	0.98	27.4	0.96	15.5	0.94	3	0.69	3	0.69	0.40
Dollar	40	0.52	21	0.61	2	0.78			2	0.78	0.61

The first two examples clearly demonstrate, that the objective, formulated in section 2, has been achieved for this data. The numbers of prototypes for GPM1 are significantly smaller than the number of training objects. On the other hand, the accuracy of GPM1 differs only negligibly from that of NN. For $p_0 = 3$, the generalized and the simple prototype method coincide. The third example demonstrates, that the generalization of the prototype method has no effect if the simple prototype method gives better results than the NN classifier. But it shows the good performance of the prototype method used for the prediction of exchange rates.

3 Stringclassification

Now the assumption that all curves are given on the same time interval is dropped, i. e. the approximating functions do not belong to the same functional space. The similarity measures and the prototype building from section 2 cannot be used. To define a proper similarity measure for the kNN classification, the approximating splines are transformed into strings. There are different ways for doing it. If typical, relevant pieces of the considered curves can be described by a set of linguistic rules, the curve can be decomposed with the help of these rules into parts. These curve parts are identified with characters of an alphabet. After that the sequence of symbols corresponds to a string.

The goal is to find a measure for the evaluation of the similarity of two arbitrary strings. Let S and T be two arbitrary strings, where the components belong to the same alphabet. S and T are converted into directed graphs the nodes of which are the characters (symbols) and the arcs between two nodes are labelled by the distances of the symbols in the string (relations). The so-called compatibility graph can be used for the construction of a similarity measure for graphs ([7]). Pairs of identical characters (one from each string) form the nodes of the compatibility graph. Two of its nodes are compatible if the corresponding characters have the same relation (distance) within their strings.

Obviously, two strings have a large similarity if the maximal induced connected subgraph (maximal clique) of their compatibility graph has a quite large number of nodes with respect to the string lengths, i. e. with the help of the cardinal number of the maximal clique a similarity measure can be defined.

The graph metric $d(S,T) = \max\{n(S),n(T)\} - n(S,T)$, $(S,T \in \mathcal{G})$, is based on the cardinal number of the maximal clique of the compatibility graph $n(S,T)$ and was introduced by Zelinka [8] and generalized by Kaden [3] and Sobik [4] to the set $\mathcal{G}$ of all finite directed labelled graphs ($n(S)$ - cardinal number of S). By this way a metric for strings is obtained, too. The methods for computing a maximal clique are NP-complete ([1]). In the present case, the task is simpler due to the fact that the compatibility graph consists of disjoint cliques.

For the curves of example 1 from section 2 linguistic rules were given. After approximating the curves, tranformating into strings, and treating by kNN, mean success rates 0.98 (for $k = 1$) and 1.0 (for $k = 3$) were obtained.

References

[1]   Bron, C./Kerbosch, J.: Finding All Cliques of an Undirected Graph. Comm. ACM 1973, Vol. 17, No. 9, 575 - 577

[2]   Haffner, C./ Kunst M./ Swiatkowski, C./Seidelman, G.: In-situ quality monitoring during the deposition of a-Si:H films. Applied Surface Science 63(1993) 222 - 226

[3]   Kaden, F.: Graphmetriken und Distanzgraphen, in: Beiträge zur angewandten Graphentheorie, Teil 1, ZKI-Informationen 1982, Akademie der Wissenschaften der DDR, 2/82, 1 - 62

[4]   Sobik, F.: Graphmetriken und Klassifikation strukturierter Objekte. in: Beiträge zur angewandten Graphentheorie, Teil 1, ZKI-Informationen 1982, Akademie der Wissenschaften der DDR, 2/82, 63 - 122

[5]   Wisotzki, C./Wysotzki, F.: Feature Generation and Classification of Time Series. in: Bock, H. H., Lenski, W., Richter M. M. (eds) : Information systems and data analysis, Studies in Classification, Data Analysis, and Knowledge Organization, Springer-Verlag Heidelberg, 1994.

[6]   Wisotzki, C./Wysotzki, F.: Lernfähige Klassifikation von Zeitreihen. in: 39. IWK, Band 3, Technische Universität Ilmenau, 1994

[7]   Wysotzki, F.: Artificial Intelligence and Artificial Neural Nets. Proc. 1st Workshop on AI, Shanghai Jiaotong-University, Sept.1990, 116 - 122

[8]   Zelinka, F.: On a Certain Distance between Isomorphism Classes of Graphs. Casopis pest. mat. 100 (1975), 371 - 373

Author Index

Lecture Notes in Artificial Intelligence (LNAI)

Lecture Notes in Computer Science